EMERGING WRITING RESEARCH FROM THE RUSSIAN FEDERATION

INTERNATIONAL EXCHANGES ON THE STUDY OF WRITING

Series Editors: Joan Mullin, Magnus Gustafsson, Terry Myers Zawacki, and Federico Navarro

Series Associate Editors: Ana M. Cortés Lagos, Anna S. Habib, and Matthew Overstreet

The International Exchanges on the Study of Writing Series publishes books that address worldwide perspectives on writing, writers, teaching with writing, and scholarly writing practices, specifically those that draw on scholarship across national and disciplinary borders to challenge parochial understandings of all of the above. The Latin America Section of the International Exchanges on the Study of Writing book series publishes peer-reviewed books about writing, writers, teaching with writing, and scholarly writing practices from Latin American perspectives. It also offers re-editions of recognized peer-reviewed books originally published in the region.

The WAC Clearinghouse and University Press of Colorado are collaborating so that these books will be widely available through free digital distribution and low-cost print editions. The publishers and the series editors are committed to the principle that knowledge should freely circulate and have embraced the use of technology to support open access to scholarly work.

Recent Books in the Series

Natalia Ávila Reyes (Ed.), *Multilingual Contributions to Writing Research: Toward an Equal Academic Exchange* (2021)

Cecile Badenhorst, Brittany Amell, and James Burford (Eds.), *Re-imagining Doctoral Writing* (2021)

Bruce Morrison, Julia Chen, Linda Lin, and Alan Urmston (Eds.), *English Across the Curriculum: Voices from Around the World* (2021)

Alanna Frost, Julia Kiernan, and Suzanne Blum Malley (Eds.), *Translingual Dispositions: Globalized Approaches to the Teaching of Writing* (2020)

Charles Bazerman, Blanca Yaneth González Pinzón, David Russell, Paul Rogers, Luis Bernardo Peña, Elizabeth Narváez, Paula Carlino, Montserrat Castelló, & Mónica Tapia-Ladino (Eds.), *Knowing Writing: Writing Research across Borders* (2019)

Sylvie Plane, Charles Bazerman, Fabienne Rondelli, Christiane Donahue, Arthur N. Applebee, Catherine Boré, Paula Carlino, Martine Marquilló Larruy, Paul Rogers, & David Russell (Eds.), *Research on Writing: Multiple Perspectives* (2017)

EMERGING WRITING RESEARCH FROM THE RUSSIAN FEDERATION

Edited by L. Ashley Squires

The WAC Clearinghouse
wac.colostate.edu
Fort Collins, Colorado

University Press of Colorado
upcolorado.com
Louisville, Colorado

The WAC Clearinghouse, Fort Collins, Colorado 80523

University Press of Colorado, Louisville, Colorado 80027

© 2021 by L. Ashley Squires. This work is licensed under a Creative Commons Attribution-NonCommercial-NoDerivatives 4.0 International License.

ISBN 978-1-64215-142-8 (PDF) | 978-1-64215-143-5 (ePub) | 978-1-64642-272-2 (pbk.)

DOI 10.37514/INT-B.2021.1428

Names: Squires, L. Ashley, editor.
Title: Emerging writing research from the Russian Federation / edited by L. Ashley Squires.
Description: Fort Collins : The WAC Clearinghouse; Louisville, Colorado : University Press of Colorado, 2021. | Series: International exchanges on the study of writing | Includes bibliographical references.
Identifiers: LCCN 2021047896 (print) | LCCN 2021047897 (ebook) | ISBN 9781646422722 (paperback) | ISBN 9781642151428 (pdf) | ISBN 9781642151435 (epub)
Subjects: LCSH: Russian language—Rhetoric—Study and teaching—Russia (Federation) | Academic writing—Study and teaching—Russia (Federation) | LCGFT: Essays.
Classification: LCC PG2475 .E44 2021 (print) | LCC PG2475 (ebook) | DDC 808/.049171071—dc23/eng/20211119
LC record available at https://lccn.loc.gov/2021047896
LC ebook record available at https://lccn.loc.gov/2021047897

Copyeditor: Don Donahue
Design and Production: Mike Palmquist
Cover Photo: "Saint Vasily Cathedral in Moscow," by Petar Milošević, used under a CC BY-SA 4.0 license
Series Editors: Joan Mullin, Magnus Gustafsson, Terry Myers Zawacki, and Federico Navarro
Series Associate Editors: Ana M. Cortés Lagos, Anna S. Habib, and Matthew Overstreet

The WAC Clearinghouse supports teachers of writing across the disciplines. Hosted by Colorado State University, it brings together scholarly journals and book series as well as resources for teachers who use writing in their courses. This book is available in digital formats for free download at wac.colostate.edu.

Founded in 1965, the University Press of Colorado is a nonprofit cooperative publishing enterprise supported, in part, by Adams State University, Colorado State University, Fort Lewis College, Metropolitan State University of Denver, University of Alaska Fairbanks, University of Colorado, University of Denver, University of Northern Colorado, University of Wyoming, Utah State University, and Western Colorado University. For more information, visit upcolorado.com.

§ Contents

Acknowledgments vii

Introduction 3
    L. Ashley Squires

PART ONE. ESTABLISHED TRADITIONS AND EVOLVING CONTEXTS

1 Academic Writing in Russia Beyond Zero Point 17
    Irina Korotkina

2 Essays in Middle and High School in Russia: Historical Background . . . 51
    Elena Getmanskaya

3 How Russian Art Historians Learn to Write 69
    Natalya Smirnova and Anna Guseva

4 They Teach Writing but They Do Not Write: Why Russian University Foreign Language Instructors Rarely Publish 99
    Svetlana Bogolepova

PART TWO. WRITING CENTER INTERVENTIONS

5 Developing Writing Centers in Russia: A Balancing Act 127
    Tatiana Glushko

6 A Russian Model of a Writing Center: The Case of HSE University 153
    Svetlana Suchkova

7 A Transnational Training Model for Peer Tutors: Authority, Rhetorical Awareness, and Language in/through Virtual Exchange Practices 171
    Olga Aksakalova and L. Ashley Squires

PART THREE. LANGUAGE MATTERS

8 Software Development for Corpus Research in English Studies 195
    Elizaveta Smirnova, Svetlana Strinyuk, and Viacheslav Lanin

9 Punctuation in L2 English: Computational Methods Applied in the Study of L1 Interference 211
    Olga Vinogradova, Anna Viklova, and Veronika Smilga

Part Four. Classroom Practice

10 From Secondary to Tertiary Education in Russia: Bridging the Academic Writing Gap 237
Tatiana Golechkova

11 Transcending Authorities: Literature and Performance in an Integrated Reading-writing Classroom in Russia 265
Irina Kuznetsova-Simpson

Contributors 295

§ Acknowledgments

The authors would like to thank Matthew Overstreet, Magnus Gustafsson, and the other editors at the WAC Clearinghouse for their stewardship of this project. We would also like to thank the anonymous reviewers for their thoughtful feedback and Emily Peters for helping us with the final stages of manuscript preparation.

EMERGING WRITING RESEARCH
FROM THE RUSSIAN FEDERATION

Introduction

L. Ashley Squires
NEW ECONOMIC SCHOOL, MOSCOW

Russia is a place where subway stops, major roads, and city squares are named after writers. Particularly in Moscow and St. Petersburg, you can scarcely take a step without walking into some scene from literary history. One of my favorite pedestrian routes in the capital takes me past Pushkin Square, a metro station named for Chekhov, a monument to the poet Sergey Yesenin, and the park where the devil arrives on Earth in the opening incident of Bulgakov's *Master and Margarita* (a sign is posted reminding visitors not to talk to strangers).

Perhaps it is at least partly due to the richness of this literary heritage that *academic* writing has only lately become part of the conversation about the future of Russian higher education. As will be evident in the chapters in this volume, it is still not remotely uncommon to encounter the attitude—dissonant in the land of Tolstoy and Akhmatova—that Russian scholars and students need help with writing. What is meant, of course, is that Russian academics need to increase the volume of research published in highly-ranked international (and usually anglophone) journals and that university instructors—like their counterparts worldwide—are frustrated with the quality of student writing. The reasons offered are many: the accretion of habits from the Soviet period in which Russian scholars were largely isolated from the global academic community (see Chapter 1 and Chapter 3), even older pedagogical traditions in which Russian writing—as in the Anglosphere—was closely linked with the study of literature and other modes of communication were neglected (see Chapter 2 and Chapter 11), lack of familiarity with the lingua franca of international education and scholarly publishing (English) and internationally accepted rhetorical norms (see Chapter 1, Chapter 3, Chapter 4, and Chapter 8), structural problems in the Russian education system with its newfound emphasis on testing (see Chapter 10), and straightforward lack of resources (see Chapter 4).

Efforts to address academic writing in Russia have become particularly urgent in the context of state efforts to converge with international education standards. In 2003, Russia entered the Bologna Process, a multi-national European agreement to align higher education systems to ensure academic mobility for faculty and students. Then in 2013, the Russian Ministry of Education initiated Project 5-100, an effort to launch five Russian universities into the top 100 of major international university rankings. This program included substantial funding for incentives for faculty who publish in international journals and for support services to help them do so.

Because English is the lingua franca of international academic publishing, the work of advancing this agenda has mostly been delegated to specialists in English for Academic Purposes (EAP) who direct and staff newly created writing centers and writing programs at Russian universities. The first American-style Russian writing center was founded at the New Economic School (NES), a private graduate school, in 2011. The Academic Writing Center (AWC) at HSE University, Russia's largest public university, quickly followed. Since then, 11 writing centers—some freestanding and some housed in language departments—have sprung up across the country, and a professional organization, the National Writing Centers Consortium (NWCC), has been established to support this burgeoning area of pedagogy and research. The NWCC hosted its first conference in Moscow in 2018, and research on academic writing has been a feature of many national conferences on the teaching of English. In short, there is a rapidly growing community in this area that did not exist ten years ago and which stands to exert some influence not only on the future of academic research and higher education in Russia but in other parts of the region, as interest in writing and writing pedagogy spreads to other parts of the former USSR (see Chapter 1).

Though Russia has its own tradition of writing in the academy and its own academic publishers and journals, to serve the current needs, writing pedagogy models have largely been adapted from abroad. This has included concepts like academic literacy and multiliteracy (see Chapter 1, Chapter 3, Chapter 8, and Chapter 10) and institutional models like the writing center (see Chapter 5, Chapter 6, and Chapter 7). This does not mean, however, that this conversation only concerns English writing or that these practitioners wish to create a siloed, privileged space for English. Rather, there is an effort to make concepts like academic literacy translingual (see Chapter 1), and many support programs offer their services in both English and Russian (see Chapter 6 and Chapter 7). Pressure to publish is intense regardless of the language scholars are working in (see Chapter 3 and Chapter 4). Nevertheless, Russian higher education must contend with the overwhelming demand for writing and writing services in English.

The Aims of this Volume

The aim of this collection is to offer the reader a broad view of the changing landscape for academic writing, writing pedagogy, and writing centers in Russia by individuals with on-the-ground experience. It includes Russian writing scholars living and working in Russian universities, Russian-born writing scholars currently teaching in the United States, and U.S.-born expatriates with experience teaching in Russia. In many ways, it can be viewed as an extension of the work done by the contributors to Pavel Zemliansky and Kirk St.Amant's (2016) *Rethinking Post-Communist Rhetoric* published when the regional conversation was still nascent. As Tatiana Glushko notes in Chapter 5 of this collection, Thaiss, Brauer, Carlino, Ganobcsik-Williams and Sinha's (2012) worldwide survey of writing programs included no entries from Russia. With a special focus on the Russian context, we show how research in this area has developed regionally since the middle of the decade—a truly productive and transformative period in terms of the establishment of institutions (like the NWCC) and the development of research, which in the Russian context has come to embrace approaches rooted in academic literacy (Lillis & Curry, 2010) as well as multilingual approaches (Korotkina, 2018).

We therefore also contribute to the growing conversation about the internationalization of higher education models (Altbach & Knight, 2007; Brooks & Waters, 2011; Rajakumar, 2018) and the field of writing studies (Arnold et al., 2017; Bazerman et al., 2012). This is in some ways a story about the importation of anglophone models of writing pedagogy that, as Christiane Donahue (2009) noted a decade ago, have been the focus of much research under the rubric of internationalization. But it is also a story about the uniquely local character of writing interventions, which has also been the hallmark of so much research in this field (Muchiri et al., 1995).

While Western-born and trained individuals like myself have been a part of the development of academic writing in Russia, much of the conversation is being driven by people whose lives and careers have been centered there. Unlike in the Middle East, East Asia, and other parts of the world, there are no branch campuses of U.S. universities in Russia (though some private universities maintain dual-diploma programs), and only a few Western-trained specialists (be they U.S.-trained compositionists or applied linguists based in Europe or the UK). While a few practitioners are familiar with the U.S.-based field of rhetoric and composition, many more are trained as ESP/EAP teachers and scholars. As the reader will see from this collection, this means that Russian writing programs are pulling together resources from a variety of places and adapting them to their own needs. It also means that the development of this field is influenced by a deep understanding of the unique structural challenges Russian scholars and teachers face, of the idiosyncrasies of the Russian educational bureaucracy, and of the unique linguistic and cultural context for writing.

A few words about my positionality as editor may be warranted here. After completing my Ph.D. at the University of Texas at Austin in 2013, I was hired as the Associate Director of the New Economic School's Writing and Communication Center (WCC), founded to support the curriculum of its elite, American-style liberal arts bachelor's program (Olga Aksakalova, the first director of the WCC, joins me in Chapter 7 of this collection). Because I have therefore been present for much of the recent history of academic writing in Russia and am also very familiar with international academic norms (including the process of publishing a book with an American university press), I am well-positioned to help mediate this discussion. However, on top of my non-Russian biography, the institution I work for is unusual in the broader landscape of Russian higher education. In addition to its liberal arts bachelor's curriculum, the faculty who teach at NES are international. Indeed, one must hold a Ph.D. from a Western university to hold the rank of assistant professor. From a Russian perspective, this is a pretty rarified environment in which to establish a writing center. NES gives us the institutional flexibility and the international orientation to serve students in the best way we know how, using methods largely adapted from the United States.

The pioneering role of NES as well as the institutional growth and leadership of HSE helps explain why there are several contributions from the faculty of those institutions (as does the fact that our funding models and teaching loads give faculty comparatively more freedom to engage in research activities). At most other institutions, writing centers, programs, and curricula must attempt to fit into the complicated bureaucratic structure of higher education and serve a constituency that is far less habituated (indeed is often quite skeptical) of Western-identified educational models. In fact, the WCC at NES remains the only bilingual writing center in Russia that serves undergraduates as its primary constituency. We also seem to have the only undergraduate program in which there are required writing-intensive courses in both Russian and English. Most of the other centers and programs exist to serve research faculty and sometimes graduate students. As this volume will demonstrate, Russian writing centers have in many cases expanded well beyond the consultancy model we use at NES to become de facto academic writing departments or programs. The aforementioned Academic Writing Center at HSE University, Moscow (described in detail in Chapter 6), for example, seeks to "meet the growing needs of our faculty for participating in the global academic community and improving the international visibility of the research and educational services provided by HSE," offering courses, workshops, and individual consultations for "faculty, researchers and students who write for international publications and take part in global research conferences" (Academic Writing Center, n.d.) Elsewhere in Moscow, the Academic Writing University Center at the National University of Science and Technology (where Director Elena Bazanova also serves as the President of the NWCC)

> Provides language support services to university PhD students, researchers and faculty for every stage of their academic career and for any kind of writing, e.g., abstract writing, conference papers, dissertation and thesis writing, grant proposal writing, research papers, etc. in English. (Academic Writing University Center, n.d.)

Writing centers and programs are also active well beyond the Russian capitals (Moscow and St. Petersburg). The Samara Academic Consultancy Center, part of the modern languages department at Samara University, was established to "provide consultations on article writing for English journals, assistance for participation in international conferences, workshops for mastering skills of foreign language communicative competence for both teaching staff and students" (Samara Academic Consultancy Center, n.d.). Far to the east in Siberia, the Center for Academic Writing "Impulse" "delivers Academic English language programs to University faculty and researchers and provides support to them in developing scientific writing skills to get published in international journals" (Center for Academic Writing "Impulse," n.d.).

The list of National Writing Centers Consortium members goes on to include writing and linguistic support centers at the I. M. Sechenov First Moscow State Medical University (Moscow), the Russian Presidential Academy of National Economy and Public Administration (Moscow), the Moscow Institute of Physics and Technology (Moscow), ITMO University (St. Petersburg), Tomsk State University (Tomsk), and Tomsk Polytechnic University (Tomsk; National Writing Center Consortium, n.d.).

My aim in this collection is therefore to offer as broad as possible a view of how writing pedagogy is conceived of and practiced, which means that much of the discussion will center on the teaching of writing to researchers and not the more familiar paradigm (for a U.S. audience) of teaching writing to late teens and young twenty-somethings (though this is dealt with in Part Four). Writing education for school children and undergraduates is, as it is in most places, a concern, but for the moment, researchers are the institutional priority and are thus where a lot of the effort is being directed. Writing pedagogy and research are therefore less focused on the freshman seminar and more focused on professional development modules offered to faculty who range from early postdoctoral researchers to experienced scholars, some of whom may indeed be reluctant to start publishing in English or conforming to international (anglophone) norms of academic communication. Writing centers, as they do in other places, offer individual consultations, but these are usually about work that is intended for publication and therefore demand different techniques than the ones used in undergraduate writing centers. This collection is therefore a unique opportunity to look at how writing pedagogy and writing center practices are being adapted for multi-lingual faculty, a constituency that has not heretofore been very visible even in the international scholarship on writing but whose needs are nevertheless real and urgent.

The writing scholars in this collection are focused on what motivates their colleagues to write and to learn about writing, on the types of interventions that work for faculty, and on the technologies that might help busy professionals save time. These concerns are deeply pragmatic and locally situated, but they have much to teach our distant colleagues. If academia is to become a kind of global public sphere in which ideas can be discussed and debated—and if English is to be its lingua franca—then anglophones will need to learn from the experiences of their international colleagues as much as those colleagues will need to adapt in order to be published (Lillis & Curry, 2010). And as I think is clear from the tenor of these essays, we the authors and our colleagues are ready for international dialogue and cooperation.

Plan of the Collection

The first section of this book presents an overview of the current context for academic writing in Russia. First, in her agenda-setting essay, "Academic Writing in Russia Beyond Zero Point," Irina Korotkina examines the challenges faced by current Russian writing programs, which must cope with the baggage of this field's anglophone attachments as well as the residue of the Soviet Union, in which the sharing of scientific research for broad audiences was discouraged. From Korotkina's perspective, Russia needs to develop a strong academic literacy curriculum in the Russian language (as well as minority languages) and not only in English.

In Chapter Two, Elena Getmanskaya examines historical precedents for today's conversation about writing in Russia. Using extensive archival resources, the author illuminates the practice of teaching writing in Russia in the nineteenth century, when the use of essay writing in secondary and tertiary education was moving from a strictly philological exercise associated with language and literature to a research activity designed to develop the overall humanitarian knowledge and civic personhood of high school graduates and university students. Getmanskaya describes the conflicts that this transition engendered and debates over best practices that foreshadow the current conversation.

In Chapter Three, Natalya Smirnova and Anna Guseva dive deeper into existing writing and pedagogical traditions by examining the learning histories and current writing practices of experienced researchers in the domain of art history. Based on interviews with six multilingual Russian art historians, Smirnova and Guseva reveal the various formal and informal ways in which these scholars have learned to write, mostly in the absence of writing courses. Participants discuss the ways in which the Soviet period shaped the rhetorical orientation of their discipline and the challenges they presently face—access to museums, libraries, and scholarly databases—that are shared by their colleagues in other disciplines.

Having established some of the ways in which the past informs present conditions, Chapter Four, "They Teach Writing but They Do Not Write," turns to a quite current conundrum: the educators tasked with teaching their colleagues in other disciplines to write research papers in English—Russian English teachers—tend not to publish their own work. Author Svetlana Bogolepova indicates that this has become an issue of special concern in the context of Project 5-100, where all faculty are expected and heavily incentivized to publish. Based on a survey of English faculty at several large Russian universities, Bogolepova offers reasons why language faculty lag behind and provides recommendations for how the issue ought to be addressed.

Because university writing centers have been created for the specific purpose of addressing these needs, Part Two focuses on the development of the writing center model in Russia. In Chapter Five, Tatiana Glushko presents the results of interviews with writing center and writing program administrators in Russia, arguing that the development of academic writing in this country is a "balancing act" between immediate needs driven by the market for academic publication and "long-term educational goals for internationalization" as well as between Russian and anglophone traditions that are sometimes incompatible.

Chapter Six then offers a close look at one of Russia's original writing centers: the AWC at HSE-Moscow. Director Svetlana Suchkova demonstrates how writing center structures and methodologies have been adapted to the Russian institutional framework in order to meet the specific needs of faculty researchers. Through data systematically collected on the effectiveness of the Center's activities, this chapter finds that the AWC model is effective and can be generalized to other institutions in the Russian Federation.

Chapter Seven brings us to peer tutoring—a core aspect of writing center work in the United States and Europe that is nascent in Russia. Olga

Aksakalova, and myself analyze the results of a collaboration among peer tutors at the New Economic School and trainees at LaGuardia Community College in New York City. During the Spring of 2018, participants were asked to take part in a series of mediated exchanges through a Wordpress blog, reflecting on their experiences. Based on our analysis of their posts and final reflections, we argue that this exercise helped inculcate a sense of transnational professional identity among peer tutors and enabled a sustained discussion of the fraught questions of authority in peer tutoring. We also make recommendations for the use of international exchanges as a training practice for writing center staff.

Though multilingualism and the need for bilingual (even tri-lingual) writing pedagogies is a feature of many of these chapters, English still looms very large on this landscape. It is the target language for most researchers seeking publication in international journals and at times a critical hurdle for them to overcome. As such, applied linguists are playing a considerable role in both the research on and the teaching of academic writing. Part Three is therefore dedicated to the language issue.

Chapter Eight presents the application Paper Cat, developed by researchers at HSE University, Perm. This program, as Elizaveta Smirnova, Svetlana Strinyuk, and Viacheslav Lanin argue, goes beyond general grammar checkers like Grammarly to identify the specific linguistic features of academic discourse based on an analysis of the existing corpus of academic writing across a variety of fields. The purpose is to assist second-language (L2) writers in the production of their own texts and to assist EAP instructors in evaluating the writing of their students and writing center clients as well as designing lessons that target the features of academic discourse that cause the most problems.

Chapter Nine continues this computational theme. Olga Vinogradova, Anna Viklova, and Mikhail Paporotskiy present the results of corpus research on first-language (L1) interference in the use of punctuation in English. Punctuation, they argue, is both understudied and under-taught to English language learners, and the results of their study of intermediate and advanced writing by Russian students shows that Russian speakers continue to apply Russian punctuation rules to English and do so in ways that make their communications less clear and effective. They note the most important differences and argue that punctuation simply cannot be ignored in language teaching, which it unfortunately often is.

Part Four discusses the teaching of writing in undergraduate classrooms. University teaching during the Soviet period largely favored oral assessment, but writing as a mode of testing students' skills and knowledge is becoming more common. Students taking the unified state exam (a university entrance exam) are now tasked with writing an essay modelled after the writing tasks on international English tests, and more top-tier universities are offering academic writing courses to their students, usually, again, in English. As Tatiana Golechkova indicates in Chapter Ten, the testing regime along with other features of secondary school preparation leads to a mismatch in expectations between students and university faculty. Golechkova applies the research on secondary-to-tertiary transition problems to the Russian context, examining the sources of these mismatched expectations and suggesting ways in which academic writing classrooms adopting an academic literacies framework can assist students in their transition to university studies.

Finally, Chapter Eleven explores the specific disciplinary context of the literature classroom, as Irina Kuznetsova-Simpson argues for the substitution of linguistic approaches with reader-response approaches to the teaching of writing to undergraduate students in literature courses. Drawing on her experience teaching an English-language drama and theatre course, Kuznetsova-Simpson further makes the case that performance in literature courses is "a very effective bridge between both skills—reading and writing— as well as a tool for sharpening students' analytical, creative, and autonomous writing skills."

Final Words

Lying beneath the surface of each one of these essays is an essential question: why write? Why write for an international audience? Why write in English? This is a question that our authors study while also seeking to answer it for themselves. That a group of scholar-teachers in Russia should want to get together to produce a volume for an American university press is not an obvious proposition. For one thing, many us are teachers who primarily transmit knowledge through the classroom. Furthermore, many of the research questions that arise do so out of local and institutional interests without always having obvious connections to broader disciplinary concerns at the international level. If they felt compelled, nevertheless, to write, our contributors could all have easily published these essays in Russian journals, and they could have done so with a much faster turnaround time than an edited collection affords. So why do this?

Some of the possible answers are unsatisfying. As Bogolepova's research suggests (Chapter 4), it may be because such writing is—through financial incentives or with the threat of job loss—demanded by one's institution and one's government. As the practitioners represented in this book attest, the case beyond professional survival is often unclear to the very writers these programs were designed to help. Yet they are motivated in their work and in their chapter contributions by the idea that there is something fundamentally satisfying and valuable about participating in a broader academic conversation. By contributing to this volume, by attending conferences abroad, by inviting prominent scholars to conferences in Russia, the members of this field are seeking not only international expertise to assist them in their own efforts but international presence and influence. It is our earnest hope that our colleagues abroad find things of value in our locally-inflected but globally-oriented work.

Perhaps the signal contribution that Russian writing programs and scholars can make is the very fact that so much of this work is being done with professional writers. To be honest, given my American bias and pedagogical interest in students and the freshman seminar, I have sometimes regarded this researcher focus as a kind of problem, as if it were drawing resources away from the urgent work of preparing the next generation. But what we are seeing here in Russia is no less than the transformation of an entire culture of academic communication, from the top down. These changes involve not only the language and modalities of communication but new standards of academic ethics and a new understanding of the purpose of writing and publishing. That this transformation should be uneven is only to be expected, but the essays presented here are evidence of the fact that it is occurring. In contrast to the inward, nationalist turn of Russian and U.S. politics seen over the past several years, the globalization of academic culture seems to be continuing apace.

References

Academic Writing Center. (n.d.). About AWC. HSE University. Retrieved October 20, 2019 from https://academics.hse.ru/en/awc/about.

Academic Writing University Center. (n.d.). Home. NUST MISIS Writing Center. Retrieved October 20, 2019 from http://awuc.misis.ru/.

Altbach, P. G., & Knight, J. (2007). The internationalization of higher education: Motivations and realities. *Journal of Studies in International Education*, *11*(3-4), 290-305.

Arnold, L. R., Nebel, A., & Ronesi, L. (Eds.). (2017). *Emerging writing research from the Middle East-North Africa region*. The WAC Clearinghouse; University Press of Colorado. https://doi.org/10.37514/INT-B.2017.0896.

Bazerman, C., Dean, C., Early, J., Lunsford, K., Null, S., Rogers, P., & Stansell, A. (Eds.). (2012). *International advances in writing research*. The WAC Clearinghouse; Parlor Press. https://doi.org/10.37514/PER-B.2012.0452.

Brooks, R., & Waters, J. (2011). *Student mobilities, migration and the internationalization of higher education*. Palgrave.

Center for Academic Writing "Impulse." (n.d.) About us. University of Tyumen. Retrieved October 20, 2019 from https://cawi.utmn.ru/eng/about/.

Donahue, C. (2009). "Internationalization" and composition studies: Reorienting the discourse. *College Composition and Communication, 61*(2), 212–243.

Korotkina, I. (2018). Russian scholarly publications in anglophone academic discourse: The clash of tyrannosaurs. *Integration of Education, 22*(2), 311–323.

Lillis, T., & Curry, M. J. (2010). *Academic writing in a global context: The politics and practices of publishing in English*. Routledge.

Muchiri, M. N., Mulamba, N. G., Myers, G., & Ndoloi, D. B. (1995). Importing composition: Teaching and researching academic writing beyond North America. *College Composition and Communication, 46*(2), 175–198.

National Writing Centers Consortium. (n.d.). Члены ассоциации [Association members]. National Writing Centers Consortium. Retrieved October 20, 2019 from https://nwcc-consortium.ru/participants/.

Rajakumar, M. (2018). *Western higher education in global contexts*. Lexington.

Samara Academic Consultancy Center. (n.d.). Welcome to Samara Academic Consultancy Center. Samara University. Retrieved October 20, 2019, from http://en.sacc.ssau.ru/.

Thaiss, C., Brauer, G., Carlino, P., Ganobcsik-Williams, L., & Sinha, A. (Eds.). (2012). *Writing programs worldwide: Profiles of academic writing in many places*. The WAC Clearinghouse; Parlor Press. https://doi.org/10.37514/PER-B.2012.0346.

Zemliansky, P., & St.Amant, K. (2016). *Rethinking post-communist rhetoric: Perspectives on rhetoric, writing, and professional communication in post-Soviet spaces*. Lexington.

Part One. Established Traditions and Evolving Contexts

1 Academic Writing in Russia Beyond Zero Point

Irina Korotkina
MOSCOW SCHOOL OF SOCIAL AND ECONOMIC SCIENCES

Before the 2010s, writing was largely considered by the Russian academic community to be the result of individual writing experience or innate talent. The term *academic writing* was used only among teachers of English and emerged in its direct Russian translation in debates triggered by the Government Decree of 2013 aimed at transforming universities into competitive global research organizations. Due to its novelty, the term was often interpreted arbitrarily; however, the debates soon involved a nation-wide audience of academics, editors, and educators, who demonstrated major concern about the poor quality of research papers written by Russian scholars. However, as in other multilingual academic communities, the problem was formulated in terms of international publications and poor knowledge of English among academics. This led to a profanation of academic writing, the multiplication of commercial services, and publications in predatory journals. The outcome of all these events is nevertheless positive because they raised awareness of academic writing as a specific set of teachable skills that may and should be developed not only in English but also in the native tongue. This awareness is still vague but likely permanent. In this chapter, I share insights based on long-term research implemented between my two doctoral dissertations on the development of academic writing in Russia, defended in 2008 and 2018. I analyze the impediments to introducing academic writing as a discipline in the national university curricula and elicit the key differences between the Russian and anglophone (globally accepted) writing traditions using the field of education as an example. Drawing from the rhetorical model of anglophone academic writing, I offer a metalinguistic approach to teaching writing, which merges anglophone methodology with the national language by focusing on the cognitive stages of rhetoric. Embracing wider audiences of educators, editors, scholars, and students, this approach can foster acceptance of the rhetorical and publishing conventions of the global academic discourse in Russia, contribute to the quality of national publications, and promote academic literacy in Russia and other post-Soviet spaces where Russian is still the lingua franca of academic communication.

Effective problem solving depends on how well the problem itself is understood. Policy analyst William Dunn (2011) points out that an error in problem structuring leads to the failure of the entire policy. When Russian educational policymakers began to analyze the problem of the diminishing status of Russian science, they defined it as the lack of international publications (Fedotov & Vasetskaya, 2013; Polikhina, 2020; Rostovtsev, 2017). Consequently, they focused their policies on research activities at universities and sought for stimuli to increase the number of quality international publications by Russian scholars. Two government decrees[1] stipulated that universities should become competitive research centers and academics should publish their research in top scholarly journals. As a result, Russia joined the "publish or perish" rush, which had by that time already embraced various geolinguistic regions (Canagarajah, 2000; Corcoran & Englander, 2016; Kuteeva & Mauranen, 2014), and just like other multilingual scholars, Russian academics found themselves under institutional pressure (Dobrynina, 2019; Zborovskij & Ambarova, 2019).

The consequences of the rush, also known in Russia as "publication fever," have long been discussed by the global academic community. The necessity to publish in English and communicate with anglophone "gatekeepers" (editors and reviewers) has led to the rise of commercial services offered by language and academic brokers; multiple publications in predatory journals; and has ultimately provoked opposition on behalf of those who claim that the dominance of English threatens the national culture (Corcoran & Englander, 2016; Lillis & Curry, 2010, 2015; Rostovtsev, 2017). The shadows of Swales' (1997) "Tyrannosaurus rex" and Phillipson's (1992) linguistic imperialism crawled into the Russian academic community and lurked in national publications (e.g., Popova & Beavitt, 2017).

However, the rush brought in some really positive consequences, such as the rise of university writing centers, the spread of English for Academic Purposes (EAP), the change in the attitudes towards teaching English, and the growing interest in academic writing. This was the point at which academic writing

---

[1] Government Decree No. 211 of 16 March 2013 and Presidential Decree No. 204 of 7 May 2018 set the goals of fostering the internationalization of science and higher education and integrating research organizations and federal universities.

started to emerge in Russia, and it is academic writing that has been crucial in defining the problems encountered by Russian science and education.

Indeed, the problem of raising the quality of research, as well as the interrelated problem concerning the status of higher education, can best be defined in terms of academic writing and literacy. According to Hyland (2007, 2011), the three main factors underlying research skills include academic literacy, socialization in a specific academic discourse community, and training in academic writing. Unfortunately, the notion of academic literacy has not been embedded in Russian academic discourse, and as a consequence has never been considered in discussions of Russian higher education (Korotkina, 2018a; Smirnova & Shchemeleva, 2015). Students' socialization in discourse communities has remained rather poor due to the general dysfunction of higher education caused, among other reasons, by the traditional gap between education and science (Sukharev, 2014). For until recently research has mainly been carried out by scientific institutes or research organizations, not universities (Fedotov & Vasetskaya, 2013). However, the major factor in the dysfunction of both education and science has been that academic writing has not been included in Russian university curricula, except for basic courses within EAP programmes found mainly in leading universities (Bakin, 2013; Bazanova, 2015; Smith, 2017; Squires, 2016; see also Chapters 7, 10, and 11).

The priority of academic writing as a fundamental skill set for all university students, largely unquestioned in Western universities, has still been the matter of argument in Russia. First of all, it has been mainly viewed as a matter of individual practice and talent; secondly, teaching writing has been associated with teaching language and literature at school, which has had little to do with research (see Chapter 2); finally, the term *academic writing* has been typically connected with teaching EAP, which has been generally seen as preparation for the International English Language Testing System (IELTS) test. As knowledge of English among students and academics has been rather poor, teaching academic writing in English may help only a limited audience (Dobrynina, 2019; Petrashova, 2017). The idea that academic writing is a specific discipline and field of study has not yet been widely accepted (Korotkina, 2018a; Smirnova & Shchemeleva, 2015).

In this chapter, I will strongly argue that developing academic writing in a country where English has not been widely used may best be achieved in the native tongue. Teaching academic writing through clear, flexible rhetorical models adopted from the well-developed anglophone writing methodology provides a much shorter path to raising the quality of higher education and promoting Russian research results on the global stage. Indeed, learning writing in the native language will help bypass the long and slow process of mastering written English, which is, in fact, a grapholect (Bizzel, 1999), or a very specific written form of academic communication which all neophytes to the academy should master regardless of their native tongues (Hyland, 2011). The specificity of a grapholect means that the language of academic discourse is universal and transdisciplinary, with its own rhetorical, syntactic, and lexical features, and therefore has to be taught not only to non-native but also to native speakers—regardless of which national language is used for teaching.

Establishing academic writing as a discipline in the national curriculum is obviously the most effective way to overcome the obscure, obsolete academese which still permeates the Russian publishing tradition and has caused the most problems encountered by writers who have learned writing by imitating this style. Butler et al. (2014) have noted that Russian students and teachers alike have transferred academic context and cultural norms from writing in Russian into writing in English. This happened because no other norms were made explicit to them; conversely, if the norms of anglophone rhetoric are made explicit, writers may follow them deliberately, both in English and Russian.

This idea has been strongly supported by Russian EAP experts who have viewed academic writing through the lenses of academic literacy (Smirnova & Shchemeleva, 2015) and bilingual or translingual approaches (Dobrynina, 2019; Khalyapina & Shostak, 2019; Rasskazova et al., 2017). Many Russian writers are willing to present their research results in accordance with globally accepted rhetorical conventions, but few have succeeded in breaking free from the influence of the old norms. Thus, the Russian academic community today faces the problem of fighting their own tyrannosaur rather than the English-speaking one (Korotkina, 2018c).

Throughout this discussion, I will have to refer to my reflections, which are the outcomes of a decade-long study. The complete analysis can be found in my papers (partially listed in the references), manual on academic writing in Russian (Korotkina, 2015), monograph (Korotkina, 2018b), and doctoral dissertation (Korotkina, 2019b) written during this period and aimed to inform the Russian academy rather than the global community.

To make my ideas explicit for the international reader, I will start with a brief overview of how academic writing in Russia became the focus of national and international discussion. I will then consider the factors underlying the problems of Russian researchers through the lens of rhetoric, systematize typical Russian mistakes drawing from sample papers in the field of education, and offer solutions for the problems. These solutions involve teaching writing for research publication purposes through methods which have been developed in the anglophone community—but in the learners' native tongue. I will conclude by demonstrating the benefits of such teaching in Russia and beyond.

Academic Writing in Russia: Views from the Inside and Outside

As a preamble to this section, I will refer to my own experience of getting familiarized with the notion of academic writing, which might give the reader a real insider's view of the situation. Like other Russian university teachers of English, I discovered academic writing in the mid-1990s. The discovery came upon me as a startling revelation, an abruptly obtained ability to explain things which were meant to be inexplicable. I immediately started to transfer those skills into my Russian writing, and ever since then, my most passionate desire has been to share this new knowledge with every writer in the country.

The first opportunity to share occurred in 2008, when I presented my views to Russian educators at a conference. The impact on the audience was similar to my own first impression, and I was strongly encouraged to defend the idea of academic writing in a dissertation (Russian candidate's degree in education, usually referred to as similar to the Ph.D.). I did, and in 2009 I introduced the terms *академическое письмо* (academic writing) and *академическая грамотность* (academic literacy) into the Russian educational discourse. At that time, the terms sounded so alien to Russian educators that the dissertation council discouraged me from using them in the title of the dissertation. After a long fight, I had to concede to the traditional Soviet wording, which can be approximately translated into English as "The development of professionally-oriented written communication of secondary school authorities in the process of professional development training"[2] — and this was the least horrible of all the proposed variants. Sadly, my research results were disregarded due to my being a novice in Russian pedagogy. Thus, the terms in their Russian translation remained as they were, in informal communication among Russian EAP teachers.

However, I continued the study with renewed vigor when I rediscovered writing as rhetoric and composition in 2013, when experts from the US started to seek teachers of writing in Russia (I will give details later in the chapter). This second discovery contributed to my own understanding and helped me promote academic writing further and much more successfully. My second doctoral dissertation of 2018 (Russian doctor in education)

---

2 "Развитие профессионально-ориентированной письменной коммуникации у руководителей школ в процессе повышения квалификации."

established academic writing as a new discipline and field of study which should be systematically developed in the country and introduced into university curricula and beyond. It was a comparative study titled *Theory and Practice of Teaching Academic Writing in Western and Russian Universities* (a close translation into English). The very difference between the two titles demonstrates the dramatic changes in the attitudes toward academic writing among Russian academics and educational policymakers that took place within just one decade.

The bitter concern among Russian academics about poor writing and research skills among students broke out into an open discussion in 2011 on the pages of the scholarly journal *Higher Education in Russia* (Kouprianov, 2011; Orlova, 2011; Perlov, 2011; Robotova, 2011; Senashenko, 2011; Stepanov, 2012; and others). The discussion followed two roundtables on academic writing organized by Arkady Perlov at the Russian State University of Humanities and Boris Stepanov at HSE University. Interestingly, I also conducted a round table on academic writing and literacy at HSE University the same year, but somehow missed the start of the discussion in the journal. However, it was the first of a series of publications in which the term academic writing was used in print by representatives of different disciplines and universities. Each of them referred to his or her own experiences and used the term according to their own intuitive understanding. The term itself in Russian was considered arguable and used in quotation marks in the titles and texts.[3]

Unfortunately, when EAP teachers joined the debate (e.g., Bakin, 2013; Bazanova, 2015; Dobrynina, 2015; Korotkina, 2013), and academic writing was defined in terms of the discipline as it has existed in Western universities, other academics ceased submitting papers on the topic. As some of the first participants later explained, they probably realized that their expertise was not professional. However, their papers were—and still are—an important source of information on how academic writing was interpreted in Russia before it became widely known.

The variety of problems raised by the first publications could be roughly divided into two issues: whether university education in Russia needs specific courses aimed at developing writing skills, and whether these skills are specific enough to be called academic writing. Some authors referred to their specific practices in teaching students to write within other courses (e.g., Kouprianov, 2011; Orlova, 2011), others pondered Russian university curricula

---

3   In the English titles that appeared in the Russian papers, authors did not use quotation marks, so in the list of references to this chapter they are not visible.

in general (e.g., Perlov, 2011; Senashenko, 2011; Stepanov, 2012). All authors agreed that teaching Russian students to write was a major issue that needed consideration at the national level because the standards of higher education stipulated the standards of written papers only formally but did not provide any information on how to achieve those standards.

Being unanimous about the necessity of teaching writing at university, the participants argued about the very idea of academic writing as a special set of skills. Precisely as in the case of my first dissertation, many did not accept the very term academic writing. Indeed, while it was not yet embedded, Perlov (2011) and Stepanov (2012) substituted it in their texts with academic work, which they intuitively considered more relevant to discussing research skills. Professor Robotova (2011), an expert in Russian language and literature, opposed the term on the grounds of language ambiguity: if "writing" means producing text in a language, and the word "academic" in Russian means pertaining to the highest degree of scientific knowledge (like in The Academy of Sciences), then academic writing means writing like classical scholars, which is nonsense. Kouprianov (2011), who did not oppose the term, noted that being deprived of explicit models for expressing their own ideas, Russian students attempted to imitate the style of nineteenth century classical scholars, whose works are usually studied in the first year. This problem also has been emphasized by anglophone academic writing experts (e.g., Bean, 2011; Young, 2006), so Robotova's fears of possible misinterpretations were partially right.

An especially puzzling interpretation of the term appeared in two monographs by Vladimir Bazylev (2014, 2015). While other authors discussed the relevance of the word academic in collocation with writing, he used the word writing in quotation marks: in both titles and texts it appears as academic "writing." One of the books had the parenthesized subtitle "theoretical aspect" (2014), the other, "methodological aspect" (2015). They opened with an overview of the above-mentioned discussion in *Higher Education in Russia*, including my own contribution and those by other EAP experts. Bazylev seemed to totally agree with us, but his books (later published as one in 2016) demonstrated a misinterpretation of writing, which he discussed in terms of the traditional Russian disciplines named "Standards of Speech," "Methodology of Science," and "Discourse Analysis." These disciplines in Russia have focused on teaching reading and stylistics, so writing has been viewed as somewhat of a side effect of these courses, which partially explains the quotation marks. A more obvious (although indirect) explanation is found in the bibliography: out of 219 references, only five are in English, one of which is on stylistics, and three on discourse; the fifth is a reference to a university website. The content of the book casts doubts on the fact that the author read Hyland's *Academic Discourse* (2009), which is one of the three; otherwise, his whole idea of writing would be different.

The only book that approached real writing in Russian was the manual From Note-taking to Dissertation by Professor Natalia Kolesnikova (2004) from the Novosibirsk State Technical University. I wondered why her terminology was so different from English, but when we met, she confessed that she did not speak English and was totally unaware of the existence of English academic writing (N. Kolesnikova, personal communication, February 5, 2009). The astonishing fact about her book was that she introduced paragraph writing with topic sentences and constructing a text of logical clusters in a way that was very close to English academic writing (in Russia, paragraphs have usually been considered mere visual divisions in page layout). Unfortunately, her book appeared to be the only positive result of my search for Russian sources. A few minor publications appeared after her book, but they generally repeated what she said and did not add much.

Probably the first account of academic writing in Russia (or rather, its absence) that became accessible to an international audience was my paper "Academic Writing in Russia: Evolution or Revolution?" (Korotkina, 2014). The study focused on potential misunderstandings in discussing writing in Russia caused by the huge gap between the anglophone and Russian understanding of writing: as rhetoric and composition—or the basic ability to write. A similar gap divided understanding of literacy, which was not—and still has not been—applied in Russia to any skill beyond basic ability to read and write. Because of this, for instance, information literacy has not been accepted as a term by Russian experts in the field, who have deliberately substituted the English term with "*информационная культура личности*" ("informational culture of an individual") (Gendina et al., 2006, p. 29).

Because Russian publications on the topic were mostly limited to the discussion described above, the only evidence I could rely on in the paper was my own experience from schooling, university education, my work as translator in science and technology, editor of a Russian scholarly issue, EFL and EAP teacher and teacher trainer, and eventually teacher of academic writing in English and Russian—the latter being a unique position. Understandably, such evidence seemed either too personal or too general to anglophone experts: at least, this is how Professor Pavel Zemliansky put it when he reviewed my first version of this paper for the journal *College Composition and Communication*, where it was not then published. Indeed, I did not even answer my own question, for neither evolution nor revolution had yet been seen. However personal or general the evidence might seem to an anglophone expert, this first account was immediately referred to in a study simultaneously conducted in Russia by a group of international researchers (Butler et al., 2014). The authors admitted the validity of my account and supported their findings with multiple references to it. Another acknowledgement, although indirect, came when the paper reached the top ten full text downloads in several educational databases during the first four months of its publication through the Social Science Research Network (SSRN). The reason was the publish or perish rush in other geolinguistic regions (especially in Asia), the rising interest in academic writing, and the lack of publications concerning Russia.

My paper was the result of reflections that followed participation in two events, both of which took place in Moscow in 2013: a course on rhetoric and composition conducted by Olga Aksakalova and Kara Bollinger at the New Economic School, and the 16th Fulbright Summer School for the Humanities conducted by a group of U.S. professors at the Moscow State University. The leaders of the latter also published their reflections on academic writing in Russia (Schleifer et al., 2016), but their publication did not reach the international reader as effectively, probably because it was issued three years after the events and in a Russian journal.

Another study was carried out at the same time by Zemliansky and Goroshko (2016), in whose survey I participated in March 2013 as it reached me through Aksakalova and Bollinger. The study encompassed Ukraine and Russia and was published in the book Rethinking Post-Communist Rhetoric: Perspectives on Rhetoric, Writing, and Professional Communication in Post-Soviet Spaces (Zemliansky & St.Amant, 2016) along with Bollinger's (2016) account of her teaching experience at the New Economic School. All the papers in the book focused mostly on the cultural differences in writing traditions and their influences on writers' attitudes to and understanding of academic writing. They also referred to the low level of English among Russian or Ukrainian students and researchers but considered it an impediment to the development of academic writing in these countries rather than a manifestation of Swales' (1997) "Tyrannosaurus rex."

There was a later publication, however, that attempted to view Russian research papers through the lens of Phillipson's (1992) linguistic imperialism. Published in the Russian *Journal of Integration of Education* (Popova & Beavitt, 2017), the research focused mainly on the formal, cliché-based writing provoked by the spread of the Introduction, Methods and Materials, Results, and Discussion (IMRaD) format. The authors, who based their research on content analysis of 200 Russian papers in chemistry indexed in the Scopus abstracts database, claim that the format diminishes the role of the Russian language in academic discourse because writers use clichés due to their insufficient knowledge of English, and their papers sound formal and impersonal. This statement is arguable if we take into account the fact that the majority of STEM scientists have tended to write in clichés in their native languages, and the IMRaD format established by Robert Day (Day & Gastel, 2016) half a century ago proved effective even beyond technical or natural sciences.

To provide two more arguments against the spread of English, Popova & Beavitt (2017) go on to discuss the disadvantages of teaching subjects in English through content and language integrated learning (CLIL), and the dangers of spreading the anglophone tradition of writing through the establishment of university writing centers. These arguments, however, have been fairly ambiguous because CLIL is not widely spread in Russian universities and thus could not have been considered a threat, while the information about Russian writing centers in the paper was given insufficiently and even erroneously. Sadly, Popova & Beavitt totally disregarded publications concerning the heated discussion around establishing writing centers in Russia, which by that time had already reached a peak on the pages of *Higher Education in Russia* and triggered a number of international conferences, workshops, and roundtables around the country.

The debate about writing centers started to emerge in Russian universities in the 2010s and focused on their functions due to the uncertainty of their institutional and methodological bases. First of all, creating writing centers was urged by national policies aimed at the internationalization of science and education, but their aim was defined as merely helping faculty publish internationally (Bazanova, 2015; Smith, 2017). Because of this, the audience for writing centers was mainly researchers, and students were involved only when a university ran international programs (Squires, 2016). Consequently, a contradiction emerged between the aims set by U.S. experts who came to help establish writing centers, basing their work on tutoring and writing center pedagogy (Smith, 2017) and the lack of knowledge about this pedagogy among the newly appointed Russian writing center directors and their colleagues. Besides, the hands-off approach is useless where the basics of academic writing are unknown.

Last but not least, as English was considered the only impediment for international publications, writing centers became the responsibility of EFL departments. However, teachers of English in Russian universities have been one of the least published groups of academics because most of them are educators rather than researchers, teach more academic hours and tend to be paid less than teachers in other disciplines, which leaves little space for research (see Chapter 4). As a result, the limitations on their own writing practice have hampered their efficacy in teaching others. As EAP experts are still rare and new to the academic community, teachers of English have continued to be looked down upon by other academics, and writing centers have been viewed as support units whose raison d'etre is to translate papers into English or correct language mistakes. Writers just do not understand that the reasons why editors of high-ranking international journals reject their papers is not bad English, but the lack of text organization, insufficient support, faulty argument, or the opaque academese they consider essential to use.

Reflections from the Discipline of Rhetoric

The language in which we think is invisible to communicators, and it works in unpredictable, nonlinear and mostly unspoken ways. The deeper our knowledge, the more things we skip as obvious, and the quicker we grasp complex problems. This is the way we conduct research and conceive new ideas. Even preparing to communicate ideas by text, we might not care about the language because no one sees how we strive to logically organize our thoughts, what kind of evidence we seek, or which style we are planning to use to present our ideas. These stages of writing, also referred to as metadiscourse (Flowerdew, 2013; Kwan, 2010), represent the writer's commitment to the study and are therefore core elements of academic writing, probably the most important and difficult to learn. Language is just the means to deliver ideas, and if no new knowledge is produced, a paper in whichever language is pointless. In Russia, however, such papers have still been published.

When in 2013, I found out that American experts use the term rhetoric and composition instead of academic writing and apply it in various theoretical and practical contexts (Enos, 2010; Leki, 1999; Lynn, 2010), I was amazed. Indeed, understanding writing as rhetoric presents it as a system of five stages described by the sophists and formulated by Aristotle millennia ago and recovered by compositionists (Jarratt, 1991): invention (hypothesizing or having an original idea), arrangement (organizing ideas and arguments logically), style (choosing the genre), memory (using content knowledge, literature and methodology of the discipline), and delivery (presenting it all as a text in a language).

Now it became clear why the discussion of academic writing from 2011 to 2014 revealed such diverse attitudes among Russian academics. Only the last stage of the five, delivery, involves what we traditionally understand in Russia as writing, while the cognitive stages of writing, metalinguistic per se, have not been considered as part of the writing process, but rather part of research. If writing is thus divided from research, it loses significance and remains the concern of linguists and philologists.

However, Russian academics are not to be blamed for their misunderstandings. The bimillennial path from the sophists to today's rhetoric and composition was not straight, and rhetoric lost its cognitive elements more than once (Enos, 2010; Ryan & Zimmerelli, 2009). Studying the history of rhetoric and composition reveals the connection between the way scholars communicate knowledge and the political environment. When a society is dominated by a religion or ideology, the first two stages erode. This happened in the Middle Ages, when new knowledge had to be thoroughly wrapped in direct quotations from canonized classics, and in the Soviet times, when it had to be supported by communist rhetoric with similar direct quotations. The quality of argument depended on the number and choice of quotations (memory) and the passionate or elaborate language (style and delivery). As logic or evidence mattered little, the preferable form of debate in such societies was oral, truth was mixed up with censored fiction, and exams in universities were oral, or, if written, then based on the same censored and canonized lists of literature. Interestingly, even speaking foreign languages has depended on ideology: in the Middle Ages scholars spoke Latin and Greek, the dead languages for quoting long dead canonized classics; in the USSR, speaking any live foreign language was suspicious and even dangerous. Ideologies have kept their borders shut and have preferred dead classics to those still alive (Korotkina, 2018b).

The tragic gap between the Western and Russian writing traditions formed in the twentieth century, when the sharing of knowledge was restricted by the Iron Curtain. This was the period of rapid development of rhetoric and composition in the US and academic writing as a field of research around the world. When in the very beginning of the century, the newly created National Council for Teachers of English (NCTE) started their fight against canonized lists of literature, and progressive education led to an understanding of writing as a set of intellectual and social skills that enable students to express their own views and ideas, Russia entered World War I and the revolution. In the 1920s, the USSR implemented the great social project of general public education and a literate society in all the multicultural regions of the vast country. In the 1930s, however, ideology strengthened, and while New Criticism evolved in the US, Soviet schools and universities fell under the directives of the government, all sources were censored, and ideas prescribed. Since then and until the end of the century, language was connected with literature, and literature was carefully selected (see Chapter 2). Like in the Harvard system that preceded progressive education, final exams in schools and entrance exams at universities paid special attention to compositions in which students were expected to express the prescribed ideas—and express them passionately, as if they were their own. In exam compositions and oral exams, the use of sources was forbidden, and students had to repeat what was said by teachers and memorize long quotations from canonized literature. Unfortunately, these practices—albeit so deeply and for so long embedded in Soviet education—have not yet been paid proper attention in Russian publications: some might still consider it common practice; others, not worth consideration.

However, a century of such practices could not be overcome in a few years—or even decades, so when eventually the Soviet state collapsed, education faced too many challenges. The fall of the Iron Curtain was immediately followed by the New Media Revolution. Learning English started to be important, and the digital divide added even more problems for teachers, who were mostly born in the Soviet era and naturally reluctant to engage new trends in curricula and methodology. New rhetoric and new requirements started to form chaotically, and educational policymakers strived to find ways through this stormy sea of trouble. Educational reforms have lasted for over two decades but have been unanimously considered unsuccessful by the academic community and either severely criticized (e.g., Sukharev, 2014) or regarded as subject to major changes (e.g., Klyachko & Mau, 2015).

Discussing writing in Russia, U.S. experts in rhetoric and composition have had to bear in mind that Soviet-style literary compositions were substituted by the unified exam only in the mid-2000s (see Chapter 2 and Chapter 10), and the idea of writing centers emerged ten years ago, when they celebrated 40 years of their successful functioning in the US.

This very brief historical overview sheds light upon the factors underlying the problems of today's Russian academic writing. First, education still has remained oral in many educational contexts, with the sage on the stage and oral exams, which have required memorizing what was said by the teacher or read in a book. Writing to express one's own idea has been a novelty, and essays in the unified exams (both in Russian and English) have been taught rather formally, focusing on language cliches. It takes at least a year to encourage newcomers to university to speak out and defend their views, for their motivation to study appears perverted (Zborovskij & Ambarova, 2019; see Chapter 10). According to state standards, most written assignments in disciplines are not essays, but papers called "рефераты," in which students should simply demonstrate the scope of their reading and proper understanding of what they read. Criticism or expression of one's own ideas has not been the aim of such writing. Because of this, research papers written later have often contained too many direct quotations and unnecessary references and lack structure.

Secondly, writing has still been associated with language and literature (a problem happily overcome in the US nearly a century ago). Courses in rhetoric, interchangeably called "standards of speech" and taught at a university level as supplementary units, have often focused on speaking, editing, and reading rather than writing. Courses in Russian called "academic writing" have also appeared as supplementary, but these have been commonly taught by professors in disciplines (for instance, faculty of psychology at the Russian Presidential Academy of National Economy and Public Administration, or sociology at the Moscow School of Social and Economic Sciences); they usually focus on literature search, referencing and meeting formal requirements. When teachers of Russian have been involved, they have taught courses according to their own perceptions, mainly grammar, punctuation, and accuracy (the aforementioned Natalia Kolesnikova (2004) being a rare exception).

Thirdly, although the number of Russian students with good command of English has grown rapidly, updated authentic learning materials have been used in a limited number of schools and universities where students' and teachers' social statuses have given them an opportunity to travel or study abroad. According to the English First English Proficiency Index (EF EPI) of 2020, Russia is still a country with a relatively low level of English (the 41st position among the 100 surveyed countries), and according to a national survey by the Levada-Center in 2015, only one of five Russian respondents with higher education admitted to speaking a foreign language, which is not necessarily English or good enough to read or write.

Finally, many academics in arts, humanities, and education cannot read English or do not think it necessary to read international publications in the original because their disciplines are more deeply embedded in local cultural contexts than STEM. This has significantly limited both their own research and the research skills they teach. In STEM and life sciences, reading in English has been essential for constantly checking the most recent research results obtained around the world. Language barriers fall when the information is crucial. For instance, Soviet advances in space exploration and nuclear physics were valued internationally despite the Russian language and format of publications: even restricted access did not prevent other scholars from reading them. Contrarily, the decades-long isolation of education as a discipline has led to immense problems in today's communication in the field: the Russian concepts are so different from English that they have prevented understanding.

The problem of poor citation and narrower readership in humanities and social sciences has been acknowledged by researchers on the international scale (e.g., Dunleavy, 2014), but when research is limited by national publications, the result for many is zero citations.

Another major problem has been the Russian publishing tradition. Until recently, publishing the same text under slightly modified titles in several journals was welcome, and fighting plagiarism in a country where it used to be solely understood as publishing an author's complete paper under someone else's name seems quixotic. In 2018 and 2019, the Russian company Antiplagiarism with the support of several influential partners held two conferences titled "Plagiarism Detection" ("Обнаружение заимствований," which is in Russian abbreviated as OZ because the term plagiarism was substituted by the less radical word, "adoptions").[4] The goal of the conference was to reach consensus on understanding plagiarism and seek ways of revealing and preventing it. I participated in both conventions and was shocked to hear that the majority of plagiarized dissertations have not belonged to government officers but university lecturers.

Hence, if the problem of Russian academic writing should be defined in terms of rhetoric, the definition should start with the first two stages, invention and arrangement (producing new knowledge and organizing ideas), then style and memory (introducing international publishing conventions, publishing ethics and referencing), and then move on to delivery. As the first four are beyond, or above, national languages, they imply metalinguistic skills, which may be taught effectively in the native tongue. Surprisingly, when we get to delivery, differences between Russian and English also appear to be diminishing because learning how to use cohesion, parallel structures, and repetition of key words, or how to avoid wordiness and nominalization may be considered fairly similar in both languages.

Thinking Russian, Writing English: Reflections from Education

Education is probably the most problematic research area in Russia and other post-Soviet states today because in the Soviet era it was the key tool for educating new generations and therefore developed under the strict ideological control of the government and in deeper isolation from the global mainstream. The consequences of this isolation for Russia have not yet been systematically studied, and publications devoted to the history of Russian pedagogy tend to value the Soviet period, considering it classical, but as I argue in this section, the resulting differences in terminology and writing

---

4   See the conference website https://ozconf.ru/oz-2020.

traditions have provided multiple examples of academically illiterate papers. Professor Robotova (2015, 2018) expresses major concern about the poor quality of papers and dissertations in Russian pedagogy, the illiteracy of writers, their careless use of terminology, and the neglect of the Russian language, which they ought to use especially well, being teachers.

I will refer to this field as a sample, but it does not mean that Russian educators are incapable of good writing or that writers in other disciplines necessarily write better. I would also emphasize the fact that Russian education researchers are not being opposed to anglophone writers in this analysis: their papers have been analyzed in terms of the requirements of academic writing and publishing, of which they have been simply unaware. The items quoted in this section come from real publications, but the authors' names or the titles of the journals will not be revealed for ethical reasons. The material presented in this section was previously published as part of a conference paper (Korotkina, 2019a) and are part of my second doctoral dissertation (Korotkina, 2019b).

When Russian educators started to participate in international programs and projects, methodological and terminological differences caused significant misunderstandings and misinterpretations. On the one hand, Russian educators rarely know English well enough to read international journals and are not familiar with English terminology; on the other hand, they are used to their own concepts, which have been deeply embedded in national publications and supported by the established authority of Soviet and Russian scholars. To find correspondences between the two terminologies has been hard enough, but to reconsider the national system has been even harder.

The very word "education" causes problems. In Russian, the field is called педагогика (pedagogy), which is reflected in multiple derivatives, such as "doctor of pedagogical sciences," "pedagogical studies," or research, and "pedagogues" as the umbrella term for all teachers from kindergarten to the postgraduate level. The term "образование" (education) is used for institutional or political purposes, like in Ministry of Education or higher education, and there is no corresponding term for educators. As for teachers, the term derived from the similar Russian verb (to teach—учить, teacher—учитель) is applied only to primary and secondary school teachers, whereas university teachers are named by a special term, "преподаватель," with the corresponding verb. A similar distinction is made between university students (студенты) and school pupils (ученики, школьники); the latter are never called students. These discrepancies are basic and therefore the most troublesome.

Examples of misunderstandings emerge in Russian publications in English, or, more often, the translated titles and abstracts in Russian journals.

Professor Sternin (2017) bitterly remarks that Russian abstracts in English have traduced Russian arts and humanities. Mechanical or word-to-word translation has been the most common reason for such terminological puzzles as "personal competences" instead of "study skills," "educational material" instead of "learning material," "pedagogical process" instead of "teaching and learning." or "valuable orientations formation" instead of "enhancing" or "evincing values." Some Russian concepts are hard to identify in English; for example, the widespread Russian term образовательное пространство (literally, educational space) means "the area with unified learning conditions and assessment standards." It is commonly used with the adjective единое (unified) and applied as nation-wide or world-wide. Other terms that seem similar or synonymous in meaning to Russian educators include learning environment, educational environment, educational context, or learning context; these may occur in Russian translations of the same term, causing even more confusion because they have distinctly different meanings in English. Unfortunately, Russian translators in education have hardly ever checked the occurrence of a term using search tools.

Another problem is the translation of whole phrases or sentences. They are often unreadable even to Russian educators with good English, and especially destructive in titles, (e.g., "Anthropological Synthesis of the Methodological Bases of Pedagogical Activity's Research," "Integration of Didactic Units of Knowledge by Methods of Activity Approach in Training of Students of Higher Educational Institutions in Mathematics," or "To the Question about the Modern Technologies of the Construction of the 'Container' Model of Society: One Example of the Existence of the Religious Clothes in the Education Institutions." These are just random examples taken from Russian journals indexed in the e-Library, the Russian database of scholarly publications. I would not embarrass the authors or editors by giving direct references, understanding the lack of professional translators and poor funding of Russian pedagogical journals.

When an abstract is written in such "Russian English" with key words that are either non-occurring or confusing, the paper will hardly be noticed by international peers. The following single sentence belongs to the abstract of one of the previously cited titles: "On the basis of the conducted research it was revealed that application of the theory of integration of didactic units of knowledge and ways of activity in training of students of higher education institutions in mathematics significantly improves quality of the knowledge gained by the students as the main time is allocated for training in ability to solve mathematical problems in the context of integration of the actions corresponding to the process of the solution of these tasks."

The problem is rooted not in poor translation, but in the Russian tradition (occurring mainly in the arts, humanities, soft social sciences and education) of writing texts in obscure, wordy academese, which permeates not only traditionally formalized texts (e.g., legal) but also many texts in humanities and social sciences (Kolesnikova, 2009; Robotova, 2015, 2018). Certainly, Russians have not been the only ones who have fallen into the trap of wordiness and excessive nominalization. As Bean (2011) wittily points out, writers get "infested with nominalization . . . through unsafe intercourse with bureaucrats, psychobabblers, and educational administrators" (p. 249). Obviously, educational administrators have been the source of this kind of infection worldwide. At least, this is what the unanimous agreement of Russian academics to Bean's statement invariably demonstrates when I quote him in my workshops.

The traditional view of academic writing as unintelligible to all but a few experts is also widely accepted not only by Russian educators. Graff (2000) argues that texts intentionally made more incomprehensible are less frequent, more peripheral, and make less impact on their fields, but some journal editors who are overworked and underpaid still accept them. As a result, some really important ideas have been made less central than others. This has been true of overworked and underpaid Russian journal editors, who would rather object to obscurely written papers but have to accept them in light of the Russian publishing tradition and respect for the authors' degrees. Russian scholars would argue that their papers are important because of the ideas but not the language and refer to their academic statuses as a proof.

The tradition of sticking to Russian terms in education has been so strong that translators often have followed the patterns of Russian discourse even when the papers are written by professionals or native speakers of English. An American colleague who teaches research writing in a Russian university complained how embarrassed she was when her article was edited by a Russian journal, and the proof was not sent to her for final approval before publication. The corrections turned her native academic English into patterns which she daily fights in her students' assignments. I felt similarly embarrassed when someone translated the title and abstract of my Russian paper into English without informing me. When I do it myself, I typically get two rather different texts, and titles may differ in syntax and wording because of terminological, not language differences. Ever since then, I have been asking Russian editors not to make any changes to my English titles and abstracts.

The impact of the tradition has also been noticed in texts written by Russians with good command of English because in writing they could not overcome it. For instance, in Popova and Beavitt's paper (2017), the Russian co-author's voice can be recognized in sentences like "In other words, one may speak about the absence of free choice in terms of the form of presentation of results of intellectual activity" (p. 57). This is a perfect example of a typically Russian collection of rhetorical faults like excessive nominalization, wordiness, multiple repetition of the preposition of, and words from spoken English, such as speak, look, or talk. Of course, the mastery of written academic English by multilingual scholars cannot compare to that of British or American writers, but texts written in co-authorship with native speakers should be polished by the more proficient co-author. Sadly, texts written by Russian co-authors often remain unpolished as well, and collaborative projects effectively become separate pieces written in separate voices. Clarity does not depend on the national language, but as language has been considered secondary to research, polishing has rarely been practiced by Russian writers (Kolesnikova, 2009).

Russian researchers are not to be blamed for writing this way. As I previously noted (and as is demonstrated in Chapter 3), Russian students and scholars develop as writers individually, most often by imitating the patterns and styles they encounter in disciplinary texts, which result in an unnaturally elaborate manner not only among Russian (Kouprianov, 2011) but also among other international students (Hyland, 2007; Young, 2006). Day and Gastel (2016), note that Western scholars who developed their writing before the 1970s also "learned only to imitate the writing of the authors before them—with all its defects—thus establishing a system of error in perpetuity" (p. xvi). This "system of error in perpetuity" is what has to be overcome in Russia—and other geolinguistic regions—today.

To fight the perpetuation of a bad tradition, the Russian academic community needs to understand why this locally embedded tradition is inappropriate for international publications and why the globally accepted rhetorical and publishing tradition should be preferred. The validity of the comparative study I conducted was supported by my 15-year experience in editing and translating Russian scholarly papers in physics, aviation and space technology, medicine, history of science and education, and 20-year experience in teaching academic writing to students and researchers in both languages. The study was carried out at two universities, the Moscow School of Social and Economic Sciences and the Russian Presidential Academy of National Economy and Public Administration. Research also included annual workshops and seminars for Ph.D.s, researchers, and academics at two leading national research universities in Moscow, HSE University and the MISiS Technical University, and workshops, regional schools, and seminars for academics and researchers at eight other federal universities and national research universities across Russia. Research results were published in Russian scholarly journals and my monograph Academic Writing Teaching Models: International Experience and National Practices (2018) and defended in my second doctoral dissertation (Russian doctor in education, 2019) Theory and Practice of Teaching Academic Writing in Western and Russian Universities.

The study (Korotkina, 2019b) involved critical discourse analysis of over 150 research papers in education and pedagogy, selected from 47 Russian journals, all of which were currently included in the database of the Higher Attestation Commission of the Russian Ministry of Science and Higher Education. The papers were analyzed alongside ten criteria formulated in terms of requirements for international publications. According to these criteria, the study identified ten major differences between the expectations of publications in English and typical Russian-language publications in the field of education:

1. **Title and abstract**

English: Titles and abstracts are considered of major importance; they should contain key words and present the focus of the paper clearly and concisely; abstracts should present research results and implications.

Russian: Titles have often been wordy, too general or ambiguous; abstracts have sometimes been too short, written formally before submission and only hinted at results.

2. **Format and organization**

English: Format requirements are normally strict; the length of the text and number of references depend on the subject and target audience of the journal; sections are required, each section and paragraph being explicitly organized.

Russian: Format requirements have sometimes been vague; papers can be too short or contain few references; texts have often been unstructured; no special requirements have been provided for the organization of information within sections or paragraphs.

3. **Originality**

English: All publications are required to be original.

Russian: The same papers or considerable parts of previously published research have been published in different journals.

4. **Purpose and responsibility**

English: The text is expected to present new knowledge to the discourse community, so editors normally rely on double-blind reviews by experts in the field who take on the responsibility.

Russian: The purpose of the text has commonly been seen as to report a publication to the institution and increase the number of an author's publications; editors have rarely required reviews from authors with degrees, and reviews for others have been limited to formal recommendations from their tutors or colleagues, often written by the authors themselves.[5]

5. Focus

English: Content should be focused on the topic; the argument should be easy to follow.

Russian: Frequent deviations from the main topic may occur.

6. Support

English: Each argument should be supported by evidence or references; definitions should be provided in the beginning of the text.

Russian: Some statements may remain unsupported as self-evident; definitions can be omitted or appear in the middle of the text.

7. References

English: References are normally listed in alphabetical order without numeration; in journal publications, in-text references are given with authors' names and dates of publication.

Russian: References have been most often listed in numerical order according to their occurrence in the text; inside the text only numbers have been given (in-text references with names and dates were only allowed by the state standard in 2008 and have not yet widely spread).

8. Sources

English: Sources should be selected according to the topic and support the argument; paraphrase should provide critique and help keep the writer's voice.

---

[5] Junk publications are not solely a Russian problem, but the publishing tradition makes them eligible and therefore appropriate. Double-blind or even peer reviews are only starting to be required by some editors.

Russian: Sources have sometimes been excessive or irrelevant; multiple direct quotations have been common; long quotations have not been marked by format (font, paragraph).

9. Style

English: The argument should be presented in a cohesive, functionally regular and persuasive manner that demonstrates respect for a non-specialist audience and other viewpoints.

Russian: Texts have often been wordy and full of academese (overloaded with terminology and formal phrases); some statements can be subjective or emotional.

10. Language

English: Language should be economical and easy-to-follow; nominalization and passive structures should be avoided; drafts are expected to be thoroughly polished.

Russian: Language has often been obscure with excessive nominalization, ambiguous impersonal structures and complicated, sometimes erroneous syntax; polishing the language has been considered insignificant.

However evident these differences may seem to the Russian eye and, at the same time, rough or exaggerated to the English, they provide a basis for analysis. Even anglophone researchers who obtain their writing skills explicitly in accordance with the requirements and expectations of the global academic discourse and practice writing under the supervision of professors who publish internationally have not always succeeded in meeting these requirements and expectations.

When Russian researchers succeed, their effort should therefore be valued highly. According to recent studies (Lovakov & Yudkevich, 2020; Polikhina, 2020), between 2012 and 2019 the number of Russian papers among top-cited world publications rose seven times, and not only the quantity, but the quality of research has risen. This means that even the first efforts undertaken in the last decade have brought positive results. To foster the quality of research publications further, the problems faced by Russian researchers need to be structured and ways of overcoming them sought—just like in medical treatment, when diagnoses are made to help, not to humiliate patients.

First and foremost, all the listed requirements refer to metalinguistic competences even when language and style are concerned because clarity, brevity, and objectivity are equally relevant in any language. The differences can be roughly divided into two categories depending on who is affected by or responsible for the changes to be made: the editors (e.g., 1, 2, 3 and 7) or the scholars, although most often both are implicated. Some of the problems refer to academic literacy and writing and can be overcome by introducing the appropriate courses in English or Russian into the Russian educational and publishing context.

The Russian tradition of republishing a single article in different journals and books has been well illustrated by the number of retracted papers when a Russian journal has accepted the international code of conduct. For instance, *Integration of Education* had to retract six such papers just in 2014 after the journal started to be indexed in Scopus.

What seems especially striking from the point of view of publishing ethics is that Russian educators and pedagogues (and many in other disciplines) have considered this practice quite natural, explaining that a scholar cannot and should not create new ideas for every publication and has a right to make his or her ideas visible for the discourse community through as many publications as possible. If the publishers accept such papers, why not publish? The practice of retraction is new to Russian editors, and self-plagiarism has been a new concept to cope with. However, the retraction of plagiarized papers (unless they are officially accepted reprints) ought to become common practice among Russian publishers, although this policy will affect many prominent professors and academics—and not only in pedagogy and humanities, but also in other disciplines.

Another major problem is referencing. The tradition of listing bibliography entries in numerical order is still used in many journals and dissertations, which significantly impedes the reading of the paper because inside the text, figures do not signal the reference, and the list of references does not provide a clear view of the bibliography. This tradition also complicates the work of the writer, who needs to arrange the references so illogically; however, it has helped some writers to conceal their lack of knowledge or inappropriate use of sources. In 2008, the Russian state standard accepted the international practice of in-text references by name and date with the bibliography entries in alphabetical order and allowed it to be applied in dissertations. Many publishers and journals have accepted this format; whether they use the American Psychological Association (APA), Modern Languages Association (MLA), or the Russian format (the position of date, italics, punctuation, etc.) is not essential. What is important is the convenience for both the writer and the reader. Although numerical order (mostly with footnote referencing) is accepted in some international journals as well, the use of in-text references is a major salutary difference.

Direct quotations, some of which are too long or combined into one overlong sentence, are also a considerable problem in Russian non-STEM sciences.

Sometimes the author's voice is hardly distinguishable from the cited sources. In my teaching practice, I make this fault explicit to my students by referring to Saint-Exupéry's The Little Prince, where the child drew a picture of a boa who swallowed an elephant. In the case of multiple direct citations, the boa is full of the undigested parts of various animals, which is even more disgusting. The metaphor works well, and students start avoiding direct quotations by paraphrase. Unfortunately, the international requirement to signal long quotations (longer than two lines) by separate paragraphs in a smaller font has not been accepted yet by Russian journals; if it is, writers will have to work on their texts more thoroughly because other authors' text will become visible. Today, it is hard to see how much is quoted by noticing the quotation marks, which are often hard to notice due to the length of multiple quotations.

The listed faults along with excessive nominalization, wordiness, and the lack of drafting and polishing relate to the purpose of publication, which is most frequently described as adding more papers to the author's institutional report rather than addressing the discourse community.

Mastering Rhetorical Conventions: The Metalinguistic Approach

Teaching anglophone rhetoric in Russian can be used as an efficient framework for educating writers on a much larger scale regardless of their English proficiency. When Russian scholars accept this rhetoric, especially in non-STEM sciences, they can contribute to the development of their disciplines and communicate new knowledge more widely and effectively. This approach can help scholars not only in Russia, but also in post-Soviet spaces where Russian still remains the lingua franca of academic communication (e.g., Central Asian states). I would also emphasize that accepting anglophone rhetoric can and should rid the academic community in this vast geolinguistic area of obsolete writing and publishing traditions and improve knowledge communication both within and between countries.

The benefit of the metalinguistic approach to teaching writing is that rhetorical skills are transferable, especially if they are accepted as best suiting writers' goals. My seminars on writing for research publication purposes in Russian, which I conducted across the country, have shown that even elderly academics with multiple publications have accepted anglophone rhetoric and composition (composition is essential here) as useful new knowledge which ought to be applied not only to their writing, but also to their teaching. The latter has often been considered even more important by lecturers in disciplines.

Mastering academic discourse and the rhetorical conventions developed by anglophone experts in academic writing requires understanding how they function and why they function this way. And again, English as the language of a particular culture has not been the issue. Academic writing models and structures required in the global academic discourse were, indeed, developed by anglophone experts and writers, but they have been most convenient for multilingual scholars who need to communicate effectively regardless of their cultural backgrounds (Cargill & Burgess, 2017; Flowerdew, 2013; Lillis & Curry, 2015). When a writer's argument is concise, cohesive, regular, and economical, it is easy to follow. The straightforward English tradition of focusing a text, widely illustrated by Kaplan's typology (Kaplan, 1966), appeared efficacious for global academic discourse, connecting researchers cross-culturally and cross-disciplinarily. As a result, academic English became no one's or, rather, everyone's language because of its functional simplicity and logic, and not because anglophone scholars just dominated in international publications.

Not only anglophone rhetorical conventions are transferable, but the methods of teaching rhetoric and composition. This means that other nations can follow them without having to invest in pioneering a totally new field of study. When I worked on my Russian manual Academic Writing: Process, Product and Practice (Korotkina, 2015), I followed the three aspects of rhetoric and composition: focus, organization, and mechanics. As mechanics involves language, I expected it to be the most difficult to present (because I would need many specific examples in Russian) but probably the shortest because it is meant to be used by native speakers of the language. In fact, mechanics appeared to be the biggest, the most difficult, and at the same time the most interesting part to write. Even now, my seminar titled "The Unknown Russian Syntax" (Korotkina, 2017) is invariably accepted as the discovery of an amazing truth about something the participants always thought they knew well. One such amazing fact is that there is no difference between English and Russian in sentence structures provided they are used properly, and no translator will ever spoil or misinterpret the texts provided similar principles of subject-verb connections, cohesion, or even punctuation—are followed by the authors. Thus, when I have created learning materials to develop particular academic writing skills, such as repetition of key words, parallelism, or topic sentences, I have had to use anglophone texts in translation because even the most brilliant Russian texts cannot be used as samples.

Changing cultural habits and traditions is hard, but in the case of academic writing we are changing not the natural native culture, but an artificially created, highly bureaucratic style and no less artificial and often illogical formal requirements inherited from the Soviet past. My extended practice, as well as that of my colleagues from the Russian EAP community, confirms the willingness of researchers and scholars to get free from the habitual use of that sort of writing. Smirnova and Shchemeleva (2015) have expressed major concern about the fact that teaching academic writing has been limited to EAP, while teaching it in Russian would be much more beneficial.

Teaching writing in the native tongue based on anglophone writing methodology has significantly alleviated the process of writing through easy-to-use models and technologies, to which writers have willingly agreed. Teaching by flexible models is different from imitating samples, following artificial prescriptions or formal rules because it allows for multiple applications across disciplines and contexts. I totally agree with the experts who claim that written academic English is no culture's language, but a grapholect that should be mastered by all researchers, whose different cultures remain in another space beyond academic communication (Bhabha, 1994; Bizzel, 1999; Flowerdew, 2013; Kwan, 2010). Good examples are the structure of an introduction, topic sentences for paragraphs, or Leki's (1999) formula of a thesis statement: "Although A, B because C".

The advantage of models in rhetoric and composition is that they can be applied universally, like algebra (which Leki's (1999) formula shows), but they are not necessarily prescriptive. For instance, in more culturally embedded studies, style might vary or even dominate. In my seminars, I often ask participants to provide me with samples of their writing so that we can edit them. This activity always works well, allowing for collective practice and individual feedback; however, once it failed. The presented piece of writing was written in English by a professor in Japanese studies; it did not follow the anglophone rhetoric in Kaplan's (1966) terms but was developed in a contemplative, measured manner around a metaphor, making his academic text sound like Japanese poetry. The style matched the content so perfectly that all we could do was admire it. I believe no anglophone editor would dare make any changes to its supposedly flawed cohesion or excessive use of co-ordination. This unity of Russian authorship, well-written English, and the flavor of Japanese philosophy is a perfect example of deep understanding of other cultures which can be found in texts on arts and humanities. I was happy that the text was not translated, but originally written in English by the Russian professor, and I am sure it was enjoyed by a multicultural academic readership.

This example shows the benefits of writing directly in English, and researchers with good command of the language should certainly be taught English for Research Publication Purposes (ERPP), the recently designed branch of EAP that best suits their needs (Corcoran & Englander, 2016;

Flowerdew, 2013; Kuteeva & Mauranen, 2014; Kwan, 2010). ERPP has been the core methodology applied and developed by Russian writing centers. Unfortunately, they rarely publish their research results for the reasons I mentioned earlier in this chapter, and I can only hope that the publish or perish pressure will urge them to share their experiences (Chapter 4). The problem, again, is not solely Russian: considering the developments in ERPP, Flowerdew (2013) has emphasized the need for publications in the field and has claimed that "it is an area that offers unique challenges and opportunities for the ESP profession to demonstrate its value" (p. 316), to which I totally agree.

ERPP is not the focus of this paper; however, competencies developed by this methodology are essential for teaching writing for research publication purposes in any language. Flowerdew (2013) systematized them as command of schematic structure, command of discipline-specific citation language, and metadiscourse, which Kwan (2010) defined as "one's degree of commitment to statements made" (p. 57). Other publication-specific skills include communication with gatekeepers, ability to identify the target journal, and strategic management of research and publishing. Although some of these competencies, such as discipline specific citation language, could be considered in terms of ESP or writing in the disciplines (WID), others are transdisciplinary and could be taught within the frameworks of academic or information literacy.

To sum up, the most effective way to introduce a clear and systematic methodology for teaching writing for research publication purposes requires several conditions. First, ERPP should be incorporated into the work of Russian writing centers not only directly but also as a framework for developing programs in the national language. The experience of other experts should be used, but they should be educated in academic writing to properly understand the part they play in the newly established discipline. Writing centers should also help educate editors and publishers, who have generally been at a loss when dealing with particular texts, for the code of conduct prescribes but does not teach how to make abstracts informative or which particular criteria reviewers should apply.

All these activities should be promoted within the more general framework of academic literacy, which could serve as an umbrella for teaching rhetorical and publishing conventions across disciplines in both English and Russian—first and foremost in Russian. This approach could be effective in overcoming the differences between the anglophone and Russian traditions and facilitate the process of internationalizing education and science in Russia. A text written in Russian along with all the rhetorical and even syntactic models of anglophone writing is not only clearer, better organized, and better focused, but also takes less effort to translate, and no translator will pervert such a text. Writers who are taught to write this way do not need the academic literacy brokering or post-submission official journal brokering described by Lillis and Curry (2015) and thus can have their papers accepted by the gatekeepers worldwide. The first steps towards establishing this approach are being made by Russian EAP and academic writing practitioners recently united into the National Writing Centers Consortium.

Conclusions

The changes in international publishing and attitudes to multilingual scholars that have taken place in the last fifteen years have shown the decline of Phillipson's (1992) idea of linguistic imperialism. Many formerly peripheral (Canagarajah, 2002) academic communities have gained a more prominent position on the global stage. Russian scholars, being a large academic community with a long history of producing new knowledge for the world, cannot and should not stay at the periphery of international communication due to the mere lack of awareness of international rhetorical and publishing conventions.

Writing in English is not the sine qua non of publishing qualitative research results in highly-ranked international journals. A much more important condition is presenting these results in accordance with the expectations of other multilingual scholars, in the form of a well-structured, clearly written text with efficacious arguments supported by sufficient, reliable, and up-to-date evidence. This requires explicit rather than implicit knowledge of rhetorical skills taught in academic writing. Although writing as a discipline was mainly developed by anglophone experts, its global popularity and acceptance has been the result of decades-long research carried out in rhetoric and composition. In his book, Teaching and Researching Writing, Hyland (2016) emphasized the key role of academic writing in the lives of millions of people around the world, helping them succeed in their education and professional development, thus becoming a valid indicator of their quality of life.

The Russian academic community has been rapidly changing its attitudes towards the new discipline of academic writing. The discussion on academic writing pioneered by the journal Higher Education in Russia in 2011 started by discussing the term; since then, hundreds of Russian publications on the topic have appeared, and their number has grown rapidly. Researchers, educators, EAP professionals, and academics present their arguments, often contradictory, but no longer questioning the idea of academic writing or the necessity of introducing it into Russian education. There still have been misunderstandings and misinterpretations, but no more resistance. I can conclude that during the last five years the Russian academic community has definitely stepped onto the road of no returning.

Today, teachers of academic writing in Russian appear to be the professionals that Russian education needs first and foremost. Russian science and education need specific programs, both professional development and academic, which will work on a bilingual or even translingual basis (Dobrynina, 2019; Khalyapina & Shostak, 2019; Rasskazova et al., 2017) and merge directive and non-directive approaches depending on the needs, qualifications, and abilities of the audience. The spread of EAP, ESP, and ERPP in Russia is certainly a good prospect, but while the majority of scholars and students cannot be taught in English, the development of similar methodologies in their native tongue remains the only option to obtain internationally accepted rhetorical skills. On the other hand, rhetorical and publishing conventions should be made explicit to Russian editors and publishers, who also rarely speak English. This could foster change in the national publishing tradition and improve the quality of national scholarly journals. Educators and university staff would be another important target group because introducing new writing programs into university curricula has largely depended on their understanding.

Rhetorical skills are interrelated with other cognitive skills, such as critical thinking, analysis, discussion, and reading skills. To introduce academic writing as a new discipline could only be effective if all these skills are incorporated into a unified system of teaching under the umbrella framework of academic literacy.

Discourse analysis of Russian texts in education has demonstrated that the language of publications by more isolated academic communities has been more vulnerable to faults like wordiness, nominalization, and syntactic incomprehensibility. Fields of study which have been more embedded in national, social, and cultural contexts will certainly need more time and effort to overcome their long isolation. The new traditions, however useful they may seem to the community at large, might be opposed by the scholars and academics who obtained their statuses in the old tradition. Overcoming their resistance may only be possible through negotiating and promoting the benefits of academic writing for Russian science and education. This work will require raising awareness of the status of academic writing as a discipline and opposing the perversion of the term academic writing by untrustworthy parties.

Developing academic writing and writing for research publication purposes in the Russian language under the umbrella of academic literacy is currently a great challenge for Russian university writing centers, but this challenge offers (paraphrasing Flowerdew (2013)) unique opportunities for Russian EAP and ESP professionals to demonstrate the value of their pioneering work. Publishing in the new field should be regarded as essential for informing the Russian academic community, editors, and educational policymakers about the centrality of academic writing in academic publishing and university education. I hope this book will contribute to a better understanding of the situation in the global community, especially U.S. experts in rhetoric and composition.

Last but not least, the metalinguistic approach to teaching academic writing could help develop programs for scholars and students not only in Russia but beyond. Russian has remained the lingua franca of international relations and academic discourse in many post-Soviet states, among which Central Asia has been the most significant geolinguistic region. Since 2018, collaboration between the academic writing and communication center of the Russian Presidential Academy of National Economy and Public Administration and the Kyrgyz State University first led to networking within the Kyrgyz Republic, and then started to emerge into a wider network connecting universities in Kazakhstan, Uzbekistan, and Tajikistan. I hope that the metalinguistic approach will help Central Asian university writing centers not only support writers in English and Russian, but also restore the statuses of their national languages in science and education.

Even as I was drawing these conclusions, I kept wondering if now I have a definite answer to the question I asked six years ago: is it an evolution or a revolution? However, one thing is certain today: the process has started and become irreversible. The Russian academic community is experiencing the emergence of academic writing in the country as the first coil of a huge spiral, which inevitably raises the dust of controversies, misconceptions, and oppositions. The dust will gradually disperse and give way to an accelerating progress. Evolution, it is.

References

Bakin, E. V. (2013). Academic writing center: Experience of establishing. *Vysshee Obrazovanie v Rossii/Higher Education in Russia*, (8/9), 112–116.

Bazanova, E. M. (2015). Laboratory of scholarly communications: Russian perspective. *Vysshee Obrazovanie v Rossii/Higher Education in Russia*, (8/9), 135–143.

Bazylev, V. N. (2014). *Akademicheskoye "pis'mo" (teoreticheskiy aspekt) [Academic "writing" (theoretical aspect)]*. SGU Publishing House.

Bazylev, V. N. (2015). *Akademicheskoye "pis'mo" (metodicheskiy aspekt) [Academic "writing" (methodological aspect)]*. SGU Publishing House.

Bean, J. (2011). *Engaging ideas*. Jossey-Bass.
Bhabha, H. K. (1994). *The location of culture*. Routledge.
Bizzel, P. (1999). Hybrid academic discourses: What, why, how. *Composition Studies*, 27(2), 7–21.
Bollinger, K. M. (2016). Introducing Western writing theory and pedagogy to Russian students: The Writing and Communication Center at the New Economic School. In P. Zemliansky & K. St.Amant (Eds.). *Rethinking post-communist rhetoric: Perspectives on rhetoric, writing, and professional communication in post-Soviet spaces* (pp. 19–42). Lexington Books.
Butler, D. B., Trosclair, E., Zhou, Y., & Wei, M. (2014). Student and teacher perceptions of academic English writing in Russia. *The Journal of Teaching English for Specific and Academic Purposes*, 2(2), 203–227.
Canagarajah, S. A. (2002). *A geopolitics of academic writing*. University of Pittsburgh Press.
Cargill, M., & Burgess, S. (Eds.). (2017). *Publishing research in English as an additional language: Practices, pathways and potentials*. University of Adelaide Press.
Corcoran, J. N., & Englander, K. (2016). A proposal for critical-pragmatic pedagogical approaches to English for research publication purposes. *Publications*, 4(1), 6. http://www.mdpi.com/2304-6775/4/1/6/htm.
Day, R. A., & Gastel, B. (2016). *How to write and publish a scientific paper* (8th ed.). Greenwood.
Dobrynina, O. L. (2015). Propaedeutics of errors in abstracts of papers written in Russian. *Vysshee Obrazovanie v Rossii/Higher Education in Russia*, 7, 42–50.
Dobrynina, O. L. (2019). Academic writing for research publication purposes. *Nepreryvnoye Obrazovaniye: XXI vek/Life-Long Learning: 21st Century*, 1(25), 1–10. https://doi.org/10.15393/j5.art.2019.4485.
Dunleavy, P. (2014). Poor citation practices are continuing to harm the humanities and social sciences. The London School of Economics and Political Science. *The LSE Impact blog*. http://blogs.lse.ac.uk/impactofsocialsciences/2014/12/09/poor-citation-practices-humanities-and-social-sciences/.
Dunn, W. N. (2011). *Public policy analysis: An introduction* (5th ed.). Longman.
Enos, T. (Ed.). (2010). *Encyclopedia of rhetoric and composition: Communication from ancient times to the information age*. Routledge.
Fedotov, A. V., & Vasetskaya, N. O. (2013). Analysis of the effective machinery in motivation the publication activity of Russian scientists. In *Universitetskoye Upravleniye: praktika i analiz/University Management: Practice and Analysis* (pp. 60–68). Urals Federal University Press.
Flowerdew, J. (2013). English for research publication purposes. In B. Paltridge & S. Starfield (Eds.), *The handbook of English for specific purposes* (pp. 301–322). Wiley-Blackwell.
Gendina, N. I., Kolkova, N. I., Starodubova, G. A., & Ulenko, Y. V. (2006). *Formirovaniye informatsionnoy kul'tury lichnosti: Teoreticheskoye obosnovaniye i modelirovaniye soderzhaniya uchebnoy distspliny* [Developing informational culture of an individual: Theoretical basis and modeling the content of the discipline].

Mezhregional'ny Tsentr Bibliotechnogo Sotrudnichestva [International Center of Library Collaboration].

Graff, G. (2000). Scholars and sound bites: The myth of academic difficulty. *PMLA, 115*(5), 1041–1052.

Hyland, K. (2007). *Writing in the academy: Reputation, education and knowledge*. Institute of Education Press.

Hyland, K. (2009). *Academic discourse*. Continuum.

Hyland, K. (2011). Academic discourse. In K. Hyland & B. Paltridge (Eds.), *The Bloomsbury companion to discourse analysis*. Bloomsbury.

Hyland, K. (2016). *Teaching and researching writing*. Routledge.

Jarratt, S. (1991). *Rereading the sophists: Classical rhetoric refigured*. Southern Illinois University Press.

Kaplan, R. B. (1966). Cultural thought patterns in intercultural education. *Language Learning, 16*, 1–20.

Khalyapina, L. P., & Shostak, E. V. (2019). Plurilingual and translingual approaches as new trends in the theory of content and language integrated learning for technical university students. *PNRPU Linguistic and Pedagogy Bulletin, 2*, 119–130.

Klyachko, T., & Mau, V. (2015). The future of universities. Article 2. Trends in Russia. *Social Sciences and Contemporary World*. (4). 5–25.

Kolesnikova, N. I. (2004). *Ot konspekta k dissertatsii [From Note-taking to dissertation]*. Flinta.

Kolesnikova, N. I. (2009). *Lingvodidakticheskaya Kontseptsiya Formirovaniya Zhanrovoy Kompetentsii Uchashchikhsya v Sisteme Nepreryvnogo Yazykovogo Obrazovaniya [The linguodidactic concept of developing students' genre competence in integrated language learning]*. Flinta.

Korotkina, I. (2013). Academic writing: On the way to conceptual unity. *Vysshee Obrazovanie v Rossii/Higher Education in Russia, 3*, 136–142.

Korotkina, I. (2014). Academic writing in Russia: Evolution or revolution? Social Science Research Network, http://ssrn.com/abstract=2435130.

Korotkina, I. (2015). *Akademicheskoye pis'mo: protsess, product i praktika [Academic writing: Process, product and practice]*. Urait Publishing House.

Korotkina, I. (2017). The logic of an academic text: The unknown syntax. In Kirillova, O. V. (Ed.), Proceedings of the 6th International Conference "World-Class Scientific Publication – 2017: Best Practices in Preparation and Promotion of Publications" (pp. 60–65). Ural University Press. https://doi.org/10.24069/2017.978-5-7996-2227-5.09.

Korotkina, I. (2018a). International studies of new literacy and problems of terminological nonconformity in Russian pedagogy. *Otechestvennaya i Zarubezhnaya Pedagogika/Pedagogy in Russia and Abroad, 3*(50), 132–152.

Korotkina, I. (2018b). *Modeli obucheniya akademicheskomu pis'mu: mezhdunarodny opyt i otechestvennaya praktika [Academic writing teaching models: International experience and national practices]*. Urait Publishing House.

Korotkina, I. (2018c). Russian scholarly publications in anglophone academic discourse: The clash of tyrannosaurs. *Integration of Education, 22*(2), 311–323.

Korotkina, I. (2019a). Russian educational research papers in international publications: The urge for academic writing. *The European Proceedings of Social and Behavioural Sciences. Future Academy*, 2018. *XLVI*, 36. 309–318. https://doi.org/10.15405/epsbs(2357-1330).2018.9.2.

Korotkina, I.B. (2019b). Teoriya I praktika obucheniya akademicheskomu pis'mu v zarubezhnykh I otechestvennykh universitetakh [Theory and practice of teaching academic writing in western and Russian universities] [Unpublished doctoral dissertation]. Institute for Strategy of Education Development of the Russian Academy of Education.

Kouprianov, A. (2011). Academic writing and academic form of life: Trying to adapt the course of academic writing in an unfriendly institutional milieu. *Vysshee Obrazovanie v Rossii/Higher Education in Russia*, (10), 30–38.

Kuteeva, M., & Mauranen, A. (2014). Writing for publication in multilingual contexts: An introduction to the special issue. *Journal of English for Academic Purposes, 13*, 1–4.

Kwan, B. S. C. (2010). An investigation of instruction in research publishing in doctoral programs: The Hong Kong case. *Higher Education, 59*, 55–68.

Leki, I. (1999). *Academic writing: Exploring processes and strategies* (2nd ed.). Cambridge University Press.

Lillis, T., & Curry, M. J. (2010). *Academic writing in a global context: The politics and practices of publishing in English*. Routledge.

Lillis, T., & Curry, M. J. (2015). The politics of English, language and uptake. *AILA Review, 28*, 127–150.

Lovakov, A., & Yudkevich, M. M. (2021). The post-Soviet publication landscape for higher education research. *Higher Education, 81*(2), 273–299. https://doi.org/10.1007/s10734-020-00541-2.

Lynn, S. (2010). *Rhetoric and composition: An introduction*. Cambridge University Press.

Orlova, G. A. (2011). Practical analytics: Teaching discourse analysis through the university curriculum. *Vysshee Obrazovanie v Rossii/ Higher Education in Russia, 7*, 127–133.

Perlov, A. (2011). "What do we want and how do we explain it": Transformations of the tutorial on preparing a research project. *Vysshee Obrazovanie v Rossii/Higher Education in Russia, 7*, 133–140.

Petrashova, T. G. (2017). Evaluation of the effectiveness of EFL instruction throughout the English language program to provide conditions for internationalization of the university: Experience of an innovative technical university. *Language and Culture, 38*, 269–284.

Phillipson R. (1992). *Linguistic imperialism*. Oxford University Press.

Polikhina, N. A. (2020). Publication activity of academic staff in Russia: Results, trends, problems. *Science Governance and Scientometrics, 15*(2), 196–222.

Popova, N. G., & Beavitt, T. A. (2017). English as a means of scientific communication: linguistic imperialism or interlingua? *Integratsiya Obrazovaniya/Integration of Education, 21*(1), 54–70.

Rasskazova, T. P., Glukhanyuk, N. S., & Guzikova, M. O. (2017). The results of English teaching as a foreign language for academic staff in the artificial bilingualism environment. *The Education and Science Journal, 8*(19), 188–203.

Robotova, A. S. (2011). Is it necessary to teach the academic work and academic writing? *Vysshee Obrazovanie v Rossii/Higher Education in Russia*, 10, 47–54.

Robotova, A. S. (2015). Absurdities in pedagogical texts. *Vysshee Obrazovanie v Rossii/ Higher Education in Russia*, 3, 145–152.

Robotova, A. S. (2018). About pedagogy, its words, concepts and texts. *Vysshee Obrazovanie v Rossii/Higher Education in Russia*, 27(7), 9–19.

Rostovtsev, A. A. (2017). The Russian and international practices of identification of irresponsible journals and authors. *Science Editor and Publisher*, 2(1), 30–37.

Ryan, L., & Zimmerelli, L. (2009). *The Bedford guide for writing tutors* (5th ed.). Bedford/St. Martin's.

Schleifer, R., Townsend, M. A., Tsiopos Wills, K. V., Aksakalova, O., Nemec Ignashev, D., & Venediktova, T. (2016). Under Lomonosov's watchful gaze: A case study of an early faculty development writing workshop in Russia. *Contrastive Linguistics*, (5), 297–309.

Senashenko, V. (2011). About academic writing and research competences. *Vysshee Obrazovanie v Rossii/Higher Education in Russia*, (8/9), 136–139.

Smirnova, N. V., & Shchemeleva, I. Y. (2015). Writing at the university level: American, European and Russian perspectives. *St.Petersburg State University Bulletin*, 9(2), 185–196.

Smith, E. (2017). *Writing centers in multilingual settings: A workbook*. Samara University Press.

Squires, L. A. (2016). The NES writing and communication center: The case for student-oriented writing centers in Russia. *Vysshee Obrazovanie v Rossii/Higher Education in Russia*, 8/9, 66–73.

Stepanov, B. (2012). On the academic writing once again: Critique of the academic criticism. *Vysshee Obrazovanie v Rossii/Higher Education in Russia*, (7), 130–138.

Sternin, I. A. (2017). Kak uvazhat' sebya zastavit'? Ucheny-filolog razmyshlyayet o nabolevshem [How to make others respect us? A philologist's reflections on grave issues]. *Poisk [Search]*, 8. https://www.poisknews.ru/magazine/22732/.

Sukharev, O. V. (2014). Disfunktsiya obrazovaniya i nauki v Rossii: traektoriya preodoleniya [Misfunction of education and science in Russia: The trajectory for overcoming]. *National Interests: Priorities and Security*, 1(208), 2–17.

Swales, J. (1997). English as Tyrannosaurus Rex. *World Englishes*, 16, 373–382.

Young, A. (2006). *Teaching writing across the curriculum* (4th ed.). Pearson.

Zborovskij, G. E., & Ambarova, P. A. (2019). The dream of quality education: Contradictions in the development of educational communities in Russian universities. *Mir Rossii [The World of Russia]*, 2, 98–124.

Zemliansky, P., & Goroshko, O. (2016). A survey of academic and professional writing in higher education in Russia and Ukraine. In P. Zemliansky & K. St.Amant. (Eds.), (2016). *Rethinking post-communist rhetoric: Perspectives on rhetoric, writing, and professional communication in post-Soviet spaces* (pp. 3–18). Lexington Books.

2

Essays in Middle and High School in Russia: Historical Background

Elena Getmanskaya
MOSCOW STATE PEDAGOGICAL UNIVERSITY

Differences between the essay writing methodology of the nineteenth and twentieth centuries have allowed us to perceive the turn of the nineteenth-twentieth centuries as a time of flourishing sophistication in school essays. The substantial humanitarian component of the school essays of that period mirrors current approaches to formulating essay topics for the school final exam. As this chapter shows, modern essay writing methodology in Russia can be seen not as a recent invention but as a return to elements of the methodology existing at the turn of the nineteenth-twentieth centuries. We can learn from similar processes that took place in the development of writing pedagogy in the nineteenth and early twentieth century, where the teaching of writing lost its special philological character. This chapter analyzes the scholarly literature on essay methodology from this period and identifies three key directions of its development: 1) an active scientific and pedagogical search related to the regulation of the school composition form and requirements for this genre of writing; 2) the expansion of journalistic topics in school essays on literature, which included multidisciplinary (non-literary) topics; and 3) the functioning of the final essay as the main form of checking the general humanitarian knowledge of the high school graduate and as a method of admission to universities without exams.

Examining the history of school essays in Russia, it has become clear that the modern Russian methodology for teaching essay writing is built on three hundred years of domestic experience with the use of essays as a key criterion for the language education of the younger generation (Brenchugina-Romanova, 2000; Chertov, 2013; Getmanskaya, 2015; Reut, 2013). In Russia, the methodology for using essays became systematic at the turn of the nineteenth to twentieth century and was transformed into an exemplary methodological model for secondary schools and universities throughout the next century, having received one essential addition in the 1920s. This addition was instigated by the social revolution of 1917, which brought about changes to the secondary school curriculum that existed at the turn of the nineteenth to twentieth century. Reforms resulted in the exclusion of then-existing language arts from the school curriculum. It was substituted by two new disciplines in the 1920s—Russian language and literature. As a result of the division, literature education developed into its modern form during the course of the twentieth century and obtained a new dominant element—close analysis of literary (mainly classical) works. Post-reform, the school essay no longer aimed to develop writing based on historical, geographical, and agricultural material and physical law as before. Ethical reflective essays became a thing of the past. At that stage educators rejected the goal of developing writing based on non-literary material and focused mainly on purely literary themes (Getmanskaya, 2013). However, due to that trend, in the twentieth century, school essays started to lose the thematic breadth that was typical of the school essay in the pre-revolutionary period, before the division of language arts into Russian language and literature.

This essay model was only strengthened throughout the twentieth century. Now the situation has changed. Currently, Russian schools have been actively returning to the thematic interdisciplinarity of essays, which has now become part of the unified state exam in Russian (see Chapter 10). The growing importance of general humanitarian themes in essays motivates scholarly interest in the methodology of the early twentieth century, when interdisciplinarity was the norm.

The differences between the essay writing methodology of the nineteenth and twentieth centuries let us perceive the turn of the century as a time of flourishing sophistication in school essays that then disappeared post-reform. The substantial humanitarian component of the school essays of that period is echoed in current approaches to the formulation of essay topics for the final exam in Russian high schools. The return of modern essay writing methodology in the present period to elements of the methodology existing at the turn of the nineteenth to twentieth centuries proves the necessity of studying that period, both its best practices and areas of controversy.

As this chapter will show based on a review of archived instructional manuals and the work of nineteenth century methodologists, teaching writing in the literature classroom before the post-revolutionary reforms was not limited to the content of the discipline "literature." One of the main pieces of evidence for this was the broad humanitarian themes of school essays even in literature classes. Historical, geographical, moral, and natural-scientific themes were widespread in high schools along with literary themes. The thematic breadth confirmed the humanitarian (non-philological) basis of teaching writing in the literature classroom.

The teaching of composition in schools became a priority for many pedagogical researchers during this period and was also included in the content of the state programs and official recommendations of the National Education Ministry. Nevertheless, as I demonstrate here, the introduction of the essay into school practice was accompanied by a number of methodological failures caused by the predominance of reproductive approaches, a significant difference between the practice of writing in school and the official ministerial recommendations, and the mass distribution of poor-quality manuals for training students to write essays.

In the first decades of the twentieth century, a number of works appeared that suggested ways to improve the school essay (Alferov, 1911; Braylovsky, 1910; Filonov, 1902; Golubkov, 1914; Larionov, 1915; Ovsyaniko-Kulikovskii, 1911; Shumilovskii, 1910). Scientists proposed the use of topics that go beyond the subject of literature, approaching writing as a kind of research problem, and a clear correspondence of the essay topics to the psychological and age characteristics of students.

Aleksandr Alferov (1911) and Vasiliy Golubkov (1914) considered the final year of high school studies to be a transitional stage before study at the university and recommended replacing essays written in class with essays written at home, raising the requirements for more advanced students. All the themes of the essays focused on the work of authors from the school curriculum. The main conditions for the success of the essay in the conception of these scholars were: individualization of themes for school composition, advanced work on the plan of the essay, as well as work on the mandatory list of literary criticism.

The final essay played an important role in determining the final knowledge of high school students and the starting level of knowledge for those who enter the university. Its significance was such that students whose essays received excellent marks were given the opportunity to enter the university without exams. The final composition, as well as compositions in earlier classes, checked the student's knowledge of style and only then the literary knowledge of students. The broad humanitarian orientation of the final school essay prepared the high school graduate not so much for the continuation of their philological education but for the execution of multiple tasks related to social and civic communication.

Modern literary education in schools now targets a wide range of knowledge in the humanities and is gradually departing from a focus on philology and literature. We can therefore learn from similar debates that took place in the development of writing pedagogy in the nineteenth and early twentieth century. As I argue in this chapter, at the turn of the twentieth century, school essay methodology in the Russian tradition was characterized by three key elements:

1. An active scientific and pedagogical search related to the regulation of the school composition form and requirements for this genre of writing;
2. The expansion of journalistic topics in school essays on literature, which included multidisciplinary (non-literary) topics;
3. The functioning of the final essay as the main form of checking the general humanitarian knowledge of the high school graduate and as a method of admission to universities without exams.

Caused mainly by the evolving practice of school essays, these processes, except for the last one, were gradually developing during the second half of the nineteenth century.

Regulating the School Essay Form and Methodology

The first high school curriculum, "Sample Curriculum of the Russian Language and Church Slavonic and Literature," was published by the Ministry of Public Education in 1890. It relegated essay writing methodology to the senior classes, where essays were included in a group of exercises in stylistics, working on speech faults and compliance with language norms. The same group (exercises in stylistics) included translations from classical languages (Greek and Latin) into Russian, written reproductions of some content in the Russian and classical languages, written reports on the study of some mandatory literary work, and analysis of the chosen literary work—its content, plan, form, style and idea (Ministry of Public Education, 1890). The methodology of essays was closely connected with translations from Greek and Latin into Russian.

The improvement of the student's writing directly depended on his or her ability to translate from classical languages. This interdependence between writing skills and translation techniques was supported by the above-mentioned curriculum (Ministry of Public Education, 1890). The program emphasized that the writing and thinking processes of students were imperfect because of their age: "due to the immaturity of students, their thoughts are rather empty, and, therefore, students' essays can be characterized by stylistic poverty and wide use of stereotypical expressions" (Ministry of Public Education, 1890, p. 104). To teach students how to use the Russian language to its full extent, lecturers also offered them exercises on the translation of abstracts from the ancient Greek and Roman literature into Russian. According to the author of this curriculum, while practicing the exact transfer of classical texts into the

Russian language, students would adopt features of their native language by constantly comparing it with the speech of Ancient Rome and Greece (Ministry of Public Education, 1890).

This recommendation could have led to the idea that the Russian language was subordinate to classical languages. However, a more detailed analysis proves that classical texts were mainly used to improve the learner's scientific and journalistic writing and to model the most important styles for writing essays (Getmanskaya, 2015). The relationship of essay writing to translation indicates that writing was predominantly an exercise in learners expressing themselves in the correct style. It should be noted that the existence of the state program, on the one hand, helped the methodology of school composition to develop, but on the other hand, the abundance of writing instructions minimized its creative component.

Due to the shortcomings of school essays, some scholars rejected this type of exercise. Academician Dmitriy Ovsyaniko-Kulikovskii wrote,

> It is time to abandon pseudo-pedagogical thoughts, writing exercises on any given or unspecified topic are beneficial. It is only a school of puzzling scholasticism, sophistry, contrivance and deception; it is a complete waste of time both for students and teachers. (1911, p. 429)

The judgmental position of Ovsyaniko-Kulikovskii was caused not so much by the weakness of practical work with essays but by the mass distribution of manuals that "facilitated" the task for students. Criticizing such manuals, Sergei Brailovskii pointed out a number of the following methodological mistakes:

- The redundancy of theoretical reasoning, while writing essays is a matter of practical skills;
- The abundance of ready-made essay samples that encouraged students to plagiarize.

Instead of developing independent approaches to the analysis of a literary work, the student was offered the results of someone else's work in the finished samples of school compositions (Brailovskii, 1910).

This reproductive approach would have been less negative if the proposed samples had been of the proper level, but the quality of outlines and texts left much to be desired. In my estimation, Alexey Semenov's (1912) book, *Outlines and Essays: The Course for the 7th Form of Gymnasiums*, is an example of just such a manual. This two-volume edition contained 116 topics and outlines for essays related to the Russian literature of the eighteenth and nineteenth centuries. It largely repeats the content of literature textbooks, in particular, Vladimir Savodnik's (1906) textbook on literature entitled *Essays on the History of the Russian Literature of the Nineteenth Century*. If students used this manual, little research would be required of them. In fact, the author offered a rigid algorithm for writing about any given topic. Students could only add "actual proofs" to the proposed scheme of analysis.

The "crisis of the genre" of the essay in high school was associated not only with the predominance of reproductive approaches, but also, in part, with overly regulated official requirements for its content. The curricula developed by the Ministry of Public Education in the 1890s contained recommendations on essay topics in high school, which, on the one hand, created useful methodological mechanisms for writing an essay, and on the other unnecessarily structured students' creative work (Ministry of Public Education, 1890, p. 80). The main recommendations were formulated as follows:

- Essay topics should correspond to the course and age of students;
- Teachers could not take essay topics exclusively from the existing textbooks;
- Teachers of Russian literature were obliged to make up their own essay topics and help students develop outlines;
- Teachers should avoid overly general essay topics embracing several historical epochs or a whole series of literary phenomena;
- Students' essays should be devoted to the literary works of the best Russian writers, "having a positive direction and truly artistic nature capable of contributing to the proper literary education of students."

In my opinion, the differentiation between research-oriented and reproductive approaches to writing essays was important for understanding how students' opinions about the literary material they were studying were introduced into their essays. In this regard, Sergey Larionov's (1915) interpretation of two main approaches to essays is of particular interest. Considering two statements—"the art of writing an essay" (p. 3) and "the drafting of an essay"—Larionov insisted on the latter (p. 3). Outlines of compositions offered by Larionov (1915) using the method "the drafting of an essay" (p. 3) show that they are designed for students who have deep knowledge of literary-historical course content. According to Larionov, essay teaching is not about writing cribs or composing texts based on a certain outline but rather developing a thoughtful and scientific understanding of the chosen topic. Larionov's typology of essays was built on the consistent complexity of literary-theoretical and literary-historical materials. In fact, it is a transitional methodology from school essays to university essays. For starters, this methodology provides complex features of certain fictional characters (i.e., simple characteristics are the study subject in primary school). Next, students should master characteristics common to a group of characters, comparative characteristics of two or more literary images or phenomena, as well as analyzing several literary works and historical facts regarding the same event (Larionov, 1915).

The outlines compiled by Larionov (1915) for these essays are characterized by their strict composition and scientific nature, but they also give room for students' independent activity. The research approach is demonstrated in an outline for the topic "The Origin and Gradual Development of Realism in Russian Literature" (Larionov, 1915). This plan has a prominent research focus. It helped students who knew the main topics of the course structurally rather than meaningfully, leaving enough room for their self-expression.

Aleksey Lebedev developed a "research-and-technological" approach to essay teaching which is similar to Larionov's (1915) methodology and was represented in his work, "Tasks of School Essays" (Lebedev, 1916). Identifying the concepts of "analysis" and "essay," Lebedev emphasized, "Analysis is a hard task that should be carried out methodically. Analysis or essay are the skills that should be taught" (Lebedev, 1916, p. 276). From Lebedev's viewpoint, any written essay should be preceded by an oral essay composed in the classroom. The scholar defined a school essay as a complex product that students must master by the end of the course, but these attempts should begin in the fifth form. Of course, Larionov and Lebedev further developed ideas from the school program of 1915. According to the program, while performing homework, senior students had to show their awareness of the content of some literary work and recommended manuals on the topic under consideration (Ministry of Public Education, 1915).

The pre-revolutionary method of writing essays was established at the First All-Russian Congress of Language Teachers (1917). Alferov and Golubkov's speeches, as well the final resolution of the Congress, thoroughly assessed the methodology of writing essays and ways to improve it. Golubkov indicated "the unsatisfactory position of school essays" based on the analysis of teachers' questionnaires (The First All-Russian Congress, 1917, p. 37). He claimed that the main shortcomings of this method were the lack of students' creativity and the presentation of material already learned, as well as the one-sided logical nature of essays that barely touched students' emotions and imagination.

Alferov and Golubkov believed that the most important methodological question was the issue of students' motivation or interest in "the stated material and methods of its communication" (The First All-Russian Congress, 1917, p. 39). Both methodologists connected ways of heightening interest with the solution to the following three main problems: the individualization of essay topics; in-depth work on outlines for essays on literary-historical topics; and the establishment of home essays as the main type of essay for students in their senior year. Based on Alferov's and Golubkov's reports, the Congress adopted a resolution on the written works of students where the main points were the convergence of topics with the personal interest of students, the development of creative abilities in the process of preparing and writing essays, and the individualization of essay topics (The First All-Russian Congress, 1917).

Extension of Journalistic Themes in School Essays

My analysis of the works of nineteenth century Russian methodologists concerned with students' essays testifies to certain difficulties that not only beginner but also experienced teachers of Russian language and literature faced in the educational process. The problems with school essays were attributed to their complex hierarchy of topics (Belyavskii, 1889; Olshamovskii, 1880; Yakubovich, 1896). Along with literary topics, school essays involved themes not directly related to literary-historical materials. Methodological works in the last decades of the nineteenth century referred to such essay topics as abstract and were based on historical, geographical, cultural, and autobiographical materials. In the modern context, one would call such essay topics non-literary or journalistic.

What general tasks were defined by methodologists in the 1880s to 1890s for essays, regardless of their literary or non-literary (journalistic) topics? Mikhail Olshamovskii (1880) in his book *Guidelines for the Introduction of Written Exercises into High Schools* highlighted the following tasks:

- To determine the most useful types of writing exercises in high schools;
- To determine the sequence in which one type of written exercise should follow the other;
- To develop teaching methods and techniques that assist students in the successful and expedient execution of written exercises.

According to Olshamovskii (1880), the analysis of literary texts should be almost exclusively an oral exercise. This statement highlights the importance of journalistic topics in students' written exercises from a new perspective.

What connection should students' non-literary essays have with the other disciplines of the main high school curriculum? Methodologists had many disputes while addressing this issue. Thus, Konstantin Yakubovich (1896) emphasized "the connection of essays with Russian literature and the sphere of morality" (p. 12). Egor Belyavskii (1889) organized all essays in the senior high school forms into two equal groups: half of them belonged to the abstract group and the other half was divided into historical and literary topics. Olshamovskii (1880) offered abstract, literary, and historical topics to senior high school students. Olshamovskii insisted that essays should have a wide range of associations with other academic disciplines, including history, geography, Russian and Western European literature, and classical Greek and Roman works studied during lessons on ancient languages. The scholar claimed that the expediency of this approach was determined by the fact that teachers could not limit the content of essays written by senior students to one sphere (literary or moral). In this case, topics from history, geography, literature, and the ancient world became an integral part of written exercises on literature. I believe that these changes transformed the essay from a genre situated within the framework of the literature discipline and into an essay of a supersubjective character. Olshamovskii's recommendations have a supersubjective basis—"topics should satisfy the following conditions: a) they should be unified, b) interesting, c) represent a short, precise and definite expression so that students do not have to wander away from the stated question" (Olshamovskii, 1880, p. 83). Yakubovich (1896) also wrote about the supersubjective basis of literature:

> Nowadays combining the whole amount of school knowledge and concentrating it around one common center is only an ideal of education. However, Russian literature utilizes data from other school disciplines for drawing its own conclusions and serves to a certain extent as a connection between heterogeneous information of general and, in particular, real education. (p. 14)

The methodological manuals of that period distributed non-literary topics into various areas in a number of ways (Kholevius, 1912; Shumilovskii, 1910). Abstract (non-literary) topics from Olshamovskii's (1880) book *Guidelines for the Introduction of Written Exercises into High Schools* are as follows:

- Education: what kind of a person can be called well-educated;
- Knowledge, learning, books, travel;
- Labor and idleness: causes of idleness;
- Happiness, misfortune, troubles;
- Poverty, wealth, stinginess, thrift. Poverty is not a vice;
- Different attitudes of people to themselves. Self-cognition;
- Mutual relations between people and nature. The influence of people on nature;

- Mutual relations between people: humane and selfish;
- Mutual relations between people and their actions. What is hypocrisy;
- Human life, cities, states. The value of rivers and seas;
- Words and writing: an individual style represents the people themselves. (pp. 83–92)

Olshamovskii (1880) emphasized that the distribution proposed above was not rigid or fixed but that abstract topics were an integral part of essays. While teaching students to write essays, he insisted that the first essays offered to children in middle school should be devoted to abstract topics (Olshamovskii, 1880). Yakubovich (1896), a literature teacher whose works left a noticeable mark on methodology, also emphasized the supersubjective nature of literature in his speech "The Significance of the Russian Language in Education Systems." Yakubovich (1896) confirmed this thought by describing school reading books on literature comprising historical stories and geographic notes besides literary works. Books for senior forms aimed to acquaint students with the most important literary techniques (Yakubovich, 1896). This situation was brought about by the fact that the objectives of studying literature at school were associated with the mastery of stylistic and grammatical norms of the Russian language rather than exact literary analysis, which became important in the twentieth century. The acquisition of literary skills was the decisive objective of introducing non-literary works in Russian schools in the late nineteenth century. The analysis of historical models used in the Russian essay in the nineteenth century demonstrates that it was not closely connected with historical and literary materials and addressed a wide range of journalistic topics.

The number of literary topics remained insignificant in the final years of high school (from the fifth to seventh forms). Students of the fifth to sixth forms studied major works of Russian literature from the eighteenth century, where moral or historical issues prevailed rather than the analysis of a certain artwork. For example, they studied "Summer and Winter Pleasures of Female Students" and "Causes and Effects of the Greco-Persian Wars" in the fifth form and "The Reasons that Caused the Development of Education in South-West Russia in the Seventeenth Century" in the sixth form (Istomin, 1891).

In my opinion, the prevalence of such near-literary topics encouraged students to approach the essay as an abstract and verbose reflection. The absence or insufficient presence of topics directly related to literary analysis led to the dominance of scholastic, general arguments about obvious truths in adolescents' essays, and did not contribute to their literary development. These topics include the following themes for the sixth form:

- Very Old Man and Infant;
- Folk Literature;
- What Constitutes the Defense of the Motherland Against External Enemies;
- True Enlightenment Inextricably Connects Mental Development with Religious and Moral Ones. (Istomin, 1891, p. 15).

The seventh form (the final year at high schools) mostly dealt with literary-theoretical and literary-historical topics, usually of a comparative nature, for instance: "Tatyana and Olga in Pushkin's Novel Eugene Onegin" and "The Comparison of D. I. Fonvizin's Comedy 'Brigadier-General' and A. N. Ostrovsky's (1885) Comedy 'It's a Family Affair—We'll Settle It Ourselves' Regarding the Idea and Separate Fictional Characters" (Istomin, 1891, p. 31).

The rapid growth of essay topics for high school in the early twentieth century prompted methodologists to classify them. One of these classifications, offered by Shumilovskii (1910), testifies to the broad humanitarian (not only literary-historical) orientation of essay topics even in high school. The methodologist determined several thematic fields for the senior year. Below are examples of specific topics:

- Literary: "Chekhov's intellectuals," "Famusov";
- Historical: "Reforms of Peter the Great," "The Founding of Saint Petersburg";
- Geographical: "A Description of My Province," "The Volga River";
- Autobiographical: "My memories of high school";
- Historical and cultural: "Life is Like a School." (Shumilovskii, 1910).

By the end of the nineteenth century, journalistic topics in the Russian school accounted for 50 percent of the overall number of school essays. The importance of non-literary material for essay writing was proved by the fact that the school reading books on literature included historical stories and geographical notes. In fact, the significant number of journalistic essays justified the universal, supersubjective character of the discipline of literature.

The Essay as Final Examination

Universities set high standards and requirements for the final school essay since it offered certain admission to the university. If a final school essay was rewarded with a "good" mark, the candidate could get enrolled at the university without entrance exams.

The methodology of essays established by the Curriculum of 1890 was supported by numerous theoretical developments. In the late nineteenth century and the first decades of the twentieth century, the works by Brailovskii (1910, 1915), Istomin (1891), Filonov (1902), Ovsyaniko-Kulikovskii (1911), Shumilovskii (1910), Larionov (1915), Alferov (1911), and Golubkov (1914) gained wide popularity. In Shumilovskii's (1910) opinion, to study in high school, one needs the ability to express, develop and justify thoughts. In other words, universities wanted to perceive their students not only as passive carriers of given knowledge but also as people who creatively assimilate such knowledge and develop it, "adding it to the circle of life" (Shumilovskii, 1910, p. 3). The latter could not be achieved without mastering the art of the word (Shumilovskii, 1910).

In the nineteenth century, the quality of literary education in high schools was mainly evaluated through the strengths and weaknesses of the final essay. Its importance was exemplified by the automatic university enrollment of those high school graduates who received high marks for their essays. Being the final test of literary knowledge, it reflected the level students achieved in high school and the starting level of knowledge of those who entered the university. The final essay "mostly tested the mastery of speech and then the knowledge of the corresponding literary-historical course, which should be taken into account when determining what literary skills high school graduates were expected to have" (Getmanskaya, 2015, p. 266).

The general list of themes of graduation essays for 1907 provides a good understanding of the degree of their productivity for the further literary development of graduates. The themes of the 1907 works can be divided into three groups:

- Reproductive topics that do not stimulate independent thoughts;
- Research essays that are not consistent with the age of students and increase the amount of work required for that age;
- Research topics corresponding to students' maturity and knowledge of Russian literature.

The theme "G. R. Derzhavin as a singer of Catherine II" (Filonov, 1908, p. 154) belongs to the first group. This topic involves considering Derzhavin solely as an apologist for the ruling monarch. This topic could help form a citizen loyal to the government, but not a humanistic thinker. The first group also included archaic topics that could not arouse students' sustained interest. For example, the topic "What requirements does Domostroy impose on a person?" (Filonov, 1908, p. 160) has nothing to do with artistic and imaginative thinking and requires only the reproduction of well-known historical information about the system of patriarchal despotism.

The second group comprised research topics that were not consistent with the age of students. For example, the topics "Indicate different ideals of Russian society through literary monuments" and "Nature in the works of first-class poets" (Filonov, 1908, pp. 90, 186).

The third group was represented by research topics corresponding to students' maturity and knowledge of Russian literature. While analyzing the presented high school essays, we could include only one essay from the Irkutsk high school among the research topics: "Peter the Great in A. S. Pushkin's poetry and prose" (Filonov, 1908. p. 186).

Thus, research topics represented a small fragment of the total number of essays. At this stage, the clichéness and repeatability of topics became a significant obstacle to high-quality final school essays. In addition, the final goals of school essays were to promote the development of logical thinking and consolidate the ideas of the literary works under study in the minds of students. However, these objectives were difficult to accomplish because an essay presented what was already learned in the class and reproduced the known material in a mechanical manner.

The new (homework) form of composition for the upper classes of the high school remedied the problems with stereotyped, mechanistic essays. These exercises gradually turned from a 90-minute classroom task in the upper classes into a homework assignment. In his textbook *Mother Tongue in Middle School*, Alferov (1911) justified the transfer of essays from classroom tasks to home assignments by the fact that the older the students were the more material they should have had to work on. Therefore, the more important homework would come at the final stages of high school education. He believed that this way of working with texts corresponded to the conditions students faced at universities (Alferov, 1911). Alferov (1911) proposed replacing several small essays in the senior year with one yearly essay prepared at home, and he raised the requirements for its quality. He developed a detailed methodology for such essays in the eighth form, including reading lists on each topic. To write the essay on "I. S. Turgenev's Main Views on His Correspondence" and "Poems in Prose," Alferov (1911) recommended reading the following books:

- *The Collection of I. S. Turgenev's Letters* (1884);
- I. S. Turgenev's *Collected Works* (1898);
- I. A. Ivanov, *I. S. Turgenev* (1896);
- I. D. Galperin-Kaminskii, *Unpublished Letters of I. S. Turgenev to Madame Viardot and His French Friends* (1900);
- D. N. Ovsyaniko-Kulikovskii, *Turgenev* (1909);
- A. A. Izmailov, *The Twilight of Godlings and New Idols* (1910). (Alferov, 1911, p. 276).

To evaluate I. S. Turgenev's views based on his epistolary heritage, students had to conduct research and analyze both the letters of I. S. Turgenev and other literary sources. The extended list of references and the long period for writing the essay (an entire academic year) brought the methodology of final essays in line with the rules for working on a scientific paper in universities.

Alferov (1911) was not the only one who proposed using references. All the high-profile manuals that aimed at the development of students' independent activity were comprised of long lists of additional literature. In particular, Shumilovskii (1910) believed that "a textbook should be followed by a popular book, which is succeeded by a scientific work" (Shumilovskii, 1910, p. 6) in the process of writing an essay.

In the early twentieth century, Russian universities and institutes introduced entrance examinations. The essay was essentially a mandatory exam for applicants to all higher education institutions, so its role increased dramatically in high school and in higher education. In general, at this historical stage, essays contributed to the strengthening of writing skills related to a wide range of humanitarian knowledge required in both philological and non-philological higher education, as well as in addressing the social and civic tasks of high school graduates and in the process of literary self-education.

Conclusion

Essays became the main form of assessment for high school students in the nineteenth and early twentieth centuries. Summarizing the development of essays in high and middle school, we should note there were significant methodological failures along with general positive trends. They can be explained by the following factors:

- The prevalence of reproductive approaches;
- Significant differences between actual school essays and generally progressive ministerial recommendations;
- The mass distribution of underdeveloped manuals (ready-made essays and outlines reproducing the content of some literary work).

These reasons conditioned the weakened position of graduation essays. At this stage, the main task was to introduce a productive essay methodology. S. N. Brailovskii (1910, 1915), V. A. Istomin (1891), A. G. Filonov (1902), D. N. Ovsyaniko-Kulikovskii (1911), L. I. Shumilovskii (1910), S. S. Larionov (1915), A. D. Alferov (1911), and V. V. Golubkov (1914) proposed a number of measures to resolve problems with the established essay practice, namely:

- The use of a wide range of topics;
- The transformation of essays into a research task;
- The clear correspondence between essay topics and the level of the students.

The development of essays during this period, their regular use in high school, and the expansion of compulsory middle school writing programs through topics and additional literature enable us to see that writing skills were the basis for continuing literary education in institutions of higher education. At the same time, graduation essays checked the formation of students' individual style and only then their literary-historical knowledge. The general humanitarian orientation of essays in high school (along with literary topics, historical, geographical, moral, and natural-science ones were used) testified to the non-special nature of teaching essays during literature lessons. This non-special nature ensured stable writing skills in any institution of higher education, including philological ones, as well as outside the walls of higher education institutions (i.e., in a wide range of social duties common to high school graduates). The simultaneous functioning of essays as the final form of checking the literary knowledge of senior students and the main evaluation criterion for entering any specialized university determined the constitutive value of essays for the Russian school throughout the nineteenth and early twentieth centuries.

After the post-revolutionary reforms, school essays lost their broad humanitarian tendency. The hypertrophy of the literary-historical course which exists in high school today is the result of a long, timely tracing of academic approaches to the study of literature in high school. In order to return school essays to the category of exercises that contribute to the creative development of students' skills and extensive humanitarian education, it is worth taking a closer look at the experience of Russian educators and pedagogical theorists in the nineteenth and early twentieth century, when the development of written language was based not mainly on historical and literary material, but on ethical, cultural and general educational subjects.

Improving the model of the final literature essay for today's high school graduates is an acute problem discussed not only in the professional teaching environment but also at the government level. What should this essay be like, given that it is already mandatory for all graduates? At the discussion stage, opinions on this issue were rather disparate: a philosophical essay, a critical reasoning essay, an essay upon a literary work, a research project based on the literary material, the analysis of a movie scene, a spoken reply to a question, a detailed commentary on a literary quotation, etc. The number of scenarios and proposals increased, but this did not clarify the situation. Nowadays, when the question of the genre of the final work has been resolved, experts still have a lot to do in order to clarify the basic expectations of an essay, its evaluation and the inclusion of the rich historical experience of using essays in Russian schools.

In this context, a retrospective analysis of the final school essay allows us to avoid those mistakes that had long been present in the domestic methodology, a struggle reflected in the success of the essay as a final test of students' knowledge. Today it should be borne in mind that the main obstacles in the historical development of the essay have included non-conformity of topics to the age abilities of pupils, the predominance of reproductive approaches (in which students could find obvious answers to essay questions in textbooks), and erroneous criteria for assessing written works.

In the twenty-first century, we have returned to a moment in which school essays are a significant component of school-leaving exams (and thus university admissions) and in which essay-writing and the teaching of writing are leaving the domain of literature and becoming more broadly humanistic in nature. The formation process of the school essay a century ago described in this chapter is in a certain parallel with the current state of the methodology and can help to overcome possible errors in the work of modern instructors and researchers.

References

Alferov, A. D. (1911). *Rodnoi yazyk v srednei shkole: Opyt metodiki* [Mother tongue in middle school: Methodological experience]. Sotrudnik shkoly.

Belyavskii, E.V. (1889). Metod vedeniya sochinenii v starshikh klassakh gimnazii [The method of using essays in high school (gymnasiums)]. *Zhurnal Ministerstva narodnogo prosveshcheniya, 4*, 29–41.

Brailovskii, S. N. (1910). O shkolnom sochinitelstve [About school essays]. *Russkii filologicheskii vestnik, 1*(2), 25–39.

Brailovskii, S. N. (1915). Staroe i novoe v metodike sochinenii po russkomu yazyku [Old and new trends in the methodology of essays in the Russian language]. *Pedagogicheskii sbornik, 1*, 1–46.

Filonov, A. G. (1902). *Sovremennoe prepodavanie slovesnosti* [Modern teaching of literature]. Tip. Rikhte.

Filonov A. G. (1908). *O temakh po russkomu yazyku dlya pismennykh uchenicheskikh sochinenii v srednikh uchebnykh zavedeniyakh* [The Russian language topics for students' essays in middle educational institutions]. Tipografiya Glazunova.

The First All-Russian Congress. (1917). *Pervyi Vserossiiskii Sezd prepodavatelei russkogo yazyka srednei shkoly v Moskve (27 dekabrya 1916–4 yanvarya 1917 g.)* [The First All-Russian Congress of Russian language teachers in Moscow middle school (December 27, 1916–January 4, 1917)]. Pechatnya A. Snegirevoy.

Getmanskaya, E. V. (2013). *Slovesnost' v srednej i vysshej shkole: tradicii preemstvennosti (istoriko-metodicheskij ocherk)* [Literature in secondary and higher schools: traditions of continuity (historical and methodological essay)]. Prometheus.

Getmanskaya, E. V. (2015). *Literatura v srednei i vysshei shkole: razvitie i preemstvennost (konets XVII – nachalo XX veka)* [Literature in middle and high school: development and consistency (the late 17th century and the early 20th century]. Izd-vo Moscow State Pedagogical University.

Golubkov, V. V. (1914). *Novyi put. Posobie dlya literaturnykh besed i pismennykh rabot* [New path. Student's textbook for literary conversations and paperwork]. Izd. A. I. Mamontova.

Istomin, V. A. (1891). Metodicheskie ukazaniya otnositelno prepodavaniya russkogo yazyka i slovesnosti v zhenskikh srednikh uchebnykh zavedeniyakh [Methodological guidelines for teaching the Russian language and literature in girl's middle educational institutions]. (1891). *Russkii filologicheskii vestnik, 1*, 1–31.

Kholevius, I. (1912). *Temy i plany dlya sochinenii* [Topics and outlines for essays] (Vol. 2). Izd. V.V. Dumnova.

Larionov, S. S. (1915). *Sbornik tem dlya sochinenii v starshikh klassakh srednei shkoly i na okonchatelnykh ispytaniyakh* [The collection of essay topics for upper middle school and final examination]. Tiflis.

Lebedev, A. M. (1916). Zadachi shkolnykh sochinenii [Tasks of school essays]. *Rodnoi yazyk v shkole, 6*, 274–276.

Ministry of Public Education. (1890). Primernaya programma russkogo yazyka s tserkovnoslavyanskim i slovesnosti [Sample curriculum of the Russian language and Church Slavonic and literature]. *Zhurnal Ministerstva narodnogo prosveshcheniya, 12*, 80–107.

Ministry of Public Education. (1915). *Materialy po reforme srednei shkole. Primernye programmy i obyasnitelnye zapiski* [Materials on middle school reforms. Sample curricula and explanatory notes]. Senatskaya Tipografiya.

Olshamovskii, M. N. (1880). *Rukovodstvo k vedeniyu pismennykh uprazhnenii v gimnaziyakh* [Guidelines for the introduction of written exercises into gymnasiums]. Tip. E. Lissner i Yu. Roman.

Ostrogorskii, V. P. (1885). *Besedy o prepodavanii slovesnosti* [Conversations of teaching literature]. Tip. V. Demanova.

Ovsyaniko-Kulikovskii, D.N. (1911). O prepodavanii teorii slovesnosti v srednei shkole [Teaching the theory of literature in middle school]. In B. A. Lezin (Ed.), *Voprosy teorii i psikhologii tvorchestva* [Questions of theory and psychology of creativity] (pp. 426–430). Mirnyi Trud.

Semenov, A. K. (1912). *Plany i sochineniya. Kurs VII klassa gimnazii* [Outlines and essays. The course for the 7th grade of gymnasiums]. Tipografiya "Poryadok."

Shumilovskii, L.I. (1910). *Rukovodstvo k samostoyatelnomu sostavleniyu uchenicheskikh sochinenii* [Guidelines for the independent conduction of students' essays] (Vol. 1). Izd. inzh. P.K. Shmulevicha.

Yakubovich, K. F. (1896). *Znachenie russkoi slovesnosti v sisteme realnogo obrazovaniya* [The significance of the Russian language in education systems]. Tip. I. I. Chokolova.

3 How Russian Art Historians Learn to Write

Natalya Smirnova and Anna Guseva
HSE University, St. Petersburg

In this chapter, we explore how writing has been taught in the domain of art history in Russia. We draw on academic literacy theory and work from two major premises: a) writing is a type of social practice and b) writing is closely linked with the knowledge-making practices in a discipline. We employed semi-structured interviews to explore how participants were taught to write in the discipline and how they have taught their students to write. The results of our study indicate that mentoring and discovery learning were the main teaching approaches and that writing was seen as purely instrumental, a skill that one acquired naturally from experience. The interview data indicates that the participants were reinventing their writing and that the major tensions in that process were closely linked to: 1) access to resources in the process of researching and producing a text, and 2) traditions of knowledge-making globally and in the particular geopolitical and socio-historic context of Russia. The findings indicate that research on the writing for publication practices of art historians has been challenging because this knowledge domain is marked by varying interpretative epistemologies within national, cultural, and or geopolitical contexts.

Academic writing for publication as a research field has been developing globally over the last 30 years (Curry & Lillis, 2015; Kuteeva & Mauranen, 2014). The majority of studies have looked into various linguistic patterns within published texts, scholarly writers' experiences and publication practices, and cultural and disciplinary variations in academic text production by academics working in hard and soft sciences (Cargill et al., 2019; Hyland, 2009; Uzuner, 2008). At the same time, little research has been carried out on how contemporary scholars learn to write academic texts within the domain of arts and humanities. In particular, research on the writing for publication practices in fields like art history is challenging because the knowledge domain of the humanities is marked by the production of mono-authored texts with distinctive authorial voices, a less rigid rhetorical structure, and interpretative epistemologies (Hyland, 2016).

Another challenge is that within all disciplines, anglophone writing pedagogy is the most researched one. For example, research into writing centers has been predominantly driven by studies which examine how U.S. writing center models are adopted or adapted in universities across the world (Shine Cain, 2011, see also Chapter 5 and Chapter 7). Yet, there have been calls in academia to acknowledge the existence of indigenous writing traditions in native languages so as to overcome the hegemony of Anglo-centric writing pedagogy (Altbach & de Wit, 2015; Canagarajah, 2005) and make local writing traditions visible to the global research community (Chitez et al., 2018; Gustafsson & Ganobcsik-Williams, 2016). Following Lillis and Curry (2010), our study explores how writing has been taught in the domain of art history in the particular geolinguistic and geopolitical space of Russia.

We draw on academic literacies theory (Lea & Street, 1998), and there are two major premises underlying our approach: a) writing is a type of social practice (Lillis, 2001) and b) writing is closely linked with the knowledge-making practices in a discipline. The chapter is based on six interviews with Russian art historians about their academic writing practices. We seek to address the following empirical questions:

- What were the educational practices in the past and what are the contemporary approaches to teaching writing in art history in Russia?
- What challenges existed and exist in knowledge-making and writing practices and how do they affect the teaching of writing?

To our best knowledge, there have been few studies which have explicitly or implicitly raised the issues of writing pedagogy in the art history knowledge domain in particular geolinguistic and geopolitical contexts. Thus, the aim in this chapter is to bring to bear understandings and questions arising from complexities in meaning making and writing in art history texts to explore contemporary Russian scholars' accounts of their educational experiences and the challenges that have significantly affected academic writing practices. In this chapter, we first address the academic literacies framework and emphasize the value of drawing on scholarly writers' experiences and perspectives on academic writing as a type of social practice. Then, we critically address art history as a contested site of knowledge production and the distinctive features of the discipline that influence its associated rhetoric. Next, we discuss the existing pedagogical approaches worldwide in this domain and reach conclusions about the state of writing and writing education in this field. We then introduce the research design and the results of the study. Finally, we discuss the key findings and draw conclusions relevant for researchers in academic writing, scholarly writers in the field, and writing instructors.

Academic Writing as Social Practice

The complexity of research on how academics produce and learn to produce academic texts is linked to the existing diversity of ideologies and theories in the field of writing for publication. Lillis and Curry (2010) have usefully suggested that there are key ideological orientations towards writers, texts, practices, and languages which underlie methodological choices for research. Thus, methodological choices in scholarly writing research have heavily depended on how writing is conceptualized and how text and context have been methodologically linked.

One key methodological strand of approaches to exploring academic text production is based on text analysis (Curry & Lillis, 2015). Text-based approaches primarily focus on variations in the linguistic features of academic texts (cross disciplinary and cross linguistic studies) with the aim of quantifying them and comparing or contrasting these features. Such studies tend to treat English-medium academic texts as a fixed norm. This methodological approach is grounded in the debatable premise that language is a transparent and bounded phenomenon (Lillis, 2013). In other words, an academic text is taken out of its context (Blommaert, 2005) and becomes the primary object of analysis.

The other key approach is ethnography-oriented research, which has been employed to explore issues related to contexts for text production and the experiences of scholarly writers in academia (Lillis, 2008). Paltridge (2017) echoes Lillis' (2003) emphasis on the idea that writing is a type of knowledge-making rather than just knowledge inscription. Such an approach is transformative in its nature because it enables both scholars and writers to explore the existing conventions and their constraining or restricting powers in the process of academic text production (Lillis, 2015). However, what constitutes context requires clarification (Blommaert, 2005), and Lillis (2008) has usefully distinguished among three levels of ethnography (as method, methodology, and deep theorizing) to indicate that there have been variations in ethnographic engagement and levels of context in the field of academic writing.

The theoretical framework for academic literacies emerged as a response to the dominance of skills-based approaches to teaching reading and writing and inequalities in access to education among students. Rooted in New Literacy Studies (e.g., Street, 2003), academic literacies theory provides a critical lens for exploring who can say what in academia and offers a viable methodological approach to learning the experiences of scholarly writers. It has a distinctive ideological and epistemological tradition (Lea & Street, 1998; Lillis & Scott, 2007). Literacy should not be treated as autonomous and "a single and universal phenomenon with assumed cognitive as well as economic benefits" (Lillis &

Scott, 2007, p. 11). Instead, it has an ideological nature: socioculturally embedded literacy practices should be taken into account along with the associated power relationships (Lillis, 2009). Thus, the high-stakes academic writing of scholars is the key component of literacy and is a social practice (as opposed to competence). It is heavily shaped by the values, beliefs, and ideologies of writers in a particular context (Barton et al., 2000; Lillis, 2001).

In *Academic Writing in a Global Context*, Lillis and Curry (2010) explore scholars' writing experiences and access to resources in four national contexts (Portugal, Hungary, Spain, and Slovakia). They reveal important resources which have been available to scholars and mobilized via local and transnational networks: contacts among scholars, information, academic materials, rhetorical resources, collaboration in writing, collaboration on research, and brokering (connections to publishing opportunities). Lillis and Curry (2006) also reveal the role of literacy brokers, a term they use to refer to actors who can influence the academic research article production and access resources in important ways, such as reviewers, editors, and translators. Other geopolitical contexts where marked center-periphery inequalities have been studied are: China (Li & Flowerdew, 2009), Spain (Pérez-Llantada et al., 2011), and Germany (Schluer, 2014).

The value of Lillis and Curry's (2010) work is its use of ethnography, a key empirical methodology of the ideological model of academic literacy. In our study of text production by Russian scholars within a particular cultural, disciplinary, and geopolitical context, the notion of writing as a type of social practice helps to identify and explore links among the objects of the research (texts, their uses, and users). Practice helps to link language with individuals at the level of the context of a situation (what is said at a certain moment, under certain conditions) and at the level of the context of a culture (what can be researched at a certain moment and under certain conditions) in three ways: 1) texts do not exist in isolation and are part of what people do (practices) in the material world; 2) these practices become the life routines of individuals and institutions when language is seen as practice-resource; and 3) academic writing shapes and is embedded in social structures (Lillis & Scott, 2007).

Art History as a Knowledge Domain

Knowledge production in the field of arts and humanities has been genuinely different from the hard sciences and social sciences (Hellqvist, 2010). Art history, like any disciplinary field, has certain features that influence meaning-making in the process of academic text production. This is a young discipline globally and is still evolving and struggling for its disciplinary boundaries. Art history has also been seen as an emerging discipline without a formal status (Grabar,

1982) and often positioned as luxury, elitist, and not meeting practical educational demands (Kent, 2012). In Russia, art history has been struggling for its independence from such root knowledge domains as literary criticism, theory of arts, and history. The standards of writing in the field have differed a lot (Sychenkova, 2014) because the cultural, epistemological, and aesthetic expectations of writers and readers have been vast and thus unmanageable.

Interpretation is important to understanding how art historians write their texts. Biglan (1973) identifies variations along the hard-soft and pureapplied dimensions. The distinction between hard and soft fields relates to the extent to which knowledge is constructed on the basis of a framework of shared assumptions. The pure sciences (hard) maintain a degree of internal unity over aims, methods of investigation and evaluation criteria, which may come to be seen as derived from reality itself, rather than constructed by disciplinary convention. The humanities and social sciences (soft), in contrast, tend to be characterized by internal discord, encouraging a view of knowledge as a matter of interpretation. Writing is a way to make meaning, yet it is surrounded by many difficulties. Grabar (1982) illustrates a few of them: fear of being obvious or doctrinaire; the risks of raising fundamental issues when there are established ways of operating which seem perfectly acceptable within the discourse community; the difficulty of choosing meaning-making and interpretation patterns from anthropology or literature; and, generally, the absence of a collectively accepted statement of what the history of the visual arts is supposed to be (p. 281).

The intellectual response to art has been constrained by the fact that each subfield has its own methods and approaches, technical vocabulary, and needs. Grabar (1982) explains that subfields in art history can be cultural, social, technical, methodological, and conceptual. He concludes that they are so different that that they need autonomy to develop, and there is no universal history of art.

The visual experiences of art historians have been central to their academic text production. Barolsky (1996) addresses the theoretical and methodological problem of how one sees in the history of art and emphasizes that seeing is a play of imagination reflected in writing. Roth (2010) addresses the future of the writing medium (when compared to visual modes) and refers to the long-standing tensions between writing and visual representation.

Writing a text in art history in the global academic context has become more difficult for art historians, and Grabar (1982) makes four key observations. First of all, the range of visual experiences offered to the historian of art has increased dramatically. There is an increased variety of historical periods and geographical areas; minor (decorative arts) and major media; paintings, photographs, and books as reproducible substitutes; and exhibitions and other visual experiences (external to the show). The second observation is that major journals publish a limited range of methodological and conceptual approaches in art history. Art forms mostly represent the Western European heritage, from late antiquity to the late nineteenth century while published papers belong either to the patronage or attribution genres. He also observes that regions outside the western world mostly have limited access to key artworks, books with reproductions, or key readings in the discipline "out of which emerge the principles of the classical history of arts" (Grabar, 1982, p. 282). Finally, what counts as knowledge becomes the outcome of educational and academic circumstances. He questions why Western art and no other artistic tradition is privileged as the mainstream in classical history.

Grabar's (1982) observations have certain implications and consequences for meaning making and writing in the discipline and emphasize the risks of cultural imperialism. Kauffmann (2004) explains that while the traditional classification of works of art is made by country and period, the political and cultural boundaries are complex, fluid, and not always transparent. He argues for establishing the geography of art as a subject and that our assumptions about the place of art should be reconsidered and reflected in narratives of art history. Many of the regions outside the Western world have their own non-Western traditions of explaining art and its history, and while the non-Western practices are recognized, the Western methodologies and terms prevail (Elkins, 2007, 2011; Van Damme & Zijlmans, 2008).

Overall, epistemology has been related to rhetoric in important ways and defines how art history writing should and can be taught as a part of the meaning-making and knowledge-making process in higher education (Becher, 1989).

Art History, Associated Rhetoric, and Writing Pedagogy

Understanding art historians' epistemological orientations and associated rhetoric is crucial for developing academic writing pedagogies in art history. For example, Adam (2014) argues that writing in art history, particularly the fine arts domain, has been rooted in subjectivity and objectivity, when "critical examination rests on embodied, subjective understandings as well as rigorous analysis and as much on creative intuition as on calculated attention" (p. 219). This epistemological orientation results in the associated rhetoric in which "written work is presented in the form of an on-going exchange between self and world, practice and theory" (Adam, 2014, p. 219). He proposes the adoption of a performative writing strategy that "reflects both the content and context of the enquiry" (2014, p. 218). Such an approach allows for the exploration of critical concepts in practice and draws on one's phenomenological experience of continually questioning, re-negotiating, re-interpreting, and representing concepts.

Research and writing in art history is an embodied process. Adam (2014) refers to the examples of Paul Ricoeur, Janet Wolff, John Wylie, and others to signal the variety of ways in which the writers construct their narrative identities in their texts by combining subjective description with critical analysis. For example, Crème and Mckenna (2010) explored the relationship between writing and identity—how writers sense themselves as writers. They used Roz Ivanic's (1998) three writing selves: the autobiographical, the discoursal, and the authorial to look for markers that indicate writers' backgrounds, disciplinary orientations, and authorial presence.

Writing a text has been closely linked to the aesthetic tastes of individual writers. Adam (2014) says that "the writings of Irigaray, Kristeva and Cixious continue to inspire me" (p. 220). Barolsky (1996) emphasizes the importance of poetry in writing, as otherwise a text lacks passion and is neutral. He argues that there are two key reasons for bad writing in the field. First, art historians have not thought of themselves as writers. Second, writers have been afraid to employ artful rhetorical forms (e.g., passion, enthusiasm, imagination, use of metaphorical language) because they will be seen as unprofessional in a context where writers have been expected to fortify their claims. Thus, to avoid the problem of dry prose and reference to facts only, Barolsky (1996) emphasizes that good writing emerges from the imitation of good writers.

At the same time, Adam (2014) highlights that conventions have been the opposite of what is expected by the discourse community (in contrast with the natural and social sciences where writing is grounded in conventions). For example, MacLeod and Holdridge (2005) explain that "the conventionally written academic thesis does not always seem appropriate for the doctorate in fine art" (pp. 23). Moreover, Barrett and Bolt (2010) argue that the particular methodologies of the discipline have been "personally situated, interdisciplinary and diverse and emergent" (p. 2). Thus, defining rhetorical patterns and conventions is problematic and requires a writer to meet traditional expectations and challenge familiar models at the same time.

Barnet (1993) explains that producing a text in art history has been rooted in existing epistemologies and that writing style is revealed in form. She explains that after the 1970s, there was an epistemological shift from decontextualized objects towards deconstruction and demystification in knowledge making and writing. Work has always been connected to social history. The writer's own contexts will also influence their interpretations.

When writing in art history, one needs to think about "what is in front of us as well as what is within us" (Barnet, 1993, p. 1). Writing becomes a way of learning and is a way to communicate our responses to the material and interest the reader in seeing the work as the writer sees it. Thus, writing a text involves such functions as observing, showing, and illuminating. Interestingly, unlike building an argument based on logic, as is traditional for the natural and social sciences, showing serves the function of argument building and is a way to convince the reader. Close analysis of form is a kind of analytic statement about "how the work means" (Barnet, 1993, p. 115). Elton and Nicolle (2009) emphasize that while there is writing development support at universities, there are certain risks of adopting approaches governed by a narrow emphasis on form. They question the transparency of the medium of language in the learning, teaching, and assessment of writing. Thus, apart from focusing on rules-led writing, it is equally important to read texts in the process of understanding and producing written texts.

Overall, while there is a growing body of research into epistemologies within the art history knowledge domain (Borgdorff, 2007), little is known about the writing and knowledge-making practices of contemporary scholars in various geopolitical and geolinguistic contexts (Lillis & Curry, 2010). There is considerable work still to be done to critically explore the complexity of issues which have surrounded the knowledge production and academic writing of scholars working in English and other languages in order to draw conclusions about writing pedagogies in the field.

Study Design and Data

Our study explored the experiences of six multilingual scholars in Russia within the context of English as the lingua franca of knowledge-making and production (Lillis & Curry, 2010). The methodology involved a text-ethnographic approach that traced the production of scholars' texts, with an empirical focus on specific texts, interviews conducted with scholars about the production of specific texts, and documentary data at the institutional, national, and international levels.

The key methodological orientation of this study was the critical framework of academic literacies with its "specific epistemological and ideological stance" (Lillis & Scott, 2007, p. 7) which was relevant for exploring high-stakes writing practices in academia. Our key aim was to foreground the writers' perspectives on text production and reveal academic writing practices with particular attention to emic perspectives in the course of cyclical talk, which "becomes part of sustained engagement in specific research sites and is set alongside other types of data" (Lillis, 2008, p. 362).

We followed the sociolinguistic premise that language is not transparent (Lillis & McKinney, 2013) and language indexes the real-life experiences of individuals. The interview data analysis involved working back and forth "from vertical (understanding the individual case) to horizontal (identifying patterns across cases) orientations to the data" (Barton & Hamilton, 1998, p. 70; see also Lillis & Curry, 2018) in order to generate themes that emerged as significant.

We used our personal contacts to trace art history scholars located in Moscow and St. Petersburg via snowball sampling, and we also traced publicly available scholars' profiles. We sought experienced writers with at least 10 years in academia who work in Russia in the field of art history. We then sent an email invitation to 12 scholars, and six participants agreed to take part in the study (see Table 3.1 for participants who agreed to participate in the study).[1] The major reasons for rejecting our participation invitation included the absence of time for the interview due to heavy workload (four scholars) and lack of desire to talk about publishing at all (two scholars). Each participant had a choice in the language of the interview (Russian or English). The interview lasted 60 to 90 minutes and covered such issues as education and academic experience, research writing experience, and the linguistic profile of writer-participants.

Table 3.1. Participant Profiles: Positions, Research Interests, Number of Academic Publications, and Years in Academia

Scholar	Location	# of academic publications	Academic position[2]	Research interests	Years
Anna	St. Petersburg	12 Russian 1 English	Docent	History of European sculpture	13
Olga	Moscow	18 Russian 5 English	Docent	History of Byzantine Art	14
Diana	Moscow	19 Russian 0 English	Docent	History of European graphic art	16
Elena	St. Petersburg	21 Russian 0 English	Docent	History of Eastern art	16
Alexander	Moscow	16 Russian 2 English 1 Chinese	Docent	History of the Western and Russian Architecture	16
Ekaterina	St. Petersburg	33 Russian 1 French	Docent	History of European Graphic art	43

1   The participants' names were anonymized.

2   Academic titles vary across countries and institutions. In Russia, there are such titles as professor (= U.S. full professor), docent (Czech Republic, Hungary, Poland, i.e., countries with academic traditions that stem from German-speaking countries = associate professor), senior lecturer (= U. S. assistant professor), and lecturer. These titles are given to faculty who both teach and conduct research in the majority of Russian universities at the moment.

In addition, we collected participants' current curricula vitae to analyze their working experiences and publications over time, along with additional documentary data that participants considered relevant for their knowledge-making and academic writing practices. For example, state and institutional initiatives about publishing in arts and humanities.

Results and Discussion: Art Historians at Work

In our exploratory study we sought to address two empirical questions. The first question was what the educational practices were and are in teaching writing in art history in Russia where we seek to make visible how and why art historians learned to produce texts and how their students learn to write now (see below Learning Trajectories: Past and Present). The second question targeted challenges which existed and exist in knowledge-making and writing practices and how they might affect the teaching of writing. We distinguished two major themes which emerged from the interview data: the importance of access to resources (see below Challenges in Writing Arising from Limited Access to Resources) and local traditions of knowledge-making and producing a text (see Challenges in Writing Arising from Disciplinary Traditions of Knowledge-making in a Particular Geopolitical and Socio-historic Context).

Learning Trajectories: Past and Present

Scholars shared their experiences of learning academic writing, and when we asked whether they were formally taught to write, all participants, except for Ekaterina and Elena, initially said no. However, in the course of interviews about their educational experiences, each scholar explicitly signaled that writing is and was a challenging experience and talked about the ways they learned to write. Ekaterina is the only participant who had formal training in writing. She said that in the academy of arts in St. Petersburg there was a compulsory course in writing, and they produced such genres as: "notes, essays, and reviews. (заметки, эссе и рецензии)."

When she was a first-year student, Elena says she had a seminar in writing for publication, but she believes that experience:

> Was a waste of time because we were first year students, and there were no writers among us at that time. (Это было мало полезное мероприятие, потому что нас учили на первом курсе, к тому моменту пишущих людей среди нас не было. Поэтому если я что-то и знала из первого курса, то я это забыла к моменту, когда понадобилось писать статьи.)

By contrast, Alexander said he had no formal classes in writing and had to learn to write by interpreting texts correctly:

> There were no such courses, it seems, anywhere. There was a lot of work with old texts that we had to understand in the contemporary context and interpret correctly. (таких курсов не было, мне кажется, нигде. Было много работы со старыми текстами, которые нужно понять с современной точки зрения и правильно изложить. Никаких приёмов письма, никаких занятий не было.)

He also recalled that although his high school classes in literature with a private tutor and first year university classes in history helped him learn to organize his ideas, thinking, and argument, he was not taught to write:

> I had, like many of us did and do now, private classes before joining the university in literature. We briefly discussed not how to write but how to organize your thinking, internal logic so that it exists in texts. There were seminars in history during the first year of studies. They were not about writing but about thinking, how to reason as a historian who is deconstructing a written text. (Я, как многие в те годы и сейчас, занимался с преподавателями перед поступлением и, в частности литературой. Мы немножко обсуждали не как писать, а как выстраивать мысль, внутренней логики, чтобы она была в текстах. были семинары на первом курсе по истории, в которых это касалось не письма, а мышления. как логически выстраивать логику мышления историка, который препарирует письменный текст.)

Writing essays was a part of a course in literary criticism, and Diana explained she produced essays which were: "A different genre, not a research article. (но это совсем другой жанр, это не научная статья.)" At the same time, due to current publishing pressure (Curry & Lillis, 2015), she said art historians have had the strong need to be able to publish research articles apart from the more common genres (e.g., notes, essays, reviews). Overall, Diana signaled that writing texts has always been a challenging experience because: "it seemed that everything you wrote was not right, and then there comes a feeling that you are doing it right. (кажется, все что пишешь, получается не так, потом возникает ощущение, что все получается.)" Diana emphasized the importance of learning to write by using the feedback from her research supervisor in the course of writing her thesis:

> I am grateful to my research supervisor. Good supervision is important, when a more experienced professional guides a novice writer. Feedback was quite harsh, but it helped me to understand how everything should be. (Я признательна своему научному руководителю. Важно умное руководство и чтобы старший специалист правильно направлял начинающего. Правка была достаточно жесткой, но она помогала понять, как все должно быть.)

When recalling how she learned to write, Ekaterina also talked about the importance of a supervisor. The reason for this was that sometimes the object of study requires a specific attitude, description, and writing style. She said that the process of learning to work with particular materials, such as engravings, was a "complex and unique process of learning" that resembled more an artisan training with its workshop style of teaching than academic classes:

> If you are holding a portrait of the sixteenth century you have to understand the context [of its making]; to know the history from the costume to philosophy and history of religion and culture. That's why every student has a supervisor. сложное, штучное обучение. обучение идет с руки, как в многих творческих профессиях. есть методические материалы, которые ты прочитываешь, но перед тобой портрет XVI века, и ты должен понимать контекст, эпоху: от костюма до философии, истории, истории религии и культуры. Тьютор закрепляется за тобой как твой наставник.)

Two participants talked about the importance of learning to write by reading texts that they like and see as exemplary in their field. Elena said she learned to write:

> By studying samples, sample papers of more experienced peers, those who I respected and who were interesting and pleasant to read. A collection of sample texts was emerging, and I followed them, and step by step I got into writing. (училась вприглядку, на образцовых статьях старших коллег, которых я уважала, которых мне было интересно и приятно читать. Из них собирался банк образцов, стараясь следовать которым я постепенно входила в писание.)

Reading exemplary texts in terms of quality of research and quality of writing was crucial for Olga, who said that she learned to write from reading and by paying attention both to the content and the style of a text:

> I consider the quality of research. If I see that the text I read is reliable, does not raise any doubts at the professional level. But I pay significant attention to the quality of writing like an editor. (Я ориентируюсь на уровень исследований. Если мне кажется, что то, что я читаю, заслуживает доверия, не вызывает у меня сомнений на профессиональном уровне в первую очередь. Но я очень обращаю внимание и на качество письма тоже, как редактор.)

At the same time, while reading exemplary texts guides some writers in producing texts, Diana signaled the challenge of finding her own way of writing a text which will differ from her teachers':

> I cannot say that I follow more experienced peers. We depend on the examples set by our teachers, but I do not try to imitate them. (не могу сказать, что я сильно ориентируюсь на старших коллег. Мы зависим от примера преподавателей, но я не стараюсь подражать им.)

Even more, Anna said she believes her texts have been produced themselves and she could hardly explain how it has happened: "Texts are born themselves, I only write them down. (сами пишутся они, я их только оформляю.)"

As Anna reports, art criticism classes were an opportunity to write more about art. Yet, she said that although she has always valued literary features in texts, there was no place for them in academic texts:

> We were specifically taught art criticism, but they never demanded literary features of texts, which I always liked. (Нас учили художественной критике специально и целенаправленно, но не требовали каких-то художественных достоинств текста, а мне это всегда нравилось.)

Finally, participants talked about their editing experiences, as they said it is a way to significantly improve their writing. Anna explains that:

> You learn when you edit. Most important is the experience of working with good editors. Not my own editing experience, but external, when my texts were edited. (учишься сам когда редактируешь. больше всего помогает опыт с хорошими

редакторами. Не мой собственный, а внешний, когда мои статьи редактировали.)

Apart from sharing their experiences of how they learned to write in art history, they also talked about how they currently teach writing to their students. First of all, five scholars talked about the lack (mostly absence) of formal training in writing for their students. It has proven problematic since writing for art historians, like in any other field in the humanities, is a way to make meaning and to make knowledge fixed in a written text. For example, Alexander said there still are no writing courses for his university students, and it has posed a serious limitation which students have inherited when they graduate from the university and pursue an academic career:

> It [writing skill] can develop naturally, but even in this case it is useful to learn. Very often, it [writing skill] does not develop at all, and there are many people who have problems with writing. It seems to them that they do not have problems, but the reader immediately sees that there are problems with logic, style, some things are completely ignored. (это может родится само, но даже в этом случае будет полезно поучится. Очень часто это не рождается совсем, и есть много людей, которые испытывают потом с этим проблемы. Им кажется, что они не испытывают, но читателю сразу видно, что у человека проблемы с логикой, с подачей, что какие-то вещи он просто не замечает.)

The second current challenge of teaching writing to students has been rooted in the fact that art history has a wide variety of subfields, each with a specific style and manner of writing. Olga explained that study books exist that can help writers in general writing issues, but since her field of research has been very narrow, she would need a special writing manual for her research focus:

> There are some manuals in research writing. Our field of research is very narrow, and nobody writes special manuals. When I was a postgraduate student, I learned some ideas from the book by Umberto Eco, How to Write a Thesis. (есть какие-то пособия по научному стилю письма. У нас очень узкая область, поэтому никто не пишет специальных работ. Я когда была аспиранткой, что-то почерпнула из работы Умберто Эко «Как писать дипломную раб»).

Overall, the experience of learning to write has appeared, for art historians, related to working within literature or history traditions. Deconstructing a text was more common than learning to compose a text. The participants signaled that writing is an ability that does not develop naturally and highlight the importance of introducing formal writing instruction to university students in such genres as notes, essays, reviews, and journal articles. Their orientation in learning to write toward more experienced, respected writers (e.g., their supervisors or from published texts of their peers) has signaled that the mentoring model of learning to write and produce meaning in an academic text—as well as their feedback—has served an important function by highlighting problems not only with writing but with meaning making in their texts. At the same time, the mentoring model allows space for the writer's voice and identity, as texts are born in the process of meaning making.

Challenges in Writing Arising from Limited Access to Resources

Talking about their writing experiences, the participants' comments explicitly signaled the importance of having access to particular resources in producing a text, namely, the limited access to research literature, the necessity of using foreign languages in research, limited access to objects of art which are under research focus, and lack of time for research and writing.

Limited Access to Research Literature

The participants talked about limited access to published books and periodicals due to lack of financial resources in higher education and poor libraries in Russia. For example, Olga said that most of the research in her field is published abroad and is not available in Russian libraries:

> Most of the studies on my topic are published abroad. Many periodicals about Italian art are not available in our libraries. Getting foreign literature is the hardest problem. (По моей тематике большинство работ выходит заграницей. Много работ по итальянской периодике, которые в наших библиотеках недоступны. Добыть иностранную литературу одна из самых сложных проблем.)

Diana explained that local libraries have received little funding and that travelling abroad or accessing electronic databases are the only ways for her to get access to published works:

> We try to increase our library, but we sometimes fail, in part due to financial reasons. A trip overseas is not only for vis-

iting museums but for visiting libraries. We have had access to electronic databases for the last three years. (Пытаемся расширять нашу библиотеку, но нам это не всегда удается, в том числе по финансовым соображениям. поездка за рубеж посвящается не только походам в музеи, но еще и посещению библиотек. у нас около трех лет есть подписка на несколько баз данных.)

When the published works appear to be limited, Olga also said that she seeks ways to freely access published works online: "Fortunately, now we have the academia.edu portal so that poor Russians can find papers from different fields. (К счастью, появился сайт academia.edu., чтобы бедные русские находили там темы по различным областям знаний.)" While working with foreign published literature has appeared crucial for one's work, seeking access to research literature, catalogues, and periodicals published in foreign languages has represented a great challenge for contemporary art historians in Russia.

Knowledge of Foreign Languages

Many participants talked about the importance of knowing foreign languages in order to do research, and some of them learned the local languages of Japan, Spain, Greece, and Portugal, because most of the research about an object of art has been published in the local language. Ekaterina says that any art historian should be able to read modern foreign texts and: "Must know all European languages because references are always made in the language. (должен владеть всеми европейскими языками, потому что справочные сведения опубликованы на языке.)" She also said that in order to work with engravings she had to learn Latin because: "It was the international language in the seventeenth-eighteenth centuries. (пришлось учить латынь, так как это язык международного общения XVI - XVIII века.)"

Sometimes scholars have sought the support of their peers when working with an object of art which has been described or represented in a foreign language. For example, Anna described how her peer has helped her with translations of Portuguese texts from the seventeenth century. Ekaterina usefully explained that the origin of the object of art has been closely linked to the language of its creation, description, and interpretation. While reading in foreign languages is a necessary part of their work, Ekaterina said that writing a text in a foreign language has been a great challenge. She believed writing a journal article in a foreign language required a degree in philology because she saw translation from Russian into a foreign language as the only way of producing a text:

> I write in Russian, and it is translated. You need to obtain a degree in philology to write in a foreign language. I believe that a non-native speaker is not able to translate except for a couple of geniuses. (Я пишу по-русски, и это всё переводят. потому нужно закончить филфак чтобы писать на языке. Я считаю, что не носитель языка не может перевести нормально, ну кроме парочки гениев.)

Scholars successfully use foreign languages to read published works and study the objects of art, but writing in a foreign language is challenging for many of them (see also the subsection below: Challenges in Writing Arising from Disciplinary Traditions of Knowledge-making in a Particular Geopolitical and Socio-historic Context).

Limited Access to Objects of Art

The visual experiences of art historians have been central to their academic text production (Barolsky, 1996). In fact, access to objects of art was an important theme raised by the participants and has been limited in different ways. Olga explained that only original objects of art could be studied: "Illustrations in books, however good they are, do not give a full understanding about the value of art objects. (иллюстрации в книгах, какими бы хорошими они не были, они не дают полного представления о том, насколько это ценное произведение.)" Diana said that she had to travel for internships in museum depositories in the US and Germany because it was the only way she was able to witness objects of art and learn about their conservation principles. By contrast, Ekaterina said that because of the tough political and economic situation in Russia she was able to travel quite late in her career:

> An art historian, like an artist, must begin with visiting the living art object. I am 60, and I visited Italy for the first time when I was 58. (историк искусства, так же, как и художник, должен начинать все свои практики с посещения живого памятника культуры. мне 60 лет, а я первый раз в 58 лет побывала в Италии.)

Olga explained the limited access to art objects in Russia has come from heavy bureaucratization and restrictive requirements in local depositories:

> Access to Byzantine works is given to an academic not only with a higher education degree but with a research degree and often with a recommendation from a western colleague. (часто византийские рукописи может получить в библиотеке

человек, имеющий высшее образование, но и имеющий научную степень. иногда еще рекомендацию западного коллеги.)

Interestingly, getting access to objects of art is also a problem for foreign scholars who research Russian art collections. For example, Ekaterina talked about providing access to Russian art collections to foreign scholars and the fact that online catalogues have appeared important in times of limited financial resources or travel restrictions:

> Many times, I heard abroad "Do you have it?" I said "Yes." They said, "I was wondering where the black hole is." Only now is there an internet catalogue, and foreigners were not allowed in the country in the past. Catalogues were handwritten in the nineteenth century. (много раз за границей я слышала «ах, это у вас есть?». Да, говорю. «Ах, я-то думал, ну где же есть эта чёрная дыра». сейчас появился интернет каталог, а раньше иностранцев не пускали в страну. А каталоги были написаны в 19 веке от руки.)

Getting access to objects of art is essential for a researcher but has presented certain challenges to art historians, as it has been limited by the financial, bureaucratic, and political factors surrounding a scholar's work.

Lack of Time

Many of the respondents stressed that difficulties in getting direct access to their research object is not the only obstacle. Time available for writing influences the rhetorical choices and knowledge-making practices of the scholars. Olga said that despite the fact that she values the literary features of academic texts, she had no time for such prose and had to write "boring" texts. She explained that meaning has been more important for her than the beauty and smoothness of the text when her time has been limited:

> There is more work, family requires more time as well, and I have no time for literary texts. I'd rather use the same word again and again to make my argument absolutely clear than synonyms that could obscure the meaning. (работы стало больше, семья тоже стала занимать все больше времени, и на литературные работы просто перестало хватать сил.)

Diana said that she allocated limited time for writing what she saw as important. While she said that writing museum catalogues is the key genre for an art historian, publishing journal articles has been seen as secondary, as universities have pressed for increased research output measured in research articles. Thus, she said she experiences tensions in meeting the university research output requirement:

> The exhibition catalogue is the key genre for a museum specialist. That is why I try to find time primarily for them and write research articles only if I can. (для музейщика более частый жанр—это выставочные каталоги. Поэтому время приходится выкраивать для них, а статьи это уже если получится.)

Overall, the scholars' accounts signal that the writing practices of art historians have been rooted in work in libraries and reading foreign language (e.g., modern and ancient) literature, travelling and witnessing objects of arts, and finding time for research and writing. While access to libraries and time have been important for research and writing in many academic spheres (e.g., Lillis & Curry, 2010), one's ability to get access to specific resources, such as using foreign languages (not only English) and seeing and witnessing objects of art located in foreign countries and in Russia, has significantly influenced Russian art historians' writing practices, both for university students and researchers.

Challenges in Writing Arising from Disciplinary Traditions of Knowledge-making in a Particular Geopolitical and Socio-historic Context

The importance of epistemological orientations in meaning making and writing has been well documented in Curry and Lillis (2010). These orientations were signaled in participants' accounts. The influence of socio-political and historic contexts on meaning making and knowledge reflects the nature of writing practices as situated and rooted in their contexts of production.

Epistemological Tensions and Rhetoric

Producing a text in the discipline has been connected to local and global epistemological tensions. For example, Ekaterina explained that there have been long standing tensions between two epistemological camps in Russia, iskusstvoznanie (study of art) and istoria iskusstv (history of art). She identified herself with a global tradition, as opposed to the two local camps, and uses the English term the history of art to signal the divide between the local camps and Western scholarship:

> In Soviet times there was mainly iskusstvoznanie, istoria iskusstv [study of art, history of art] but it was not history of art [uses English term]. [Study of art and art history] were descriptions, emotions, literary studies. There were big terminological battles [in Soviet Russia] between iskusstvoznanie and istoria iskusstv [study of art and history of art]. Study of art was interpretation, art criticism, and new social and philosophic views. I do not like it. (В советское время было в основном искусствоведение, история искусств, но она не была хистори оф арт. Это было описание, эмоции, литературоведение. Были большие терминологические битвы—искусствоведение или искусствознание. Искусствознание—это интерпретация, арт критика, новый взгляд социальный, философский. Я это не люблю.)

Different epistemological camps have set certain standards in research writing, and certain tensions during the publication process have appeared. Anna indicated that when her texts have undergone review and have been edited by peers, she has seen the existing tensions between the epistemological and rhetorical orientations of editors and her own in the process of publishing a paper:

> Editors cut papers, and we cut with them. With editors from different fields, philologists, you understand that your paper is edited as a philology text, a text in literary history. Some editors work in natural sciences and explain to you that the order of images should be the following because you refer first to this and then to that picture, but they should match. (редакторы грызут статью и ты вместе с ними. Когда редакторы из разных областей—филологи, которые работают в основном с филологической литературой, и ты понимаешь, что твою статью пытаются отредактировать так, как принято редактировать филологические статьи, статьи по истории литературы. Кто-то работает с естественнонаучной литературой, начинает тебе объяснять, что последовательность картинок должна быть такая-то, потому что ты ссылаешься сначала на эту картинку, а потом на эту, и что они должны соответствовать.)

Epistemological orientations are at the core of the rhetorical choices in art history writing. Anna provided an example of how an art object does or does not define the research rhetoric and how she had enjoyed both approaches in her own writing:

> A contemporary art object can fully construct the language of the researcher. If we believe that the research object does not construct the language of the researcher, then, in art criticism it is the opposite: the language is created by the object. I follow this approach, take both sides. I like moving close and further from the object, being under its language power and getting free from it. (Говорить о произведении современном, которое может полностью конструировать язык исследователя. Если мы считаем, что объект исследования не должен конструировать язык исследователя, то в критике наоборот язык должен конструироваться объектом. я стараюсь занять позицию, взяв и оттуда, и оттуда. Мне нравится перемещаться ближе к предмету, дальше от предмета, то есть попадать во власть его языка или выходить оттуда.)

While there are certain types of disciplinary rhetoric, scholars, like Anna in her account above, have talked about their individual rhetorical choices to express what is important in their texts. This reflects Adam's (2014) argument that writing in art history, particularly the fine arts domain, has been rooted in subjectivity and objectivity. For example, Diana talked about the important role of the context, the epoch when working and writing about an art object: "In my papers it is important for me to sense the epoch's nerve, put the art object into the epoch's context. (В своих статьях мне важно уловить нерв эпохи, вписать произведение в контекст эпохи.)" Anna said she employs a type of rhetoric which she calls "provocation" (e.g., see Crème & Mckenna, 2010, Ivanic, 1998, for a discussion of ways in which the writers construct their narrative identities in their texts). She said she learned it from reading English-medium papers written by one anglophone center art historian and which she liked very much. She called this type of rhetoric provocation because she could discuss the social aspects of art when this focus was not common in Russia:

> One of most interesting texts was written by a professional art historian. It was written in such a way that it was pure social history of art, even more than I do. The reader must make certain efforts while reading a text, follow the same discovery road as the writer did. (Когда возможно, я предпочитаю эссеистику. Один из самых интересных текстов, который я

читала был написан профессиональным искусствоведом. Он был написан таким образом, хотя там была в чистом виде социальная история искусства ещё больше, чем у меня. Читатель должен делать усилия при прочтении текста, пройти путь автора в открытии.)

Scholars' accounts suggest that local and global disciplinary traditions and epistemological orientations are key to producing research texts in art history in addition to the individual rhetorical decisions of the writers. Yet, at the local level, sometimes these orientations clash and result in writer's frustrations with the process of publishing a research paper. At the global level, there are also tensions since while the non-Western practices are recognized, the Western methodologies and terms prevail (Elkins, 2007, 2011; Van Damme & Zijlmans, 2008).

The Heritage of the Soviet Union

Knowledge-making and writing traditions in the discipline are rooted in their socio-historical and political contexts (Lillis & Curry, 2010). In Soviet times, Ekaterina explained that research on art was problematic. She recalled that when she was doing her postgraduate exam in the Soviet era, an examiner asked her about her future research topic. She said that she wanted to study English books of the eighteenth century, and he started questioning her patriotism.

> Science was made undercover. He said "don't you know that we are responsible for the North-West of the country and are allowed to research only national books. Do you say you want to move to England?" (наукой в советское время занимались подпольным образом. На что он мне сказал 'Мы отвечаем за Северо-Запад страны и можем заниматься только отечественной книгой. Вы что, в Англию собираетесь уехать?')

Being the most experienced participant in our study, she explained that the fact that Soviet academics were isolated from international scholarship and rarely able to travel abroad resulted in, what she called, "paper art history." She says academic texts were published without any illustrations of the objects of art:

> Paper art history—people wrote monographs about Rembrandt but never saw a single painting in real life. All my teachers— we had no other way—studied art history by reproductions. (Бумажное советское искусствознание—люди писали мо-

нографии о Рембрандте ни разу произведение вживую не видев. Все мои учителя, у нас не было другого выхода, искусствоведением занимались по репродукциям.)

This political and socio-historical context has resulted in certain rhetorical traditions. Ekaterina believed that the majority of Russian art history texts have been full of lengthy descriptions and lack analysis. She said she saw it as a consequence of the rhetorical essayistic tradition of art history in the nineteenth to early twentieth century which continued to exist in the Soviet times. Ekaterina commented that:

> The tradition of Soviet times was marred by descriptions from the nineteenth century, unsupported by any historical contexts. Not because they were bad researchers but because they were not allowed to. Sociocultural context reigns in the twentieth century in the West, but we were not allowed to study Western art. We were seen as dissidents because we read foreign literature. (традиция советского времени грешит описательностью 19 века, не подкреплённой какими-то историческими контекстами. Не потому что были плохие исследователи, а потому что этого нельзя было сделать. Социокультурный контекст на Западе весь 20 век, а у нас нельзя было заниматься западным искусством. На нас смотрели как на диссидентствующих людей, потому что мы читали западную литературу.)

Such ideological pressure on the art history knowledge domain and writing practices of scholars has brought about certain challenges in knowledge-making and writing when they are in the position of making decisions about their rhetorical choices (Barnet, 1993). For example, Anna referred to a powerful genre which, as she said, has almost totally disappeared in Russia—"Sbornik statey"[3]:

> In collections of papers published by the Russian Academy of Arts I felt very free, I did not want extra scientificness, there are many such papers there, and nobody will be trying to verify my experience. It's a somewhat provocative strategy. (в сборниках академии художеств я себя чувствовала достаточно свободно, поэтому мне не хотелось лишней научности и

---

3   Sbornik statey is a collection of papers which are published as conference proceedings or under any topic developed by a university or other art institution.

наукообразности, потому что там и без меня такого полно, и никто не будет тогда пытаться верифицировать мой опыт. немного провокаторская стратегия.)

Small Community

Certain rhetorical orientations emerged as participants' accounts signaled that the community of art historians has generally been small both locally and globally. Moreover, each historian has worked in a very narrow field of research which has been further narrowed by the object of art. The intellectual response to art has been constrained by the fact that each subfield has its own methods and approaches, technical vocabulary, and needs (Grabar, 1982). For example, Olga says that: "Today, there are few researchers, and each works in their own field. (сегодня не так много исследователей, и все занимаются разными материалами.)" All participants say that the small professional community results in the related problem of limited readership for their texts. Olga says that in Russia and in the world: "My texts are read by very few people. (что я пишу, читает очень мало людей.)" According to scholars' accounts, this small community is becoming even smaller, as there have been closed communities built around major art history institutions which have required different epistemological, rhetorical, and educational standards that define the rhetoric of historians. Ekaterina said that:

> These are closed communities. Sometimes the editor could happily say to me "you did not study with us, that is why you put a comma here, while a semicolon is needed." Writing samples and education in the university and academy of arts that teaches art historians are different. (это закрытые сообщества. иногда, редактор радостно мог сказать «вы у нас не учились, поэтому вы поставили здесь запятую, а нужно было точку с запятой». образцы письма и образование Университета и Академии художеств, которые готовят искусствоведов, отличаются.)

Grabar (1982) explains that subfields in art history can be cultural, social, technical, methodological, and conceptual. When a professional community is small yet highly diverse, there arises a question of who art historians write for and who reads their papers if their research foci are so different and they work in very narrow fields of research. Given the publishing pressure on academics when research articles are expected to meet the journal standards (Hazelkorn, 2015), what should these standards be?

The scholars' accounts signal the impact of their epistemological orientations as well as of the socio-political and historical contexts on their meaning making and rhetorical choices. Their accounts signal the variety of indigenous local and global knowledge-making traditions and their associated rhetoric. Yet, at the same time, this desire to write differently (which is enacted in different ways) has resulted in the existing disciplinary tensions with other writers within the small professional community of art historians, each working within a particular educational, institutional, epistemological, and theoretical context.

Conclusions and Implications for Writing Theory and Practice

In our study we addressed two major empirical questions. The first one was how contemporary art historians in Russia learn to write. At the beginning, all scholars said they were not taught to write academic texts. Consequently, the accounts of the scholars revealed that learning to write was not straightforward, but, in the course of reflection, they identified particular learning trajectories. Some experiences were related to traditions of working with a written text in literature and history when both the writer's ideas and the textual form were valued.

The accounts of scholars referring to the importance of reading exemplary texts and receiving feedback from more experienced peers indicate that the implicit mentoring model has been dominant in the field both when they write in Russian and English. At the same time, participants' comments about how they learned to write and how they have taught their students signal that they were reinventing their writing pedagogies (see Bartholomae, 1985, and Lillis & Scott, 2007 for the idea of "reinventing" the university and associated literacy practices). The lack of explicit writing instruction and attention to text production issues in art history education in Russia has forced scholars to intuitively identify and read the already existing variety of rhetorical codes in the discipline.

Scholars' accounts signaled that writing ability rarely develops naturally, and they have seen explicit writing instruction as important. At the same time, writers look for opportunities to express their voices as well as identities, as texts are born in the process of meaning making. This finding echoes Halsall's (2012) argument that aesthetic judgement plays a key role in the production of an art history text because the writer's judgements of taste lie at the very heart of art history practice.

The second empirical question targeted challenges in writing, and the scholars' accounts signal that there have been significant challenges in meaning making and writing a scholarly text. The major tensions in the process of meaning making and writing were closely linked to: 1) access to resources in the process of researching and producing a text and 2) traditions of knowledge-making globally and in the particular geopolitical and socio-historic context of Russia.

The scholars' accounts indicated that access to international books and periodicals, knowing foreign languages, the ability to see (experience) objects of art, editing experiences, and time available for writing significantly impact their meaning making and writing practices. Limited access to resources has been highly consequential for knowledge-making in the field. While writing pedagogies rarely have centered around the issue of getting access to resources, we believe that these are important issues to consider.

The scholars signaled particular challenges in writing arising from traditions of knowledge-making globally as well as the particular geopolitical and socio-historic context. Writing has been an essential part of the process of meaning making and knowledge production. Writing has been essential to knowledge construction and to the creation of academic and professional communities. Writing practices and rhetorical choices have been significantly defined by the existing tensions between global and local epistemological camps (e.g., literature, literary criticism, history, art history) when writers belong to different camps. Scholars talked about tensions between the current demand for empiricist research writing and the longstanding essayistic tradition based on the dialogic nature of texts (Lillis, 2011). This finding resonates with Borgdorff's (2007) argument that contemporary art historians portray themselves in their texts and either follow or resist any form of academization out of the fear of losing the distinctiveness of their intellectual work.

Importantly, knowledge-making and writing traditions in art history have been rooted in its socio-historical and political contexts. The scholars' accounts indicate that the Soviet period and its heritage have had an impact on contemporary art history. Scholars commented that description-driven texts often have prevailed over argument-based papers in part due to the Soviet art history writing tradition and due to the absence of training in research methodology and academic writing in modern universities.

No less important were the comments that rhetorical orientations have emerged in response to the small size of the professional community of art historians in Russia and worldwide. The scholars' comments revealed that there have been few local and international researchers, and they all research different materials (objects of art). These challenges indicate that writing as well as teaching writing in art history should be centered around making scholars aware of each other, facilitating their participation in meaningful conversations, and exposing writers to a variety of rhetorical choices and their consequential nature.

Exploring meaning making and writing practices through the lens of the academic literacies framework, where writers' voices are placed center-stage, enabled us to make the writing and knowledge-making practice of art historians more visible. In times of increasing exclusion of arts and humanities from global knowledge production (e.g., Hazelkorn, 2015; Savelieva & Poletaev, 2009), in our chapter we made an attempt to signal the need to make these practices more visible. Our findings indicate that researching the writing for publication practices of art historians is challenging because this knowledge domain has been marked by the production of single-author texts with distinctive authorial voices, less rigid rhetorical structures, and varying interpretative epistemologies within a national and cultural context and across the globe. We believe our methodological approach and key findings can be used to set an agenda for and guide the inquiry into the academic writing practices of other humanities disciplines and across various indigenous national and cultural contexts of art history knowledge production and writing. Such an approach allows overcoming the hegemony of Anglo-centric writing pedagogy (Altbach & de Wit, 2015; Canagarajah, 2005) and making local writing traditions visible to the global research community.

Acknowledgments

We express our deep gratitude to all the scholars who participated in our study of academic writing for their time, valuable insights, and generous accounts of their writing experiences. We are also grateful to Ashley Squires for the opportunity to publish in this edited collection and for her continuous support throughout the preparation process. We thank Magnus Gustafsson and two anonymous reviewers for valuable feedback which helped improve our chapter.

References

Adams, S. (2014). Practice as research: A fine art contextual study. *Arts and Humanities in Higher Education, 13*(3), 218226. https://doi.org/10.1177/1474022213514549.

Altbach, P. G., & de Wit, H. (2015). Internationalization and global tension: Lessons from history. *Journal of Studies in International Education, 19*(1), 410. https://doi.org/10.1177/1028315314564734.

Barnet, S. (1993). *Writing about arts: A short guide to writing about art*. Harper.
Barolsky, P. (1996). Writing (and) the history of art. *Art Bulletin, LXXVIII*(3), 398400.
Barrett, E., & Bolt, B. (2010). *Practice as research:* Approaches to creative arts enquiry. IB Tauris.
Bartholomae, D. (1985). Inventing the university. In M. Rose (Ed.), *When a writer can't write: Studies in writer's block and other composing-process problems* (pp. 134-166). The Guilford Press.
Barton, D., & Hamilton, M. (1998). *Local literacies: Reading and writing in one community*. Routledge.
Barton, D., Hamilton, M., & Ivanic, R. (2000). *Situated literacies: Reading and writing in context*. Routledge.
Becher, T. (1989). *Academic tribes and territories: Intellectual inquiry and the cultures of disciplines*. The Open University Press.
Blommaert, J. (2005). *Discourse: A critical introduction*. Cambridge University Press.
Borgdorff, H. (2007). The debate on research in the arts. *Dutch Journal of Music Theory, 12*(1), 1–17.
Cain, K. S. (2011). From comfort zone to contact zone Lessons from a Belfast writing centre. *Arts and Humanities in Higher Education, 10*(1), 67–83. https://doi.org/10.1177/1474022210385276.
Canagarajah, A. S. (2005). *Reclaiming the local in language policy and practice*. Routledge.
Cargill, M., Burgess, S., & Arnbjörnsdóttir, B. (2019). Editorial: Publishing research internationally: Multilingual perspectives from research and practice. *Publications, 7*(3), 47. https://cpb-eu-w2.wpmucdn.com/blogs.brighton.ac.uk/dist/c/2106/files/2016/05/H-Borgdorff-The-Debate-on-Research-in-the-Arts-14d694g.pdf.
Chitez, M., Doroholschi, C. I., Kruse, O., Salski, L., & Tucan, D. (2018). *University writing in central and eastern Europe: Tradition, transition, and innovation*. Springer; Cham.
Crème, P., & Mckenna, C. (2010). Developing writer identity through a multidisciplinary programme. *Arts and Humanities in Higher Education, 9*(2), 149167. https://doi.org/10.1177/1474022210361456.
Curry, M. J., & Lillis, T. (2015). The dominance of English in global scholarly publishing. *International Higher Education, 46*, 6–7. https://doi.org/10.6017/ihe.2007.46.7948.
Elkins, J. (Ed.). (2007). *Is art history global?* Routledge.
Elkins, J. (2011). Why art history is global. In J. Harris (Ed.), *Globalization and contemporary art* (pp. 375–386). Willey-Blackwell.
Elton, E., & Nicolle, C. (2009). Now you see it, now you don't. *Esri, 9*(August), 32–54. https://doi.org/10.1109/GLOCOM.2002.1189015.
Grabar, O. (1982). On the universality of the history of art. *Art Journal, 42*(4), 281–283. https://doi.org/10.2307/776687.
Gustafsson, M., & Ganobcsik-Williams, L. (2016). Writing centres and the turn toward multilingual and multilitercy writing tutoring. In Hyland, K. (Ed.), Shaw, P. (Ed.), (2016). *The Routledge handbook of English for academic purposes*. Routledge, https://doi.org/10.4324/9781315657455.

Halsall, F. (2012). Making and matching: Aesthetic judgement and art historical knowledge. *Journal of Art Historiography*, 7. https://arthistoriography.files.wordpress.com/2012/12/halsall-aesthetics.pdf.

Hazelkorn, E. (2015). Making an impact: New directions for arts and humanities research. *Arts and Humanities in Higher Education*, *14*(1), 25–44. https://doi.org/10.1177/1474022214533891.

Hellqvist, B. (2010). Referencing in the humanities and its implications. Journal of the American Society for Information Science, 61(2), 310–318. https://doi.org/10.1002/asi.21256.

Hyland, K. (2009). Introduction. In *Academic Discourse: English in a Global Context* (pp. viii–x). Bloomsbury Academic. https://doi.org/10.5040/9781474211673.0004.

Hyland, K. (2016). Methods and methodologies in second language writing research. *System*, *59*(July), 116–125. https://doi.org/10.1016/j.system.2016.05.002.

Ivanic, R. (1998). *Writing and identity: The discoursal construction of identity in academic writing*. John Benjamins.

Kent, E. F. (2012). What are you going to do with a degree in that?: Arguing for the humanities in an era of efficiency. *Arts and Humanities in Higher Education*, *11*(3), 273–284. https://doi.org/10.1177/1474022212441769.

Kuteeva, M., & Mauranen, A. (2014). Writing for publication in multilingual contexts: An introduction to the special issue. *Journal of English for Academic Purposes*, *13*(1), 1–4. https://doi.org/10.1016/j.jeap.2013.11.002.

Lea, M. R., & Street, B. V. (1998). Student writing in higher education: An academic literacies approach. *Studies in Higher Education*, *23*(2), 157–172. https://doi.org/10.1080/03075079812331380364.

Flowerdew, J., & Li, Y. (2009). English or Chinese? The trade-off between local and international publication among Chinese academics in the humanities and social sciences. *Journal of Second Language Writing*, *18*(1), 1–16. https://doi.org/10.1016/j.jslw.2008.09.005.

Lillis, T. (2001). *Student writing: Access, regulation, desire*. Routledge.

Lillis, T. (2003). Student writing as "academic literacies": Drawing on Bakhtin to move from critique to design. *Language and Education*, *17*, 192–207. https://doi.org/10.1080/09500780308666848.

Lillis, T. (2008). Ethnography as method, methodology, and "deep theorizing": Closing the gap between text and context in academic writing research. *Written Communication*, *25*(3), 353–388. https://doi.org/10.1177/0741088308319229.

Lillis, T. (2011). Legitimizing dialogue as textual and ideological goal in academic writing for assessment and publication. *Arts and Humanities in Higher Education*, *10*(4), 401–432. https://doi.org/10.1177/1474022211398106.

Lillis, T., & Curry, M. J. (2006). Professional academic writing by multilingual scholars: Interactions with literacy brokers in the production of English-medium texts. *Written Communication*, *23*(1), 3–35. https://doi.org/10.1177/0741088305283754.

Lillis, T., & Curry, M. (2010). *Academic writing in a global context: The politics and practices of publishing in English*. Routledge.

Lillis, T., & Curry, M. (2018). Trajectories of knowledge and desire: Multilingual women scholars researching and writing in academia. *Journal of English for Academic Purposes, 32*, 53–66. https://doi.org/10.1016/j.jeap.2018.03.008.

Lillis, T., & McKinney, C. (2013). The sociolinguistics of writing in a global context: Objects, lenses, consequences. *Journal of Sociolinguistics, 17*(4), 415–439. https://doi.org/10.1111/josl.12046.

Lillis, T., & Scott, M. (2007). Defining academic literacies research: Issues of epistemology, ideology and strategy. *Journal of Applied Linguistics, 4*(1), 5–32. http://oro.open.ac.uk/17057/1/JAL_Lillis_and_Scott_pdf.pdf.

MacLeod, K., & Holdridge, L. (2005). *Thinking through art*. Routledge.

Paltridge, B. (2017). Context and the teaching of academic writing: Bringing together theory and practice. In J. Bitchener, N. Storch, & R. Wette (Eds.), *Teaching writing for academic purposes to multilingual students: Instructional approaches* (pp. 9–23). Routledge.

Pérez-Llantada, C., Plo, R., & Ferguson, G. R. (2011). "You don't say what you know, only what you can": The perceptions and practices of senior Spanish academics regarding research dissemination in English. *English for Specific Purposes, 30*(1), 18-30. https://doi.org/10.1016/j.esp.2010.05.001.

Roth, N. (2010). Writing as pretext: On the way to an image. *Arts and Humanities in Higher Education, 9*(2), 256264. https://doi.org/10.1177/1474022210361455.

Schluer, J. (2014). Writing for publication in linguistics: Exploring niches of multilingual publishing among German linguists. *Journal of English for Academic Purposes, 16*, 1-13. https://doi.org/10.1016/j.jeap.2014.06.001.

Street, B. V. (2003) Foreword. In R. K. Blot & J. Collins (Eds.), *Literacy and literacies: Text, power, and identity* (pp. xi–xvi). Cambridge University Press. https://doi.org/10.1017/CBO9780511486661.001.

Sychenkova, L. A. (2014) Pervye ėksperimenty v sfere iskusstvovedcheskogo obrazovaniiā: nezapolnennyĭ probel v istorii nauki ob iskusstve [The first experiments in art historical education: Unfilled gap in history of art science]. *Uchenye zapiski Kazanskogo universiteta. Seriya Gumanitarnye Nauki [Proceedings of Kazan University. Humanities Seiries], 156*(3), 223–239. https://www.elibrary.ru/item.asp?id=22633643.

Uzuner, S. (2008). Multilingual scholars' participation in core/global academic communities: A literature review. *Journal of English for Academic Purposes, 7*(4), 250-263. https://doi.org/10.1016/j.jeap.2008.10.007.

Van Damme, W., & Zijlmans, K. (2008). *World art studies: exploring concepts and approaches*. Valiz.

4 They Teach Writing but They Do Not Write: Why Russian University Foreign Language Instructors Rarely Publish

Svetlana Bogolepova
HSE University, Moscow

Since Russia entered the Bologna process in 2003, the pressure to publish in Russian universities has been steadily increasing. Language instructors supposedly have had the advantage of being proficient in English, so they may be hypothesized as productive in terms of academic publications. Despite the requirements imposed by Russian universities and the support they provide, it has not been the case. To reveal the factors that have prevented this large group from being represented in academic journals and the factors that may encourage them to write for publication, a survey was administered to language teachers representing 37 universities based in different parts of Russia. One hundred and forty instructors completed the survey. The results of the survey allowed the researcher to compare the language instructors who have had a considerable publication track record and those who have not in terms of attitudes, skills, and practices. The survey results were supplemented by the findings of semi-structured in-depth interviews with 10 successful writers. Results showed that time constraints, research incompetence, unfamiliarity with Anglo-American academic conventions, the absence of a supportive environment, and low motivation pose major difficulties. Implications for institutional policies and individual strategies were extrapolated from the analysis of the results. The findings may be relevant to contexts where English is taught at the university level and where publication activity is an institutional requirement for university language instructors.

Faculty at universities around the world live in the "publish or perish" paradigm. Considerable research has focused on how faculty deal with this challenge in different contexts (Bardi, 2015; Duszak & Lewkowicz, 2008; Gea-Valor et al., 2014; Gnutzmann & Rabe, 2014). Some studies have looked

DOI: https://doi.org/10.37514/INT-B.2021.1428.2.04

at the hurdles academics in different fields have had to overcome to be more academically productive (Martin et al., 2014). Research has demonstrated that Russia has lagged behind many other developed and developing countries in terms of the number of publications in internationally recognized journals (Macháček & Srhole, 2019). However, there has been little research into how university instructors in Russia enter the international academic dialogue and what difficulties they have experienced while doing so.

Russian universities have done their utmost to increase their research productivity. In the majority of universities, a publication track record has been a must for every member of the faculty. Recruitment procedures have posed strict requirements for the venue and the quality of publications as universities have aspired to get to the top of international rankings. They have provided bonuses to those who publish and have offered the services of academic writing centers. Unlike other faculty, university language instructors have hardly responded to these initiatives. Those who have actually taught writing in English to their students have not produced academic papers themselves.

Historically, in Russian universities language teachers were perceived as practitioners who were supposed to publish only if they choose the academic track for growth. Now the requirement to have a publication track record has been extended to all teaching staff. So far little has been done to investigate the research and publication practices of linguists and language teachers (e.g., Dikilitas & Mumford, 2016; Sato & Loewen, 2018; Schluter, 2014). This shortage may stem from the contextual specificity of the problem, as only in some countries has English been an obligatory subject taught to everyone at the university level irrespective of their major. As the needs of this considerable group cannot be ignored, it is necessary to answer the following research questions:

- What are the factors that inhibit university language instructors' publication activity in Russia?
- What can be done to encourage university language instructors to publish in higher-tier journals?
- What strategies do more prolific authors use, and in what way are they different from their less successful peers?

In search of the answers to these questions, I administered a survey to English language instructors in 37 universities around Russia. Its analysis revealed inhibiting and possible motivational factors for university language instructors' publication activity. Apart from that, the survey results allowed me to study prolific writers' attitudes, strategies, and routines. They were supported by interviews in which university language instructors who had a track record of international publications participated. Based on the findings, institutional support policies and individual strategies are suggested in the paper. The findings may be relevant to contexts where English is taught at the university level and where language instructors constitute a significant portion of academic staff.

Literature Review

Barriers to Writing

A number of factors have been thought to inhibit research productivity (Boice & Jones, 1984; Lee, 2014; Liebowitz, 2015; McGrail et al., 2006). These reasons have either an extrinsic or intrinsic nature.

One of the possible external reasons has been the lack of institutional policies conducive to publication activity. If the institution does not have a research policy that has required all lecturers to engage in scientific inquiry, or it cannot provide infrastructural facilities and resources to support lecturers involved in research, or it does not financially support the incentives to write for publication, academics will not conduct and publish research. What also has decreased research productivity has been the lack of available time, as considerable teaching or administrative loads conflict with writing (Hemmings & Kay, 2010). If instructors have to bear a heavy teaching workload, they may be physically unable to focus on other activities.

Low research productivity and publication rates have been accounted for by the lack of exposure to research on the institutional level. University instructors in some contexts have not realized how research could enhance teaching and have little or no access to current research (Sato & Loewen, 2018). Without access to academic journals and deprived of a supportive academic environment, instructors have not been able to participate in academic dialogue and remain aware of what is current or what ideas are worthy of publication. Lack of mentoring and group support has been an example of the absence of a conducive environment as well. In non-English speaking universities, researchers have rarely been trained to write for publication in English (Rezaei & Seyri, 2019).

External factors influence research productivity. For instance, at-desk rejections have not always had to do with the quality of the paper, as they may have been caused by the disparity of standards between academics and reviewers (Min, 2014). Researchers still have not developed uniform criteria on what a research article should look like (van Enk & Power, 2017). The decision to reject an article could also have political reasons (Rezaei & Seyri, 2019).

The intrinsic factors have depended on the individual. The absence of relevant knowledge and skills has served as an example of such a factor. Not only the knowledge component but a person's attitude could predict whether they will participate in an activity. University instructors have not been necessarily interested in research and publication activities and work in the tertiary sector for other reasons. Not everyone has been confident in their skills and the outcome of the endeavor. Some have been put off by the fear of rejection or the daunting prospects of lengthy reviewing and redrafting periods, high rejection rates, and limited readership. Some have opted for publishing in the local language to make their work known locally and have attracted a readership (Duszak & Lewkowicz, 2008). Lack of intrinsic motivation may lead to task avoidance even when extrinsic factors are present.

Any skill is acquired through constant practice, and writing is no exception. Once an academic stops writing, it is difficult to get back on track. Some individuals have faced a writing block conditioned by a negative experience, fear of criticism or perfectionism (Crosby, 2003). Furthermore, writing has required focus, so distractions and lack of discipline may get in the way. Not only does it take time to develop writing routines, but it has also been increasingly difficult to catch up with those who write successfully (Boice & Jones, 1984). The Matthew effect, by which more famous scholars get more opportunities to publish, has had its place in academia (Merton, 1968).

More issues have emerged in non-anglophone contexts. In academic environments where English is a non-native language, insufficient linguistic competence and unawareness of Anglo-American academic conventions have been identified as the dominant issues (Frumina & West, 2012; Gea-Valor et al., 2014; Min, 2014; Olsson & Sheridan, 2012). Even researchers from European countries have experienced difficulties on the levels of lexis, grammar, and rhetoric (Perez-Llantada et al., 2011). Academics have been "linguistically constrained in writing their papers in English," and this has been felt as "burdensome" (Perez-Llantada et al., 2011, p. 206); therefore, scholars "heavily rely on external help to cope with linguistic issues" (Fernandez & Varela, 2009, p. 159). In humanities and social sciences, linguistic demands may be higher than in hard sciences (Gnutzmann & Rabe, 2014). There has been a fear that the incorrect use of English could impede reviewers' understanding of the main message (Min, 2014), which actually has happened at times and has led to rejections.

In some cases, language has not been the major concern (Belcher, 2007; see also Chapter 1). Culturally determined thinking patterns have influenced the way authors have structured their writing (Kaplan, 1966; Leki, 1992), so non-native speakers have had to come to grips with alien academic and writing conventions. The style of composition and even the strength of claims is culturally specific (Flowerdew, 1999). It has been a challenge to find topics relevant to the global community, as local issues may not appeal to the wider readership (Min, 2014). Authors from non-anglophone contexts have been overly focused on their local contexts, and therefore their research findings have not appealed to the international academic community (Flowerdew, 2001).

The failure to appropriate Western academic conventions has inhibited the publication productivity of non-native English speakers even if their general language proficiency has been high. As Hyland (2006) has reasonably put it, it is necessary to communicate in the manner accepted by the community to become part of that community. Writing mechanics may have been an issue, such as lack of skill in citing references (Liebowitz, 2015). On the level of syntax, authors have had to handle two competing goals in EFL academic writing: explicitness and conciseness (Wu et al., 2020). The effort invested in the writing of various elements of an article may differ. For example, Spanish scholars have reported that the discussion section has been the most challenging part to write (Martin et al., 2014). Actually, both L1 and L2 writers have had a tendency to mix discussion with results (Shen et al., 2019). Literature reviews and the identification of research niches could pose a problem for writers whose cultural conventions have not presupposed critical discussion and evaluation of arguments in writing (Uzuner, 2008). Journal editors have found introductions and literature reviews composed by non-native speakers to be "not structured appropriately" (Flowerdew, 2001, p. 136).

Publication of research is only a part of research activity, which also involves networking, collaboration, research management and completion, and evaluation of research (Kyvik, 2013). As the primary reason for rejections has been the flaws in research (Martin et al., 2014), the lack of research and data analysis skills may inhibit instructors' publication activity. Not trained in how to plan, conduct, and analyze research, language teachers have seen no value in it and no connection to their classroom practices (Bai, 2018).

Support and Strategies

Support and motivation have been inextricably linked with the barriers university instructors have come across when writing for publication. Thus, the factors that could help university instructors be more academically productive have been primarily targeted at the elimination of these barriers. They are:

- Availability of time and other resources;
- Exposure to research in the field;
- Development of relevant skills;
- Understanding of how empirical research should be conducted;

- Increased awareness of what is topical and can be researched;
- Understanding of Anglo-American academic writing conventions;
- Increased English language proficiency.

Institutional policies understandably have relied on reward and punishment initiatives. The former has included bonuses awarded for publications or the opportunity of promotion, the latter could manifest in contract termination. Threats of contract termination or promises of financial rewards have had some effect on research productivity; however, such factors as previous experience and mentoring have been more effective (Reyes-Cruz & Perales-Escudero, 2016).

Keen (2007) has suggested that support should be provided at the stages of preparation, actual writing, and submission. At the preparation stage, authors could be provided with information or access to scientific journals. At the writing stage, support could take the form of courses, coaching, or collaborative writing groups. At the submission stage, formatting and proofreading services could be provided.

McGrail and colleagues (2006) have considered different types of interventions aimed at increasing academic publication rates. The researchers looked at writing courses, writing support groups, and writing coaches. Writing courses seemed to attract novice writers, while writing groups appealed to more experienced ones. However, it was difficult to gauge the efficiency of those interventions as individuals already committed to writing for publication participated in the activities. Intrinsic drives, such as the desire to understand a topic in depth, the ambition to reach one's potential or to increase one's confidence, should supplement external training (Liebowitz, 2015).

Some studies have looked at the strategies researchers have implemented while participating in the publishing process. When identifying a research niche, Taiwanese social science scholars have considered the topics relevant to the local public, which also have been of interest to a wider community (Li & Flowerdew, 2009). For Iranian doctoral students, reading similar articles extensively seemed to be the most efficient strategy at the preparation stage; they also usually asked their supervisors and more proficient friends to edit their articles before submission (Rezaei & Seyri, 2019). Spanish medical scholars familiarized themselves with the journals in the field and their writing conventions when preparing for writing (Martin et al., 2014). They preferred the help of expert editors familiar with the field before submitting the publication. Ho (2017) found out that Taiwanese doctoral students resorted to each other's help as well as the aid of experienced mentors. It has been possible to resort to the English translation of the manuscript (Luo & Hyland,

2019) though direct translation may be inappropriate due to the difference in writing conventions and rhetorical patterns.

At least partly, motivation to write academic papers should come from within. One of the things that constitutes a professor's job satisfaction is having an impact on the scientific community (Larsson & Alvinius, 2019). As Lee (2014) rightfully puts it, "we don't just publish to keep our jobs, but to become contributing members of the academic/research community, to advance knowledge in the field, to gain personal satisfaction, and to make a difference" (p. 260). One can hypothesize that prolific writers are motivated to carry out research and write for publication. They have regular engagement with research input in the English language; therefore, these academics are aware of the features of academic written discourse.

Though writing in English should not be an issue for university language instructors, other challenges are likely to be present. Revealing the most significant factors that inhibit this cohort's publication activity in the context of Russian tertiary education may help to find a way to decrease those barriers. Finding out the motivational aspects that could encourage language teachers to publish more could help decision-makers to develop the relevant policies. If detected, the strategies more prolific researchers use to be more productive publication-wise could shed light on the best practices.

Method

Russian universities have provided foreign language (predominantly English) classes to all students irrespective of their major. This has been the reason why university language instructors have constituted a significant part of academic staff. Trying to enter international rankings and increase their visibility in the international scientific community, universities have required that their staff publish regularly and in internationally recognized journals. It has been shown that poor proficiency in the English language has prevented Russian scholars from successful participation in the international academic dialogue (Frumina & West, 2012). Language instructors supposedly have had the advantage of being proficient in English; therefore, one might suppose them to be productive in terms of academic publications. In reality, it has not been so. A tertiary language instructor with a publication track record has been more of a rarity than a rule. So, quite a few language instructors have had to settle for short-term contracts with hourly pay without being able to enjoy the perks of full employment.

There may be several reasons for such a situation. Traditionally, language instructors have been considered craftsmen who are trained to do their job—teaching—well without being required to delve into scientific endeavors. They may not have undergone rigorous scientific training. If they have, this may have happened in a different paradigm. Research methods in humanities and social sciences, as well as the written academic discourse that prevailed in Soviet times, have been quite different from what international norms have required (see Chapter 1 and Chapter 3). Anyway, language instructors in Russian universities and in many other contexts (as is described in Bai, 2018; Dikilitas & Mumford, 2016; Sato & Loewen, 2018) have constituted a large group who have needed support and development. Therefore, it is necessary to study what barriers they have faced when writing for publication and the motivations and strategies that could urge them to do it more successfully.

Research Design and Participants

Stage 1

The literature review formed the basis of the questionnaire administered to university language instructors. Surveys and questionnaires are instruments widely used to reach out to a large number of respondents, and academics are no exception here (see, for example, Martin et al., 2014).

The questionnaire included: One open question in which the participants were asked to identify the university they work for, six multiple choice items, and six Likert scale-based items.

The multiple-choice questions pursued a number of goals. The first one asked about the respondent's publication history: "Have you published articles in international peer-reviewed journals?"(the questions are a direct translation from the survey in Russian). The possible options included *Yes, one article*, *Yes, several articles*, *No, but I want to*, and *No, and I have no desire to*. The second question asked the respondents if publication activity was a demand imposed by their universities. Three more multiple choice questions dealt with the challenges language instructors faced when they conducted research and wrote for publication, and the possible motivational factors. The choice of options was based on the issues and strategies discussed in the literature review. The respondents had the opportunity to type in their own answers to the multiple-choice questions. The final question required the participants to select the stage of the publication process which they considered the most challenging one.

The Likert scale-based items looked specifically at the factors that may have been characteristic of the population in focus. They touched upon language instructors' attitudes ("I prefer teaching to researching and writing for publication, I want to share my knowledge with the international community"), their practices ("I regularly read articles in English"), and necessary knowledge and skills ("I am aware of the particular features of Anglo-American academic discourse;" "I am aware of the demands of each element of an academic article in terms of content and language;" "Language teachers are not taught how to conduct research and write for publication"). The continuum ranged from 1 (*totally disagree*) to 5 (*completely agree*).

The questionnaire was piloted among three university language instructors who were asked to give feedback on the wording and clarity of questions. Feedback was also sought from the head of the HSE Academic Writing Centre (see Chapter 6). As a result, two items were discarded, and three questions of a different type were added.

The link to the online questionnaire was sent to university language instructors by e-mail. One hundred and forty teachers responded to the questionnaire. They were representatives of 37 universities based both in Moscow and beyond (Krasnoyarsk, Novosibirsk, Ryazan, Rostov, Irkutsk, Tambov, Ulyanovsk, Vologda, Tuva, Tomsk, etc.). More information on the represented institutions can be found in Table 4.1.

Table 4.1. Represented Universities

University	Number of respondents
HSE University (Moscow)	46
Moscow State Linguistic University	18
Samara State Technical University	13
National University of Science and Technology (Moscow)	12
Buryat State University	9
Siberian Federal University	5
Cherepovets State University	5
Other universities	33
Total	140

The quantitative results were statistically analyzed using descriptive statistical characteristics such as mean and median values, and standard deviations. Pearson correlations were also calculated. The results of this stage informed the design of the second stage of the study.

Stage 2

Semi-structured interviews are a commonly used tool to understand individual and group beliefs, attitudes, and practices (Wu, 1967). Such interviews were conducted with those language instructors who had a track record of publications both in Russian and in English ($n = 10$). These instructors have published at least three articles in highly ranked international journals within the last five years. The informants were one male and nine females, aged 27–42, including senior lecturers and associate professors. Each interview lasted for about 15 minutes and touched upon the issues and motivations revealed at Stage 1. Each participant answered questions that revealed:

- How they balance their workload and research writing;
- What kind of routine they have for writing;
- How they select the publication venue;
- How they decide on the topic of research and set research questions;
- What they do about data analysis;
- What kind of motivation boosts their academic productivity;
- What kind of instruction they had that allowed them to publish internationally;
- How they deal with rejections and overcome the block that may be provoked;
- If they prefer individual or collaborative writing.

Next, the recorded interviews were transcribed, analyzed, and thematically coded. The data was received in Russian, and the results were translated into English.

Results

Stage 1

Figure 4.1 illustrates the experience the respondents have had with academic publications. As can be seen, less than half of the participants ($n = 56$) had a publication history (one or more articles published in international peer-reviewed journals). A more considerable but comparable number ($n = 84$) had not published in international journals yet, though a significant majority of those were determined to publish ($n = 73$). Apart from the analysis of the results for the whole cohort, it makes sense to focus on the comparison of these two groups. I will refer to those who had already published as Group 1, and those who had not as Group 2.

When asked whether publication activity was a requirement at their universities, the overwhelming majority (83.2%) confirmed the requirement, and only 6.8% of the respondents answered that it was not.

■ yes, one   ■ yes, several   ■ no, but I want to   ■ no, and I am not going to

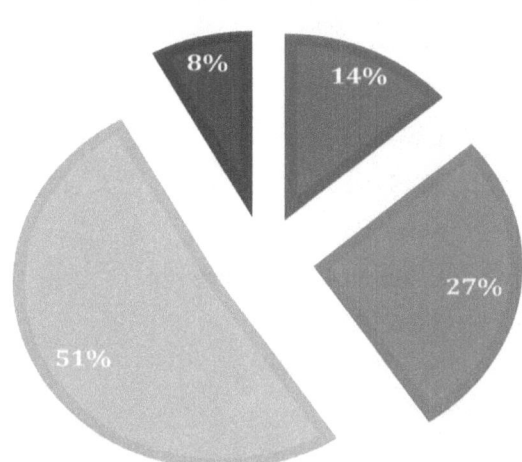

Figure 4.1. Respondents' publication histories and intentions.

The following questionnaire items were informed by the factors singled out when research on the topic was analyzed. The multiple-choice items aimed to reveal the main obstacles that prevented language instructors from research and publication, as well as the factors that could have given them the opportunity to publish more.

As can be seen from Figure 4.2, the major issue for the representatives of both groups was allocating enough time for thorough research (75.4%). A participant wrote that "a heavy teaching load and academic productivity are not compatible." This factor significantly outweighed the other aspects, including the choice of research topic, which came in second place (32.6%) closely followed by self-motivation (31.9%) and setting the research question (29%). Approximately a quarter of the respondents reported having difficulty analyzing qualitative data statistically. Group 1 and Group 2 respondents did not significantly differ in what they considered the main obstacles to their research activity.

When it came to writing for publication, the major difficulty seemed to be the choice of journal (see Figure 4.3). This task was equally challenging for the inexperienced (63.4%) and the experienced writers (60.7%). It presented a challenge for almost two-thirds of the cohort (63.2%). Almost half found it difficult to write the text in compliance with Anglo-American discourse conventions. Both experienced and inexperienced writers reported having difficulty with text editing (37.5%), accessing scientific sources (29.4%), and working with editors (27.2%). Text editing was slightly more challenging for inexperienced writers. Overall, the two groups had coinciding opinions about the major issues they have when writing for publication.

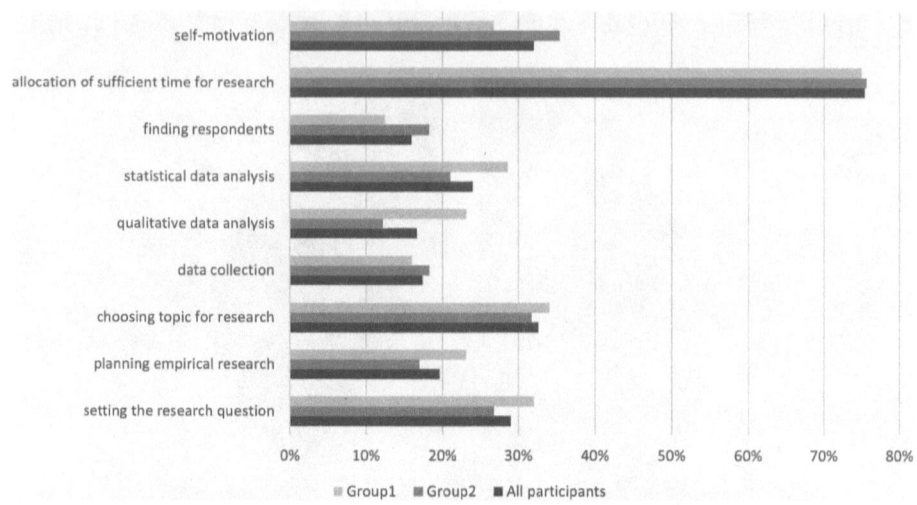

Figure 4.2. Major obstacles in research (all respondents, Group 1, Group 2).

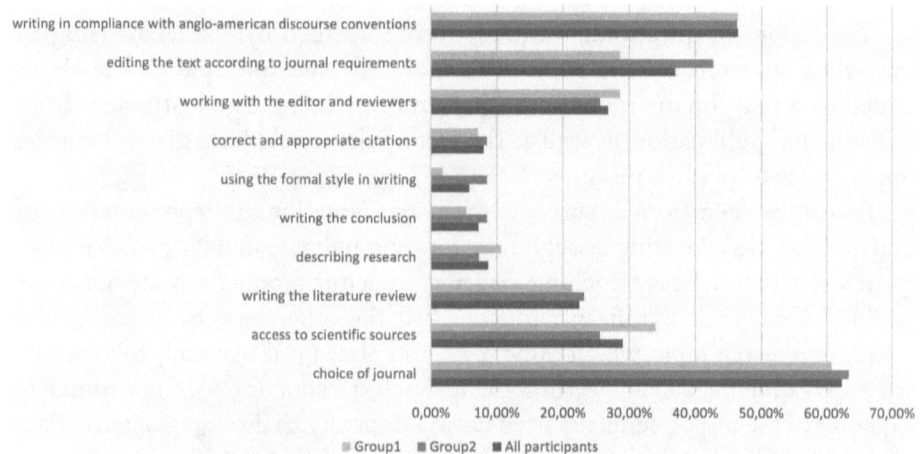

Figure 4.3. Major difficulties in writing for publication (all respondents, Group 1, Group 2).

The open responses suggested by the teachers who took the survey mentioned lack of support from administration, lack of a conducive academic environment, the absence of experience, and their considerable teaching load as inhibiting factors. One respondent noted that it was not just the choice of topic that was the problem but the identification of a theme that could be of interest to the broader academic community.

When it came to possible motivational factors, the profiles for the two groups did not coincide (see Figure 4.4). Both cohorts selected the reduction of the teaching workload and the opportunity to focus on writing most often, though these factors were more significant to Group 1 respondents. Almost half of the participants were encouraged by financial rewards, and this option was selected by both experienced and inexperienced writers. Career prospects and outside help, such as the support of a mentor or of a group, were more appealing to the participants without a track record of international publications. Targeted instruction and recruitment requirements seemed the least attractive of all the options.

The Likert scale-based items looked specifically at the crucial factors that may have been relevant to this particular sample—university language instructors based in Russia. They shed light on language teachers' knowledge, practices, and attitudes.

When it came to attitudes, the vast majority of teachers agreed that they preferred teaching to writing for publication (M = 4, Mdn = 5; see Table 2). The desire to share their findings was on an average level for both groups (M = 3, Mdn = 3). As for practices, regular engagement with academic publications was not typical of the cohort (M = 2, Mdn = 3).

When relevant knowledge and skills were in focus, the respondents mostly agreed they were aware of the features of Anglo-American academic discourse (M = 4, Mdn = 4). However, they were not at all sure what different elements of an academic paper should look like (M = 3, Mdn = 3). All respondents uniformly agreed that language teachers were not usually instructed in research methods and writing for publication (M = 5, Mdn = 4).

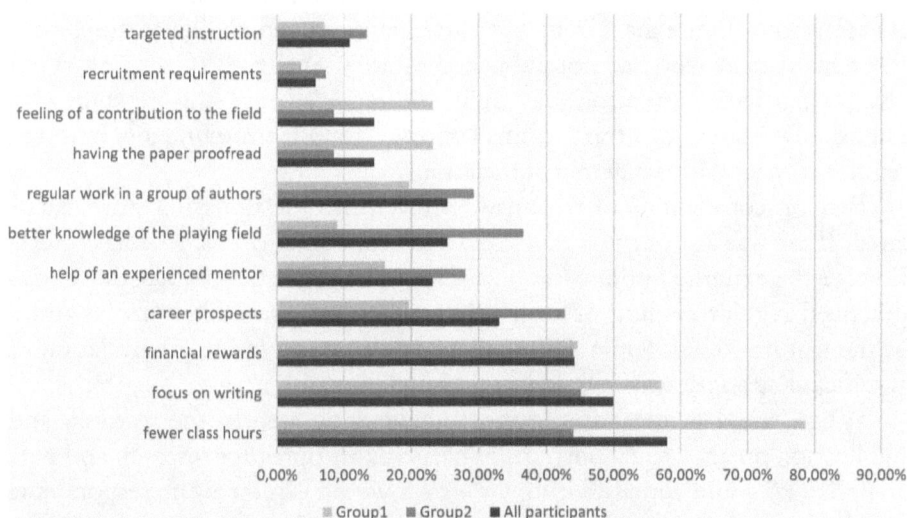

Figure 4.4. Factors that can encourage language instructors to publish more (all participants, Group 1, Group 2). Table

4.2. Likert Scale Items Analysis for the Sample

Item	M	Md	SD
Q1. I prefer teaching to researching and writing for publication.	5	4	1.205
Q2. I regularly read articles in English.	2	3	1.217
Q3. I am aware of the particular features of Anglo-American academic discourse.	4	4	1.273
Q4. I am aware of the demands of each element of an academic article in terms of content and language.	3	3	1.244
Q5. Language teachers are NOT taught how to conduct research and write for publication.	5	4	1.439
Q6. I want to share my knowledge with the international community.	3	3	1.276

If these answers are compared across the two groups, those who had a track record of publications in international journals observably differed from those who did not. Group 2 respondents were slightly more adept at writing in compliance with Anglo-American academic conventions. They also self-reportedly read more academic papers in English.

The contrast becomes stark if one compares two subgroups within Group 1: those who had only one article published in international journals (Group 1_1) and those who had a considerable track record of publications (Group 1_2). As seen from Figure 4.5, Group 1_1 participants shared similar features with those instructors who had not published internationally yet (Group 2). What attracts particular attention was their self-reported non-engagement with published research. Contrary to this cohort, Group 1_2 respondents reported regular contact with academic publications.

Pearson correlations of the answers given in Questions 1–6 were calculated. There was a strong ($r = .7, p < .01$) and very strong ($r = .8, p < .01$) correlation for the extreme options in Questions 2 and 3. In other words, those who practiced regular reading of academic publications were likely to be aware of the features of academic discourse, and vice versa. No other correlation of significant strength was revealed.

When asked to identify the most challenging step in the research and publication process, equal portions of participants opted for research and data analysis (37%) and actual writing (37%). However, Group 2, the respondents who had no publication record yet, got stuck at the first stage more often. The more experienced group found the subsequent steps more challenging.

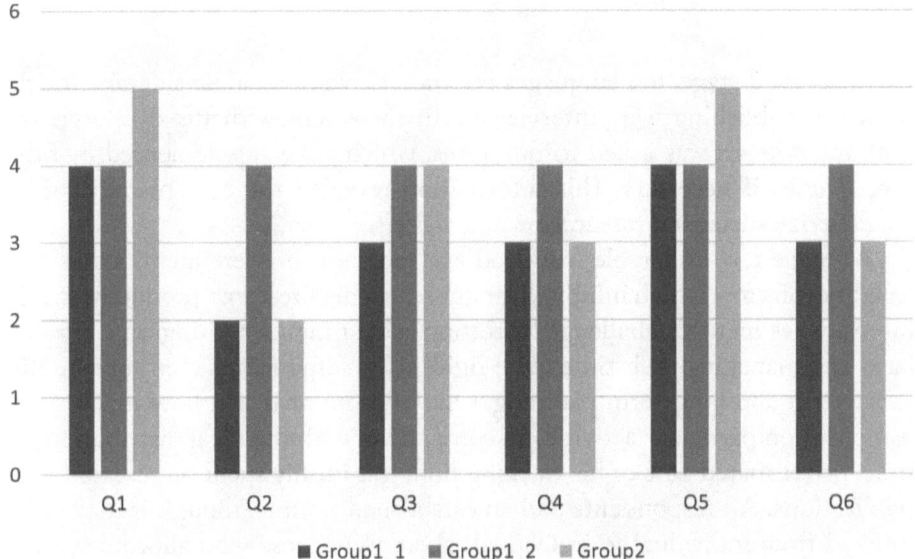

Figure 4.5. Comparison of median values for subgroups.

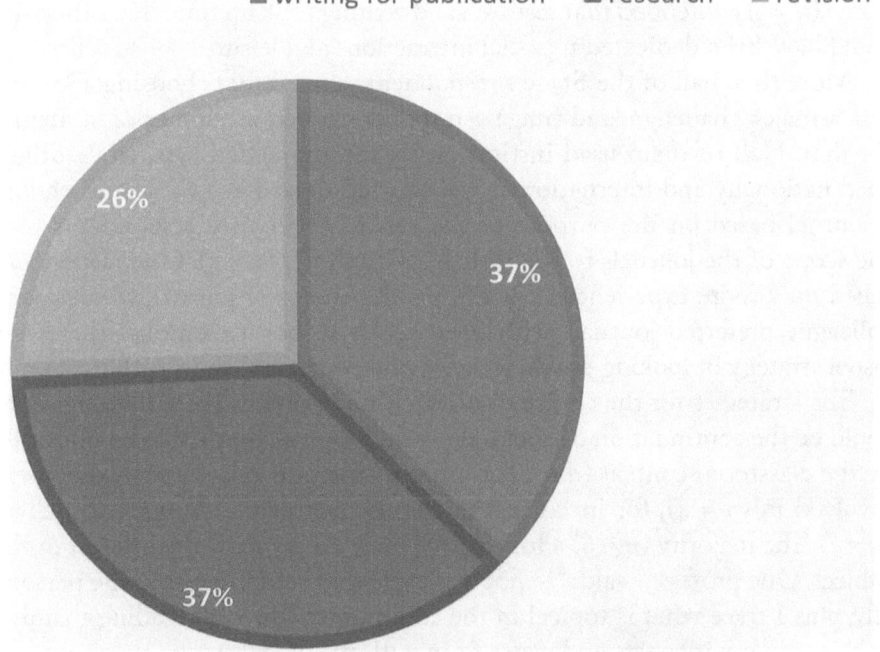

Figure 4.6. The difficulty evaluation of different stages of publication preparation.

Stage 2

At the second stage, ten languages instructors who had a considerable track record in publishing were interviewed. In these semi-structured interviews, each interviewee was asked 10 questions, which were supplemented by further queries if necessary. This information revealed the best practices that characterize successful researchers and writers.

At Stage 1, considerable workload and lack of time were identified as the weightiest factors which inhibited language teachers' research productivity. All interviewees met this challenge by setting aside time for writing on a regular basis and managing their time quite rigidly. The respondents mentioned both short-term and long-term planning. One of them analyzed how much time was spent on particular activities in comparison with the ideal distribution of time; he estimated 20% of his working time was ideally spent on research and publications. All respondents had an established routine, though it may have differed from individual to individual. There were those who allocate several days when other commitments were not that demanding to immerse in writing ($n = 3$). Some mechanical tasks (e.g., literature search, formatting) could be carried out in "unproductive" moments, after classes, and in the evenings. Some ($n = 3$) contended that research and writing took up time that otherwise could have been dedicated to social interactions and leisure.

More than half of the Stage 1 respondents agreed that choosing a journal was a major challenge, and Stage 2 respondents had a number of strategies for that. Half of them used institutionally recommended lists, while others used nationally and internationally recognized databases ($n = 5$) and choose a journal based on the purpose of the article. Obviously, respondents read the scope of the journals to see if their research fits ($n = 5$). One respondent relied on a more experienced partner for the choice of journal, whereas one colleague preferred journals with open access to boost citations. There was also a strategy of looking at where successful peers publish ($n = 3$).

The strategies for the choice of research topic varied. These investigations could be the continuation of doctoral research ($n = 2$), they could be informed by the classroom context ($n = 2$) or other instruction-related tasks they were involved in ($n = 4$), for instance, the courses instructors design and deliver ($n = 2$). The majority ($n = 6$) admitted to being led primarily by interest in the subject. One professor said: "I choose a topic that is of interest to me personally, plus I trace what is topical in the community (through reading mainly), in this way, my interests and views fit in with the global trend."

This interplay of intrinsic interest and practicality characterized the motivation that most interviewees have drawn upon when conducting research and writing for publication. On the one hand, for all participants, the motivation to research and to write research came from the inside, as they were genuinely interested in what they were studying. The male respondent contended that a researcher fulfills a mission by sharing their research with the community. On the other hand, the respondents were mostly guided by institutional requirements: "Extrinsic motivation plays a positive role, as you publish to keep up with university requirements and to have your contract prolonged." In the words of another respondent, "Extrinsic motivation is important, but I would not write without intrinsic motivation."

One respondent was sure that intrinsic motivation was a myth, as writing should become a habit, an integral part of one's professional life. The opinion was expressed that instructors need to enjoy writing, not only research.

As already mentioned, data analysis was a skill that the language teachers were not apt at. Successful colleagues mostly solved this problem by combining self-study with targeted instruction. Three respondents attended a basic course at a university abroad. Two of them took a course in the workplace. Other strategies were mentioned, such as cooperation with more knowledgeable colleagues ($n = 4$) and the outsourcing of such tasks ($n = 3$). The benefits of cooperation were highlighted by one of the respondents in the following manner: "As much research is interdisciplinary now, collaboration with people from other spheres can only strengthen your contribution. More to that, it widens the scope of your research and the number of possible publication venues."

For some, the gap in knowledge and skills was revealed when they received reviews on their articles ($n = 3$). Even when a rejection was received, reviewers may have advised on methods that could strengthen one's research, they said.

Overall, the interviewees perceived rejections as an opportunity to learn. Though half of them agreed that rejections were a blow to their self-esteem, they quickly overcame the disappointment and improved the paper using reviewers' feedback. As one of the respondents said, "Any rejection is a move forward—it gives you an understanding of what to do next, especially if you analyze the reasons for rejections."

Knowledge of Anglo-American academic conventions and discourse features, unlike data analysis methods, seldom became reasons for rejections in their cases ($n = 1$). All interviewees uniformly agreed that reading published research was the best way to increase awareness in this particular realm. Four respondents suggested that one should start writing in order to write—but not without reading extensively before that. One instructor contended that writing the first paper may be challenging and time-consuming, but gradually you become more involved and more proficient. An opinion was expressed that analysis and sometimes replication of parts of good articles could substitute for academic writing courses. The strategy a younger instructor implemented was learning bits of good articles by heart, which helped her write her papers better.

Speaking about the most preferable way to study in order to be able to write for publication, half of the respondents mentioned a combination of formal education and self-study; however, the rest opted for informal or hands-on learning, as "formal education is not focused, it's for everyone, so there is very little useful information." Two respondents who usually have written research with an established partner spoke about peer learning and teaching.

The preferences of whether to write individually or in collaboration split the cohort into four segments. There were those who always worked on their own ($n = 3$), as they wanted to be in control of everything. Two respondents work with long-standing partners. They valued the opportunity to discuss research and writing, rely on each other's strengths, and divide responsibility. Two instructors usually participated in group projects. Four respondents said they work in various modes, though "it is difficult to work in collaboration with colleagues from Russia, as their academic discourse competence is not good enough, too much rewriting is needed."

Discussion

Difficulties and Motivations

In this paper, the major obstacles that have prevented university language instructors based in Russia from publishing in internationally recognized journals were discussed. An analysis of possible motivational factors was conducted, and the practices used by those language teachers who have had a track record in publications were identified.

When it comes to obstacles, several issues come to the fore. The hypothesis that language teachers lack research competencies was supported by questionnaire results and proved in the interviews. Our findings support the claim that "most staff will not at any stage of their career, whether as a student or a staff member, be directly taught how to write for publication in refereed literature" (McGrail et al., 2006, p. 24). University teachers agreed they had not received instruction in research methods and academic writing. They have had difficulty setting the research question and analyzing the results. Because there had been no sound research, there had been no publication suitable for a high-tier journal.

As can be seen, the major difficulties our target group has faced do not have a purely linguistic nature (see also Chapter 1, Chapter 3, and Chapter

6). It has seemed challenging for them to come to grips with Anglo-American research and writing conventions. The problem may have historical roots. Science in Soviet countries evolved on its own trajectory, separated from the rest of the world by the Iron Curtain. It developed its own academic conventions and traditions, especially in the humanities. When the Iron Curtain fell and researchers had to integrate into the global community, they had to appropriate a different mindset, and many are still struggling with the appropriation. Education could help researchers to adapt to the dominance of Anglo-American research and writing conventions in academia, but as language teachers have admitted, it has not been provided to them, and they themselves have not believed in the successful outcomes of formal instruction.

The problem has been aggravated by the fact that language instructors have not read others' research. Having a broad view of a research area often gleaned through extensive reading has been essential for research productivity (Hemmings & Kay, 2010). Authors need to read research in their specialization not only for content and the identification of a research niche, but also to internalize fixed expressions used in articles in their field (Gnutzmann & Rabe, 2014). Extensive reading in one's specialization is also a way to choose a journal one's study would be appropriate for or to identify the topics that would be of interest to the international academic community. Reading extensively to stay up to date and to enrich one's linguistic repertoire takes considerable time, and it may not be possible in situations when other commitments prevail.

The opportunity to focus has been indispensable for writing (Larsson & Alvinius, 2019). Our respondents felt that they did not have this opportunity. Preoccupied with the need to earn a living today, language instructors have chosen to teach more class hours rather than invest time in a risky enterprise with postponed results such as writing for publication.

For a major part of our respondents, actual teaching was more appealing than research. They had difficulty motivating themselves for research writing. We cannot but agree with Bai (2018) who stated that "for language teachers to embrace research, they must be intrinsically motivated, and the underlying beliefs held by language teachers about what counts as research and what value research has must be addressed" (p. 119).

Writing groups and the supervision of an experienced mentor were a preferable option for language instructors without publication experience. Not only could these groups guide the writer and provide them with invaluable feedback, but also work as a substitute for the scientific environment and motivate instructors to write for publication. However, these initiatives will not work if institutions do not make sure their academics have both tools and time to conduct research and write for publication. When it comes to publication activity, institutional support and the availability of time and relevant resources could play a crucial role (Sato, & Loewen, 2018).

Publication Strategies

Our findings align with the literature analyzing the factors that contribute to publication output worldwide. Such strategies as extensive reading of other articles in the field of specialization (Rezaei & Seyri, 2019), co-operation with native speakers (Cho, 2004), and sacrifice of leisure time for research and writing (Reyes-Cruz & Perales-Escudero, 2016) were applicable to our respondents.

Those language teachers who found their way to international journals appeared to be distinctive in a number of ways. Apart from being avid readers of published research, they developed certain routines that help them to be more productive publication-wise. These academics manage their time quite rigidly. Research has shown that the most prolific writers have no more time and no fewer commitments than those who do not publish, they just manage their time wisely (Boice & Jones, 1984).

They were more adept at identifying the topic and the niche for research. They drew inspiration from their teaching context or their scientific interests. These prolific writers had an inner sense of what is topical in the field, probably due to the fact that they read more of others' research. At least self-reportedly, they were more familiar with the features of Anglo-American discourse and the structural peculiarities of an academic paper. This group was more motivated from within and eager to share their findings internationally.

The most potent factor influencing publication output has been research self-efficacy, that is, confidence in one's own ability to perform research-related tasks (Forester et al., 2004). Self-efficacy for research and research writing has depended both on training and intrinsic motivation. If motivation is low, self-efficacy will be, and if motivation is high, self-efficacy would be correspondingly high (Bailey, 1999). Our interviewees, like other professors with the highest sense of self-efficacy, were perseverant, resilient, strategic, and willing to sacrifice leisure time for the sake of research (Reyes-Cruz & Perales-Escudero, 2016). They considered rejections an opportunity to improve and reach out for assistance.

Implications for Institutional Policies

Some implications for institutional policies can be deduced. Though our respondents reported being motivated by financial rewards and career prospects, with language teachers, pure extrinsic motivation does not work. Not only have they needed support to conduct and publish their research, but they have had to develop a positive attitude about research (Bai, 2018). Training programs should, among other things, aim at a change of research dispositions and the strengthening of self-efficacy beliefs (Hemmings & Kay, 2016). The creation of a socio-constructivist learning environment via mentor-supported collaborative groups (Dikilitas & Mumford, 2016) may be helpful here. Though not every academic may embrace the opportunity to have their papers read and discussed by other people (McGrail et al., 2006), the participants decrease "anxiety from having had a community of peer writers with which to share their concerns, ideas, and frustrations" (Kirkpatrick, 2019, p. 33). The awareness raising of what classroom research is and how to conduct it will not only improve their teaching practice, but it will also give language teachers the content to write about.

Instructors at Russian universities have had to balance conflicting demands imposed by their administrations. Juggling heavy teaching loads and being active publication-wise has not always been possible. Managerial efforts may involve a focus on balancing time around teaching and research, lightening the teaching load, or raising awareness of the importance of research (Hemmings & Kay, 2016). If the load is impossible to lighten, it will be up to managers to "implement time management programs for those wrestling to find an appropriate balance among research, teaching and service activities" (Hemmings & Kay, 2010, p. 193). Those able and willing to invest a greater amount of work time to executing research tasks could be much more inclined to produce scholarly products (Hemmings & Kay, 2010). If university management needs to prioritize, support could be focused on those interested or already trained in writing for publication.

Universities in Russia have established writing centers to provide support for the lecturers in their publication endeavors (Korotkina, 2018, see also Chapter 5 and Chapter 6 of this volume). However, workshops and training courses have offered their services to all academic staff irrespective of the discipline. Instruction may be targeted at specific groups of academics with similar needs and gaps in knowledge. It may be more successful because research and writing traditions may differ in different disciplines (Yakhontova, 2006), even the requirements for the language of papers may be dissimilar (Hynninen & Kuteeva, 2017). On the structural level, the moves and the functional language used in the same parts of articles have differed across disciplines (Basturkmen, 2012).

Different approaches may be implemented by researchers at different stages of their academic career. At an early stage in their career, junior researchers could be shown how writing can be done with limited skills, but sophistication could be added to their writing later (Okamura, 2006). Our respondents clearly demonstrated they were not interested in formal instruction, as they preferred hands-on learning through a personalized approach, accounting for their lacks and needs.

As can be inferred from the interview data, institutional requirements bear fruit. The extrinsic motivation they create does not contradict but complements the intrinsic motivation successful writers have. Challenging goals fuel effort, and satisfaction derived from achievement fosters an intrinsic interest in research and writing (Reyes-Cruz & Perales-Escudero, 2016). Though accused of subjectivity, lists of recommended journals could guide the choice of publication venue. They may force academics to make pragmatic choices about what to publish and where to publish. However, if the demands are too stringent, knowledgeable practitioners may be demotivated, so a separate developmental track for those who demonstrate excellence in teaching but no inclination towards academic work may be provided.

Finally, as early provision of experience and formation of interest in research play a more important role than support for programs and related activities (Hemmings & Kay, 2016), language teachers should have access to international research as early as when they are trained for teaching. The awareness of internationally recognized research approaches and writing conventions should become part of language teacher training programs.

Conclusion

There is no one definite recipe for how to develop a strong track record of research and publications. Successful writing for publication has involved an interplay of factors, as

> Linguistic proficiency is one resource in the complex architecture of expertise required for effective research dissemination, alongside with methodological versatility, critical writing ability, awareness of editors' agendas, participation in wider research networks, and learning the practice of writing by more writing. (Bardi, 2015, p. 98)

Some other characteristics can be added to the list, such as perseverance, time management, and strategic thinking. It is a competence that evolves with time. Once an academic gets the grasp of the sophisticated publishing process, it becomes easier to be productive.

As for now, university language instructors have seemed to be losing the publish-or-perish battle. Both the change of mindset and institutional support can help language instructors start publishing more and more successfully. While institutional support has been something manageable and plannable, mindsets are not easily manipulated. Further research and a greater sample can shed light on these deep-rooted issues.

References

Bai, L. (2018). Language teachers' beliefs about research: A comparative study of English teachers from two tertiary education institutions in China. *System, 72*, 114–123. https://doi.org/10.1016/j.system.2017.11.004.

Bailey, J. G. (1999). Academics' motivation and self-efficacy for teaching and research. *Higher Education Research & Development, 18*(3), 343–359. https://doi.org/10.1080/0729436990180305.

Bardi, M. (2015). Learning the practice of scholarly publication in English—A Romanian perspective. *English for Specific Purposes, 36*, 47–59. https://doi.org/10.1016/j.esp.2014.08.002.

Basturkmen, H. (2012). A genre-based investigation of discussion sections of research articles in dentistry and disciplinary variation. *Journal of English for Academic Purposes, 11*(2), 134–144. https://doi.org/10.1016/j.jeap.2011.10.004.

Belcher, D. (2007). Seeking acceptance in an English-only research world. *Second Language Writing, 16*, 1–22. https://doi.org/10.1016/j.jslw.2006.12.001.

Boice, R., & Jones, F. (1984). Why academicians don't write. *Journal of Higher Education, 55*(5), 567–572. https://doi.org/10.1080/00221546.1984.11780679.

Cho, S. (2004). Challenges of entering discourse communities through publishing in English: Perspectives of nonnative-speaking doctoral students in the United States of America. *Journal of Language, Identity, and Education, 3*(1), 47–72. https://doi.org/10.1207/s15327701jlie0301_3.

Crosby, C. (2003). Writer's block, merit, and the market: Working in the university of excellence. *College English, 65*(6), 626-645. https://doi.org/10.2307/3594274.

Dikilitas, K., & Mumford, E. (2016). Supporting the writing up of teacher research: Peer and mentor roles. *ELT Journal, 70*(4), 371–381. https://doi.org/10.1093/elt/ccw014.

Duszak, A., & Lewkowicz, J. (2008). Publishing academic texts in English: A Polish perspective. *Journal of English for Academic Purposes, 7(2)*, 108–120. https://doi.org/10.1016/j.jeap.2008.03.001.

Fernandez, P., & Varela, M. (2009). English for research purposes at the University of Santiago de Compostela: A survey. *Journal of English for Academic Purposes, 8*, 152–164. https://doi.org/10.1016/j.jeap.2009.05.003.

Flowerdew, J. (1999). Problems in writing for scholarly publication in English: The case of Hong Kong. *Journal of Second Language Writing, 8*(3), 243–264. https://doi.org/10.1016/S1060-3743(99)80116-7.

Flowerdew, J. (2001). Attitudes of journal editors to nonnative speaker contributions. *TESOL Quarterly, 35*, 121–150. https://doi.org/10.2307/3587862.

Forester, M., Kahn, J. H., & Hesson-McInnis, M. S. (2004). Factor structures of three measures of research self-efficacy. *Journal of Career Assessment, 12*, 3–16. https://doi.org/10.1177/1069072703257719.

Frumina, E., & West, R. (2012). *Internationalisation of Russian higher education: The English language dimension*. British Council.

Gea-Valor, M.-L., Rey-Rocha, J., & Moreno, A. (2014). Publishing research in the international context: An analysis of Spanish scholars' academic writing needs in the social sciences. *English for Specific Purposes, 36*, 47–59. https://doi.org/10.1016/j.esp.2014.05.001.

Gnutzmann, C., & Rabe, F. (2014). 'Theoretical subtleties" or "text modules"? German researchers' language demands and attitudes across disciplinary cultures. *Journal of English for Academic Purposes, 13*, 31–40. https://doi.org/10.1016/j.jeap.2013.10.003.

Hemmings, B., & Kay, R. (2010). University lecturer publication output: Qualifications, time and confidence count. *Journal of Higher Education Policy and Management, (32)2*, 185–197. https://doi.org/10.1080/13600800903575520.

Hemmings, B., & Kay, R. (2016). The relationship between research self-efficacy, research disposition and publication output. *Educational Psychology, 36*(2), 347–361. https://doi.org/10.1080/01443410.2015.1025704.

Ho, M. (2017). Navigating scholarly writing and international publishing: Individual agency of Taiwanese EAL doctoral students. *Journal of English for Academic Purposes, 27*, 1–13. https://doi.org/10.1016/j.jeap.2017.02.004.

Hyland, K. (2006). *English for academic purposes: An advanced resource book*. Routledge.

Hynninen, N., & Kuteeva, M. (2017). "Good" and "acceptable" English in L2 research writing: Ideals and realities in history and computer science. *Journal of English for Academic Purposes, 30*, 53–65. https://doi.org/10.1016/j.jeap.2017.10.009.

Kaplan, R. (1966). Cultural thought patterns in intercultural education. *Language learning, 16*, 1–20. https://doi.org/10.1111/j.1467-1770.1966.tb00804.x.

Keen, A. (2007). Writing for publication: Pressures, barriers and support strategies. *Nurse education today, 27*, 382–388. https://doi.org/10.1016/j.nedt.2006.05.019.

Kirkpatrick, K. J. (2019). Online doctoral students writing for scholarly publication. *Computers and Composition, 52*, 19–36. https://doi.org/10.1016/j.compcom.2019.01.012.

Korotkina, I. B. (2018). University writing centers in Russia: Balancing unity and diversity. *Higher Education in Russia and Beyond (HERB), 2*(16), 6–7. https://herb.hse.ru/data/2018/07/21/1151527123/1HERB2(16).pdf.

Kyvik, S. (2013). The academic researcher role: Enhancing expectations and improved performance. *Higher Education, 65*, 525–538. https://doi.org/10.1007/s10734-012-9561-0.

Larsson, G., & Alvinius, A. (2019). "An undisturbed afternoon of writing": A qualitative study of professors' job satisfaction. *Journal of Applied Research in Higher Education, 11*(4), 719–732. https://doi.org/10.1108/jarhe-10-2018-0216.

Lee, I. (2014). Publish or perish: The myth and reality of academic publishing. *Language Teaching, 47*(2), 250–261. https://doi.org/10.1017/S0261444811000504.

Leki, I. (1992). *Understanding ESL writers: A guide for teachers.* Boynton/Cook.

Li, Y., & Flowerdew, J. (2009). International engagement versus local commitment: Hong Kong academics in the humanities and social sciences writing for publication. *Journal of English for Academic Purposes, 8*(4), 279–293. https://doi.org/10.1016/j.jeap.2009.05.002.

Luo, N., & Hyland, K. (2019). "I won't publish in Chinese now": Publishing, translation and the non-English speaking academic. *Journal of English for Academic Purposes, 39*, 37–47. https://doi.org/10.1016/j.jeap.2019.03.003.

Macháček, V., & Srhole, M. (2019). Globalisation of science: Evidence from authors in academic journals by country of origin. http://globalizationofscience.com/.

Martin, P., Rey-Rocha, J., Burgess, S., & Moreno, A. (2014). Publishing research in English-language journals: Attitudes, strategies and difficulties of multilingual scholars of medicine. *Journal of English for Academic Purposes, 16*, 57–67. https://doi.org/10.1016/j.jeap.2014.08.001.

McGrail, M., Rickard, C., & Jones, R. (2006). Publish or perish: A systematic review of interventions to increase academic publication rates. *Higher Education Review and Development, 25*(1), 19–35. https://doi.org/10.1080/07294360500453053.

Merton, R. (1968). The Matthew effect in science. *Science, 159*(3810), 56–63. https://doi.org/10.1126/science.159.3810.56.

Min, H.-T. (2014). Participating in international academic publishing: A Taiwan perspective. *TESOL Quarterly, 48*(1), 188–200. https://doi.org/10.1002/tesq.154.

Okamura, A. (2006). Two types of strategies used by Japanese scientists, when writing research articles in English. *System, 34*(1), 68–79. https://doi.org/10.1016/j.system.2005.03.006.

Olsson, A., & Sheridan, V. (2012). A case study of Swedish scholars' experiences with and perceptions of the use of English in academic publishing. *Written Communication, 29*(1), 33–54. https://doi.org/10.1177/0741088311428566.

Perez-Llantada, C., Plo, R., & Ferguson, G. (2011). "You don't say what you know, only what you can": The perceptions and practices of senior Spanish academics regarding research dissemination in English. *English for Specific Purposes, 30*, 18–30. https://doi.org/10.1016/j.esp.2010.05.001.

Reyes-Cruz, M., & Perales-Escudero, M. D. (2016). Research self-efficacy sources and research motivation in a foreign language university faculty in Mexico: Implications for educational policy. *Higher Education Research & Development, 35*(4), 800–814. https://doi.org/10.1080/07294360.2015.1137884.

Rezaei, S., & Seyri, H. (2019). Iranian doctoral students' perceptions of publication in English: Motives, hurdles, and strategies. *Journal of Applied Research in Higher Education, 11*(4), 941–954. https://doi.org/10.1007/s10734-019-00478-1.

Sato, M., & Loewen, S. (2018). Do teachers care about research? The research-pedagogy dialogue. *ELT Journal, 73*(1), 1–10. https://doi.org/10.1093/elt/ccy048.

Schluter, J. (2014). Writing for publication in linguistics: Exploring niches of multilingual publishing among German linguists. *Journal of English for Academic Purposes, 16*, 1–13. https://doi.org/10.1016/j.jeap.2014.06.001.

Shen, L., Carter, S., & Jun Zhang, L. (2019). EL1 and EL2 doctoral students' experience in writing the discussion section: A needs analysis. *Journal of English for Academic Purposes*, *40*, 74–86. https://doi.org/10.1016/j.jeap.2019.06.004.

Uzuner, S. (2008). Multilingual scholars' participation in core/global academic communities: A literature review. *Journal of English for Academic Purposes*, *7*(4), 250–263. https://doi.org/10.1016/j.jeap.2008.10.007.

van Enk, A., & Power, K. (2017). What is a research article?: Genre variability and data selection in genre research. *Journal of English for Academic Purposes*, *29*, 1–11, https://doi.org/10.1016/j.jeap.2017.07.002.

Wu, Y. C. (1967). The research interview and its measurement. *Social Work*, *12*(3), 79–87. https://doi.org/10.1093/sw/12.3.79.

Wu, X., Mauranen, A., & Lei, L. (2020). Syntactic complexity in English as a lingua franca academic writing. *Journal of English for Academic Purposes*, *43*, 100798. https://doi.org/10.1016/j.jeap.2019.100798.

Yakhontova, T. (2006). Cultural and disciplinary variation in academic discourse: The issue of influencing factors. *Journal of English for Academic Purposes*, *5*(2), 163–157. https://doi.org/10.1016/j.jeap.2006.03.002.

Part Two. Writing Center Interventions

5　Developing Writing Centers in Russia: A Balancing Act

Tatiana Glushko
JACKSON STATE UNIVERSITY

> Using grounded theory methodology, I take a snapshot of Russian writing centers in the process of development. I explore how writing centers build their relationships with the institutions and writers they serve and position themselves as sites of writing pedagogy. Through interviews with writing center directors and the analysis of writing center mission statements, I identify four tensions in writing center work: (1) between the immediate demands of academic capitalism and long-term goals for internationalization; (2) between Russian and anglophone academic and rhetorical traditions; (3) between Western writing center pedagogies and the needs of local writers; and (4) between serving in the niche of English for research and publication and the desire to establish itself as a field. These tensions present a fertile ground for further research on the development of writing pedagogies in an international context.

In 2012, the WAC Clearinghouse published a collection of essays on writing programs across the world (Thaiss et al., 2012), which included a green map where the location of each writing program selected for the collection was marked with a white flag. Indeed, it was a map of writing in many places, from North and South America to Australia and New Zealand and from Northern Europe to Africa. Not a single flag, however, dotted the vast green swath of Russia.

Seven years later, at the time of writing this essay, researchers in the US may still find that English-language publications about academic writing in Russia have been few (see, for example, Bollinger, 2016; Butler et al., 2014; Korotkina, 2018; Squires, 2018, among the few). At the same time, in my native Russia, conversations about academic writing have been gaining momentum: publications in the Russian-language *Journal of Higher Education in Russia*, the emergence of the National Writing Center Consortium, and the *Journal of Academic Literacy and Research Skills*, and a regularly held conference. Newly established centers for academic writing, whose number had grown from one in 2011 to 15 in 2018 (Squires, 2018), have been hubs for these conversations.

As Irina Korotkina says in Chapter 1, writing center practitioners do and will play a significant role in the way the teaching of academic writing develops. The mission of Russian writing centers, the range of services they have provided to faculty and, in some cases, to students (Bakin, 2013; Bazanova, 2015; Korotkina, 2013, 2016b), and their advocacy for teaching academic writing at all levels and across disciplines in English and Russian (Bazanova & Korotkina, 2017; Korotkina, 2016a, 2018) suggest that these writing centers have the potential to develop into full-fledged writing programs.

As Russian writing center practitioners work to enable researchers to enter professional conversations in their fields internationally, they, too, through publications and international conference presentations, have begun to position themselves among the international writing center community, to which this edited collection is a testament. Thus, they contribute to the process of the internationalization of writing studies both in Russia and the US even as Russian writing centers appear on the map.

This is an opportune moment to take a snapshot of writing centers in Russia to understand how writing pedagogies have developed in an educational context different from the US. At this early stage, I want to understand how writing centers have related to their institutions, how their pedagogies have developed, and how they have developed as a profession. I argue that in Russia this process has been a balancing act between the "order of fast capitalism" (Lu, 2004, p. 16) and long-term educational goals for internationalization, between Russian and anglophone academic and rhetorical traditions that often have been in conflict, between existing writing center pedagogies and unique local educational needs, and finally between serving in the niche of English for research and publication and the desire to establish itself as a field.

Internationalization of Academic Writing in Russia and the US

Internationalization within Russian higher education (Frumina & West, 2012; Ganzler et al., 2009; Lebedev, 2014) and the dominance of English-language publications in the world (Canagarajah, 2002; Lillis & Curry, 2010; Pennycook, 1994; Rafoth, 2015) have created pressure for Russian academics to write in English. Internationalization in Russian higher education has involved, among other things, an increased number of citations in the Web of Science, a citation-indexing service, and Scopus, an abstract and citation database that includes English-language peer-reviewed journals. This pressure has created problems in three primary areas: language learning, writing pedagogy, and rhetoric.

The low rate of English-language proficiency among academics in Russia has been one of the problems. With only 14% of faculty fluent in English (Volkova & Shmatko, 2018), many faculty members, if required to publish in English-language journals, may not be able to do so without language support. Another problem has been the lack of formal teaching of writing in higher education, where "oral methods of instruction and assessment" with lectures, seminars, and oral exams have been preferred (Zemliansky & St.Amant, 2013, p. 252). Throughout my own education in Russia in the 1990s, I never received a syllabus or assignment guidelines (except those in textbooks). My professors communicated their expectations, instructions, and feedback orally.

Yet another problem has lain in the differences between rhetorical traditions and publication practices in Russia and in the West (Korotkina, 2018, see also Chapter 1). Unlike their Western counterparts, Russian professionals have spent less time on the writing process and have paid less attention to the audience and more attention to grammar and style (Zemliansky & St.Amant, 2013). Opaque writing (Korotkina, 2018; Yakhontova, 1997) has continued as the legacy of the Soviet style of communication when the state had strict control over the dissemination of scientific knowledge, and thus professional communication was limited to an internal audience. Zemliansky and St.Amant (2013) explain,

> It is probably true that the Soviet regime consciously worked to limit the free flow of information and the ability of its citizenry to communicate with people in other countries. It also makes sense that, to achieve these goals, the Soviet ideological machine might have curtailed the teaching of foreign languages, particularly as a means of communication. But this theory fails to satisfactorily explain the lack of structured writing instruction in the native languages of the USSR under the Soviet higher education system. (p. 252)

Furthermore, they argue that in the USSR, "a culture of writing in relation to language—and the teaching of language—never emerged" (Zemliansky & St.Amant, 2013, p. 252).

The growing understanding of difficulties that Russian-language writers have experienced when writing for publication in English has provided a rationale for institutionalizing writing support and establishing writing centers. With the support of the Russian federal government, universities participating in Project 5-100 (see Introduction) had an opportunity to establish centers for academic writing to meet the needs of faculty and graduate students who write in English. The goal of the project has been "to maximize the competitive position of a group of leading Russian universities in the global research and education market" (Ministry of Science and Higher Education of the Russian Federation, n.d.) and place at least five Russian universities among the top 100 universities in the world.

Ashley Squires (2018) notes that the emergence of writing centers in Russia has reflected "the traditional relationship between the academy and the state" in that "writing centers have been established to serve specific state ends related to the international integration and prestige of Russian higher education" (p. 19). Thus, from the outset, the goal of writing centers was to participate in creating a competitive advantage for their universities in particular and for Russian higher education in general. However, instructors of English seized this opportunity to build a stronger case for incorporating writing at all levels of higher education (see Korotkina, 2018).

In the US, writing centers have also expressed interest in internationalizing, as suggested by the recent calls from the International Researchers Consortium and from the International Writing Center Association to conduct international research in writing and to build writing center partnerships. At the same time, writing center scholars in the US have been questioning their lore, calling to reconsider the theoretical grounding of writing center work (Nordlof, 2014) and the non-directive approach to tutoring (Denny et al., 2018; Salem, 2016). To reconsider our existing practices and find new meaning in what we do, it may be helpful to make the familiar unfamiliar again by turning our gaze to writing centers in other countries, non-English speaking in particular. Christiane Donahue (2009) reminds us that international writing research and partnerships will have to focus on what can be learned rather than on what has been missing or lacking. Focusing on gaps, Donahue says, has been less constructive and productive for researchers who want to participate in conversation without "othering" (p. 214). Following Donahue's advice, in this study I sought to enrich my own understanding of writing center pedagogy, which at present has been limited by my experiences of writing centers in the US even though I was educated in Russia.

Researcher Reflection: My Writing Center Experience

As someone who grew up, received education, and became an English-language teacher in Russia, I was overjoyed when I learned about writing centers being established there. Although my views on writing pedagogy and writing center work have been shaped in the US, my interest in this field began in 2001 when I worked as an instructor at the Amur State University in the Russian Far East. At that time, I attended a summer workshop on academic writing and began introducing writing into my own teaching. When I came to the US in 2006 and began to work as a tutor in a writing center, I soon realized the immense pedagogical possibility writing centers hold for developing both writers and writing pedagogies.

Writing centers have served as contact zones (Pratt, 1991) where writers from all social, linguistic, and cultural backgrounds have engaged in conversation about their writing, speaking, or research projects with peer tutors. Through these conversations, writers could develop ideas and begin to acquire academic and disciplinary discursive practices (Bizzell, 1994; Bruffee, 1995). For multilingual writers, this process has also involved negotiation of differences between two or more languages (Canagarajah, 2012; Creese & Blackledge, 2010; Lu & Horner, 2012; Matsuda, 2015; Rafoth, 2015). In the non-hierarchical context of the writing center, tutors have not acted as teachers; they have become "brokers" (Canagarajah, 2012, p. 276) who help prepare scholars to "negotiate the competing discourses" among academic audiences worldwide (Canagarajah, as quoted in Rafoth, 2015, p. 81). For tutors, this kind of engagement has required developing rhetorical skills such as listening, asking critical questions, and responding. For writers, these conversations have helped develop rhetorical attunement (Leonard, 2014) and flexibility. The process of attunement has often required writers to reflect on the political and historical contexts in which they learned to write. Thus, they become attuned not only to writing practices in another language and culture but also to "the political and historical trajectories of [their] literate practices" (Leonard, 2014, p. 238), thereby developing reflexivity and critical consciousness.

I recognize that this understanding of writing centers has been culturally constructed and that, as Donahue (2009) says, "our frames of reference may or may not be meaningful in contexts with different histories and structures" (p. 232). As a community of practice, each writing center has functioned within its own sociocultural and educational context, and within each context, the needs of participants have generated "knowledge, theories, and policies from practices" (Canagarajah, 2012, p. 272). The methodological frame that best suits the purpose of generating knowledge from practices is grounded theory (Charmaz, 2006), which would allow us to take a snapshot of writing centers in Russia in the process of development.

Using Grounded Theory in Writing Center Research

A qualitative research method, grounded theory allows for developing an analytical framework to explain a process or phenomenon based on the experiences of research participants (Creswell, 2007). It is inductive, drawing interpretations from practice rather than theory and is thus well suited for research on writing (Leonard, 2014; Magnotto, 1996) and writing centers (Neff, 2002) and for interpreting and explaining our practices. This method is also recursive, and reflexive (Charmaz, 2006), like writing itself. It focuses on the process of developing a theory rather than on the result, which allows researchers to exercise flexibility by adding sites and new data as the study unfolds.

To begin generating knowledge about writing centers in Russia from their practice, I interviewed five directors of academic writing centers from November 2018 through January 2019 and collected mission statements and descriptions of services from centers' websites. Three of the five writing centers were in Moscow, one in the south east, and another one in Siberia. Four of the participants I interviewed have directed writing centers at public universities participating in the 5-100 Project. The five centers have been the longest in existence and therefore could provide richer data. Four of these centers have served faculty and graduate students, and one has served undergraduate students because it was established to support the undergraduate curriculum at a private university modeled after a U.S.-style liberal arts college. This center, therefore, has been atypical among the Russian writing centers. All five participants were experienced teachers of English with advanced degrees. Some have led academic departments and faculty professional development programs and co-authored textbooks on academic writing.

Four interviews were conducted in Russian and one in English. The interviews were semi-structured (see Interview Guide in the appendix) and lasted from 45 to 90 minutes, resulting in 36,866 words of transcribed data. After I recorded and transcribed the interviews, I used line-by-line coding, looking for verbs describing action and coding these segments of data with gerunds to reflect the focus on action and process (Charmaz, 2006). When I coded segments of data using participants' words verbatim, I translated those words or phrases into English. I also translated quotes that were later included in this essay. I had gone through several cycles of coding and writing analytical memos, describing my interpretations of the data until I began to see core themes or categories emerging from the data and could determine connections among them.

A Snapshot of Writing Centers in Russia

The data analysis resulted in four possible theoretical categories from which to describe the current moment of writing centers in Russia. Writing centers

1) facilitate internationalization by creating a competitive edge for their universities; 2) function as mediators in the clash of expectations, rhetorical traditions, and academic identities; 3) ground their pedagogy in localized, situated practice rather than borrowed theoretical concepts; and 4) contribute to the professionalization of their field. While these categories are not stable (Charmaz, 2006) and reflect my interpretation both at the current stage of research and the stage of development of writing centers, each category provided some insight.

Writing Centers Facilitate Internationalization by Creating a Competitive Edge for Their Universities

The mission of most writing centers in Russia has been guided by the need for internationalization and integration of faculty into the international academic community. One center, for example, has stated on its website that its mission has been to contribute towards "increasing the number of publications in international journals." A statement on the website of another center has emphasized that their trained tutors have used practices that may open opportunities for faculty to begin to publish in "prestigious international journals" and thus "enable [doctoral students and junior researchers] to compete for limited journal space with native speakers from some of the best universities in the English-speaking world." Yet another center has described its mission as support for those who "write for international publications and take part in global research conferences." Enabling faculty's participation in global research communities and giving their universities a "competitive edge," as one participant expressed it, in international higher education has driven the mission of most writing centers in Russia. Although the decision to establish writing centers was top-down, the idea of a writing center had been around in the English-language teaching community even before. One participant, for example, recalled:

> You know we had this movement in Russia when academic writing and different programs began to develop. My colleagues and I were involved and participated in different seminars and conferences on academic writing, so the idea of creating writing centers was growing from the ground up.... We were beginning to think about ways to start an academic writing center as a separate unit or part of another center or department. We were not sure how to do it. And then the university administration initiated this; they understood the

> importance of [a writing center] in creating, how do I say it, a "competitive advantage" to participate in this global project.

The administrative decision, however, was necessary to get the centers off the ground, to hire administrators and staff, and to provide space and budget. Therefore, continued administrative support has been essential to the continued functioning of writing centers.

Participants talked about how the need to improve writing for publication was recognized by their administration. Yet in the experience of one director, her administration did not accept the idea of long-term programmatic support for faculty writers, and her proposal for a writing center was met with resistance:

> It's difficult to move forward, with the lack of financial and administrative support, to accomplish what we could have done in three or four years. . . . Our administration wants results here and now. They don't want to wait three or four years until we start seeing the results.

She further argued that, to facilitate internationalization at her university, they need to adopt a language policy that would provide continued support for language learning and academic writing, both necessary for international communication:

> I presented a proposal for a language policy, but again my administration did not support it. The proposal clearly outlined language competencies, who needs them and how those are developed, and, of course, everything was based on academic writing because, whatever they say, academic writing, in English in particular, is at the basis of international communication in academia.

As this participant suggested, a "language policy" that would connect internationalization, language learning, and academic writing might provide a long-term solution to the institutional efforts for improving academic writing for publication.

Even when faced with resistance, writing centers, in the words of one participant, "filled the niche" by offering services that had not been offered before, and, in the words of another participant, provided an "exclusive" service that other universities did not: "It's such an exclusive service. It's not something that is mass produced. [Writers] feel privileged that they can request an individual consultation like this, that we work with them one-on-one. It's not a production line." A sense of uniqueness about writing centers was also expressed by another participant:

> We are a very unique place, where a lot of things intersect because we have writing-in-the-disciplines needs, we're teaching in a fully bilingual space, where every student is a native speaker of Russian who also speaks English as a second or third or fourth language. So I think we have the ability to do some really interesting things here.

By occupying this exclusive niche and by offering unique services that were "not mass produced," these writing centers have been serving the purpose of raising their universities' prestige. This connection between the university's prestige and the work of the writing center promises a greater attention to the teaching of writing at all levels and may ultimately position writing centers as central to the overall success of the university. At this time, however, as one director observed, the writing center is perceived as a peripheral rather than global project for the university: "We are a supporting unit, and although everyone understands the importance of [writing in] English, we are not the priority." Nevertheless, from this peripheral position, the writing centers have worked toward the global task of internationalization by providing centralized support for faculty in writing and publishing their research in English.

Writing Centers Function as Mediators in the Clash of Expectations, Rhetorical Traditions, and Academic Identities

Even as Russian writing centers work under pressure to fulfill the goal of their institutions to increase international publications, the directors described the mission of their centers as long-term and educational rather than short-term and service oriented. Carrying out this mission involved mitigating conflicts that result from new expectations, differences in rhetorical traditions in Russian and English, and developing a new academic identity that writing in a foreign language may require. Therefore, writing center work could be described as that of mediator negotiating these conflicts.

The first clash writing center practitioners have dealt with has been that of expectations. Administrators and faculty seemed to look for fast results, but writing centers saw their goal as "long-term" and "educational." They understood that the results of their work may be "intangible":

> It's understandable that the result is intangible, . . . like any teaching. We can't say that tomorrow people, because of our

help, will start sending articles for publication. Of course, we understand this process can take a long time.

In other words, the desired publication in higher-ranking journals may not happen even if a faculty member works with a consultant in the writing center.

Meanwhile, writing centers were assessing their work by faculty satisfaction with consultations, seminars, and courses. They also were tracking the number of visits and number of pages they worked on with researchers. In addition, they were asking faculty to update them on whether their article had been submitted and to which journal. They noted if the article was published or rejected. While they were keeping track of faculty publishing activities, the directors resisted evaluating their work by the number of publications. As one director said, "Luckily I was able to convince the administration that my work will not directly affect publication numbers . . . when they tried to include this measure into my evaluation."

Even with the support of top administration, writing center directors have had to work to establish the reputation of their center within the university community and address initial skepticism about the ability of English instructors to consult on writing in fields outside their own. To diffuse skepticism, directors again have had to work from the top down and first seek the support of department chairs and directors of research institutes. As one participant recalled, a director of a research institute attended her seminar and sat with his eyes closed and arms crossed, listening to what was going on around him. Once he was convinced that the seminar was worthwhile, the members of his institute began to attend.

The new idea of a writing center and its mission has to be communicated abundantly to the university community through center websites and university publications, in meetings, and by reaching out to departments whose faculty members had not yet been using their center. One director recalled,

> I sent out information letters to each department about what we do and how we provide consultations. Because the first reaction was that people would bring us their text and we would translate it. We had to explain that we do not translate. . . . I met with people, spoke at departmental and other meetings, explaining what we do and how we do it so that people understand and have the right expectation.

This director also described the work of her center as the work of enlightenment—using the Russian adjective *prosvetitelskaia*, from the word *svet*, or light—which suggests that writing center work involves disseminating knowledge about academic writing and writing center support.

Furthermore, faculty sometimes expected writing centers to translate their articles as a quick solution to the problem of having to publish in English-language journals. As participants said, faculty believed translation could be done quickly by an English-language specialist, not realizing the differences between the work of a translator and that of a writing consultant. One director explained that translation required knowledge of the discipline, but finding a translator who had the required qualifications may be difficult and expensive, and translations done by non-specialists often did not make sense.

Another director found translation problematic because the translator would become, in a sense, a co-author, and this may have raised issues of authorship:

> They ask me to translate their article. I say, sure, but then make me a co-author because [to rewrite it in English] I will have to change the article conceptually. It doesn't just involve putting information into another language, translating it from one language to another. Submitting to a different journal often means that you have to change the concept of the article. Yes, the results may be the same, but conclusions, key concepts, categories, and criteria may need to change dramatically. But [the faculty] don't believe this.

For this participant, rewriting an existing Russian article in English involved a substantial conceptual revision of the original and thus warranted including her name as a co-author. The researchers to whom she offered co-authorship did not, however, expect any major revisions as a result of the translation. The idea that academic writing in another language required understanding linguistic, cultural, and rhetorical conventions—and making authorial choices about those—seemed novel to these faculty writers.

The second clash writing centers in Russia have had to address has been that of rhetorical traditions and practices in academic writing. Participants pointed out that writers have assumed that if the grammar was good then the writing must be good, not realizing the importance of understanding new rhetorical conventions (e.g., creating a context for research, explaining why the study is important, articulating research questions, and discussing suggestions for future research). As one director aptly put it when summarizing writers' difficulties, "We don't understand why [we do research] and we don't understand what to do with it," referring to the writers' struggle to articulate the purpose and significance of their research for a new audience. In the experience of this director, Russian researchers have not usually thought about the application of their research:

> They don't make their thoughts surface on paper. They don't talk or write through their ideas. It's like a cauldron in which their ideas are stewing. And then, some brilliant idea comes to the surface. Anyone interested, say from some organization in the West, can lift the lid of the cauldron with this delicious stew and spoon out whatever they like. But no one here would think to use these ideas to feed our country.

As the comment suggests, Russian researchers have tended to underestimate the pragmatic value of their research, which has then translated into difficulties with articulating the significance of their studies when they write in English.

The problem of "not talking through ideas," as one participant described it, may be inherent to the Soviet style of communication when researchers withheld information for political and economic reasons. As the same participant said, "Never, almost never, will a Russian researcher talk about suggestions for future research. They say, 'Why would I discuss this?'" This comment implies that Russian researchers may be unwilling to write about their future research because, as Zemliansky and St.Amant (2013) explain, many of them have not been used to a free exchange of ideas and feedback from an external audience. Perhaps this is also why, according to some participants, researchers have hesitated to share drafts of their papers with tutors from the West, preferring Russian consultants.

Learning, understanding, and negotiating social norms different from one's own involves changing, redefining, or expanding one's identity and authority. One of the directors explained, "Even though everyone understands the importance and significance of [writing in English], they say, we'll lose our identity, we'll lose the characteristics of Russian academic writing because of the different approach." Writing in English has been easier for younger researchers and graduate students, most participants noted, but may have been particularly difficult for established faculty, who may feel threatened by the new requirement to publish in English: "The aging generation of scholars, they are resistant. . . . You have to understand what it is like to become a student again when you are already a doctor of science. You have to have courage." In a way, experienced researchers have become neophytes again (Yakhontova, 1997) and have had to give up their authority and may lose confidence, even if temporarily.

The difficulty of writing in a foreign language brings about strong emotions, from tears of joy to anger and resistance. One writing center director described how she worked with a seasoned researcher who had just written his first article in English by himself. Before that, he would have his writing translated from Russian into English:

> When he wrote this article—we worked on it for a long time and it was finally published—he came to me, and he almost cried, he was so happy: "It's my first article in English!" Since then, instead of writing in Russian first, he's been writing in English.

Another participant recalled the opposite reaction of a professor confronted with having to conceptually change his article: "One professor told me: 'If that is so, then they need to learn Russian. I am not writing in English.' And he is a doctor of physics and mathematics, full professor. It's difficult to deal with this mindset."

It is not surprising, perhaps, that some writing center directors said that learning to write in another language required courage and that they saw their task as helping writers gain confidence. Thus, writing centers may function as safe houses (Canagarajah, 1997) that allow writers space to be vulnerable, to practice writing in a different language without fear of rejection, and with support from more experienced language users before they submit their manuscripts to a journal. With their own long-term goals of developing independent writers on the one hand and with faculty seeking quick solutions through translation on the other, writing centers can work towards mediating these conflicting orientations and developing new pedagogies.

Writing Center Pedagogy Is Constructed Through Everyday Practice Grounded in Local Needs Rather Than Borrowed Theoretical Concepts

A writing center is a practice situated in a local context. Even though my participants collaborated with U.S. specialists to study the work of writing centers in the US and some of them visited writing centers at Harvard University, MIT, and Purdue University, they found that U.S. writing center pedagogy has not fit their context. As one director observed,

> Our approach is different because we work with a different group of people . . . with teaching and research faculty. We are not involved with students yet. This is what makes us different and, at the same time, presents problems because we are working with writers who had no formal training in writing for publication. We would be in a better position if they were trained and took courses in academic writing.

Therefore, the approach to tutoring has to reflect the unique needs of these writers, which participants described as follows: addressing language proficiency issues, creating a collaborative environment appropriate for working with faculty, many of whom are already experienced researchers; offering various forms of instruction and staying flexible to accommodate writers' busy schedules; and encouraging and motivating faculty to increase their confidence when writing in a foreign language for a new audience.

According to the participants, faculty have to understand the norms for writing for publication in international spaces (e.g., citation practices and responding to editor's feedback); differences between academic and non-academic writing; requirements for good academic writing; and rhetorical differences between Russian and Anglo-American discourses. Understanding conventions of different academic genres, such as articles, conference abstracts, and proposals was also mentioned as important. Participants pointed out that, with the added problem of low language proficiency, they may discuss grammar issues more than in the US.

When working on these issues, participants approached faculty as partners rather than instructors. This approach, it seems, may offer a non-hierarchical, non-threatening way of introducing faculty to new concepts and conventions and might help to reduce faculty's initial resistance. One participant described her approach in the following way:

> When a faculty member or researcher comes to us, I understand that we are in a peer relationship. I may have expertise in English, but I am not an expert in their field. In other words, I respect what they do . . . I understand that their thinking is different. . . . So we have to have a conversation. I can't tell them . . . I mean I can express my opinion, I can make a recommendation, but I respect when they want to do it in their own way. So I have to find a common language, to reach a compromise. . . . It's a dialog between equals.

She explained that this dialog has been necessary to understand writers' ideas and not to take away their authorship.

Writing center directors also seem to value the collaborative, peer-like nature of their work for the learning environment it allows them to create. One director, for example, described how some of her seminars have brought together faculty from different disciplines and of different ages and experiences: "The writing center brings together people that may not otherwise get together in one classroom: young and experienced, physicists and lyricists, they all come with a different level of English proficiency."

She described how this combination has resulted in a "synergy," a productive dialog that enriches faculty's understanding of their own research. As she stated, researchers begin to "like what they do even more." Furthermore, this environment seemed to allow researchers to develop an ability to talk about their writing across disciplinary and generational differences: "Young researchers have a different attitude, they ask [older] professors tricky questions that make them think." Another director noted that tutoring sometimes has resulted in collaborations between faculty writers and writing consultants. It appears that the collaborative forms of interaction with writers can help faculty become more comfortable with communication outside their usual discourse community and produce generative forms of collaboration.

Another need that influences writing center pedagogy is that faculty have busy lives. Therefore, writing centers have to stay flexible as to accommodate faculty time constraints and multiple responsibilities. Writing centers have offered different forms of engagement, from individual consultations to more direct forms of instruction, like short seminars and longer courses, thus blending a collaborative, non-directive approach with a directive approach. One director, for example, said that her center has offered seminars every two weeks, 20 seminars per semester. Faculty have preferred to sign up for shorter seminars because longer courses require a great deal of preparation. They also seem to prefer face-to-face rather than online courses because the dropout rate in online courses is high. Another director commented that they had "shifted away from weekly workshops, which were inefficient, to short courses, which are better attended."

Having to work within faculty's time constraints, writing centers have varied the mode of engagement (e.g., online, face-to-face, asynchronously) and the length of sessions. Some have not set a time limit for consultations and continue until the writer and the consultant have achieved the expected result—the finished product, which satisfies both. One director said, for example:

> A consultation can last two or three hours. And if it's online, 24 hours. I can send my feedback and say, "Take a look." They get excited. They send it back to me [with changes] and say, "Please have another look."

To keep the writing momentum, a consultation has often become a long, extended conversation through email exchange or a series of sessions.

Consultations themselves have required preparation for consultants, as described by one of the participants:

> You may understand that the process is not that simple because we are not native speakers. We have to read [the article] first.... Also the articles may be from different fields: physics, mechanical engineering, sociology. So when the clients arrive we are ready to talk with them.

Another director (who has worked in the writing center for students) said she may give students assignments before their sessions, particularly when students have come to practice conversation in English, a service this writing center also has provided. The assignment may have included reading or watching the news in English.

Writing in a foreign language for a new audience with new expectations requires encouragement and motivation. As one participant said, the goal of her writing center has been to "make writers who don't write, write." Motivation may involve following up with authors who have used the center, reminding them that the writing center is there to support them. Three of the participants mentioned that writers have needed a push: "Administrative push is needed in Russia." One of them even wished that writing center courses were mandatory so that faculty could receive continuous instruction and move forward faster. It appears that the non-hierarchical approach to encourage writers has worked alongside the need for an administrative push.

The result of this pedagogy, participants said, is that faculty begin to perceive writing centers positively, and their awareness of the concept of academic writing has been growing. Furthermore, as one participant said, writing in English adds "system and logic," or organization and clarity, to writing in Russian. Another participant noted that even if articles they worked on were rejected, they have not been rejected because of issues with the writing.

Although all participants acknowledged the need for student writing, they did not focus much on writing pedagogy when talking about students, except one participant, who directed the student-oriented center. Many noted, however, that students have needed more writing assignments and more motivation to write. Among the ways to increase student engagement in writing, participants mentioned holding writing contests for students, involving graduate students in writing and publishing, and rewarding students with extra points for consultations in the writing center. The director of the student-oriented center also talked about developing a peer consulting program and making consulting prestigious among students.

To summarize, writing centers have taken a measured approach to the U.S. idea of a writing center by focusing on the needs of writers at their universities, such as developing language proficiency, increasing motivation, and offering different forms of engagement to accommodate faculty's busy lives. In a way, they have functioned as multiliteracy centers, offering faculty not only speaking and writing support, but also instruction in practices that surround the work of an academic, from the use of databases and citation indexes to responding to editors' comments. Even though Russian writing centers have worked in a different linguistic and cultural context with a different group of writers, the collaborative, flexible approach that would encourage writers to write seems similar to the approach used in the US perhaps because this approach has helped best when we address writerly problems. These problems have not been specific to those who write in a non-native language and have had to do more with experience of transitioning from one discourse community to another.

Writing Centers Serve as Places of Professionalization

As writing centers have participated in internationalization, their educational goals, the range of issues they address, and the variety of modes of instruction they have provided to faculty from all disciplines have positioned them as writing programs (although for faculty rather than for students). Participants described that to be able to manage these programs, they sought opportunities for their own professional development as center administrators and experts in academic writing, provided training to other instructors and writing consultants, and built their own professional network.

Managing a writing center has been a new but welcome challenge for the participants. One director recalled that she was questioning her abilities to serve as director: "It was not something I've been doing all my life." For some directors, managing a center and learning how to be a consultant rather than a teacher was new:

> It was important to understand this shift from a teacher to a consultant because when we work with professors and researchers, they look at you as an instructor, but not quite in the same sense as when we work with students. In other words, one must have certain skills and competencies to be able to work with researchers.

The participants also talked about needing to build confidence of their own and credibility and trust within the university to be able to do their work. In the words of one director,

> To understand that I have the credentials, the expertise [to work with researchers], . . . I had to present a clear argument

> that my suggestions [for revision] wouldn't compromise the article. This has to be openly discussed with writers because there are disciplines in natural sciences that sort of look down on us in the humanities.

Working with writers, who sometimes may be more experienced researchers, has also put pressure on the directors themselves to raise their expertise in academic writing. One participant shared that becoming a writing center director motivated her to fulfill her dream of studying Anglo-American rhetoric at Harvard University. She believed this new learning experience would give her more authority and credibility among faculty writers and would allow her to give feedback to them with greater confidence.

The directors shared that their position has involved multiple responsibilities that often have not been clearly defined and that pull them in different directions. They have often been invited to other universities to conduct workshops. Some had to divide time between teaching and directing the center, running the center on different campus locations, and managing center staff. With these responsibilities, participants had difficulty finding time for professional development and research. Two participants, for example, noted a desire to do research, yet they could not find time to analyze the data they had been collecting.

A main concern for directors, however, has been finding consultants with a sufficient level of English-language proficiency and creating a steady cohort. For example, one director, while discussing how Russian writing centers have differed from their American counterparts, said: "We are faced with different issues. Our main issue is to find [consultants] who can speak English first and foremost. Other issues are of secondary importance." Some directors have relied on their English departments for a pool of candidates for consultants; others have trained their English department faculty as consultants. Yet others have sought prospective tutors among participants of their workshops and seminars. The student-oriented center has handpicked teaching assistants who have demonstrated interest and have brought ideas of their own about the writing center.

Creating a pool of trained tutors is a slow process. As one director noted,

> We find people and train them. Their numbers are growing. It's just such a slow process that requires a great deal of time. But we are getting to the point where we have a group of tutors that can train other tutors.

Training may take different forms: apprenticeship, observation, or a conversation about the structure and content of seminars, workshops, and consultations. One center that has functioned as a lab within a language department has conducted tutor training as part of professional development for the departmental faculty. Another center has recently piloted a professional development program to train instructors for academic writing centers. In the student-oriented center, the director has offered a non-credit course to students and has assigned classical writing center literature from the US. She also has trained tutors to identify specific issues and common problems, including grammar.

The problem for the existing centers, then, is to sustain their efforts and continue their work by developing a reliable staff, so that the work of the writing center does not rely solely on the director, as one participant expressed it:

> My big task in my first two years as a director was get us in a place that was sustainable because due to the financial crisis here in 2014 and pressures to cut back, I had concerns about how we're going to maintain adequate staff and also what might happen if I should leave at some point whether it was for a different job or for family reasons.

The question of continued financial support, after the 5-100 Project money has run out, has also been raised by the participants: "Right now we are funded by the 5-100 program, but every year, we are discussing what to do once the program is over: Would the center become one of the university-supported units and be funded from the university budget?" Considering the future of writing centers, participants also mentioned that many universities have had trouble in moving forward in their thinking about the teaching of academic writing. Although there has been interest in helping faculty to write and publish in English, there has not been enough interest, as one participant noted, in writing centers for students, and funding them would be difficult.

As they seek ways to sustain their work, these writing centers have also been building their own association of academic writing experts, the National Writing Center Consortium, which now has organized an annual academic writing conference. They have maintained an active website for the organization and a Facebook page, and have invited each other to their universities to conduct writing seminars and tutor training workshops, thus growing their network and influence. In the words of one participant, "When we were establishing the Consortium, it was important for us to be able to discuss our experience, to have a community of like-minded people, to support each other in what we do." In the words of another participant, a strong professional organization would also help to assert their position in higher education and advocate for adding writing to the higher education curriculum:

> Our association will work to draw the attention of the Ministry of Education to the teaching of writing, to the need to change the higher education paradigm, and not only in higher education but also in secondary education, where writing is also a missing component.

The "paradigm change," as this participant implied, has required governmental support, and the organization might help coordinate the efforts of individual educators in garnering it. Yet, as another participant observed, there has not been much discussion about extending the teaching of writing beyond writing in English for publication: "So much [is] focused on English, and in the disciplinary sense, so much of it is being driven by English."

To summarize, the writing centers in Russia have worked towards creating a larger cohort of trained writing consultants and promoting a greater awareness of the need to teach academic writing in higher education. This might, however, present a point of tension because the concept of teaching academic writing seems to be firmly connected to teaching writing in English, specifically for publication. Therefore, extending the concept of academic writing beyond a niche service for faculty may require a broader discussion that addresses student writing and writing in Russian.

Developing a Bigger Picture from the Snapshot

The snapshot of writing centers in Russia has captured the remarkable progress made in just a few years. Currently, they seem to have been able to find a balance among conflicting expectations. Set up to respond to the demands of academic capitalism, they were able to create space and time to begin to establish a culture of writing in an educational setting that did not promote it. What started as a goal to develop writing for publication among faculty may then extend beyond it to include writing for students.

Writing centers in Russia have served as places where rhetorical traditions and academic discourses rooted in often conflicting social, political, and cultural values come into contact. As writing centers have mediated these conflicts, they have developed pedagogies to support writers as they develop greater rhetorical flexibility necessary for negotiating differences between discourse communities. As faculty writers develop a greater understanding of rhetorical differences in academic writing and thus become more attuned to and more comfortable with the differences in writing across fields, languages, and cultures, they may also reflect on how they write in Russian. How might the characteristics of anglophone discourse, for example, influence their writing in Russian? Furthermore, faculty who participate in writing center consultations, seminars, and classes, may develop a greater awareness of the writing process and of the need for using writing to support student learning. How might they be applying concepts and practices they acquire in the writing center to their own instruction?

Writing centers in Russia have sought to develop their pedagogy on their own terms instead of borrowing pedagogies from the U.S. First, they have applied the idea of a centralized writing support to faculty rather than students, and secondly, they have blended both collaborative and more directive methods of instruction to meet the needs of faculty writers. While U.S. writing centers have still been developing their pedagogies for multilingual writers (Rafoth, 2015) and very few have positioned themselves as multilingual (see, for example, Lape, 2019), Russian writing centers started as centers to meet the needs of writers for whom English was not a native language and have now been moving towards greater understanding of rhetoric and composition in language teaching.

Despite the obvious differences between Russian and U.S. writing centers, one may observe fascinating points of connection that writing researchers and practitioners both in Russia and the US may want to explore. For example, researchers in the US may be intrigued by the potential of writing centers to develop into full-fledged writing programs for faculty. Another opportunity involves exploring tensions identified in Russian writing centers that are also common in U.S. writing-across-the-curriculum programs and writing centers: administrators' desire for fast results versus writing faculty and tutors' commitment to longer-term results. Also, with a growing understanding of English as lingua franca and as a multitude of local Englishes, writing centers and programs have played a role in developing multilingual dispositions, important for predominantly monolingual cultures like Russia and the US. This development, however, has been sometimes met with resistance in both countries, as the Russian writing center directors reported in this study, and as writing center directors in the US also have experienced in their practice, albeit in a different way, when they have encountered negative attitudes towards local varieties of English in academic writing (Griffin & Glushko, 2016). It would be interesting to see how these tensions are negotiated in both countries.

Russian writing centers as places of professionalization seem to operate within a niche field of English for research publication purposes. Extending this field into a larger discipline might require creating a bilingual framework for teaching academic writing, as Irina Korotkina (2018) has proposed. Meanwhile, in the absence of professional departments and formal education in writing studies, Russian writing centers have been developing professional consultants through apprenticeship, collaborations, and tutor-training workshops—methods that may serve well the purpose of centers whose work is to deliver sessions that are not mass produced but fine-tuned to the needs and circumstances of faculty at their universities. Professionalization, however, would eventually require a theoretical framework from which to approach the teaching of writing in Russia, one that would reflect the values of writing center work and be congruent with the goals for higher education in Russia. Conducting a meta-analysis of current literature on academic writing and writing centers in Russia might contribute to that while also helping international researchers on writing see where Russia enters the conversation on teaching writing in higher education.

References

Bakin, E. V. (2013). Tsentr akademicheskogo pis'ma: Opyt sozdaniya [Creating a center for academic writing: Sharing experience]. *Higher Education in Russia/Vysshee obrazovanie v Rossii, 8–9,* 113–116. http://vovr.ru/upload/8-913.pdf.

Bazanova, E. M. (2015). Laboratorija nauchnoj kommunikacii: Rossijskij opyt [A laboratory for scholarly communication: Russian experience]. *Higher Education in Russia/Vysshee obrazovanie v Rossii, 8–9,* 136–143. http://vovr.ru/upload/8-915.pdf.

Bazanova, E. M., & Korotkina, I. B. (2017). Rossijskij consortsium tsentrov pis'ma. [Russian consortium of writing centers]. *Higher Education in Russia/Vysshee obrazovanie v Rossii, 4,* 50–57. http://vovr.ru/upload/4-17.pdf.

Bizzell, P. (1994). *Academic discourse and critical consciousness.* University of Pittsburgh Press.

Bollinger, K. M. (2016). Introducing Western writing theory and pedagogy to Russian students: The Writing and Communication Center at the New Economic School. In P. Zemliansky & K. St.Amant (Eds.), *Rethinking post-communist rhetoric: Perspectives on rhetoric, writing, and professional communication in post-soviet spaces* (pp. 19–42). Lexington Books.

Bruffee, K. (1995). Peer tutoring and the "conversation of mankind." In C. Murphy & J. Law (Eds.), *Landmark essays on writing centers* (Vol. 9) (pp. 87–98). Routledge.

Butler, D. B., Trosclair, E., Zhou, Y., & Wei, M. (2014). Student and teacher perceptions of academic English writing in Russia. *The Journal of Teaching English for Specific and Academic Purposes, 2*(2), 203–227. http://doi.org/10.2139/ssrn.2735380.

Canagarajah, A. S. (1997). Safe houses in the contact zone: Coping strategies of African-American students in the academy. *College Composition and Communication, 48*(2), 173–196. https://doi.org/10.2307/358665.

Canagarajah, A. S. (2002). *A geopolitics of academic writing.* University of Pittsburgh Press.

Canagarajah, A. S. (2012). Teacher development in a global profession: An autoethnography. *TESOL Quarterly, 46*(2), 258–279. https://doi.org/10.1002/tesq.18.

Charmaz, K. (2006). *Grounded theory: A practical guide through qualitative analysis.* Sage.

Creese, A., & Blackledge, A. (2010). Translingualing in the bilingual classroom: A pedagogy for learning and teaching? *The Modern Language Journal, 94,* 103–115. https://doi.org/10.1111/j.1540-4781.2009.00986.x.

Creswell, J. W. (2007). *Qualitative inquiry & research design: Choosing among five approaches.* Sage.

Denny, H., Nordlof, J., & Salem, L. (2018). "Tell me exactly what it was that I was doing that was so bad": Understanding the needs and expectations of working-class students in the writing center. *The Writing Center Journal, 37*(1), 67–98. https://www.jstor.org/stable/26537363.

Donahue, C. (2009). "Internationalization" and composition studies: Reorienting the discourse. *College Composition and Communication, 61*(2), 212–243. https://www.jstor.org/stable/40593441.

Frumina, E., & West, R. (2012). *Internationalization of Russian higher education: The English language dimension.* British Council. https://www.britishcouncil.ru/sites/default/files/internationalisation_of_russian_higher_education.pdf.

Ganzler, S., Meister, S., & King, C. (2009). The Bologna process and its impact on higher education at Russia's margins: The case of Kaliningrad. *Higher Education, 57,* 533–547. https://doi.org/10.1007/s10734-008-9187-4.

Griffin, K. R., & Glushko, T. (2016). Caught between the promise and the past: A view from the writing center. *Composition Studies, 44*(2), 167–171. https://compstudiesjournal.com/fall-2016-44-2/.

Korotkina, I. B. (2013). Ot lingvisticheskogo tsentra k tsentru akademicheskomu. [From a linguistic center to the center for academic writing]. *Higher Education in Russia/Vysshee obrazovanie v Rossii, 8–9,* 120–124. http://vovr.ru/upload/8-913.pdf.

Korotkina, I. B. (2016a). Problemy adaptacii amerikanskoj modeli centra pis'ma. [The problem of adaptation of the American model of a writing center]. *Higher Education in Russia/Vysshee obrazovanie v Rossii, 8–9*(204), 56–65. http://vovr.ru/upload/8-9-16.pdf.

Korotkina, I. B. (2016b). Universitetskie centry akademicheskogo pis'ma v Rossii: Celi i perspektivy. [University centers for academic writing: Goals and perspectives]. *Higher Education in Russia/ Vysshee obrazovanie v Rossii, 1*(197), 75–86. http://vovr.ru/upload/1-16.pdf.

Korotkina, I. B. (2018). Russian scholarly publications in anglophone academic discourse: The clash of tyrannosaurs. *Integration of Education, 22*(2), 311–323. https://doi.org/10.15507/1991-9468.091.022.201802.311-323.

Lape, N. (2019). From English-centric to multilingual: The Norman M. Eberly multilingual writing center at Dickinson College. *Composition Forum, 41.* https://compositionforum.com/issue/41/dickinson.php.

Lebedev, S. A. (2014). Russian science and education: Problems and prospects. *Russian Education and Society, 56*(1), 57–69. https://doi.org/10.2753/RES1060-93935 60106.

Leonard, R. L. (2014). Multilingual writing as rhetorical attunement. *College English*, *76*(3), 227–247. https://www.jstor.org/stable/24238241.

Lillis, T., & Curry, M. J. (2010). *Academic writing in a global context: The politics and practices of publishing in English*. Routledge.

Lu, M.-Z. (2004). An essay on the work of composition: Composing English against the order of fast capitalism. *College Composition and Communication*, *56*(1), 16–50. https://doi.org/10.2307/4140679.

Lu, M.-Z., & Horner, B. (2012). *Translingual literacy and matters of agency*. Plenary address presented at Penn State Conference on Rhetoric and Composition: Rhetoric and Writing Across Language Boundaries, State College, PA.

Magnotto, J. N. (1996, March 27–30). *Grounded theory: Research as praxis*. Paper presented at the 47th Annual Meeting of the Conference on College Composition and Communication, Milwaukee, WI. https://files.eric.ed.gov/fulltext/ED398573.pdf.

Matsuda, P. K. (2015). Writing involves the negotiation of language differences. In L. Adler-Kassner & E. Wardle (Eds.), *Naming what we know: Writing at the threshold* (pp. 68–70). Utah State University Press.

Ministry of Science and Higher Education of the Russian Federation. (n.d.). *5–100 Russian academic excellence project*. World-Class Russian Education! Retrieved September 10, 2019 from https://5top100.ru/en/universities/.

Neff, J. (2002). Capturing complexity: Using grounded theory to study writing centers. In P. Gillespie, A. Gillam, L. F. Brown, & B. Stay (Eds.), *Writing center research: Extending the conversation* (pp. 133–148). Erlbaum.

Nordlof, J. (2014). Vygotsky, scaffolding, and the role of theory in writing center work. *The Writing Center Journal*, *34*(1), 45–64. https://www.jstor.org/stable/43444147.

Pennycook, A. (1994). *The cultural politics of English as an international language*. Longman.

Pratt, M. L. (1991). Arts of the contact zone. *Profession*, *91*, 33–40. https://www.jstor.org/stable/25595469.

Rafoth, B. (2015). *Multilingual writers and writing centers*. Utah State University Press.

Salem, L. (2016). Decisions . . . decisions: Who chooses to use the writing center? *The Writing Center Journal*, *35*(2), 147–171. https://www.jstor.org/stable/43824060.

Squires, A. (2018). Writing centers and academic professionalization in the Russian Federation. In M. Rajakumar (Ed.), *Western higher education in global context* (pp. 1–22). Lexington Books.

Thaiss, C., Bräuer, G., Carlino P., Ganobcsik-Williams, L., & Sinha, A. (Eds.) (2012). *Writing programs worldwide: Profiles of academic writing in many places*. The WAC Clearinghouse; Parlor Press. https://doi.org/10.37514/PER-B.2012.0346.

Yakhontova, T. (1997). Bakhtin at home and abroad. *JAC: A Journal of Composition Theory*, *17*(1), 83–94. https://www.jstor.org/stable/20866112.

Volkova, G. L., & Shmatko, N. A. (2018, October 24). *Znanie inostrannyh jazykov rossijskimi uchenymi*. [Knowledge of foreign languages by Russian scientists]. Institute of Statistical Studies and Economic Knowledge. HSE University. https://issek.hse.ru/news/226574939.html.

Zemliansky, P., & St.Amant, K. (2013). The state of technical communication in the former USSR: A review of literature. *Technical Writing and Communication, 43*(3), 237–260. https://doi.org/10.2190/TW.43.3.b.

Appendix: Interview Guide

1. How and why was your writing center established?

    [Follow-up questions: Who initiated the establishment of the writing center? What was the role of the university administration? How did you become the director? What was your experience with teaching writing prior to becoming director? How did the university express the goals to be accomplished by establishing a writing center? What is the administrative structure of the writing center? What's the reporting structure and budget? Where is it located?]

2. Could you please describe the work of your writing center?

    [Follow-up questions: Who is the writing center for? What does the writing center do? What are the director's responsibilities?

3. How many tutors do you have? Who are they? What are the tutor's responsibilities? How are the tutors chosen? Are they trained, and, if yes, how? What are your goals in tutoring? How do you go about accomplishing these goals?

4. What does a typical day/tutoring session in your writing center look like? What documentation is used in your center (e.g., forms, reports)?

5. What difficulties do you encounter in your writing center as director? How do you overcome them? Where or who do you go to if you have difficulties, questions, or want to talk through ideas? What resources and publications do you use to develop ideas about your center?]

6. How do you envision the future of your writing center?

    [Follow-up questions: In what way (if any) does the writing center affect views on teaching writing/composition in English and in Russian? What professional organizations do you and your center participate in? What is your relationship with the National Writing Center Consortium?]

7. Is there anything important about your center or the teaching of academic writing at your university that I haven't asked about?

8. Are there any questions you'd like to ask me?

6

A Russian Model of a Writing Center: The Case of HSE University

Svetlana Suchkova
HSE University, Moscow

The writing center movement is a fairly new concept to Russia. The movement started in the 2010s as a response to government initiatives aimed at making the publications of Russian researchers more visible in the global arena. Many Russian writing centers are still in search of their identities and operational modes. This chapter is an attempt to analyze one model of a Russian writing center, the Academic Writing Center (AWC) at HSE University (HSE), as a case. The HSE AWC was established in 2011 and became a pioneer in launching university-supported programs for faculty. Unlike many American and European writing centers, the HSE Academic Writing Center works only with faculty and high-potential groups of researchers. The Center provides educational services to help researchers to master their academic writing and public speaking skills via courses and workshops. It also offers individual consultations on draft papers. To better cater to the needs of the HSE researchers, the AWC has regularly conducted surveys and designed educational programs on demand. The collected data on event attendance and feedback on the organized events allow us to evaluate the effectiveness of this type of model. The analysis of writing needs and challenges that Russian adult learners face when writing papers for publication could contribute to the discussion about effective integration of multi-lingual researchers into the global research community.

The influence of publications in peer-reviewed journals on institutional reputation and global rankings has generated an ever-increasing pressure on faculty to write and publish, particularly in English. The chapters in the first section of this volume as well as the broader literature have shown more and more understanding that faculty struggle to meet writing-related challenges and require institutional support. "For faculty who are hampered by anxiety

DOI: https://doi.org/10.37514/INT-B.2021.1428.2.06

about writing and publishing, who struggle to make time to write, or who simply feel too exhausted to write, writing programs can make the difference between a *promising* and a *successful* career." (Gray et al., 2013, p. 95). Faculty may have little practice of scholarly writing beyond writing dissertations and need to develop their literacy skills and strategies for publication (Flowerdew, 2015; Geller & Eodice, 2013; Lillis & Curry, 2010). In this respect, writing centers and teaching excellence centers have great potential to accommodate the diverse needs of university faculty.

Having had a long history of working with students, American writing centers now have expanded their support to faculty by providing them with a range of programs for their professional development as writers (Geller & Eodice, 2013). Many American writing centers advocate for various literacy events: writing support groups (Clark-Oats & Cahill, 2013; Eodice & Cramer, 2001), writing retreats (Anson, 2013; Shendel et al., 2013), immersive writing residences (Moore et al., 2013), publication-focused workshops, editing consultations, and panels with prolific writers (Baldi et al., 2013). These programs have differed in their scope and depth. The available accounts of successful practices have shown that such programs have promoted and sustained writing in academia. They have helped build a community of writers and hone faculty's facility in writing for publication.

The problem of seeking ways to assist faculty in writing has seemed especially acute in many multi-lingual centers that work in cultures where English is an additional language (Burgess & Cargill, 2013; Cho, 2009; Englander & Corcoran, 2019; Li et al., 2018). As English-medium journals have a leading role in the research publishing market (Lillis & Curry, 2010), English as an additional language (EAL) scholars are strongly advised to write papers in English. And this inevitably adds an extra burden on EAL faculty. Academics can be well-published in their first language (L1) but have to acquire a different way of communicating their research contributions internationally. The challenges EAL academics face stem not only from lower English facility than that of anglophones (Flowerdew, 1999), but also from different culturally bound thought patterns (Friedlander, 1997; Kaplan, 1966) and "the clash between the two writing traditions" (Korotkina, 2018, p. 320), which academics may not be aware of. Besides, it is known that in comparison with native speakers of English, non-native speakers need more time to produce a written text (Flowerdew, 1999). Realizing the challenges EAL academics encounter, many institutions commit to providing focused support programs in the booming field of English for research publication purposes (ERPP). ERPP is defined as "a branch of EAP addressing the concerns of professional researchers and post-graduate students who need to publish in peer-reviewed international journals" (Cargill & Burgess, 2008, p. 75), but it is much broader and more complex, especially for those who use English as an additional language. Work within this field requires writers to be aware of genre characteristics and academic rhetorical features, international standards for publication, the steps in the publication process, and etiquette for communication with editors and reviewers (Flowerdew, 2015; Reid, 2010).

Russia is also part of the race for higher university ratings. Government initiatives aimed at making the publications of Russian researchers more visible in the global arena resulted in the Russian writing center movement, which started in the 2010s (see Chapter 1 and Chapter 5). Now, Russian writing centers are gaining momentum; however, many of them are still in search of their identities and operational modes. Many emerging centers find themselves at a crossroads: choosing whether to introduce translation and proofreading services to researchers or to offer various educational programs. The cultural and institutional contexts, the aims writing centers pursue, and the resources they have, inevitably lead to a range of writing center models. Obviously, there is no universal blueprint for a faculty-focused writing center. However, sharing successful approaches could be helpful for other writing centers that explore opportunities for integrating multi-lingual researchers into the global research community.

In this chapter, I will describe the operational model of the Academic Writing Center (AWC) at HSE University, Moscow. Part of the HSE internationalization policy is creating a stimulating environment for the faculty so that they can publish papers in international peer-reviewed journals, thus enhancing the institutional profile and visibility (HSE University, 2020). The university has built a system of faculty professional development in which the AWC plays an important role. The operational model of the Center is based on the assumption that it should satisfy the needs of academics, employing strategies that are effective for cultivating their professional career growth. The major principles of the model are institutionalized support for the Center's educational services, developing customized client-oriented programs, and ensuring equal and free access to all HSE employees.

Among the key indicators of the success of the AWC, I consider the rise in usage, clients' positive evaluation of the Center's services, and the Center's ability to adapt to the changing environment. I will describe the AWC's activities, share clients' feedback, and also present data on the writing needs and challenges of Russian scholars, which the Center collected from 2015 to 2019.

I suggest that a university committed to faculty support should develop a well-thought-out strategy and create optimum conditions for professional development. I assert that the model of the HSE Academic Writing Center proves to be effective in assisting scholars to cope with a demanding reality and can be generalizable to other faculty-focused writing centers given institutional support.

This article could also contribute to the heated debate on the idea of a writing center (Bouquet & Lerner, 2008; Salem & Follet, 2013) by adding another cultural perspective. Writing centers can work not only with students but can also offer and facilitate a spectrum of customized programs for faculty development. Centers can be agents of change by having an impact on the writing culture of the university.

Russian Cultural Context for Writing Centers

Although the role of writing centers is increasing in Russia, they still have a long way to go in coping with the challenges the Russian cultural context imposes on them. One of the major challenges is that the ambitious, top-down goals of increasing the international visibility of Russian scholars' research have not been supported by the system of education itself. As academic writing in English has yet to be developed as a discipline in Russia and introduced into university curricula (Korotkina, 2017, 2018; see also Chapter 1, Chapter 3, and Chapter 5), scholars' prior education does not provide much practice with composed writing in English, which is typical of many other EFL/ESL writers (Leki, 1992). Russian academics' writing skills in English are usually limited. Consequently, many writing centers have to take on the responsibility of filling the gaps in their clients' formal education. In addition to fixing mechanical problems, writing centers have to teach basic process writing skills, facilitate researchers' critical reading skills in English, and stimulate their academic vocabulary development.

Another challenge all Russian writing centers experience is lack of qualified staff to assist academics in their research writing, which may not be an issue in U.S. centers. Russian centers have tried to employ native speakers of English, but not all universities can afford this. Usually, Russian teachers of English serve as tutors, very often as part-timers. The paradox of the situation in Russia is that very often the blind lead the blind: teachers of English, having an instrumental use of the language do not publish much but have to teach others how to publish internationally (Bogolepova, 2016; see also Chapter 4). Writing instructors themselves need training in order to offer ERPP courses, "those that teach the genres of the English language research article and associated activities, with the primary goal of enhancing the participants' ability to write for international publication" (Li et al., 2018, p. 117).

Having directed two writing centers, I realize how hard it is to find an instructor who has profound knowledge of EAP/ESAP/ERPP. Until recently, there were almost no degree specialists in the area of academic writing or in rhetoric and composition, as pedagogical universities train would-be instructors for secondary schools focusing on teaching general English. Pedagogical university graduates often have no formal training in academic writing in English and learn in the process of teaching. Being employed as university instructors, they explore various opportunities for self-development in order to master their ESP/EAP teaching skills. We definitely need a network of writing professionals to support each other.

Yet another challenge is the demand for quick results, both on the part of universities and faculty themselves. Being busy multi-taskers, academics are practical and results oriented (Bogolepova et al., 2017; Harmer, 2007; Knowles, 1984, 1990), critical, and demanding. They are likely to be very selective and self-directed, which implies that writing centers need to offer services that can help them achieve results in the shortest possible time. However, academics' low level of English can be an inhibiting factor for publication success in English (Frumina & West, 2012). As many authors have used the services of professional translators or teachers of English for years, they often perceive emerging writing centers as free translation agencies or "fix-it shops" (North, 1984, p. 435). It would be a generalization to state that all Russian academics have a low level of English (Korotkina, 2017); however, academics should realize that learning to write in English is a better strategy than just translating or proofreading texts with the help of others. It takes time and institutional policy to change such perceptions and persuade academics to invest effort in mastering their writing skills in English.

As my observations as a writing instructor show, Russian English has a range of distinctive features: sentences tend to be long and wordy, paragraphs unfocused; Russian writers overuse passive voice and synonyms, making referents unclear; writing is non-linear and less guided; there are many unsupported generalizations and weak arguments; and the authorial voice is often not developed. These claims are supported by some studies on Russian undergraduates' writing (Chuikova, 2018; Pospelova, 2016; Terenin, 2015; see also Chapter 8). Even those who are well versed in English need focused training on higher-order concerns before brushing up on language accuracy. As Korotkina (2018) has argued, "in Russia, the deeply rooted tradition of opaque and wordy writing that developed in the period of the Soviet isolation, creates more problems for scholars than the lack of English" (p. 320). We all, including Russian writing instructors, need to acquire a different argumentation paradigm and awareness of the reader's expectations. We all need to consciously apply editing strategies to make texts intelligible and more accessible to international readers.

Many of these culture-specific factors, however, can be overcome, as our experience has indicated. Centers need to raise clients' awareness of cultural differences of academic discourse and teach researchers to conform to international conventions of research writing to fulfill editors and reviewers' expectations. Centers need to offer customized services, taking into consideration clients' writing facility and specific writing needs. It seems more efficient to promote life-long learning strategies than to orient authors toward quick results. There are definitely multiple ways of investing in writing support initiatives, and there is no model that fits all. I would like to contribute to the discussion about faculty support by sharing one model of a writing center that can work well given institutional investment.

HSE's Model of a Writing Center

The HSE Academic Writing Center was established in 2011 at the initiative of the university administration. From the very beginning, the Center was designed as a space for professional development to enable academics to get their papers in print. The AWC gradually introduced short-term courses: six in the period from 2011 to 2013. The Center also organized 30 lectures and 140 proofreading sessions in the same period (Bakin, 2013). The first trial-and-error steps helped the Center shape up its philosophy and policy from investing money in papers to investing it in developing the skills of writers. The Center has been rapidly advancing in four major directions: as a research lab, an educational hub, a consultancy service, and a resource center.

Structurally, the Center is part of the HSE Academic Development Department, supervised by a vice-rector and financially supported by the university. According to the Center's policy, all services are free for the HSE faculty. Operationally, we have organized all the events on the Moscow campus and have reached other campuses online. All the events have required online registration. The Center has regularly advertised its services and events on the Center's site, via corporate email, and on social media. We have also participated in adaptation programs for new faculty and organized the Academic Writing Center Day to promote the Center's activities.

The Center is governed by a full-time director and two managers. On a contract basis, we employ four consultants and from five to 10 trainers annually. Three consultants are native speakers of English, and one is bilingual, who was invited in response to a consistent client demand for a Russian-speaking consultant. The consultants come from various educational backgrounds, all having editing experience as a pre-requisite. They run individual consultations and sometimes do workshops. The trainers who conduct courses and seminars are primarily Russian university teachers of English. We carefully select both trainers and consultants and provide them with on-going training, support them methodologically, create resources and training materials, and thoroughly monitor the quality of services. The predicted downstream effect of the professional development of trainers may be improvement of academic writing programs for students, too.

In 2019, we launched a new project—School of Trainers—with the aim of enabling university teachers of English to develop self-study materials and conduct workshops for academics in the field of research writing. We have just opened a resource center, and now we are seeking ways to engage more clients with self-study materials.

Target Audience

HSE academics, like those in other Russian universities, have a jagged language profile. There are no institutional employment requirements concerning the level of proficiency in English; however, the faculty are encouraged to publish their research in high-profile international peer-reviewed journals. To cater to the different language needs of the faculty, the university created a system of multi-level English professional development (PD) programs to provide an opportunity for faculty to improve their general language skills. The AWC deals more with writing for publication problems.

We were interested in the language level of our clients. To identify their readiness for academic communication in English, the Center launched a diagnostic module for the university talent pool program participants in 2018 (n = 106) and in 2019 (n = 100). They have been our primary audience. The fact that all of them were selected for this university-supported program indicates that all of them were ambitious, career-focused, and goal-oriented. For this group, publications in English are crucial for getting financial bonuses from the university. The module aimed to identify researchers' language needs so that we could make informed decisions about targeted PD programs for the clients. Another objective of the module was to provide each participant with personalized feedback about the level of English and recommendations for improvement.

The module results showed that the majority of this group of high achievers had Common European Framework of Reference for Languages (CEFR) scale scores of B2 (Council of Europe, 2014) and higher (see Table 6.1). Although the B2 level, which corresponds to independent users of the language, seems like the very minimum for efficient academic writing, these intermediate level learners need both linguistic support and training in anglophone conventions of research writing. They were unlikely to be formally trained in writing an article in English; therefore, they also needed focused training on genre features, rhetorical patterns, and navigating the publication process to meet journal submission requirements.

Table 6.1. Level of Language Proficiency According to CEFR

Level		A1	A2	B1	B2	C1	C2
Speaking	2018	–	5%	8%	36%	32%	8%
	2019	–	7%	17%	42%	27%	7%
Writing	2018	–	4%	13%	37%	27%	10%
	2019	2%	7%	31%	37%	17%	6%

Asking participants directly about their particular writing difficulties for publication (Brookes & Grundy, 2009; Flowerdew, 1999) can give valuable information about each individual researcher's problems and the strategies they use to cope with these problems.

The respondents to the Center's survey on consultations (n = 104) identified three top language challenges as barriers to English-medium publications: grammar and syntax (61.5%), punctuation (55.8%), and clarity of expression (41.3%). Participants reported particular difficulty with articles, sentence structure, sequence of tenses, and word combinability. We obtained the same results from the diagnostic module participants. Answering the question about their writing challenges, all diagnostic module participants voiced the concern that they lacked native-like fluency of expression, and grammar and vocabulary were stumbling blocks that prevented them from writing clearly. These findings confirm that lexicogrammatical features of academic discourse are typical challenges for all EAL writers (Flowerdew, 1999). While learners focus more on lower-order concerns, trainers have observed that the problems often lie much deeper: learners have had problems with audience awareness, paragraphing, organization of ideas, stating an argument clearly, text coherence and cohesion.

I have already emphasized the importance of planning the Center's work in accordance with the audience profile. The AWC puts a premium on analyzing clients' needs and challenges. In order to collect the most comprehensive data, we have developed a system of evaluation criteria and feedback collection from clients. We conduct several surveys annually to identify clients' requests and measure their level of service satisfaction. All these data are vitally important for the Center's success, as "the most effective materials are those which are based on thorough understanding of learners' needs, that is their language difficulties, their learning objectives, their style of learning, the stage of their conceptual development . . ." (Jolly & Bolitho, 2011, p. 128). Drawing on the survey results, we decide on the topics, design courses and seminars, and tailor materials to clients' particular needs, which helps us to improve our services overall.

In the next section, I will describe these activities in more detail and present some data collected by the Center, which might be interesting to other faculty-focused writing centers.

Educational Services

Having the aim of empowering faculty's academic writing and public speaking skills, the Center provides such educational services as courses, workshops, and individual consultations. We offer 10 annual professional development courses in English, which vary in learning outputs, length (from 12 to 36 academic hours), and format (face-to-face, blended, or online). The courses are tailored to accommodate our clients' requests. All the courses are offered on a competitive basis and require a letter of motivation. They target learners with a certain level of proficiency in English, starting at the B2 level. Some of the courses focus on the structure of a research article and anglophone conventions of research writing (e.g., "Introduction to academic writing," "Basics of writing an empirical article"). Others involve analysis of journals and readership, writing and revision strategies (e.g., "Writing a draft for publication"). Other courses incorporate more work on lexicogrammatical features of academic discourse and acquisition of the particular register (e.g., "Syntax of academic writing," "Vocabulary-building strategies").

The number of course participants remains stable—around 150 people per year. Although the quality of the courses have been positively evaluated by participants (the mean score was 9.2 out of ten in 2019) we have had quite a high rate of dropouts (around 20%). The major reasons for quitting the courses, as surveys have shown, have been clients' big workloads, frequent business trips, lack of free time, inconvenient schedule, and tough home assignments, which involve writing, rewriting, and editing. We have still been looking for solutions to cope with the issue of dropouts.

All our surveys show that the clients favor short-term educational services more, as they are not as time consuming as courses. This has prompted us to increase the number of workshops and seminars. We organize them every two weeks (20 per year). They are four-hour interactive and practice-oriented classes. The evaluation mean of workshops and seminars in 2019, which was 8.8, indicates clients' engagement and interest. The data collected by the Center show that attendance rates at seminars and workshops grew from 153 people in 2015 to 591 people in 2019. Seminars have attracted not only Russian scholars but also international faculty employed by HSE. Such growth in attendance can be explained not only by the increase in the number of seminars but, most importantly, by improved advertising techniques and a broader scope of topics.

Surveys serve as a rich source of seminar topics to cover. The most frequently requested topics since 2017 have included typical mistakes of Russian writers, features of a research article, argumentation, dealing with reviewers, punctuation, grammar, and academic vocabulary. Demand for oral academic communication has been persistently strong since 2015, including conference presentations and giving lectures in English. Based on these data, we have created a range of seminars to meet these needs. Primarily, we have focused on the global issues of research writing, article genre requirements, and language problems. One of the most recent requests is organizing seminars in narrow discipline fields: law, philosophy, history, and mathematics. Due to the lack of resources and expertise, we cannot accommodate the needs connected with specific kinds of discipline-oriented discourse (Swales, 1990) fully. Nevertheless, we have attempted to invite HSE discipline specialists with a good command of English and organized a series of seminars for researchers from law and energy engineering departments. Collaboration with prolific discipline writers seems promising, as our experience has shown.

As indicated by our surveys, the most popular service has been the one-on-one consultation. Consultations have been gaining more and more popularity over the past three years—the number of consultations went up from 261 in 2015 to 847 in 2019. It took us a while to change clients' do-all-the-fixing-for-me attitude and to make them primary agents of the sessions. At the beginning, consultations were called proofreading sessions, requiring little effort from authors. Gradual systematic work led to a change in the situation. We have written detailed guidelines for both consultees and consultants. We encourage our clients to finalize their draft research papers or conference proposals before scheduling a session. We recommend self-editing their texts first. Authors are also required to study target journal standards and requirements. Such home assignments may influence the amount of text that is processed during one-hour sessions. What is important for administering consultations is the number of sessions necessary to complete the editing of one draft. The survey results on consultations showed that 33.7 percent of clients completed editing their draft papers within two consultations (two hours); but the majority needed more sessions. The time largely depends on the language quality of the initial draft. In general, the Center's users (64.4%) have come to consultations with one paper per year. Usually, we do not register clients for consecutive meetings, and the number of sessions should not exceed three per month. Such rules were established to accommodate the needs of as many clients as possible and avoid providing services to a limited number of faculty members.

Now the sessions focus on assisting academics in their development as writers by providing authors with text-specific comments on their scholarly texts. In line with tutor pedagogy (Reynolds, 2012), the consultations provide a dialogic space where authors are encouraged to actively participate in improving their texts. Using the constructivist approach, the consultants lead authors to construct new knowledge based on their previous experiences (Hoover, 1996). The consultants help to identify language problems and offer guidance for correcting them in order to strengthen the readability of the text. They also provide strategies for revision, additional resources and recommendations for further development. The sessions help writers to not only make the text mechanically sound but also to ensure its rhetorical effect. Importantly, the content of the paper entirely remains the responsibility of the author.

The working language of consultations is English, as we believe that "languaging" (Swain, 2006) creates an opportunity for authors to be engaged in discussion about the language and develop collaboration and negotiation through the medium of English. However, if authors opt for a session with a Russian expert, the session can be conducted either in English or in Russian. Russian is usually chosen by authors with less speaking facility.

It is vital to monitor the quality of consultations. In the fall of 2018, we conducted two surveys. The first survey was aimed at clients who used the consultancy services in 2018; 104 people responded to this survey online. The questionnaire was designed to find out how consultations contribute to the development of authors' writing skills and whether consultations help in the publishing process. Our findings show that 83.7 percent of respondents stated that consultations helped them to develop their writing skills. In particular, the respondents noticed improvement in lexicogrammatical aspects, especially in the use of articles (85%) and punctuation (65.5%), which appeared to be the most challenging issues. The respondents also developed their self-editing skills (50.5%) and became more conscious of sentence length (50.5%), which led to overall clarity of the text.

To a set of questions about publication activity, the respondents answered that 90 percent of papers that went through the consultancy service in 2018 had been accepted for publication. Forty-nine percent of these were published in journals indexed in Web of Science (WOS) and Scopus in such discipline areas as economics, education, business, computer science, sociology, mathematics, statistics, applied linguistics, etc. This number may imply the high quality of the consultancy service; however, we clearly realize that such publication success cannot be attributed to the language "cure" alone. Certainly, very much depends on the quality of the research itself and the right choice of the journal.

The second survey we conducted over the course of three months from January to April 2019 was to get insights into the quality of consultations and to receive feedback on the consultants' performance. Paper-based questionnaires were distributed to 165 clients immediately after their consultations. Clients evaluated sessions given by our four consultants according to such criteria as interactivity, clarity of explanation, pace, atmosphere, and efficiency. The results were really impressive: the respondents rated consultants' overall performance as 3.92 on a 4-point scale; three consultants received a maximum score for clarity of explanation, pace, and atmosphere, which suggests their high level of expertise.

The consultants have used various techniques, which have included Socratic questioning, asking for clarification, explaining rules, giving examples, or asking the researcher to read the paper aloud. The choice of techniques has depended on the consultant as well as on the clients' preference. All the consultants explained difficult points (40–68%) and invited learners to join a discussion (45–72%). The findings on effective techniques help us recommend our visitors to the consultant whose approach suits them best.

After eight years of the Center's work, I can state that the writing center model that was developed over the years can be regarded as successful in accomplishing the goals the Center sets for itself. Surveys conducted with the help of the Center of Institutional Research in 2015, 2017, and 2018 allowed us to trace the dynamics and focus on general trends in the Center's development. The results of the surveys revealed significant growth in awareness of the Center and its services among the university faculty from 76 percent in 2015 to 96 percent in 2018.

An important indicator of the Center's progress is the attendance rate of its users, which we regularly collect. As can be seen from Figure 6.1, the attendance steadily increases with a slight drop in 2016, which can be accounted for by a change in the managerial team.

A Russian Model of a Writing Center

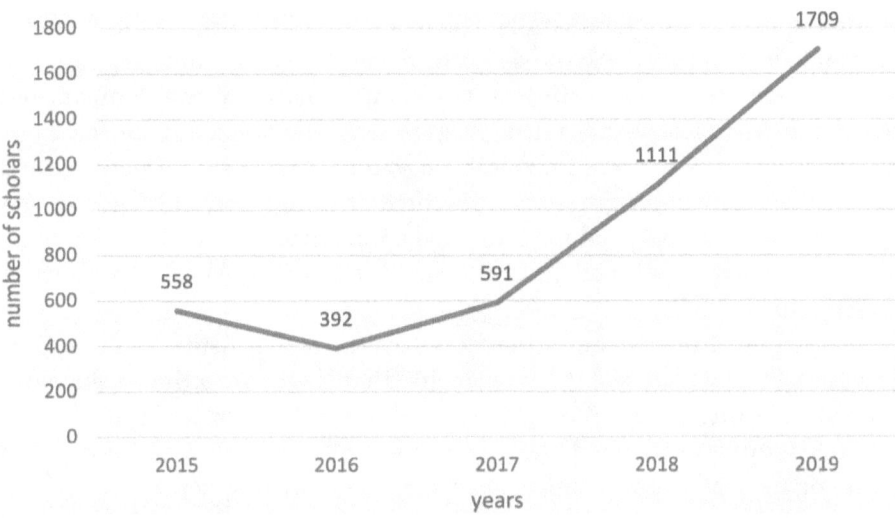

Figure 6.1. Number of scholars attending the AWC events per year.

Overall, the Center has become more noticeable in the university. There is a demand for expanding the Center's services to students. We sometimes consult with university teachers on students' writing assignments. We were also able to meet certain challenges the Center experienced at the beginning. For instance, more faculty from specific departments use the Center's services; we observe an increase in the number of applicants for the courses; we have gathered a group of writing instructors. We have also managed to create a collaborative space and make consultations educational. Yet, some problems still remain unsolved: we would like to have a wider reach on other campuses, to better cater to field-specific requests, and to offer more online events.

Necessity for Collaboration

I strongly believe that having similar goals and challenges, Russian faculty-focused writing centers should channel their efforts into networking. For the sake of creating opportunities for professional development, the National Consortium of Writing Centers was established in 2016. It aims to unite all writing instructors in Russia, disseminating the best practices and resources via conferences, on-site seminars, and courses (Bazanova & Korotkina, 2017).

All centers can benefit greatly from cooperation and expertise sharing. That is why we often invite Russian and international speakers from other writing centers and universities, experts in academic writing, textbook writers, journal editors, American fellows, and prolific writers in English.

Invited speakers run seminars and courses to contribute to the Center's program development. At the same time, as the AWC director, I receive frequent invitations from different Russian universities to run seminars and courses for the faculty and writing center staff. The geography of the Center's outreach is very wide, from Kaliningrad to Vladivostok. I have trained teachers in many universities and presented at summer schools and writing institutes and national and international conferences in Russia and abroad. These Center outreach activities demonstrate that the AWC experience is in demand.

I clearly realize that not all centers have as much institutional support and as many resources as HSE University. That is why we strive to share our experience. Recently, the AWC has offered internships for teaching instructors and writing center staff and received several applications. Although the local contexts of Russian universities vary, each writing center has gained considerable experience. We need to learn from each other and adopt and adapt best practices.

Conclusion

Having put considerable pressure on researchers to publish internationally, universities should bear this burden too and create a conducive environment for academic work. Assisting faculty as writers can take different forms and models, as the literature has shown. Russian writing centers have a promising future in offering writing services to faculty, given institutional support and collaboration. However, writing centers need clear, well-thought-out policies to operate effectively. All the services should be based on a thorough analysis of clients' needs. No matter how diverse the conditions may be, investing time and effort in helping faculty to "publish and flourish" (Gray et al., 2013, p. 96) seems to be an important mission of writing centers.

The model employed by the Academic Writing Center at HSE University appears to be efficient in achieving the goal of assisting academics to communicate their research results internationally. The Center has created formal and informal spaces for diverse collaboration and expertise sharing. The chosen university strategy of investing time, effort, and resources in facilitating the professional development of the faculty will pay off in the long run.

The AWC has great potential for growth and development to engage with the broader global community, launching international projects, and participating in international conferences. I do hope that the Center's experience can be useful for other faculty-focused centers, especially those that operate outside the anglophone world.

Acknowledgments

I would like to thank the managers of the HSE Academic Writing Center, Ksenia Maryasova and Sophia Voronina, for their enthusiasm and hard work at the Center and helping to collect and analyze the data.

References

Anson, C. (2013). Beyond the curriculum. Supporting faculty writing groups in WAC programs. In A. E. Geller & M. Eodice (Eds.), *Working with faculty writers* (pp. 21–37). Utah State University Press.

Bakin, E. V. (2013). Tsentr akademicheskogo pis'ma. Opyt sozdaniya [Creating a center for academic writing: Sharing experience]. *Vysshee obrazovanie v Rossii [Higher Education in Russia], 8–9*, 113–116. https://cyberleninka.ru/article/n/tsentr-akademicheskogo-pisma-opyt-sozdaniya.

Baldi, B., Sorcinelli, M. D., & Yun J. H. (2013). The scholarly writing continuum. A new program mode for teaching and faculty development center. In A. E. Geller & M. Eodice (Eds.), *Working with faculty writers* (pp. 38–49). Utah State University Press.

Bazanova, E. M., & Korotkina, I. B. (2017). Rossijskij consortsium tsentrov pis'ma. [Russian consortium of writing centers]. *Vysshee obrazovanie v Rossii [Higher Education in Russia], 4*, 50–57. http://www.vovr.ru/upload/4-17.pdf.

Bogolepova, S. (2016). Textbook evaluation as a means of discovering learners' and teachers' needs. *Journal of Language and Education, 2*(4), 14–23. https://doi.org/10.17323/2411-7390-2016-2-4-14-23.

Bogolepova, S., Oshchepkova, T., Shadrova, E., & Suchkova, S. (2017). English for academics concept: Course principles in teaching EAP to researchers. *Journal of the IATEFL ESP SIG, 9*, 22–37. https://www.researchgate.net/publication/320620409_English_for_academics_concept_Sourse_principles_in_teaching_EAP_to_researchers.

Bouquet, E. H., & Lerner, N. (2008). Reconsiderations: After "The idea of a writing center." *College English, 71*(2), 170–189. https://www.jstor.org/stable/25472314.

Brookes, A., & Grundy, P. (2009). *Writing for study purposes* (12th ed.). Cambridge University Press.

Burgess, S., & Cargill, M. (2013). Using genre analysis and corpus linguistics to teach research article writing. In V. Matarese (Ed.), *Supporting research writing: Roles and challenges in multilingual settings* (pp. 55–71). Woodhead Publishing.

Cargill, M., & Burgess, S. (2008). Introduction to the special issue: English for research publication purposes. *Journal of English for Academic Purposes, 7*(2), 75–138. https://doi.org/10.1016/j.jeap.2008.02.006.

Cho, D. W. (2009). Science journal paper writing in an EFL context: The case of Korea. *English for Specific Purposes, 28*(4), 230–239. https://doi.org/10.1016/j.esp.2009.06.002.

Chuikova E.S. (2018). Assessing academic texts authenticity in EFL Classes. *RUDN Journal of Psychology and Pedagogics, 15*(4), 500–511. https://doi.org/10.22363/2313-1683-2018-15-4-500-511.

Clark-Oats, A., & Cahill, L. (2013). Faculty writing groups: Writing centers and third space collaboration. In A. E. Geller & M. Eodice (Eds.), *Working with faculty writers* (pp. 111–126). Utah State University Press.

Council of Europe. (2014). Common European framework of reference for languages: Learning, teaching, assessment (CEFR). https://www.coe.int/en/web/common-european-framework-reference-languages.

Englander, K., Paltridge, B., Corcoran, J. N., & Starfield, S. (2019). *English for research publication purposes: Critical plurilingual pedagogies*. Routledge. https://doi.org/10.4324/9780429053184.

Eodice, M., & Cramer, S. (2001). Write on! A model for enhancing faculty publication. *Journal of Faculty Development, 18*(4), 113–121. https://www.semanticscholar.org/paper/Write-On!-A-Model-for-Enhancing-Faculty-Eodice-Cramer/e6749a06f21356dcf59f7fe364c35fdb51b8e7cc.

Flowerdew, J. (1999). Problems in writing for scholarly publication in English: The case of Hong Kong. *Journal of Second Language Writing, 8*(3), 243–264. https://www.sciencedirect.com/science/article/pii/S1060374399801258.

Flowerdew, J. (2015). Some thoughts on English for research publication purposes (ERPP) and related issues. *Language Teaching, 48*(2), 250–262. https://doi.org/10.1017/S0261444812000523.

Friedlander, A. (1990). Composing in English: Effects of a first language on writing in English as a second language. In B. Kroll (Ed.), *Second language writing* (pp. 109–112). Cambridge University Press. https://doi.org/10.1017/CBO9781139524551.012.

Frumina, E., & West, R. (2012). *Internationalization of Russian higher education: The English language dimension*. British Council. https://www.britishcouncil.ru/sites/default/files/internationalisation_of_russian_higher_education.pdf.

Geller, A. E., & Eodice, M. (Eds.) (2013). *Working with faculty writers*. Utah State University Press.

Gray, T., Birch, A. J., & Madson, L. (2013). How teaching centers can support faculty writers. In A. E. Geller & M. Eodice (Eds.), *Working with faculty writers* (pp. 95–110). Utah State University.

Harmer, J. (2007). *The practice of English language teaching*. Pearson Education.

HSE University (2020). ROADMAP for Implementing the Global Competitiveness Programme of the National Research University "HSE University" in 2013–2020 (SUMMARY). HSE University. https://strategy.hse.ru/en/summary.

Hoover, W.A. (1996). The practice implications of constructivism. *SEDL Letter 9*(3). http://www.sedl.org/pubs/sedletter/v09n03/practice.html.

Jolly, D., & Bolitho, R. (2011). A framework for materials writing. In B. Tomlinson (Ed.), *Materials development in language teaching* (pp. 107–134). Cambridge University Press.

Kaplan, R. B. (1966). Cultural thought patterns in intercultural education. *Language Learning, 16*(1–2), 1–20. https://doi.org/10.1111/j.1467-1770.1966.tb00804.x.

Knowles, M. S. (1984). *Andragogy in action: Applying modern principles of adult education*. Jossey-Bass.

Knowles, M. S. (1990). *The adult learner: A neglected species*. Gulf Publishing.

Korotkina, I. B. (2017). Writing centers in Russia: Limitations and challenges. SSRN. https://ssrn.com/abstract=2939495.

Korotkina, I. B. (2018). Russian scholarly publications in anglophone academic discourse: The clash of tyrannosaurs. *Integration of Education, 22*(2), 311–323. https://doi.org/10.15507/1991-9468.091.022.201802.

Leki, I. (1992). *Understanding ESL writers: A reference for teachers*. St. Martin's Press.

Li, Y., Flowerdew, J., & Cargill, M. (2018). Teaching English for research publication purposes to science students in China: A case study of an experienced teacher in the classroom. *Journal of English for Academic Purposes, 35*, 116–129. https://doi.org/10.1016/j.jeap.2018.07.006.

Lillis, T., & Curry, M. J. (2010). *Academic writing in a global context: The politics and practices of publishing in English*. Routledge.

Moore, J. L., Felten, P., & Strickland, M. (2013). Supporting a culture of writing: Faculty writing residencies as a WAC initiative. In A. E. Geller & M. Eodice (Eds.), *Working with faculty writers* (pp. 127–141). Utah State University Press.

North, S. (1984). The idea of a writing center. *College English 46*(5), 433–446. http://www.jstor.org/stable/377047.

Pospelova, T. (2016). The influence of self-editing on micro skills development in academic writing in English as a second language. *Journal of Language and Education, 2*(1), 30–38. https://doi.org/10.17323/2411-7390-2016-2-1-30-38.

Reid, N. (2010). *Getting published in international journals: Writing strategies for European social scientists*. Norwegian Social Research.

Reynolds, D. W. (2012). *One on one with second language writers. A guide for writing tutors, teachers, and consultants*. University of Michigan Press.

Salem, L., & Follet, J. (2013). The idea of a faculty writing center: Moving from troubling deficiencies to collaborative engagement. In A. E. Geller & M. Eodice (Eds.), *Working with faculty writers* (pp. 50–72). Utah State University Press.

Shendel, E., Callaway, S., Dutcher, V., & Griggs, C. (2013). Assessing the effects of faculty and staff retreats. In A. E. Geller & M. Eodice (Eds.), *Working with faculty writers* (pp. 142–162). Utah State University Press.

Swain M. (2006). Languaging, agency and collaboration in advanced second language proficiency. In Byrnes H. (Ed.), *Advanced Language Learning: The Contribution of Halliday and Vygotsky* (pp. 95–108). Bloomsbury Academic. https://doi.org/10.5040/9781474212113.ch-004.

Swales, J. (1990). *Genre analysis: English in academic and research settings*. Cambridge University Press.

Terenin, A. (2015). Unity of writing as the problem of Russian learners of English. *Procedia – Social and Behavioral Sciences, 191*, 2735–2739. https://doi.org/10.1016/j.sbspro.2015.04.683.

7

A Transnational Training Model for Peer Tutors: Authority, Rhetorical Awareness, and Language in/through Virtual Exchange Practices

Olga Aksakalova
LaGuardia Community College, New York

L. Ashley Squires
New Economic School, Moscow

In Spring 2018, students in Olga Aksakalova's "Seminar in Writing Education and Peer Tutoring" course at LaGuardia Community College in New York City and writing peer tutors in the Writing and Communication Center at the New Economic School in Moscow, directed by Ashley Squires, collaborated in a number of online activities that aimed to enrich their understanding and practice of peer tutoring. The aim of this project was to provide practicing and aspiring writing peer tutors with an opportunity to learn about how peer tutoring functions in different academic and geographic locations and across linguistic divides. From the global rhetorical and civic perspectives, this collaboration was an attempt to de-center a U.S.-based discourse on writing and facilitate instead a global dialogue between peer tutors as they get ushered into the profession of teaching writing and as each of them constructs a writerly consciousness in their own student lives. While the neo-liberal orientation of higher education on both sides of the Atlantic works to commodify and cement linguistic hierarchies of the nation states, facilitating a conversation between two groups of peer tutor trainees on equal footing seemed particularly important in the peer tutoring context. Guided by the discussion of these pedagogical goals and the outcomes they generated, this essay will present a case study of our collaboration. We analyze our assignments and student responses, as

DOI: https://doi.org/10.37514/INT-B.2021.1428.2.07

well as our reflections on the project. These artifacts will reveal whether and how the process of navigating the professional space of peer tutoring can be enriched and problematized by an international collaboration.

As most chapters in this collection illustrate, academic writing instruction and its institutional positionality in Russian higher education have revealed a transnational ethos. In this chapter, we understand the term *transnational* as a pedagogical disposition that "both highlights and works to build connections, crossings, and spaces between the existing national, ethnic, racial, and linguistic boundaries" (You, 2018, p. 2) for both educators and students. In the last decade, the emergent culture of writing centers in Russia has demonstrated a great deal of crossings between Russian and U.S. educational systems. By virtue of their name, writing centers in Russia (and other parts of the world) recall the long history of student-centered writing centers in the US. At the same time, Russian writing centers grapple with local institutions' agendas to expand the scope of Russian scholars' international publications through writing center consultations and seminars (Korotkina, 2017; Squires, 2018; see also Chapter 5 and Chapter 6). Thus, in Russian writing centers, decisions concerning staffing, training, pedagogy, types of services, policy, and languages of instruction usually consider multiple national and institutional models.

A similar awareness of multiple cultures and languages has been present in U.S. writing centers that have attended to students' and consultants' language varieties (Dvorak, 2016) and offered tutoring in multiple languages (Lape, 2013). Thus, the experience of attending or working at the writing center transcends national, cultural, and linguistic boundaries, making it necessary for tutor training programs to address transnationality and transculturalism. U.S. tutor training programs, such as peer and director observations, mentoring, and tutor training courses, (Bleankney, 2019), usually have allocated space to approaches for working with multilingual students (Bruce & Rafoth, 2009; Lape, 2013), while Russian writing centers have combined U.S.-based literature with Russian resources on writing (NES WCC Handbook, 2016). In other words, both U.S. and Russian tutor training environments have engaged in transnational work indirectly through writing center training literature, the presence of international students, and English language learners.

This chapter examines a transnational tutor training model that facilitates a direct interaction between peer tutors residing in different countries. We discuss an online exchange between peer tutors at the New Economic School (NES) in Moscow and enrollees in a peer tutor training course at LaGuardia Community College of the City University of New York (LGCC) in spring

2018. We argue that this project contributed to the professional development of our peer tutors and trainees by 1) cultivating a sense of transnational, translingual professional identity; 2) prompting them to sharpen rhetorical skills which they can implement in tutoring by modeling the practice of active reading, listening and advice-giving; and 3) enabling a sustained discussion of the fraught questions of authority inherent to peer tutoring, especially in a multi-lingual environment. As a training practice, we believe this also benefits local writing center communities in multilingual environments by positioning writing as a cognitive and rhetorical activity rather than merely a language skill, a conceptual framing that has emerged as a particular priority in the Russian scholarship on academic writing, as is evident in many of the chapters in this volume (see Chapter 1, Chapter 3, Chapter 4, and Chapter 10).

Institutional Contexts and Project Motivation

The concept of the writing center arrived in Russia—and in the former Soviet Union more generally—with the establishment in 2011 of the Writing and Communication Center (WCC) at the New Economic School (NES), an internationally oriented institution originally founded in 1992. Since its inception, the WCC has been led by U.S.-trained directors but has employed Russian and international consultants. In the last eight years, writing centers have spread more generally throughout the country; almost all of them serve faculty and graduate student researchers as their primary constituencies. The WCC at NES has remained unique in that it primarily serves students, particularly undergraduates enrolled in the joint bachelor's program run cooperatively between NES and HSE University. As an American-style liberal arts program with a mostly Western-trained faculty, the joint program has remained the closest to American educational norms. The NES WCC is a truly bilingual writing center, offering consultations in Russian and English and assisting students with writing projects in both languages (Aksakalova et al., 2016). However, as the majority of the writing done in the program is performed in English, English tends to be the predominant medium of writing center consultations (Bollinger, 2016).

The LaGuardia Writing Center has offered services in English to the linguistically and culturally diverse student population situated in one of the most diverse New York City neighborhoods, Long Island City. The staff has comprised largely professional tutors and several peer tutors, the majority of whom have attended LaGuardia. Currently, there are 28 tutors, seven of whom have taken a for-credit writing center pedagogy course. Tutors who have attended LaGuardia have provided particularly valuable insights to students and serve as role models. On campus, writing center tutors have participated in language and writing events where they share their perspectives on student learning.

During the Spring of 2018, peer tutor groups from NES and LaGuardia Community College participated in a series of guided reflections and interpersonal exchanges on Wordpress. In many regards, these tutor groups were quite different from each other. First, peer tutors at the NES WCC are drawn from the NES-HSE joint bachelor's program. All students in the program—and therefore most of the peer tutors—have been native Russian speakers who have been required to achieve a certain level of proficiency in English in order to take English-medium courses and write an English-language thesis. The NES WCC participants in the online exchange were the first to hold the position of peer tutor in Russian history. While the majority had learned English in school, one of these tutors was a dual citizen of Russia and the United Kingdom and spoke both languages with native proficiency. Additionally, an American international student from HSE who was also an experienced WCC consultant assisted with content moderation and contributed occasional posts.

LaGuardia students who enrolled in the upper-level elective course English 220: Seminar in Writing Education and Peer Tutoring were mainly English majors and shared a native or near-native fluency in English. The course encompassed a rigorous curriculum in composition and writing center theory, combined with actual tutoring and mentoring experiences. Students observed writing center tutorials and tutored their peers under supervision. Upon successful completion of English 220, students could apply for tutor positions at the Writing Center or another tutoring center on campus, such as the Reading Lab.

Though created to deal with local needs, the NES peer tutoring program has necessarily relied on Western models for its institutional form and training ethos. Peer tutors have read classics from the canon of American writing center scholarship, refer to the *Bedford Guide for Writing Tutors* (2016), and have learned practices pioneered at American universities. One of the problems, of course, has been that this pedagogical model imported from abroad has often seemed like an awkward fit for the Russian context, where authority matters and there has not been a strong tradition of collaborative learning or egalitarianism in education. Russian peer tutors may struggle to understand their identities as peer tutors, which may conflict with their self-image as students. This may especially be the case when Russian peer tutors have been called upon to tutor in their second language. Indeed, without a deep sense of the context in which these texts and practices that underpin the peer tutoring model were produced, Russian peer tutors can develop a stereotyped sense of what peer tutoring entails, one which they must either awkwardly conform to or resist. Exposure to their counterparts in the US presented an opportunity to construct a peer tutoring identity in relation to a more realistic and diverse set of models and even to act as authorities on the subject of peer tutoring.

For LaGuardia students, peer tutoring was a more familiar terrain; the practice is well known in the US, and several campus tutoring centers employ peer tutors. However, it was important for English 220 students to understand a larger, international context for teaching and tutoring writing and develop the habit of learning from peers abroad so as not to conceive of the composition and writing center fields as U.S.-centric. The virtual exchange project for LaGuardia students was a response to Christiane Donahue's (2018) call to broaden the horizon of composition and rhetoric and prepare students for succeeding in a globally interconnected world:

> We need to know that (1) we are not alone—other work on higher education writing can help us sharply articulate our own strengths and challenges—and (2) all students must grapple with questions of language and English if they are to be truly and fully prepared. (p. 21)

Operating in a bilingual environment, NES peer tutors could provide an important framework for working with international students or English language learners through such practices as code-switching. LaGuardia celebrates the cultural and linguistic diversity of its students, encouraging faculty and tutors across the campus to capitalize on students' language resources and develop translingual approaches. Thus, communication with Russian peer tutors brought a fresh perspective into LaGuardia campus efforts to promote resources for multilingual learners.

Online Writing, Cosmopolitanism, and Peer Tutoring

The growing culture of global online communication has presented a range of rhetorical and discursive needs that must be addressed in writing classrooms and tutorials. It has reconfigured the role of audience, placing it in the position "to quickly and directly respond to our ideas," redefining the rhetorical triangle that now includes not only reader, writer, and text, but also "location and modality" (Rice & St.Amant, 2018, p. 4). Writers and their instructors have thus considered "[w]here and who our audience is," as well as "what tool they're using to access our content" (Rice & St.Amant, 2018, p. 4). In response, writing tutors have targeted multiple literacies (Balester et al., 2012), and online platforms have supported tutor-student interactions (Lerner 2014; McKinney 2009). To assist their peers in acquiring multiple literacies necessary for thriving "in a globalized world and understanding its cultural, linguistic, and communicative complexities" (Hawisher et al., 2009, p. 55), writing tutors need to learn to navigate these complexities themselves. To this end, we combined video presentations with blog postings in our exchange.

The act of reflecting on their practice for and with the global audience of peer colleagues enabled tutors to construct and participate in the globally networked learning environment (GNLE) defined by global learning scholar Doreen Starke-Meyerring (2014) as "robust partnerships extending across institutional, linguistic, national, or other boundaries in order to facilitate faculty and student participation in the shaping of an emerging global social and economic order" (p. 308). As active agents in constructing GNLEs through transnational reflection, peer tutors were in the position to develop a "*kairotic* approach of working to contact participants in just the right way, to convey just the right information, and to connect with readers at just the right time in a sustained or even transactional process" (Rice & St.Amant, 2018, p. 3). This attunement to the communication needs of the audience was key to effective tutoring and a source of growing confidence for new peer tutors.

The pedagogy of international virtual exchange (IVE) has enabled not only rhetorical and digital literacies, but also an active form of global learning. IVE, also known as collaborative online international learning (COIL), virtual exchange, or telecollaboration, is a teaching method whereby geographically separated classes engage in meaningful collaborative projects using digital tools. By placing students in direct interaction and collaboration via synchronous or asynchronous means, IVE facilitated what Suresh Canagarajah (2013) calls "practice-based dialogical cosmopolitanism" (p. 196). It is a form of global citizenship that has enabled communication across difference and fosters the "cooperative disposition" to be "open to others' difference, and yet achieve community" (Canagarajah, 2013, p. 196). When envisioned in the peer tutoring context, the concept of dialogical cosmopolitanism has been particularly pertinent because it has emphasized negotiation, plurality, and dialogue, all of which have been essential for engaging in tutoring with confidence. Its major premise has been key to rhetorical and pedagogical literacies embedded in peer tutoring: "[I]t is not uniformity of values that achieve community, but the ability to align disparate values and features for common goals" (Canagarajah, 2013, p. 196).

The process of working together across difference is vital for peer tutoring in local and global contexts. Citing the work of Lev Vygotsky and Michael Oakeshott, Kenneth Bruffee (1978) has illustrated that conversation—internal and social—is a key mechanism in the thinking process, concluding that teachers must create opportunities for students to construct knowledge in dialogue with each other both in the classroom and at the writing center. This way students participate in "each other's intellectual, academic and social development" (Bruffee, 1978, p. 447) and develop interdisciplinary thinking and problem-solving skills, among others (see Lunsford, 1991). In the US, peer tutoring emerged in the early 1970s in response to college students' poor academic preparation and reluctance to seek tutoring offered by professional tutors on campus; students responded more positively to peer assistance (Bruffee, 1984). Currently, peer tutoring has been a common practice in writing, as well as in other subjects, across U.S. colleges and universities where students are offered on-the-job training or specialized courses that can employ methods for learning transfer and thus "aid in students' learning of writing, interpersonal, and metacognitive skills that can transfer to broad educational, professional, civic, and personal contexts" (Driscoll, 2015, p. 154).

While most writing center scholars and practitioners across the globe have recognized the value of collaboration enabled by peer tutoring, the question of authority has remained prominent, especially in countries like Russia that have more hierarchical educational cultures. In U.S. writing center discourse, scholars have approached this question from the methodological perspective of directive (tutor-centered) and non-directive (student-centered) methods. Thus, Peter Carino (2003) has warned against hierarchical relationships in writing center practice, but he also asserts, "to pretend that there is not a hierarchical relationship between tutor and student is a fallacy, and to engineer peer tutoring techniques that divest the tutor of power and authority is at times foolish and can even be unethical" (p. 98). The directive- non-directive continuum has particularly been problematized in the context of multilingual tutoring, where non-directive models may actually deprive writers working in their second language of valuable information about standard usage (Blau et al., 2002; Myers, 2003). Carino (2003) calls for a flexible tutoring model, whereby a tutor and a student switch smoothly between directive and non-directive methods and adhere loosely to the following principles: "More student knowledge, less tutor knowledge = more nondirective methods" and "Less student knowledge, more tutor knowledge = more directive methods" (p. 110). Similarly, citing the work of J. G. Grutch McKinney (2013), Roberta D. Kjesrud (2015) reminds us that "conferences yield more effective outcomes when tutors move within the entire continuum" of directive and non-directive methods (p. 35).

In Europe, Ella Grieshammer and Nora Peters (2011) report, institutions have resisted peer tutoring by questioning its efficacy and legitimacy.

Grieshammer and Peters have offered a list of common arguments against peer tutoring practice and possible rebuttals (2011) and, as one of the undercurrents for such skepticism, have suggested the perception of peer tutoring as "a threat to the established academic teaching system and to those who are part of it" (p. 123). In Russia, peer tutors have often been seen as inherently inferior to professional consultants, a mentality that has been observable among other students and faculty and sometimes internalized by NES peer tutors. Conversations about how peer tutoring might help get student-focused writing centers off the ground at other institutions (where demand is high but the supply of available teachers to provide staffing is low) tend not get off the ground themselves.

Methodology

Considering peer tutoring's varied histories and roles across national and institutional domains, understandably, the works outlined above tackle the relationship between authority and learning from different angles; but they have remained focused on individual locations and present the writing center scholar-administrator perspective. We wished to add another note to this existing conversation by inviting aspiring and practicing peer tutors themselves to analyze their own collaborative tutoring practices and formulate concerns and approaches to authority in peer tutoring.

Our project took place in April and May of 2018, and during that period, participants were given four initial assignments (see Appendix for full prompts): a group introduction video, a response to the partner group's video, a reflection on collaborative learning in the writing center, and a reflection on multilingualism in the writing center inspired by the Ohio University Writing Center's video series, "Becoming an Ally" (Ryerson & Phillips, 2020). Text posts were between 300 and 600 words and were designed to engage participants in conversations in which they could pull from recent experiences in their training as well as in actual consultations. However, at the time of this collaboration, the NES peer tutors were the only ones who had performed consultations independently. Participants were thus required to respond to other blog posts. Upon completion of the project, the students were asked to complete a 500-word reflection on the overall experience.

After student responses had been gathered, we analyzed and coded them according to how they addressed the main objectives of the project while also remaining open to themes that the participants introduced on their own. In this sense, while professional identity was certainly present in much of the discussion, the question of peer tutor authority—whether and how a peer is qualified to provide writing advice—proved both particularly fraught and important. Though we were also interested in how peer tutors understood and negotiated lines of authority in peer tutoring from the inception of the project, this question was never explicitly presented to the participants. In the first two assignments (video introduction and blog post #1), we gave students the freedom to select their own areas of interest. Two subsequent assignments focused on the implicit aspects of authority in peer tutoring: mutual learning and language use.

Findings

In the remainder of this chapter, we analyze the posts themselves in terms of these three themes—professional identity, rhetorical awareness, and authority—as they unfolded in response to each prompt.

Introduction Video and Blog Post #1

The first ice-breaker assignment (video introduction) offered a chance to envision one's professional self as a transnational figure. Namely, after introducing themselves and their local environments, many participants moved beyond our prompt to name an area of interest or challenge and pose questions to their partners (discussed below). Responses could potentially enrich their local tutoring experience. To come up with a question, they had to imagine the contours of their partners' environment, that is to move mentally across the world, and then situate the partners' advice in their local setting.

Although the assignment was open-ended in asking the participants to name any aspect of tutoring work of special interest or challenge, a majority of project participants on both sides (four out of six of LaGuardia students and two out of four of NES peer tutors) chose to reflect on various authority issues. Two LaGuardia students anticipated the hardship of guiding peers in areas that may not be their strongest suits, such as outlining. One LaGuardia student identified the difficulty of explaining "abstract . . . concepts," a perceived weakness that can potentially undermine his confidence, while the other student conveyed a more explicit awareness of the "power dynamic" of peer tutoring that is "hard to dismantle": "I am twenty-one. What makes another 21-year-old a greater writer than someone else?" One NES tutor pointed out the challenge of dealing with students whose level of English proficiency is higher than the tutor's.

In one exchange, two participants engaged with the question of authority so deeply and passionately that their rhetorical performance became exuberant. A NES tutor explored the "apparent contradiction" inherent in peer-to-peer interactions: "The very name 'peer consultant' contains some kind of contradiction. . . . '[P]eer' assumes horizontal relationship between people while 'tutor' or 'consultant' assumes vertical relationship between people because one teaches another." The tutor wondered how this contradiction can be "resolved in different contexts and in different environments." In formulating his question, the tutor showed awareness of his international peer audience's institutional and national context and hedged his claims in order to reflect the limitations of his experience. He also contextualized peer tutoring at NES—"Here at NES students generally expect that peer consultants would behave just like regular consultants"—and proposed a plausible comparison: "Probably in some other places peer consultants are more expected to give more informal, feedback." While the tutor was aware of the locale-specific differences, he was careful not to cement them; rather he transcended them by pointing out the duality in peer-to-peer tutoring relations. This is a good example of what Canagarajah (2013) has called the *cooperative disposition* or respectful attitude toward national or cultural differences and understanding of the shared values to "achieve common goals" (p. 196); in this case the goal was to conceptualize the dual role of peer tutor regardless of their geographic location. The tutor's respectful openness to difference and attempt to find a common ground, paired with his descriptive language about directionality of authority, illustrate not only his intellectual and linguistic investment in this subject-matter (i.e., authority as a pressing issue), but also his ability to create a comfortable kairotic space for his international peers to engage in dialogue.

Rhetorically and conceptually, he succeeded at sparking the full attention of one LaGuardia student who devoted her entire blog post to his question about authority. She admitted to selecting it after having reviewed "all of the questions posted" on the blog and then proceeded to survey two basic premises of peer tutoring that could help to disrupt the dichotomized view of power relations between the tutor and the tutee. She wrote,

> 1. The tutor is not the one who marks the paper. The writer makes his or her own corrections to the paper during the consultation. I feel like this establishes ownership of the paper and it shoes [sic] that the tutor is giving advice and guidance rather than just grading a paper.
>
> 2. There is always a conversation. The tutor is always engaging the writer and they work together to find solutions. The conversation creates an area of learning for both the tutee and the tutor.

She concluded the post with this sentence: "I hope this post helps build the bridge between you and the student and puts you on the same level." This response indicates that the NES tutor's ideas resonated with her and encouraged her to connect what she was learning in the course (e.g., non-directive tutoring style, collaborative learning, respecting student's ownership of their writing) with the unsettling question about student expectations from peer tutors. Rhetorically, she was responding to an eloquent and confident peer, so her own rhetorical act was charged. Her assertive tone, terse writing, and final sentence indicate the ability to create a peer-to-peer explanation that was clear, confident, suggestive, and conclusive, the kind of ability associated with competent tutoring.

This blog post was not the only one that contained peer advice, partly because the assignment prompt asked participants to suggest strategies or ideas in response to their international peers' questions and inquiries. Our assignment sought to create opportunities to engage in the learning-by-doing practice of advising peers, which we hoped would build participants' confidence in their own tutoring practice. For example, the experienced NES tutor who served as moderator explored how a writer's voice can be preserved through truly collaborative effort:

> My best tip for helping a tutee maintain and find their voice is to ask them to explain their thoughts or to restructure a sentence out loud. While they speak, I like to write down the words that they use. If the meaning of the sentence is clear, the student can include it in their paper. If there are still some issues, we can discuss them in the framework of the new explanation that they have just given.

She described a hypothetical session wherein the tutor decided which route to take and roles to assign in facilitating the student's thinking process. In making a valuable connection between this sentence-level work and the broader principle of Socratic questioning ("I've also found that this strategy can be very helpful for guiding students to create a structure for their essay through the use of targeted questioning."), she reminded her audience of the tutor's leading force in the session. At another level, she succeeded at giving clearly demonstrated advice to her audience of peer tutors by providing examples of the questions she might ask in a session: "What's your main point? What evidence do you have to support it? How does one piece of evidence differ from another?" Her post itself served as an example of a rhetorically successful peer-to-peer explanation: clear, developed with examples, and well-paced.

In asking students to respond to each other's concerns, we were mindful of the fact that a successful tutoring practice requires a synthesis of experiences: deep engagement with theoretical concepts, one's own experience as a writer and learner, peer review and other writing activities practiced in college classes, non-academic writing in multiple media, and tutoring observations. We share a conviction that a successful tutor training program must facilitate practice in synthesizing these knowledge sources in productive ways. Our project established the framework of an international dialogue as a way to loosely simulate tutoring session conditions that required deep contextualization, a high level of detail to illustrate points, and acknowledgement of and openness to difference. In her discussion of digital notebooks in cross-cultural exchanges, Josephine Walwema (2018) insists that "[i]ntercultural interaction is . . . not only situated and dynamic; it also 'requires high levels of sensitivity and a genuine mutual search for reciprocal understanding' (Ujitani & Volet, 2008, p. 297). And that mutual search for reciprocal understanding is rhetorical" (p. 21). A rhetorical situation constructed in and through a transnational space requires and enables the kinds of rhetorical work that define successful tutoring.

LaGuardia participants were not yet practicing tutoring at the time of writing their first posts, so in responding to their international peers' questions, they drew from their experiences as students of writing and their course material. One LaGuardia student relied on his own experiences with writing and peer reviews to provide confident and substantive advice. He responded to his peer's question about ways of addressing tone in a tutoring session by providing three major lines of advice: ensuring the writer's tone is consistent throughout the paper; checking for sweeping generalizations, "emotional and inflammatory language," and colloquial expressions; and helping to align the writer's tone with the "assignment's contextual nature." Parenthetical examples helped clarify his points, and active first-person clauses "I recommend" (mentioned twice)," "I explain," and "I help" revealed the student's confidence in the material he had already learned and practiced with peers. The closing line addressed to the audience ("I hope this helps!") makes it clear that the post was actually a response to a question posed in the video and a self-conscious attempt at mutual understanding.

The responses emerging from NES participants were more grounded in tutoring practice. They highlighted crucial examples of how tutor authority can be challenged, but also how these moments could be turned into productive learning experiences. One tutor identified the challenge of "helping people improve their works on topics that are completely unfamiliar to us." He proceeds to contextualize his work and difficulty:

> In our university many people have a very strong understanding of economics, and it is not rare for the papers to be filled with the analysis of subjects completely unfamiliar to me. It can be very confusing when you see a significant portion of the vocabulary for the first time, when you are unable to differentiate between set phrases and grammar errors and when not only the argumentation, but even the point being made in the text is unclear[;] however it is vital to understand, that none of said limitations fully prevent you from providing useful feedback for the students.

The tutor reminded his peers that they can still support the tutees by commenting on structure and "logical inconsistencies." He insists, "it is necessary to remember and demonstrate that your lack of knowledge in a specific field, does not diminish your English writing authority in any way" and proceeded to recommend:

> Be clear about what you know and what you don't, because definitions of new vocabulary and set phrases can simply be looked up online, while the act of pretending to understand new concepts can result in personal humiliation, or simply bad advice.

The determination with which this tutor provided advice mirrors the content of his advice to "be clear about what you know" and his awareness of the audience's needs. Along the same lines, another NES tutor offered confidently articulated, pointed suggestions on how to combat "the lack of confidence that you can help students" due to being younger in age. He encouraged his peers to "understand your strength," "prepare in advance to a consultation," and accept that "confidence appears with experience." Another lively post from a NES tutor colorfully sums up the ideas implied in her peers' posts: "A peer consultant is not the person of encyclopaedic learning, but somebody who can give the independent feedback."

One NES student noted that there are even situations in which peer authority can carry more weight than that of a "professionally trained consultant." Constructing a hypothetical situation based on the tutor's own experiences, the writer suggested that peers can leverage their "capital" in cases where pedagogical ideals conflict with a student's pragmatic concerns about the word volume of an essay or its ultimate grade:

> In cases, where a student's motivation is unclear or complicated, peer tutors can make learning happen even more seam-

lessly than some professional consultants. Trading off some professionalism for a deeper integration into the student body therefore is a right choice for some writing centers to make.

Noteworthy here was the tutor's explicit mention of the rhetorical work embedded in the tutor-tutee interaction: "tutors can employ ethos of their peer status to convince the student to take their side of the table." What seemed to be implied here was a tutor's agency in the session that could potentially help to enhance their confidence.

Blog Post #2

In the second blog post, participants reflected on effective collaborative practices and strategies to deal with student resistance to collaboration. While both groups discussed assignment tasks and document types specific to their local tutoring contexts, such principles as respecting the writer's ownership of their work and mutual assistance, helped establish the common ground between the two institutionally and nationally distant environments. The blog contributions helped establish that as a teaching principle, collaboration emphasizes interdependence between tutor and tutee. One NES tutor noted: "The most difficult consultations happen when the students simply expect the tutor to edit his work and do not take part in the process." He shared a useful strategy: "In such cases I usually explain to them that I cannot know what is on their minds and therefore cannot properly edit the text without their cooperation." The success of the tutor's work thus depended largely on the engagement level of the student. In fact, one LaGuardia student echoed this principle through a Benjamin Franklin quote: "Tell me and I forget. Teach me and I remember. Involve me and I learn."

The emphasis on mutual learning figured in both sets of posts. One NES tutor noted,

> Despite the fact that I'm a peer tutor, I'm also learning from them how to write. For instance, a year ago I didn't have much experience of writing CV and CL. However, I have seen many such texts during this year. Sometimes, when I find a problem in a student's writing, I understand that my texts have similar issues. So, looking at the writing of other people, we have a great chance to understand our personal mistakes because lookers-on see more than players. For this reason, now writing a CV or a CL for an application, I feel more confident.

Interestingly, here the learning of the tutor himself became the source of his confidence as a writer and, by extension, as a tutor as well. A LaGuardia student also noted what tutors may learn from their tutees: "We may learn small things such as a new word or a new type of diction but we can also learn larger things about topics in various subjects." One sentence in this post was particularly useful in pointing out that mutual learning is not unique to a tutoring situation or its cultural context, but rather a part of human interactions: "I also feel that we as humans learn from one another." Our fairly straight-forward question about collaborative learning elicited ample discussion about a range of approaches to collaboration, as noted above. But most importantly, the discussion further reconfigured a common view of authority as a rigid hierarchical construct and presented it as a process-driven, fluid construct that can shift between the student and the tutor. The stress on mutual learning implies that authority is not something to be chased, but rather noticed and negotiated as it emerges in the tutoring process. The topic of collaborative or mutual learning also moved the experience of teaching and learning out of specific linguistic, cultural, and institutional contexts, and let participants see each other as part of the same global profession.

Blog Post #3

Questions of authority were also implicit in tutors' discussions of multilingualism, though they emerged in many different ways. LaGuardia participants occasionally doubted their ability to cope with the demands of tutoring multilingual students. One writer described his first experience tutoring English as a Second Language (ESL) students as "frightening," echoing a lot of the emotionally charged language that has appeared in the literature on the tutoring of multilingual students by monolingual consultants (Blau et al.'s [2002] "Guilt-Free Tutoring" is a paradigmatic case). Despite this trepidation, LaGuardia participants embraced the concept of "allyship" as modelled in the Ohio State video series (Ryerson & Phillips, 2020) as well as strategies like code-switching (shifting between languages or dialects) in a consultation. However, they continued to use somewhat more emotional language and to emphasize the role of these practices in creating a good relationship between tutor and tutee as well as making the tutee feel "comfortable." Said one writer:

> By code-switching, students can feel like the tutor is their ally in writing a paper because the tutor is speaking to them and explaining things in the student's first language. . . . International or bilingual students who come to English speaking

> schools may find sanctuary in knowing there is someone in a position of authority who has a similar background as them. It also provides reassurance to have someone else understand you and be able to help you in your own language.

In this sense, the LaGuardia participants understood the tutor-tutee interaction as one in which the tutor must proactively avoid or disrupt the authority structures that are implied in the context of anglophone hegemony, in which a representative of an anglophone writing center is perceived as a de facto authority on the English language. Code-switching, in this context, could disrupt this dynamic and help the tutee feel less at a disadvantage.

On the other hand, NES students tended to emphasize the utility of such practices and were less interested in the social justice aspects of allyship. This may be due to the cultural and political context in which they were working and studying, but a bigger contributor to this difference was likely the fact that these peer tutors shared the same language background as the students they worked with and therefore tended to reflect on their own experiences of learning the English language when discussing their approaches as tutors. Furthermore, because they offer consultations in two languages, using English within the consultation is always an explicit choice. One Russian consultant said that students were "often resistant to speaking English" with her, "as they know me as a native Russian speaker. Therefore, they sometimes try to switch the language of the consultation." She believed it was important to insist that the consultation be conducted in the language of the document being discussed, as in her opinion, students in her program did not get enough speaking practice and also needed more opportunities to "develop thinking in English":

> I think most multilingual people are acquainted with a three-step path in our brain: we see the object or think about it, then as a first association comes is the word in our mother tongue, and only after that we translate it into second language.

Learnership thus has become another source of knowledge and authority and often became a tool with which NES participants could both inform their U.S.-based peers (who they may have assumed to be monolingual) and contested the notion that insisting on standard English was oppressive. The aforementioned post was quoted at length by one of the LaGuardia participants, who, after discussing the importance of allyship with multilingual writers, accepted the idea that insisting on standard English facilitates communication both within the consultation and in the broader context of international academic communication: "English is recognized globally with many different dialects and having a standard of writing makes it easier for us to communicate. It is not a tool of oppression."

What was somewhat remarkable was the fact that native speakerism did not seem to play a significant role in any of these reflections. Multilingual tutors (in both Moscow and New York) did not express doubts about their own authority with regard to English. If anything, the multilingual NES contributors to this project evinced fewer anxieties and fears surrounding language in consultations since they could appeal to their own experiences as learners and their knowledge of what challenges speakers of their native language might face when they learn English.

Students' Final Reflections and Our Conclusions

The foregoing is a demonstration of how an international collaboration can facilitate the development of peer tutors' awareness of the contextual nature of their practices while at the same time seeing themselves as part of a shared pedagogical enterprise that transcends borders and language. Even though rhetorical acts happened across national borders and professional contexts, the nature of the peer tutor's experience (e.g., negotiation of authority, confidence, rhetorical and intellectual effort to build knowledge collaboratively) was essentially the same. Different national and institutional perspectives simply highlighted different levels of experience and in doing so provided a deeper understanding of the tutoring job. A LaGuardia participant delivered this point well in his reflection: "Having the perspective of another writing center, especially one in another country, helped shape the idea of a unified writing initiative to assist in creating better writers." The same tutor noted that "people across the world [were] doing similar things if not exactly. The twist is that they are doing it with another completely different language and writers" and concluded, "It was a marvelous experience seeing the world in a closer environment."

In their final reflections, some tutors suggested that the collaboration had changed the way they conducted consultations or given them some new things to try, but the practical benefits seemed less significant than the reflective ones. As one Russian tutor aptly said, the discussion "made me seek formal justifications to my intuitive practices." Participants also showed developing rhetorical awareness in writing in an online format for their international partners. One NES participant described self-consciously moderating his typical academic style and adopting a more conversational tone, showing awareness of the fact that "operating in a different tone means invoking different rhetorical techniques and strands of vocabulary." Furthermore, because his "idea of the LGCC students was vague at best," he avoided any attempts at irony or humor that could have been misinterpreted or given offense. Conversely an LGCC participant mentioned avoiding "colloquialisms that they [his Russophone colleagues] would not understand."

At the same time, this collaboration was subject to many limitations. One LaGuardia tutor commented on the asynchronous nature of communication:

> The hardest part of this was the fact that we were communicating through blog posts and it wasn't always easy to get conversations flowing. I would have loved to have an option to live chat with that so we could have gotten responses quicker.

Though this was logistically difficult, future iterations of this project might include more synchronous interactions through video-conferencing or real-time text chat options, either in groups or partners. Secondly, while we the authors feel that the prompts helped focus and direct the discussion, some participants found these constraining. One NES participant in particular would have appreciated a more "argumentative element" and found that the generally irenic environment of the collaboration did not allow for any deep interrogation of some of the fundamental premises of peer tutoring. Rather, it tended to foster uncritical repetition of the agreed-upon virtues of the writing center format: "talking right things about how tutoring sessions 'establish student's ownership of the paper,' 'preserve the voice of the student,' etc." and foreclosing "more serious discussion of why this format is effective or at least a hint of comparison with other means of teaching." We would suggest that this was also a limitation of the participants' inexperience. Having had little time to put their learning into practice, it was difficult for them to develop informed critiques.

Based on the above findings and tutor recommendations, we would like to suggest that international collaboration can be a productive form of ongoing professional development for peer tutors. We recommend, however, that tutors are given opportunities to evaluate their experience not only at the end, but throughout the collaboration. As facilitators, we had regular check-ins with each other during the project and we also checked with our peer tutors, but having a structured, perhaps anonymous, written reflection could have enriched our understanding of the participants' experience. In the same vein, participants could also take a more leading role in facilitating the discussion; for example, they could contribute questions or even suggest the form of online activity.

Finally, we suggest that one broader benefit of this type of professional development for peer tutors is that it can offer ways of conceptualizing writing studies as a global, rather than narrowly Anglo-American, field (Donahue,

2018) and help to "connect writing center worlds to multiple relevant worlds outside the center" (Severino, 2016, p. ix). It can also point to the common ground between different national and institutional tutoring environments and thus allow peer tutors to discern professional and personal connections with colleagues whom they could otherwise perceive as the Other.

References

Aksakalova, O., Bollinger, K., Eubanks, I., & Squires, L. A. (2016). *NES WCC handbook. Training manual.* New Economic School.

Balester, V., Gimm, N., McKinney, J. G., Lee, S., Sheridan, D. M., & Silver, N. (2012). The idea of a multiliteracy center: Six responses. *Praxis: A Writing Center Journal, 9*(2). http://www.praxisuwc.com/baletser-et-al-92.

Blau, S., Hall, J., & Sparks, S. (2002). Guilt-free tutoring: Rethinking how we tutor non-native-speaking students. *Writing Center Journal, 23*(1), 23–44.

Bollinger, K. M. (2016). Introducing western writing theory and pedagogy to Russian students: The writing and communication center at the New Economic School. In P. Zemliansky & K. St.Amant (Eds.), *Rethinking post-communist rhetoric: Perspectives on rhetoric, writing, and professional communication in post-Soviet spaces* [Kindle edition]. Lexington. http://www.amazon.com/Rethinking-Post-Communist-Rhetoric-Communication-Globalization-ebook/.

Bruce, S., & Rafoth, B. (Eds.). (2009). *ESL writers: A guide for writing center tutors.* Boynton/Cook.

Bruffee, K. A. (1978). The Brooklyn plan: Attaining intellectual growth through peer-group tutoring. *Liberal Education, 64*, 447–68.

Bruffee, K. A. (1984). Collaborative learning and the "conversation of mankind." *College English, 46*(7), 635–652.

Canagarajah, S. (2013). *Translingual practice: Global Englishes and cosmopolitan relations.* Routledge.

Carino, P. (2003). Power and authority in peer tutoring. In M. A. Pemberton & J. Kinkead (Eds.), *Center will hold: Critical perspectives on writing center scholarship* (pp. 96–113). Utah State University Press.

Donahue, C. (2018). Writing program administration in an internationalizing future: What's to know? In S. K. Rose & I. Weise (Eds.), *The internationalization of U.S. writing programs* (pp. 21–43). Utah State University Press.

Driscoll, D. L. (2015). Building connections and transferring knowledge: The benefits of a peer tutoring course beyond the writing center. *The Writing Center Journal, 35*(1), 153–181.

Dvorak, K. (2016). Multilingual writers, multilingual tutors: Code-switching/mixing/meshing in the writing center. In S. Bruce & B. Rafoth (Eds.), *Tutoring second language writers* (pp. 101–122). Utah State University Press.

Grieshammer, E., & Peters, N. (2011). Fighting for peer tutoring in writing: Learning how to respond to scepticism. *Journal of Academic Writing, 1*(1), 120–125.

Hawisher, G. E., Selfe, C. L., Kisa, G., & Ahmed, S. (2009). Globalism and multimodality in a digitized world: Computers and composition studies. *Pedagogy: Critical Approaches to Teaching Literature, Language, Composition, and Culture, 10*(1), 55–68. https://doi.org/10.1215/15314200-2009-020.

Kjesrud, R. D. (2015). Lessons from data: Avoiding lore bias in research paradigms. *Writing Center Journal, 34*(2), 33–58.

Korotkina, I. (2017). *Writing centers in Russia: Limitations and challenges.* Working paper, Social Science Research Network. https://ssrn.com/abstract=2939495.

Lape, N. G. (2013). Going global, becoming translingual: The development of a multilingual writing center. *Writing Lab Newsletter, 38* (3–4), 1–6.

Lerner, N. (2014) Writing center pedagogy. In G. Tate, A. R. Taggart, K. Schick, & H. B. Hessler (Eds.), *A guide to composition pedagogies* (2nd ed.) (pp. 301–316). Oxford University Press.

McKinney, J. G. (2013). *Peripheral visions for writing centers.* Utah State University Press.

McKinney, J. G. (2009). New media matters: Tutoring in the late age of print. *Writing Center Journal, 29*(2), 28–51.

Myers, S. (2003). Reassessing the "proofreading trap": ESL tutoring and writing instruction. *Writing Center Journal, 24*(1), 51–70.

Rice, R., & St.Amant, K. (2018). Introduction. In R. Rice & K. St.Amant (Eds.), *Thinking globally, composing locally: Rethinking online writing in the age of the global internet* (pp. 3–11). Utah State University Press.

Ryan, L. & Zimmerelli, L. (2016). *The Bedford guide for writing tutors* (6th ed.). MacMillan.

Ryerson, R., & Phillips, T. (2016). *Becoming an ally: Tutoring multilingual writers.* Ohio University Graduate Writing & Research Center. https://www.ohio.edu/graduate/graduate-writing-and-research-center/becoming-ally-film.

Severino, C. (2016). Beyond the how-to's: Connecting the word and the world. In S. Bruce & B. Rafoth (Eds.), *Tutoring second language writers* (pp. ix–viii). Utah State University Press.

Squires, L. A. (2018). Writing centers and academic professionalization in the Russian Federation. In M. Rajakumar (Ed.), *Western curricula in international contexts: An edited collection* (pp. 1–22). Lexington Books.

Starke-Meyerring, D. (2014). From "educating the other" to cross-boundary knowledge making: Globally networked learning environments as critical sites of writing program administration. In D. S. Martins (Ed.), *Transnational writing program administration* (pp. 307–331). Utah State University Press.

Walwema, J. (2018). Digital notebooks: Composing with open access. In R. Rice & K. St.Amant (Eds.), *Thinking globally, composing locally: Rethinking online writing in the age of the global internet* (pp. 15–34). Utah State University Press.

You, X. (2018). Introduction: Making a transnational turn in writing education. In X. You (Ed.), *Transnational writing education: Theory, history, and practice* (pp. 170–186). Routledge.

Appendix: Assignment Prompts

1. Group Introduction Video: In a video of approximately 10 minutes, introduce yourselves to your international peers. In addition to any personal information you wish to share (name, major, interests, what you enjoy/find challenging about peer tutoring), please provide an institutional context where you practice/observe tutoring. Also, provide some details about your institution's writing center: student demographic, common writing concerns, language in which writing is presented, policies, and whatever else seems important. Finally, what aspects of peer tutoring do you find particularly interesting and/or challenging?

2. Blog post #1: Write a response to your international peers' video. Which concerns and interests about peer tutoring did they share with you? Based on your experience as a writing student, observer of tutoring sessions and/or practicing peer tutor, can you suggest any concepts or practices that might address these? (350–600 words; complete by Tuesday 4/24)

3. Blog post #2: A major feature of peer tutoring is collaborative or mutual learning. It can create exciting opportunities for both tutors and tutees. For example, writers may feel less inhibited to express their concerns to a peer than to an instructor and tutors may find themselves exploring new writing genres or content areas. Keeping this in mind, in your experience as a practicing tutor or observer, what types of assignments and concerns do students bring to the writing center? What strategies do peer tutors use to support the students without compromising opportunities for collaborative learning? Do you see student writers' resistance to collaborative learning? If yes, how do tutors handle it? (350–600 words; complete by May 3)

4. Blog post #3: Please watch this collection of videos about working with multi-lingual writers: https://www.ohio.edu/graduate/graduate-writing-and-research-center/becoming-ally-film and review this article: https://www.chronicle.com/article/We-Must-Help-Students-Master/243079

Which scene(s) in the video made a strong impression on you? Why? Which scene(s) are relevant to your tutoring context (LaGuardia)? How so?
Drawing on the video and the article, as well as your own experience, reflect on when it might be productive and unproductive to deviate from standard English or code-switch during a session. (350–600 words, May 20)

Final Reflection

Please reflect on your COIL experience, using the following questions to guide your narrative. Your reflection should be at least 500 words.

1. Review our blog and your notes. Which ideas revealed by your international peers about peer tutoring were familiar to you? Which were new?
2. Did your perspective on peer tutoring change as a result of participating in the COIL collaboration? Please use specific examples to illustrate your point(s).
3. Did the COIL collaboration illuminate anything new about your culture? About the culture of your international peers?
4. Did you have to adjust your communication habits when building a connection with your international peers? Why or why not? Think about whether/how your written, oral, body languages had to be modified to communicate successfully.
5. What aspect of this collaboration was challenging for you?
6. Overall, what was the most interesting and useful learning moment for you in your collaborative activities with international peers?
7. What is your major take-away from this collaboration that might help you in any aspect of your education, professional and life experience?

Part Three. Language Matters

8 Software Development for Corpus Research in English Studies

Elizaveta Smirnova
HSE UNIVERSITY, PERM

Svetlana Strinyuk
ADMIRAL MAKAROV STATE UNIVERSITY OF MARITIME AND INLAND SHIPPING, SAINT PETERSBURG

Viacheslav Lanin
HSE UNIVERSITY, PERM

In recent years, English has become the lingua franca of the spheres of higher education and science in Russia: more and more university courses are delivered in English, university students and academics take part in international conferences and workshops, and Russian scholars strive to publish their research findings in international peer-reviewed journals. Such a shift in focus has made the ability to write a high-quality academic text a necessary skill in the modern academic environment. However, as our experience as English for Academic Purposes (EAP) practitioners shows, Russian speakers writing in their second language (L2), having a good command of general English, often find it challenging to conform to the conventions of English academic discourse when writing their research papers or project proposals. Despite the existence of various types of software which can check the grammar and style of a text (e.g., Grammarly, Ginger, Language Tool), detect rhetorical moves in a text (Pendar & Cotos, 2008), and even provide feedback about errors (see, for example, Dreschler et al., 2019; Napolitano & Stent, 2009), to our knowledge, there are no programs focusing on the linguistic characteristics of an academic text. Besides, in the existing literature there appears to be no clear rubric for academic writing assessment. The application Paper Cat, developed by a team of teachers and students from HSE University, Perm, Russia, is aimed at facilitating students' and researchers' writing in English by identifying the most significant features of academic discourse. We used the world-accumulated knowledge in EAP to develop a software that is able to assess an academic text against a set of criteria (i.e., academic discourse markers selected from academic style guides, handbooks and research articles on EAP). Evaluating the "quality of academic discourse" of the text in terms of style can be automated by using software to tag style markers in that text. At the heart of this approach is creating a repository of patterns which are needed to extract the markers mentioned above. The quality of L2 academic writing is assessed against a set of criteria based on an analysis of competent writing features.

English has become the lingua franca for the academic world (Drubin & Kellogg, 2012; Garfield, 1967; Meneghini & Packer, 2007). It dominates scientific literature, which means that a manuscript published in English immediately becomes more visible and significant (Drubin & Kellogg, 2012). Russian universities, being a part of the international academic community, strive to create an English-speaking environment to teach their students reading and writing skills in academic English by using English as a medium of instruction. Students find reading scientific literature and listening to lectures in English difficult, but exposure to the language in the educational environment does ultimately develop students' receptive skills. The battle which Russian learners of English typically have lost is with academic writing, which is demonstrated to some extent by the results of international exams: according to data from the official International English Language Testing System (IELTS) website, the mean overall and individual band scores achieved by 2019 Academic Training test takers of IELTS show that academic writing even in the simple form of a short essay and diagram description pose a serious difficulty for Russian students (see Table 8.1).

Table 8.1. Mean Band Score for the Most Common First Languages (Academic)

First language	Listening	Reading	Writing	Speaking	Overall
Russian	6.75	6.74	5.87	6.51	6.53
German	7.86	7.64	6.62	7.44	7.45
Italian	6.90	7.30	6.20	7.17	6.74
Tamil	6.87	6.43	5.98	6.53	6.52
Hindi	6.69	6.17	5.93	6.33	6.34

(International English Language Testing System, 2019)

The table shows that even though writing scores were lower than those for the other exam sections among all test-takers, Russian-speaking candidates have done worse in writing than speakers of other languages, even when they have a higher overall band (see, for example, the results of Hindi and Tamil-speaking candidates).

Therefore, as established in the first section of this book, increasing the level of students' English for academic purposes (EAP) writing skills has recently become a highly topical issue, since the ability to write a high-quality academic text is seen as a necessary skill in the modern academic environment. However, even those second language (L2) writers who have achieved a relatively high level of language proficiency have often found it challenging to conform to the conventions of academic discourse when writing their research papers in English (see Chapters 1, Chapter 3, Chapter 4, and Chapter 6). Writing in an appropriate academic style involves the use of particular lexical, grammatical, and syntactic structures associated with this type of discourse. Despite the existence of a large number of textbooks and study guides in academic English along with software which can check the grammar and/or style of a text (e.g., Grammarly, Ginger, Language Tool), teaching writing in a proper academic style remains a major challenge for EAP practitioners. To solve this problem, a research team from HSE University (thereafter HSE) in Perm, Russia has made an attempt to create a software that conducts a multidimensional analysis of academic English. We assume that the software can play an important role in analyzing academic discourse as well as in teaching English for academic purposes. The approach is based on data-driven learning (DDL; Johns, 1991, 2002), which involves giving learners access to language data to meet their learning needs. This approach uses large amounts of data (language corpora) in order to develop students' language skills and raise their stylistic consciousness. Using DDL in EAP classrooms has proven to be an effective way of developing learners' genre knowledge and discipline-specific writing skills (see, for example, Anthony, 2016; Cotos et al., 2017; Feak, 2016).

The main aim of this two-year project was to develop software capable of assessing an academic text against a set of criteria (i.e., academic discourse markers). The motivation behind the development of the software was to assist HSE students and lecturers with writing their papers in English.

Project Motivation and Development

In their final year, HSE students take a course in Academic Writing in English and write a research proposal as their final assessment. The research proposal is a draft of the students' diploma project written in English and edited according to American Psychological Association (APA) and Institute of Electrical and Electronics Engineers (IEEE) style (depending on the major: social sciences or information technologies) and comprises roughly 2500 words. As teachers of this course who spend a great deal of time marking students' texts, we have concluded that the major difficulties students face in this work are not connected with content or grammar but with academic style in general (i.e., the use of lexical bundles and syntactic constructions expected in academic texts). During this short EAP course, they cannot master academic English at the necessary level. What is more, misleading instructions provided by handbooks in EAP which fail to clearly represent variations in conventions of academic English in different subject domains only add to the problem. For example, according to researchers, explicit evaluation through evaluative attributes has been more common in humanities and social sciences than in natural sciences, while modality as a way of expressing personal stance is more typical of natural sciences (Sotesbury, 2003). Clausal features occur more frequently in arts and humanities than life and physical sciences (Staples et al., 2016). However, these differences are not usually reflected in EAP textbooks.

Our software tool, developed using General Architecture for Text Engineering (GATE), is aimed at aiding students as they write. So far, learning programs have automatically detected rhetorical shifts (namely, establishing a territory; establishing a niche, occupying the niche) in academic texts (Pendar & Cotos, 2008); provided trigger questions and "gloss" (i.e., feedback content, which are supposed to help learners to reflect on and therefore improve their writing (Villalón et al., 2008); and identified and classified morphological and syntactic errors, suggesting ways of correcting them (Napolitano & Stent, 2009). Ours is different because 1) it is focused on academic discourse markers which are expected in advanced writing in a particular field; 2) it compares a user's text against a corpus of research articles in the same subject, which ensures a discipline-specific approach; 3) it uses statistics on the use of these markers, which contributes to the robustness of the assessment. Our tool identifies the most significant features of academic discourse within the subject domain based on corpus research and then uses that information to provide feedback to writers. It will also allow tutors to evaluate the quality of student papers against a number of standardized formal criteria.

The software also targets our colleagues who teach at HSE and are writing their own research papers in English for peer-reviewed journals. Writers could use this application to get real-time feedback during this challenging task. The application will be published as a publicly available service for comparing a user-provided text with text corpora. Since the program is based on GATE (Cunningham et al., 2011), which is free to use, the application is free as well.

GATE was chosen for several reasons. First, it provides a development environment (GATE Developer) with many basic processing resources (e.g., tokenizers, sentence splitters, morphological taggers) as well as an object library that can be used to write plugins specifically for the task (GATE Embedded). The main feature of GATE is a wide range of tools for text processing. The most useful tool for our project is the Java Annotation Patterns Engine (JAPE) transducer, which allows the user to describe regular expressions over GATE annotations. On the one hand, JAPE expressions can be used to find simple markers; on the other hand, we can write Java codes for complex markers ourselves.

The first version of the software tool was developed as a set of plugins for GATE Developer. Most of the plugins are used for finding style markers. At the same time, some plugins are aimed at statistical calculation and visualization. Based on acquired experience, we are now developing the second version of our tool as an internet research portal. Our portal will be able to perform a full circle of text processing from document and corpora management to building statistical reports. Due to its service-oriented architecture, the heterogeneous components of our solution can be seamlessly integrated together. Natural Language Processing (NLP) services are built on the GATE Embedded tool. Also, we have developed special tools such as a visual editor for JAPE expressions based on an ontological description. The portal can be used both for research and study aims.

We assume that evaluating the quality of the academic discourse of a text in terms of style can be automated by using software to tag style markers in that text. Creating a repository of patterns is at the heart of this approach, but it demands close attention. Therefore, at the first stage, it was necessary to make a list of patterns needed to extract the markers mentioned above. Evaluation of the statistical bounds of markers' occurrence requires using the methods and tools of corpus linguistics. In order to assess the quality of an academic text, the system compares it with a corpus of research papers published in leading peer-reviewed journals in different disciplines (i.e., a reference corpus).

So far, we have compiled 12 corpora—six of professional writing and six learner corpora in management, economics, history, political science, law, and computer science. The papers in the expert corpora were published between 2013 and 2020, and the sizes of the corpora and the journals the papers were retrieved from are presented in Table 8.2. Following Swales (1990), we believe that a paper published in a peer-reviewed journal can be seen as a model for L2 writers to follow, an academic text which "has a dynamic relationship" with various research-oriented genres, such as dissertations, monographs, presentations (Swales, 1990, p. 177). The research papers and research proposals written by HSE students have a similar macrostructure: they describe the topic of the research, the knowledge gap, give a literature review on the topic, data, and methods, and present the results of the analysis (or anticipated results in some cases). It should be noted that a research proposal is the closest type of writing in English the student writers will do during their studies, because they go on to undertake and write up the research they proposed in their native language. Besides, the practice of comparing learner academic texts with professional writing is well established in EAP literature (see, for example, Aull et al., 2017; Lee & Chen, 2009; Smirnova, 2019). So, we believe that the corpora are comparable and can be used for our purposes.

Table 8.2. Sources of Texts and Sizes of the Expert Corpora

Discipline	Number of texts	Number of words	Journals
Economics	57	654,373	Quarterly Journal of Economics Journal of Financial Economics International Journal of Production Economics
Management	61	683,287	Journal of Management Journal of Management Studies Academy of Management Journal
Political Science	73	654,628	American Political Science Review American Journal of Political Science Journal of Politics World Politics Comparative Political Studies Political Analysis
Law	91	738,383	European Law Journal European Law Journal Criminal Justice Studies Journal of Crime and Justice Contemporary Justice review
History	65	621,723	The American Historical Review The Journal of African History The Historical Journal the Journal of Modern History Contemporary European History
Computer Science	86	705,271	Artificial Intelligence Review European Journal of Information Systems Computer Science Education International Journal of Digital Earth

Features that are used for the analysis are selected from academic style guides and other methodical literature (e.g., Hamp-Lyons & Heasly, 2010; Siepmann et al., 2011; Wallwork, 2016). They can be divided into three groups: lexical markers, grammar markers, and syntactic markers. The lexical markers include terminology, abstract semantic verbs, desemantisized verbs, intensifying adverbs, hedges, exemplification, and transition words. The grammar markers comprise the passive voice, present tenses, subject pronouns, and anaphoric expressions. The syntactic markers are pre- and postpositive attributes, it-clefts, pseudo clefts, non-finite clauses, adverbial clauses, th-wh constructions, and attitudinal clauses. It should be noted that the list is not full and is still being extended. A number of previous works (see, for example, Gray, 2015; Hyland, 2008; Staples et al., 2016) have demonstrated that there are significant disciplinary differences in the use of different lexical patterns and syntactic constructions in academic discourse. Therefore, the software we are developing is based on the discipline-specific approach.

User Experience and Application

Currently, our application offers three options: it is capable of annotating texts with the listed markers, providing statistics on their use, and assessing a user's text against a set of formalized criteria. Figure 8.1 shows logic connectors found by the software in an academic text.

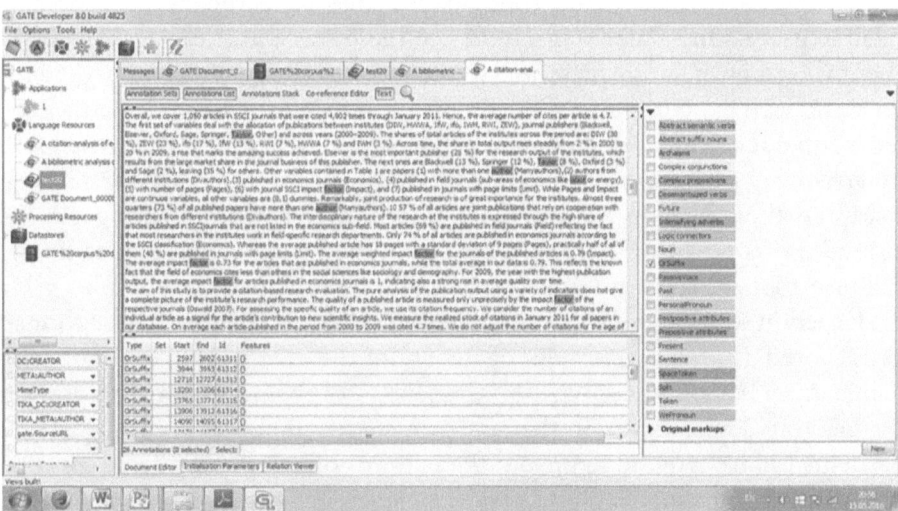

Figure 8.1. Logic connectors.

For the use of each marker, a student can get a maximum of ten points for the normal use of each marker of academic style. The norm is expressed quantitatively as the normalized frequency of a marker per thousand words in the reference corpus multiplied by the number of words in a student's work. A 10 percent deviation is possible for getting the maximum score. However, a larger deviation from the norm means a lower mark.

For example, the normalized frequency (occurrence per 1,000 words) of adverbial clauses in the reference corpus is seven. The work under consideration is 2,300 words long. Therefore, the usage norm for adverbial clauses for this work will be 7 times 2.3, which equals approximately 16. So, if there are 16+/- two adverbial clauses in the text, the student will get ten points for the use of this marker. If there are only ten adverbial clauses in the text, which is about 35 percent less than the norm, the student will get only 4 points. However, it should be mentioned that a tool like this should never actually be used for grading but possibly for self-regulation and formative feedback. This software is used in EAP classrooms at HSE in different ways.

Generating Study Materials

The compiled corpora of both expert and student writing can be used to generate study materials to assist in the classroom and in students' autonomous work. The use of concordances heightens the salience of linguistic units which the teacher or student wishes to focus on and thereby makes them more noticeable, which is a crucial factor in intake (Schmidt, 1990, 1994). Another benefit is that demonstrating concordance lines to learners can encourage them to process the material in a more profound way and to draw conclusions about the language units presented by themselves (Bernadini, 2004), thereby fostering learners' autonomy. Concordances showing the usage of some patterns aim not at providing students with answers but at giving them the tools for arriving at an independent solution to the problems they face when trying to express themselves in English (Johns, 2002). Moreover, presenting a lot of examples of a language feature in a concentrated way (i.e., in corpus lines), can save a lot of classroom time (Cobb, 1999; Hoey, 2000).

Expert writing corpora are extremely useful for creating various exercises as well as finding examples of the use of the identified markers of academic style. For instance, Table 8.3 demonstrates the most common uses of the hedging device *suggest* in the reference corpus of papers in management. Students can be asked to figure out the patterns of its use from some concordances on their own.

Table 8.3. Instances of *Suggest* in the Reference Corpus in Management

1.	We	***suggest***	*that, when a coercive pressure is introduced to adopt a new practice that is interpreted negatively by key institutional constituents.*
2.	*Our data*	***suggest***	*that decision makers take more time to comply with coercive pressures the more complexity they face.*
3.	*Trust between entrepreneurs and their investors has often been*	***suggested***	*to be key to their cooperation and the success of their partnership.*
4.	*A climate in which it is safe to speak up and take risks is*	***suggested***	*to complement the adaptation and implementation of innovation.*
5.	*The pattern of mediation that we uncovered*	***suggests***	*the possibility of other pathways such as affect.*
6.	*This*	***suggests***	*the potential for organizational interventions designed to bolster an individual's self-esteem level to potentially counteract ostracism's negative effects on self-esteem level.*

Based on the examples, learners are supposed to notice three patterns suggest is used in: somebody or something suggests that (1, 2); something is suggested to do something (3, 4); somebody suggests something (5, 6).

The learner corpora can also be used for generating error correction and text editing exercises. For examples, Table 8.4 shows examples of students' inaccurate use of anaphoric expressions, which can be employed for creating an error-correction exercise.

Table 8.4. Learners' Use of Anaphora

1.	Methods are effective only if it brings results in accordance with the goals and objectives.
2.	To obtain more specific information on each point I will select criteria and make a comparison of results according to it.
3.	The coach reflects the client's actions and helps to transform it into autonomous abilities (functions).
4.	The main idea in the third sub-group of corporate citizenship is that corporations can take its rightful place in society, next to other "citizens".
5.	The interview questionnaire will be developed on the basis of the reviewed literature, and it will help in gathering all the relevant data from this major informants.

Demonstrating Academic Discourse Markers in Use

The software can be used in an EAP classroom in order to demonstrate significant markers of academic style relevant to the discipline they are studying. For example, Figure 8.2 demonstrates the use of nouns and the passive voice in an academic text, which can serve as a colorful illustration for learners.

Moreover, the software can show typical discrepancies on the use of various markers in expert and learner corpora in a clear and catchy way (see Figure 8.3). This might allow teachers to prevent possible problems with the use of the markers in the future. The software can also be used to search for particular examples when studying certain markers of academic discourse.

Figure 8.2. The use of nouns and the passive voice.

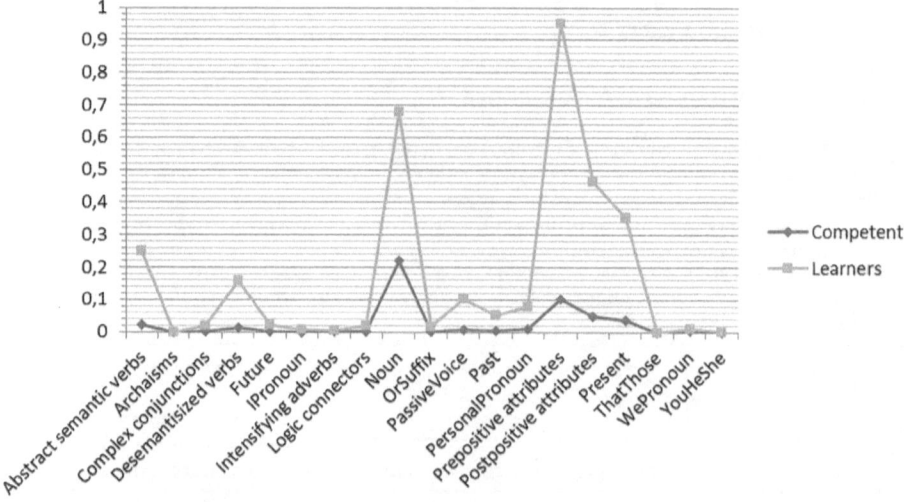

Figure 8.3. Comparison of learner and expert corpora by markers.

Motivating Learners' Autonomous Work

Finally, the software can be employed to motivate learners' autonomous work. The teacher can ask the students to find examples of some markers or identify some patterns of their use by themselves. Students are also able to upload their own academic text in order to get an automated, data-informed assessment of their work and subsequently try and improve it on their own.

While working on the project, we analyzed a lot of language data that allowed us to work out some practical recommendations that might be useful for EAP practitioners. According to our findings, not all syntactic features mentioned in EAP textbooks and study guides are frequently used by professional writers. Such rarely used syntactic constructions are, for example, it-clefts, pseudo-clefts, th-wh constructions, and adverbial clauses of purpose and manner. This might suggest that that under the conditions of limited classroom time, EAP teachers may exclude them from courses in academic writing or allocate the constructions to learners' self-study.

Conversely, our analysis informs us about which constructions ought to be prioritized depending on the learner's discipline. For instance, when teaching academic writing to learners in the hard sciences, it is important to allocate enough time for adverbial clauses of place, condition, and result because they are extensively used in comments for calculations, models, and formulas. For example:

1. Thus, the optimization formulation follows Eq. (4), where P and t are the decision variables.
2. If we apply the change of variables r we have that RIo xo; yo and, therefore, the Russell output measure of inefficiency is equivalent to an additive-type measure.
3. For convenience, we multiply the Amihud illiquidity measure by −1 so that the timing coefficient based on this measure has the same interpretation as that from the Pástor-Stambaugh liquidity measure.

On the other hand, courses in academic writing for learners who are studying soft disciplines should focus on adverbial clauses of time, contrast, and concession. It should also be mentioned that our research showed that learners do not use adverbial clauses of all types as frequently as professional writers do, sticking to simple sentences, for example:

4. Some of enterprises try to make and implement their own business processes models. Others try to use existing analysis and improvements models.
5. Logistics appeared in the Roman Empire. Its main task was the distribution of food.

This might suggest that this syntactic marker of academic style deserves close attention.

In contrast, complex sentences with which, who, and whose are used by students and professional writers with similar frequencies, but learners often use them incorrectly, for example:

6. External marketing of the employer brand is the second step that is needed to attract potential employees, which may become loyal employees in the future.

Another structure that was overused by novice writers, according to our research, was attitudinal clauses (in the analyzed learner corpora, they were used several times as often as in the expert ones). This finding suggests that students should be taught that these constructions can be used in their text once or twice only.

A particularly difficult structure for students turned out to be non-finite clauses; they are used by learners much more rarely than by professionals. This construction is quite frequent in the reference corpora and deserves special attention in EAP classrooms.

Anaphora also deserves the close attention of academic writing teachers because almost all types of anaphora have been underused by students. Thus, in students' works, there have been a lot of repetitions that could have been avoided with the help of anaphora, for example:

7. Although respondents are likely to be understood and to allow that such goods will be more expensive, but for ensuring environmental safety respondents agree to pay.
8. The first group of theories consists of utilitarian theories.

Our findings showed that the only type of anaphoric expressions overused by learners was demonstrative pronouns:

9. However, this paper supposes the use of customer development methodology for several reasons. Firstly, this method was adapted to IT-projects, for example, this technique involves the use of the approach of agile software development. Furthermore, this method is the least resource-consuming and it allows to test the hypothesis on a real market, using MVP. Finally, this technique was actually applied in practice in the majority of successful start-ups that participated in start-up accelerator of Russian internet Initiatives Development Fund.

The example demonstrates that students use it whenever they can, which might be due to an attempt to avoid errors related to the use of articles. This implies that even though the use of articles is studied at a basic level in EFL courses, this topic should be revisited in EAP classrooms as well.

A large number of errors were connected with the use of plural nouns, even though this topic has also been studied at basic levels. Our experience shows that it requires repetition in academic writing courses in order to prevent possible errors, like the ones in the examples below.

10. To obtain more specific information on each point I will select criteria and make a comparison of results according to it.
11. This beliefs and expectations produce norms that powerfully shape the behavior of individuals and groups in the organization.

Reflexive pronouns require revision as well, according to our data:

12. Therefore, the manager not only itself has to adhere to ethical standards, but also has to provide their observance in the organization in general.

Hedges, which are seen as a lexical marker of academic style, have been generally underused by learners. Special attention should be paid to the use of the modal verbs may and might, which are rarely used in students' texts, along with the words seem and possible, which are abused by students.

As our corpus analysis suggests, students demonstrate incorrect usage of hedging devices, the most typical errors being related to the use of suggest with an infinitive:

13. The author suggests to approach the question from various perspectives of analyzing the market.

The use of the phrase "become possible," which is a word-by-word translation from Russian; and the use of several hedges together:

14. In future it seems possible to put theory into practice, and develop new technologies to establish a new business.

Conclusion

To conclude, writing style plays a pivotal role in presenting the results of research, and to be published, scholars have to meet the strict requirements of scientific journals. Researchers who are not native speakers of English struggle through manuals and guidelines for academic writing, but even so, materials are often rejected due to the low quality of the writing. Special courses in EAP or picking up language from academic papers are not always sufficient remedies due to the natural limits of time and effort. Students taking English for Academic Purposes as a subject at university face an even more difficult situation due to strict deadlines and limited time in which to conduct a thorough literature review (which is practically the only type of academic reading they usually do). These limitations prevent them from processing and picking up the language in the most natural way—through extensive analytical reading. Digging in handbooks and manuals in EAP cannot sort out the problem since such studies are time consuming and usually require the assistance of a competent writer.

The application could solve this problem by assessing academic writing and providing those who would like to master academic writing with quality feedback. The application solves manifold tasks, namely, it may be used in corpus and contrastive research in order to analyze the L2 academic writing of both novice and competent writers; it can be used for teaching EAP in class and also for creating study materials. All these functions are fulfilled through the implementation of corpus research based on specific domain corpora which makes both teaching and researching more reliable.

References

Anthony, L. (2016). Introducing corpora and corpus tools into the technical writing classroom through data-driven learning (DDL). In J. Flowerdew & T. Costley (Eds.), *Discipline-specific writing: Theory into practice* (pp. 162–180). Routledge.

Aull, L., Bandarage, D., & Miller, M. R. (2017). Generality in student and expert epistemic stance: A corpus analysis of first-year, upper-level, and published academic writing. *Journal of English for Academic Purposes, 26,* 29–41. https://doi.org/10.1016/j.jeap.2017.01.005.

Bernadini, S. (2004). Corpora in the classroom: an overview and some reflections on future developments. In J. Sinclair (Ed.), *How to use corpora in language teaching* (pp. 15–36). John Benjamins.

Cobb, T. (1999). Breadth and depth of lexical acquisition with hands-on concordancing. *Computer Assisted Language Learning, 12*(4), 345–360. https://doi.org/10.1076/call.12.4.345.5699.

Cotos, E., Link, S., & Huffman, S. R. (2017). Effects of DDL technology on genre learning. *Language Learning & Technology, 21*(3), 104–130. https://lib.dr.iastate.edu/engl_pubs/103/.

Cunningham, H., Maynard, D., & Bontcheva, K. (2011). *Text processing with GATE (Version 6).* University of Sheffield.

Dreschler G., Ontrust, M., & de Jong, N. (2019, July 1–4). *Digital individual support for writing skills across the disciplines* [Conference session]. The 2019 Conference for the European Association for the Teaching of Academic Writing. https://easychair.org/smart-program/EATAW2019/2019-07-03.html#talk:106283.

Drubin, D. G., & Kellogg, D. R. (2012). English as the universal language of science: Opportunities and challenges. *Molecular Biology of the Cell, 23*(8), 1399. https://doi.org/10.1091/mbc.E12-02-0108.

Feak, C. B. (2016). EAP support for post-graduate students. In K. Hyland & P. Shaw (Eds.), *The Routledge handbook of English for academic purposes* (pp. 513–525). Routledge.

Garfield, E. (1967). English—An international language for science. *The Information Scientist, 76,* 19–20. http://www.garfield.library.upenn.edu/essays/V1p019y1962-73.pdf.

Gray, B. (2015). On the complexity of academic writing: Disciplinary variation and structural complexity. In V. Cortes & E. Csomay (eds.) *Corpus-based research in applied linguistics: Studies in honor of Doug Biber* (pp. 49–78). John Benjamins.

Hamp-Lyons, L., & Heasly, B. (2010). *Study writing: A course in writing skills for academic purposes.* Cambridge University Press.

Hoey, M. (2000). A world beyond collocation: New perspectives on vocabulary teaching. In M. Lewis (Ed.), *Teaching collocation: Further developments in the lexical approach* (pp. 224–245). Language Teaching Publications.

Hyland, K. (2008). As can be seen: Lexical bundles and disciplinary variation. *English for Specific Purposes, 27*(1), 4–21. https://doi.org/10.1016/j.esp.2007.06.001.

International English Language Testing System (2019). www.ielts.org.

Java Annotation Patterns Engine (JAPE). (n.d.). Retrieved April 18, 2019 from https://gate.ac.uk/sale/tao/index.html#x1-2020008.

Johns, T. F. (1991). From printout to handout: Grammar and vocabulary teaching in the context of data-driven learning. In T. Odlin (Ed.), *Perspectives on pedagogical grammar* (pp. 293–313). Cambridge University Press. https://doi.org/10.1017/CBO9781139524605.014.

Johns, T. (2002). Data-driven learning: The perpetual challenge. In B. Kettemann & G. Marko (Eds.), *Language and computers: Teaching and learning by doing corpus analysis. Proceedings of the fourth international conference on teaching and language corpora, Graz* (pp. 107–117). Rodopi.

Lee, D., & Chen, S. (2009). Making a bigger deal of the smaller words: Function words and other key items in research writing by Chinese learners. *Journal of Second Language Writing, 18,* 149–165. https://doi.org/10.1016/j.jslw.2009.05.004.

Meneghini, R., & Packer A. L. (2007). Is there science beyond English? *EMBO Reports, 8*(2), 112–116. https://doi.org/10.1038/sj.embor.7400906.

Napolitano, D. M., & Stent, A. (2009). TechWriter: An evolving system for writing assistance for advanced learners of English. *Calico Journal, 26*(3), 611–625. https://www.jstor.org/stable/calicojournal.26.3.611.

Pendar, N., & Cotos, E. (2008). Automatic identification of discourse moves in scientific article introductions. In Tetreault, J, Burstein, J., & De Felice, R. (Eds.), *Proceedings of the Third Workshop on Innovative Use of NLP for Building Educational Applications* (pp. 62–70). Association for Computational Linguistics. https://www.aclweb.org/anthology/W08-0908.pdf.

Schmidt, R. W. (1990). The role of consciousness in second language learning. *Applied Linguistics, 11*(2), 129–158. https://doi.org/10.1093/applin/11.2.129.

Schmidt, R. W. (1994). Deconstructing consciousness in search of useful definitions for applied linguistics. In J. H. Hulstijn & R. Schmidt (Eds.), *Consciousness and second language learning: Conceptual, methodological and practical issues in language learning and teaching, thematic issue of AILA review—Revue de l'AILA* (pp. 11–26). Free University Press

Siepmann, D., Gallagher, J. D., Hannay, M., & Mackenzie, J. L. (2011). *Writing in English: A guide for advanced learners.* UTB.

Smirnova, E. A. (2019). Referential coherence of academic texts: A corpus-based analysis of L2 research papers in management. *Journal of Language and Education, 5*(4), 112–127. https://doi.org/10.17323/jle.2019.9688.

Staples, S., Egbert, J., Biber, D., & Gray, B. (2016). Academic writing development at the university level: Phrasal and clausal complexity across level of study, discipline, and genre. *Written Communication, 33*(2), 149–183. https://doi.org/10.1177/0741088316631527.

Swales, J. M. (1990). *Genre analysis: English in academic and research settings.* Cambridge University Press.

Villalón, J., Kearney, P., Calvo, R. A., & Reimann, P. (2008, July 1–5). Glosser: Enhanced feedback for student writing tasks. In *2008 Eighth Institute of Electrical and Electronics Engineers (IEEE) International Conference on Advanced Learning Technologies* (pp. 454–458). IEEE. https://doi.org/10.1109/icalt.2008.78.

Wallwork, A. (2016). *English for writing research papers.* Springer.

9 Punctuation in L2 English: Computational Methods Applied in the Study of L1 Interference

Olga Vinogradova, Anna Viklova, and Veronika Smilga
HSE University, Moscow

This chapter presents the results of learner corpus observations of punctuation misuses in English language writing by learners with Russian as their native language. The observations were carried out across research datasets extracted from the texts of essays from English examinations written by Russian university students. The research question concerned the possibility of first language (L1) interference as a cause of punctuation mistakes, so Russian punctuation conventions were introduced for comparison. The statistical results confirmed the strong influence of the native language in making decisions about the uses of punctuation marks. The conclusions highlight the importance for English as a Foreign Language (EFL) professionals of drawing their students' attention to the similarities and differences in applying punctuation marks in L1 and L2 starting with quite early stages in their acquisition of the new language.

"Loads of people hate punctuation, don't know why we should use it and don't really understand the purpose of it." This is how Joanne Rudling, the author of the online course *Beginners Guide to Punctuation*, starts her introduction.[1] This attitude to punctuation has been around for a long time, as there have been arguments over the general importance of punctuation or over this or that convention ever since the appearance of the first guides and stylesheets for authors in all English-speaking countries (there are many references to such arguments throughout the book by the English journalist Henry Hitchings

---

1 This research was carried out as part of the HSE University Research Foundation project «2021 - Автоматизированная проверка текста, написанного на английском языке русскоязычными авторами»

The Language Wars: A History of Proper English, published in 2011). In the unpublished manuscript, *How to Punctuate*, by R. L. Trask and L. D. Wale (as cited in Jones, 1997), the authors start by addressing questions common in the 1990s—which are still relevant today in the age of texting and Twitter:

> Why should you learn to punctuate properly? After all, many people have made successful careers without ever learning the difference between a colon and a semi-colon. Perhaps you consider punctuation to be an inconsequential bit of decoration, not worth spending your valuable time on. Or perhaps you even regard punctuation as a deeply personal matter—a mode of self-expression not unlike your taste in clothes or music. (p. 9)

Rudling, as well as Trask and Wale, attempt to refute such arguments, and they successfully demonstrate the importance of punctuation, as does Lynne Truss (2003) in *Eats, Shoots and Leaves: The Zero Tolerance Approach to Punctuation*. In spite of the popularity of Truss's book among the broader public, there are many papers both in the second-language acquisition (SLA) community and in computational linguistics whose authors emphasize the fact that punctuation—both the conventions of usage among native speakers and the teaching of them to language learners—still remains hugely understudied. In "What's the Point? A (Computational) Theory of Punctuation," Bernard Jones (1997) attempted to make English learners aware of English punctuation conventions by studying the distributions of native speakers' uses of punctuation through extensive corpus research. A similar approach was applied to study punctuation uses in a recent paper by Markov et al. (2018), but with advanced computational methods. It shows that punctuation uses in learner English were good predictors of a learners' native language, as native language continues to influence punctuation use even after a high proficiency level in a non-native language is achieved. The implications for SLA professionals are serious, suggesting that punctuation may need to be highlighted in English-language instruction in ways that it currently is not. Our research, the focus of which is not on identification of learners' first language (L1), but on relating the problems with English punctuation uses by Russian learners to Russian punctuation conventions, also confirms the insufficiency of attention paid to English punctuation in English as a foreign language (EFL) teaching traditions.

In the following chapter we review the punctuation approaches that are expressed in English punctuation guides and stylesheets, and as the main part of the research, we examine misuses of English punctuation in Russian learners' texts in English and decide whether they stem from the standard punctuation usage in Russian. At the same time, we look into and take into consideration the cultural background and educational practices in Russia in comparison to those in English-speaking countries. We specifically look at the writing of Russian learners of English in academic settings because the need to stick to the set of conventions is stronger there than in less formal settings and the conventions themselves are more uniform than in informal production. Against the background of the well-known set of conventions (see reference sources), the research reveals which specific deviations from those conventions can be connected to the phenomenon of L1 transfer. This constituted the second goal for our study of punctuation misuses in learners' English, because EFL instructors in Russia need to be aware of which areas of punctuation their Russian learners of English have to be taught.

The research was carried out in three stages. First, we extracted research datasets for each of four major punctuation marks used in learner essays—commas, semicolons, colons, and dashes. Depending on the size and special features of each dataset, we worked out a separate method of analyzing the uses and misuses for each punctuation mark. In the set of comma errors, which was by far the largest, we implemented randomized sampling; in the set of sentences with dashes we excluded those used for numeric spans and other types of range (e.g., April–June period; 55–65 years old, etc.); in the dataset with colons, we did not take into consideration their mathematical uses between numbers. The analysis across the datasets, and the statistical results of our observations are presented in the next section. At the next stage, we annotated the uses of these four punctuation marks as correct or incorrect by comparing learner uses with the rules outlined in our reference materials. Sets of sentences with erroneous uses of the four punctuation marks were analyzed and classified. We also provide information on the corresponding Russian punctuation rules and on the ways Russian students study punctuation at the secondary school level while discussing the possibility of L1 interference among the identified punctuation deviations from the accepted norms in the English language. Methodologically, we followed the directions outlined in the seminal work of Sylvian Granger (2012). The last part summarizes all the conclusions concerning violations of punctuation rules which Russian learners of English most frequently make in their academic writing. We also point out the possible implications for approaches to teaching English punctuation.

Research Materials, Datasets, and Methodological Approach

This study was conducted on a learner corpus, REALEC (Russian Error-Annotated Learner English Corpus), of about 6,000 essays (roughly 1,463,000 words total) written in English by university students of HSE University, Moscow as part of their second-year English examinations.[2] The examination includes two essay tasks: an argumentative essay of about 250–350 words and a 150–250-word description of graphic materials. The native language of the vast majority of the authors is Russian.[3] Most of the writers were between 19 and 21 years old at the time they sat for the examination. Some essays were written by hand, and some were typed on the computer during the examination. The errors made by students in their texts were initially annotated manually by students specially trained to identify errors in English grammar with the help of reference materials, and the total number of annotations in the corpus is over 106,400.

The initial datasets were set up by extracting all sentences from the corpus in which student authors used the following punctuation marks—commas, semicolons, colons, and dashes. The distribution of the data across the four punctuation marks is shown in Table 9.1. It is clear from the summary statistics that the available data with commas exceed those with colons, semicolons, and dashes many times over, so to make all datasets comparable, we had to randomly select five sentences out of each hundred with commas (5%). As a result, we obtained 1,930 sentences with commas for the initial comma research dataset.

A different approach had to be applied to the set of all sentences with dashes. Close to half of the 5,340 sentences with this mark used a dash with spaces around it in place of a hyphen (as in "up – to – date" instead of "up-to-date"), which we excluded, so the initial number was 3,187 dashes in 2,643 sentences. Of those, we then chose to exclude the cases in which dashes introduce spans for numeric or other values (i.e., 1940–2040, 15%–59%, or A - Z). The resulting number of sentences in the dataset was thus only about a sixth of the total count of uses of this mark.

In the set with colons another elimination was applied—we decided not to consider the uses of colons in cases like "the ratio was 3:2" (there were five of them).

---

2   The essays are available in a learner corpus called REALEC (Russian Error-Annotated Learner English Corpus), which is provided open access at http://realec.org/index.xhtml#/exam/.

3   For a few residents of the RF, Russian may be their second language, but as they will have studied at least some subjects in Russian at the secondary school level, and as the language of instruction in their studies at HSE University is Russian, their proficiency in Russian will be very close to that of native speakers; besides, overseas students with different native languages do not take the English examination from which we get written essays for the learner corpus.

The dataset with semicolons was made up of all uses of this mark in the corpus except for eight sentences in which this punctuation mark was used in misspelled words.

For each of the four punctuation marks under observation, we counted the number of sentences in which a certain punctuation mark was included in the error span which annotators identified with the Punctuation tag, the fourth most frequent type of error annotated in REALEC (8,056 occurrences out of 106,401 manual annotations in the corpus). In Table 9.1, summary statistics are shown for each mark.

Table 9.1. Statistics of Data Extracted from REALEC and of the Sets Chosen for the Research

	Comma	Dash	Colon	Semicolon
# marks in the corpus	60,165	3,187	1,779	474
# sentences in the corpus with the mark	38,599	2,643	1,729	342
# sentences extracted for the research dataset	1,929 (5% random selection)	926 (not in spans)	1,724 (not between numbers)	334
# sentences with **Punctuation** tag	87	11	20	27

However, we have to admit that annotating with the Punctuation tag in the corpus—at least for some annotators—was not completely consistent, and the corrections conform to the rules in the reference materials only in clear and unambiguous cases, as the annotators themselves were students and learners of English and thus prone to the same weaknesses in the use of punctuation. Therefore, for the sake of bolstering the reliability of the data, the research team of three EFL experts annotated the sentences in each dataset to identify correct and incorrect uses of punctuation on the basis of the authoritative reference sources—Jones (1997), Huddleston and Pullum (2002), and Straus and Kaufman (2008). For unclear cases, we used additional reference sources on the following websites:

- https://dictionary.cambridge.org/grammar/british-grammar/punctuation
- https://www.ef.com/wwen/english-resources/english-grammar/punctuation/
- https://www.grammarbook.com/punctuation_rules.asp
- https://linguapress.com/grammar/english-punctuation.htm

While making decisions about whether or not a particular use of a punctuation mark is appropriate, we also worked out classes of punctuation misuses. The statistics on errors identified by our team of EFL instructors on the basis of reference sources is shown in Table 9.2 along with the percentage of sentences that were considered erroneous.

Table 9.2. Statistics on Comma, Dash, Colon, and Semicolon Uses and Misuses in Research Datasets.

	Comma	Colon	Dash	Semicolon
# sentences extracted for the research dataset	1,929	1,724	926	334
# sentences chosen to be in the research dataset[4]	1,873	1,638	863	269
# sentences marked correct in the use of the punctuation	1,300	1204	574	171
# sentences marked incorrect in the use of the punctuation	573	434	289	98
percentage of errors	31%	36%	33%	36%

Categorization of punctuation errors in Russian learner texts

In all four datasets, we noted cases when a different punctuation mark was required instead of the one used by the author of the text; we also counted redundant uses of each punctuation mark; whenever possible, we noted absent punctuation where the mark was necessary. By far the largest set of punctuation errors is composed of comma misuses. The analysis of the comma research dataset resulted in identifying five classes of the most frequent mistakes and five more classes of mistakes that appeared with lower frequency, but we can say that there were nevertheless enough errors represented in the corpus to consider them characteristic for Russian learners. We also identified two classes of errors which border on a variation of the norm rather than being considered erroneous, but because the rules related to these last two classes are included in the majority of the reference materials (see the discussion in the last section of this paper), we chose to take them into consideration along with the other ten. As a result, we worked out 11 different classes of punctuation errors that are listed in Table 9.3 together with examples from the essays in the learner corpus.

---

4   We eliminated sentences with a low level of proficiency in English in which the meaning was totally incomprehensible to our team.

Table 9.3. Categorization and Examples of Errors in the Use of Commas in REALEC[5]

	Class of errors	Examples
1	A redundant comma after the main clause in front of a subordinate clause	But we can't ignore the fact**,** that the main aim of high education is to bring up great proffesionals.
		And the problem raises**,** when it concerns young people who are truly believe in their own independence.
		For them it is normal**,** when there are more male or female students in subjects.
2	Confusion with commas around relative clauses	From the graph it can be noted that the proportion of the population aged 65 and over increases from 1940 to 2040 years in all countries**,** which are presented.
		Thirdly, such equality would negatively affect not only a person**,** who was not accepted by university, but also a person**,** who was.
		Firstly, there are faculties**,** where men's qualities are incredibly needed.
3	Confusion with commas around discourse-organizing units	All in all_ the graph shows**,** that the amount of people aged 65 and over is not static between 1940 and 2040, it changes dramatically and in whole is going up.
		If universities ever would count gender as a decisive factor, the whole education system would be broken_ in my opinion.
		Comparing the proportion of populations_ it can be seen that since 1940, the average levels had grown up from 5 to 10% to more than 25%.
4	Absence of comma to coordinate independent clauses with *and/but/or* etc.	In conclusion, I would like to emphasize that both man and woman should be able to choose their subject independly_ and the amount of people to every discipline by no means should be determined by universities.
		First of all, in modern world every person should have the same rights as others_ and any discrimination is prohibited.
5.1	Colon required instead of comma	All in all the graph shows**,** that the amount of people aged 65 and over is not static between 1940 and 2040, it changes dramatically and in whole is going up.
5.2	Semicolon required instead of comma	To draw a conclusion, we may say that not only social or economic tendencies, but also government policies might cause certain changes in social proportions**,** consequently, these policies and tendencies should be accurately governed.

---

5   NB: All words in the sentences in Tables 9.3 and 9.5–9.7 are represented with the author's spelling, grammar, and vocabulary fully preserved; punctuation marks regarded as incorrect are bolded; for erroneous absence of a punctuation mark, we underline the space where the mark is needed.

	Class of errors	Examples
5.2	(*continued*) Semi-colon required instead of comma	So we may notice that all of the lines go up, it means that proportion of population aged 65 and over within years will be higher and higher.
		Some people believe that it's inappropriate, to make universities accept equal numbers of male/female students, others agree that it will improve current situation in education.
5.3	Dash required instead of comma	Maybe this way we will miss a gender equality, but we will achieve a much more important thing, the people equality.
		What is worth doing, is worth doing well, it is unwise to forbid it.
6	Redundant comma in different contexts (not the same as in Class 1)	That's why I suppose that universities have to try to accept equal numbers of representatives of both sex, for every subject.
		Some people believe that it's inappropriate, to make universities accept equal numbers of male/female students, others agree that it will improve current situation in education.
		What is worth doing, is worth doing well, it is unwise to forbid it.
		To specialize on a type of work you're best at, is the most efficient way to organise society.
7.1	Confusion with commas around appositives	To sum up, everyone_ both males and females_ has a right and opportunity to choose their profession and study in a place they want.
7.2	Confusion with commas around attributive participial construction	Compared to LinkedIn, Instagram is more used by young people, aged from 18 to 29.
		Some people, living in far regions, haven't got a cinema near.
		Nowadays when peoples health is affected by different dangers, caused by the development of humanity, this topic is especially problematic.
8	Confusion with commas in comparative constructions	First of all, in that situation all of students should feel better, than in the situation, when in class there are more girls or boys.
		It is interesting that LinkedIn is as popular among 65+ users, as among 18–29 users.
9	Oxford comma	So, you should stop drinking a lot, spend holidays with your son or dauther_ and try to be a good example for him.
10	Absence of comma after a subordinate clause in front of the main clause	If the weather is good all over the year_ then it is not the problem to provide the population with food, because you can seed all the year.
		Secondly, most music fans, if they like the group_ will buy the T-shorts or something like that with photos of favourite groups.
11	Ellipsis	The persantage of unemployment stood unchanged in N. Africa at 12,5%, in S. Asia_ at 3,9%.

For comparison with similar prior research, Table 9.4 gives a list of common rules taught in the American EFL tradition; it was compiled by Israel et al. (2012, p. 286) by looking through guidebooks and stylesheets available for American EFL professionals (rules concerning use of punctuation in special categories like numerals, titles, and proper nouns rather than in the sentences are omitted in our representation).

Table 9.4. Common Comma Uses (in American EFL Practices)

Rule	Example	Corresponding error classes from Table 9.3
Elements in a list	Paul put the kettle on, Don fetched the teapot, and I made tea.	Absence of comma to coordinate independent clauses with *and/but/or*, etc., class 4
Initial word/ phrase	Hopefully, this car will last for a while.	Confusion with commas around discourse-organizing units, class 3
Dependent Clause	After I brushed the cat, I lint-rollered my clothes.	Absence of comma after a subordinate clause in front of the main clause, class 10
Independent Clause	I have finished painting, but he is still sanding the doors.	Absence of comma to coordinate independent clauses with *and/but/or*, etc., class 4
Parentheticals	My father, a jaded and bitter man, ate the muffin.	Confusion with commas around appositives, class 7,1
Conjunctive adverbs	I would be happy, however, to volunteer for the Red Cross.	Confusion with commas around discourse-organizing units, class 3
Contrastive Elements	He was merely ignorant, not stupid.	Confusion with commas in comparative constructions, class 8

It is clear that practically all the classes of errors we identified in Russian learners' writing were the same as the classes of recommended uses of commas on the list compiled by the American authors, whose research aim was to achieve highly efficient automated identification of punctuation errors in EFL learners' writing.

The distribution of the occurrences of erroneous uses of commas in our research dataset is given in Figure 9.1. The numbers next to the lines for each class of errors demonstrate how many sentences contained this type of error from the 573 sentences that were regarded as erroneous by the three EFL experts. This subset of 573 sentences was a little under a third of the original 1,980 sentences. The rest of the sentences were 1,300 sentences with correct uses of punctuation (two-thirds of the research dataset) and 56 erroneous sentences in which the level of the author's proficiency was clearly so low that we had enough ground for doubts about his or her awareness of any punctuation in the English language at all.

Some of the labels we have applied in the distribution in Figure 9.1 constitute specific classes of errors identified in the comma dataset—namely, the four types of errors most frequently made by Russian learners of English:

- a redundant comma after the main clause and in front of the subordinate clause;
- confusion with commas around different types of relative clauses;
- confusion with commas around different discourse-organizing units;
- absence of a comma before a conjunction coordinating indenpendent clauses (and, but, or).

One more frequently made mistake was using a comma where another punctuation mark (e.g., dash, colon, or semicolon) was required instead of the comma. Other types of errors were less frequent in comparison with the first five, and four types out of six included a few specific types of a similar nature, so the count was carried out for all of them as a class.

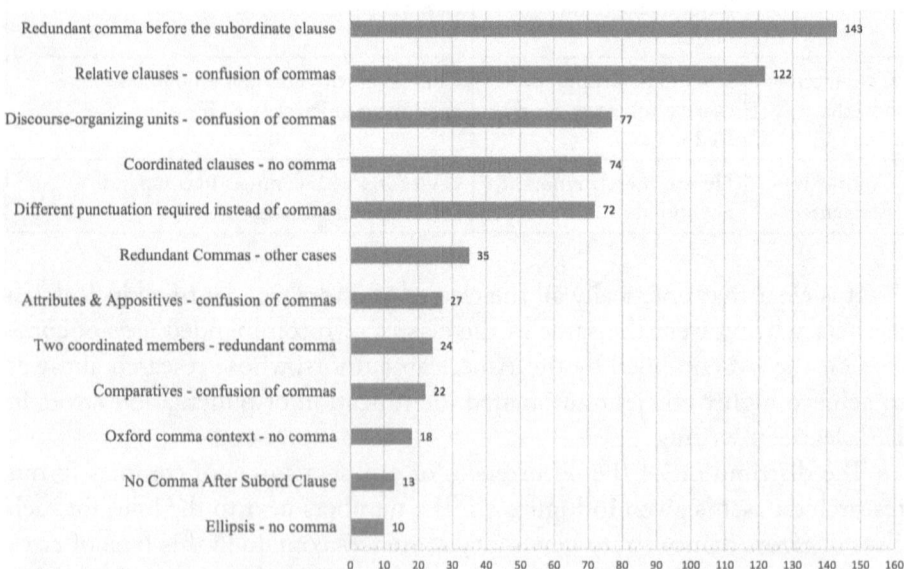

Figure 9.1. Distribution of classes of punctuation errors in the use of commas.

Examples concerning the other three punctuation marks are presented in Tables 9.5, 9.6, and 9.7.

Among the incorrect uses from the research datasets for the three other punctuation marks for many contexts, there was often a question of the variability of dashes and colons, or colons and semicolons, or even of all three marks. For two examples from Huddleston and Pullum (2002), for example, three native English speakers regarded the following punctuation uses as equally appropriate:

- He had forgotten the thing he needed most: a map.
- He had forgotten the thing he needed most – a map.
- He had forgotten the thing he needed most; a map would have saved him a lot of trouble.
- He had forgotten the thing he needed most – a map would have saved him a lot of trouble.
- All students had to take a language: Sue took French.
- All students had to take a language; Sue took French.
- All students had to take a language – Sue took French.

Our decision was to regard any sentence similar to those in the examples here as correct. The only choice we applied was the following (and it may possibly look suspicious to some experts, but it consistently proved preferable in our search in corpora of writing produced by native speakers): in cases of general expression followed by a list of specific entities (noun groups, verb groups, etc.), a dash has to introduce the illustration, and a colon has to be used for explanation. Prototypical examples of erroneous uses of a colon are represented in Table 9.5 with a number of similar occurrences out of 434 sentences (see Table 9.1) given in parentheses. The misused colons in the examples are given in red.

Table 9.5. Examples of Errors in the Use of Colons in REALEC

	Type of error (#sentences out of 434)	Examples
1	Dash required instead of colon (206)	From 194 to 1960 the number rose steadily in both countries: in the USA and in Sweden, while Japan experienced a slight fall in the number of old people by 4 per cent.
2	Comma required instead of colon (58)	On my opinion: the main purpose of social media is communication.
		For example: 70% males and only 30% females got post-graduate diploma.

	Type of error (#sentences out of 434)	Examples
3	Semicolon required instead of colon (64)	A good worker should share the interests of the company: if he does not, he will not work for success.
		If the goverment decided to increase the number of sports facilities it does not mean that all people decided to go in for sport: some of them, moreover, are not able to do it.
4	Redundant colon (106)	From position of airlines we can argue that: air market is not very high profitable, attentional taxes will decrease amount of passengers and increase price of tickets.
		And there is a task: how to grow the level of people health?

Next we give examples of dash misuses in Table 9.6, and then in the last section we go on to discuss why Russian learners produced strange sentences with redundant dashes, which we counted separately in our annotation of errors (21 out of 104 total redundant uses of dashes).

Table 9.6. Examples of Errors in the Use of Dashes

	Type of error (#sentences out of 289)	Examples
1	Comma required instead of dash (74)	The more reposts — the more audience, listeners and followers.
		When you make copies of film or a music without author's permission — you can be punished.
2	Colon required instead of dash (61)	That is why import is necessary — it allows people to choose that they want to eat from the wide range of products.
3	Semicolon required instead of dash (14)	To my mind, the last position is not right at all — it sounds like a feminism.
4	Redundant dash (83+21)	The last group — of children was only 14,3% and is going to descend to 11,5%.
		Using hi-tech to motivate people be more active — is a possible solution.
		In addition, the first small step for public health — restrictions on fast food.

The dataset for semicolons in REALEC was the smallest dataset in this study, as there were only 98 sentences in which the researchers identified misuses of semicolons. In many sentences there was no ground whatsoever for using a semicolon, so in the end we considered the errors in the use of semicolons to be typos rather than inappropriate decisions to use a semicolon. This must have happened, for one, in this case: "However; in airbus usually people sleep." Besides, Russian punctuation conventions for semicolons cover fewer cases than English rules do. As a result, there was little ground to suspect L1 interference. However, to make a certain claim, we need to be confident that we have sufficient data, and the dataset was too small. Out of 98 sentences with erroneous uses of a semicolon, in the majority—61—we came to the decision that a comma was required instead of a semicolon.

Table 9.7. Categorization and Examples of Errors in the Use of Semicolons

	Type of error (# sentences out of 98)	Examples
1	Comma required instead of semicolon (61)	The number desktop users accounted for approximately 130 million in 2012; whereas it fell slightly by 2013 accounting about 130 million users.
		As we know, sport can normilise blood pressure; help your heart work and prevent the development of obesity.
		The positive point of starting university studying after finishing school is that you will learn new science; and get new information.
2	Dash required instead of semicolon (14)	The population has been broken into two main types; general and prison.
		In 2000 the highest amount of children without access to primary school education was in Africa; 23,7 million girls and 20 million boys.
3	Colon required instead of semicolon (10)	In 2015 there was a slight decrease of this rate in the Middle East; it decreased by 1,4%.
		The second place was occupied by 26 - 40 year olds people; their figure accounted 30 %.
4	Redundant semicolon (13)	The positive point of starting university studying after finishing school is that you will learn new science; and get new information.
		And I 'm absolutely sure that only strong measures in each field; may lead us to result, which consists in unpolluted nature and health nation.
		The tendency towards such a 'passive' way of participating is growing more and more popular, which has led to a great amount of agrument; whether it is worth doing at all.

Discussions Concerning English Punctuation Acquisition

While trying to establish the types of errors that may have been made under the influence of learners' native language, the researchers compared the systems of punctuation rules for English and for Russian. Table 9.8 summarizes the results of the comparison with short made-up examples with the same meaning in English and Russian. Columns "Eng" and "Rus" have a plus if a rule that mandates the use of punctuation exists in English or Russian correspondingly, and they have a minus if there is no such rule. The third symbol used in columns "Eng" and "Rus" is "+/-," and it means that there is a rule prescribing when to apply and when not to apply a punctuation mark in the corresponding context. However, Table 9.8 only includes cases in which the distribution in using or not using punctuation is different for English and Russian. The table is followed by detailed explanations of the different conventions in each language.

In the examples in the last column, the punctuation mark or its absence—according to the rule—is enclosed in brackets, and when the rule prescribes no use of a mark, there is just space in brackets. So, it is clear which areas correlate in the English and in the Russian equivalents. The optional uses of a punctuation mark are enclosed in parentheses.

Table 9.8. Differences in English and Russian Punctuation Conventions for the Same Contexts

	Presence of punctuation		Examples
	Eng	**Rus**	
A comma after the main clause in front of the subordinate clause	-	+	I will tell you this[ ] when you come. Я расскажу тебе это[,] когда ты придешь.
Commas around relative clauses	+/-	+	I know a rule[] which works here. Я знаю правило[,] которое здесь работает. I know this rule[,] which is hard to apply. Я знаю это правило[,] которое применять трудно.

	Presence of punctuation		Examples
	Eng	**Rus**	
Punctuation around discourse-organizing units	comma/ semi-colon	comma/-	I know this[,] however[,] I don't know what to do. OR I know this[;] however[,] I don't know what to do. Я это знаю[,] однако[,] я не знаю, что делать. It is difficult to work with him[,] however[,] it is also nice. Работать с ним трудно[,] однако[ ] и приятно.
Comma after discourse-organizing units introducing lists	+	-	You will want to bring many backpacking items[,/;] for example, sleeping bags, pans, and warm clothing. Вам следует взять много походных вещей[,] например[ ]_спальные мешки, сковородки и теплую одежду.
Commas after fronted units	+/-	-	Right from the start[(,)] I knew the rules. С самого начала[ ]я знал эти правила.
Comma for coordinating independent clauses with *and/but/or*, etc.	+/-	+/-	I learned about these rules[(,)] and it was helpful. Я узнал про эти правила[,] и это было полезно.
Punctuation after subject clause introduced with *wh*-word or expressed by the infinitive.	-	comma/ dash	What you know[ ] is true. Что (То, что) ты знаешь [, /—] (это) правда. To tell her[ ] is the hardest thing to do. Сказать ей [—] это самое трудное.
Comma after the infinitive of purpose after the predicate	-	+	He came there[ ] to see her. Он пришел туда[,] чтобы ее увидеть.
Commas around attributive participial constructions	+/-	+	People[ ] living in remote regions[ ] haven't got electricity. У людей[,] живущих далеко[,] нет электричества. Living in remote regions[,] people travel more. Живя в отдаленных районах[,] люди ездят больше.

	Presence of punctuation		Examples
	Eng	Rus	
Commas in comparisons with *than*	−	+	To tell her is much harder[ ] than to conceal it from her. Сказать ей гораздо труднее[,] чем скрыть это от нее.
Punctuation in cases of ellipsis	comma	dash	In 1920, the highest percentage was shown by the elderly, but in 2010[,] by the young. В 1920 самый высокий процент показали пожилые, а в 2010 [—] молодые.

The first convention in Table 9.8 covers the class of comma misuses most frequently demonstrated in Russian student essays written in English (see Table 9.3, class "Redundant comma in front of the subordinate clause after the main clause"). These errors constitute the first area in which the phenomenon of language transfer begs to be explored, and the following considerations are the reasons for thinking that it is indeed L1 interference. First, in Russian a comma introduces and completes any subordinate clause, no matter whether the dependent clause comes before or after the main clause. This rule is rigid, and absence of a comma before or after the dependent clause in a Russian sentence is seen as a blunder by native speakers of Russian. This punctuation rule is taught in Russian classes at the secondary school level. Russian punctuation gets even more important in Russian grammar classes in the final years in Russian high schools, as all students take their obligatory school-leaving examination in the Russian language, and violations of punctuation conventions are strictly penalized. The results of this examination are submitted (along with the results of a few other examinations) in applications for university studies. As a result, knowledge of Russian grammar, including punctuation, is of much importance, at least for those students who apply for university programs. This means, in turn, that students graduating from secondary schools remember the main punctuation rules very well—as the Russian saying has it, "they know it well even if they are woken up in their sleep." The result for the acquisition of English as a foreign language is that it has become very difficult for Russian learners of English not to automatically separate any subordinate clause with commas in their writing in English—hence a lot of erroneous commas in contexts like "think, that" or "fact, that" or "do it, when".

The additional proof of L1 interference is the fact that a comma is always recommended after a subordinate clause of longer than four to five words introducing a main clause (see Dependent Clause type among "American EFL comma rules" in Table 9.4). Russian learners almost never omit this comma—out of 573 sentences with errors in the use of commas, there were only 13 in which the dependent clause was not separated from the main clause with a comma. Compare this number with 143 sentences with a redundant comma in front of the subordinate clause after the main clause. In our view, this has to do with the same strict rule in Russian—a subordinate clause always has to be separated from the main clause with a comma, on both sides if applicable, so students overwhelmingly do it in English too, not differentiating the use of commas for subordinate clauses positioned before and after the main clause, nor looking at how many words there are in the subordinate clause. In the end, the phenomenon of L1 transfer in this particular area appears to be positive for one sequence of clauses but clearly negative for the other.

The next row in Table 9.8 also relates to the frequent error, "Confusion with commas in relative clauses" (the second in frequency of occurrence) in Table 9.3. The reason for the frequency is the fact that relative clauses constitute an especially difficult grammar area for Russian learners, and again, interference with L1 is certainly at play. In Russian, there is no differentiation of relative clauses, and the Russian equivalents to English relative clauses (traditionally called attributive subordinate clauses) are always separated from the main clause with a comma. Furthermore, they all are introduced by one and the same conjunction in Russian equivalents of defining and non-defining relative clauses, and the Russian equivalents of coordinate clauses are introduced by a completely different conjunction. Accordingly, acquisition of the last type of relative clause poses no difficulty at all for Russian learners, while the notion of the division of clauses into defining and non-defining types presents an entirely new concept. It should not be surprising, then, that it requires more time and much more exposure to authentic English sentences with relative clauses than most students usually get at the university level. Moreover, relative clauses also require sensitivity towards linguistic subtleties on the part of teachers of English so that they can draw their students' attention to all the differences between defining and non-defining relative clauses when they come across them in authentic texts, tests, and other materials. Furthermore, sensitivity towards subtle differences is sometimes lacking even in texts written by native speakers of English[6]—misused commas

---

6   There is a comment on that feature in relation to punctuation around relative clauses in Moore, 2016, p. 2.

around relative clauses can be identified in authentic English written production. A simple experiment proved this: the search for "which" in a corpus of British academic writing in English[7] returned among the first 20 sentences (out of 29,167) two sentences with errors in the use of commas around a relative clause. The sentences are copied here with the error spans for the comma and the conjunction in brackets:

1. In conclusion racism, which can be defined as an ideology which categorises people as inferior according to their race, and is put into practice through many policies and actions[,] which seek to exclude non-whites from many areas of society, can still be seen in today's society.
2. The few hospitals set up to provide for the working classes were poor quality, and the women were subjected to harsh treatments, which the upper classes[ ] who could afford to pay for superior treatment[ ] were not.

In sentence (1), the relative clause is in our view defining because it restricted the set of all policies and actions to those that seek to exclude non-whites, so no comma was required in front of the relative clause; however, the comma after the relative clause was justified because it is also the end of the long non-defining relative clause, starting with "which can be defined." In sentence (2), the relative clause introduced with "who" was non-defining, in our opinion, as "upper classes" in this sentence was the opposite of "working" classes, namely, people who are not poor and who can thus "afford to pay," so the relative clause required commas both before and after it.

The second conclusion concerning relative clauses is that, just as in the prior case involving subordinate clauses, Russian learners appear to benefit from applying the rule of obligatory commas around relative clauses transferred from Russian punctuation when they apply it to English non-defining and coordinate clauses. However, the same Russian rule causes redundant commas in the case of defining clauses, which—unfortunately for Russian learners—are more frequent than the first two types.

In the third and fourth rows in Table 9.8, we again have contexts in which errors in the use of commas occur very frequently—commas around discourse-organizing units. It is true that Russian and English separate these

---

7   The search was carried out on the platform called SketchEngine, which hosts many language corpora and is equipped with tools for searching contexts for separate words, phrases, or sophisticated combinations of elements of the text, and the results of the search were received from the British Academic Written English Corpus (BAWE).

expressions with commas in very similar ways, and in both languages, there are words used as discourse-organizing elements that sometimes have commas around them and sometimes do not. The problem is that the rules prescribing different comma behavior with such words differ in English and in Russian. Furthermore, the rules are sophisticated, and applying them, again, requires linguistic sensitivity, and for some speakers they become a sort of grey area in English punctuation conventions. We can quote here Straus and Kaufman's (2008) well-known American grammar book with a large chapter devoted to punctuation:

> Use either a comma or a semicolon before introductory words such as namely, that is, for example, e.g., for instance when they are followed by a series of items. Use a comma after the introductory word. Examples: You may be required to bring many items, for example, sleeping bags, pans, and warm clothing. OR You may be required to bring many items; for example, sleeping bags, pans, and warm clothing. OR You may be required to bring many items, e.g., sleeping bags, pans, and warm clothing. (pp. 57–58)

In the end, a reader is left with the idea that it does not matter whether or not the discourse-organizing units given before the list of items are followed by a comma, but a corpus search in any large collection of native English writing demonstrates that at least "namely," "that is," "for example," and "for instance" are indeed overwhelmingly followed by a comma.

The differences between English and Russian comma conventions with discourse-organizing units are shown in Table 9.8 with examples of English "however" and Russian "однако." The former has to have commas around it "when they are used as interrupters" (Straus & Kaufman, 2008, p. 57) and does not require commas when used in the same way as "how" ("however you do it"), or with an adjective or adverb following it ("however difficult it may seem"; "however smartly you solve it"). The latter, the Russian equivalent, is always introduced with a comma, but is followed by a comma only when there is a complete clause after it and is not followed by a comma when there is a coordinated member, and not a complete clause, after it (literally: "hard however nice"). Given that Russian students had substantial difficulty differentiating the two uses in Russian, it is not surprising that they have overgeneralized both the "Russian" and the "English" conventions by applying them in writing in English and getting, as a result, confusion with commas of the following two types—with a comma or semi-colon in front of "however," but lacking a comma after it: "In other words, some people find happiness in their family, however others prefer to be alone;" and with a redundant comma like "He tries to solve a problem, however, difficult it may seem."

Another example of the difficulty with punctuating discourse-organizing units is that words like "thus" get a comma when they appear at the beginning of a sentence but can do without commas in the middle of a sentence like in this example: "He overcame his incertitude and thus won the respect of his classmates." In Russian, there are two equivalents of "thus"—one is a word combination "*таким образом*," which always requires commas after it or on both sides, and the other is just one word "*так*," which can be used in exactly the same two ways as "thus" in English—as a discourse-organizing unit at the beginning followed by a comma, or as an adverbial modifier without commas around it. If a certain learner bears the first equivalent in mind, he or she will develop redundant commas in "He overcame his incertitude and[,] thus[,] won the respect of his classmates." If the learner thinks of a one-word equivalent of "thus," their use of commas with this word in English may turn out correct.

The next context from Table 9.8 that needs explaining is when two clauses get coordinated with the help of conjunctions "and," "but," "or," "as well as," and some others. According to Straus and Kaufman (2008, p. 55), the comma is optional when two coordinating clauses are independent in English: "Use a comma to separate two strong clauses joined by a coordinating conjunction—and, or, but, for, nor. You can omit the comma if the clauses are both short." When two subordinate clauses get coordinated, the English convention is not to have a comma in front of "and," "but," "or," and "as well as," but if the first clause is long, it often has other constructions in it, and a comma at the end of some constructions often falls on the position in front of the coordinating conjunction. This may explain the fact that not many sets of punctuation tips include the rule that a comma should not be placed between the two coordinated subordinate clauses. As a result, in English coordinating clauses of both types—dependent and independent—a comma is somewhat optional. In Russian, on the contrary, the rule for a comma in coordinating clauses is very strict: if the two clauses are independent, then the comma is obligatory, while the comma is forbidden in coordinating two subordinate clauses. The same rule, but with different variations, makes coordinating English clauses an error-prone area for Russian learners.

One more class in Table 9.8—"Comma after subject clause introduced with 'wh'-word or expressed by the infinitive"—correlates with the classes "Comma required instead of dash" and "Redundant dash" in Table 9.6. Errors in these two classes are clearly caused by interference with Russian practices. The first of the examples in Table 9.8 represents a clause introduced by "what" to express the subject of a larger clause. The rule in English forbids ever separating a subject from a predicate with a comma. However, the same construction in Russian obeys the rule that requires separating any clause with commas, including a subject clause. Nevertheless, the Russian language allows for the alternative of omitting the predicate when it is expressed by the verb "BE" in the present tense (and it is omitted in almost all such cases); as a result, a dash appears instead of the omitted verb, and it may be followed by the Russian equivalent to "this." The same thing happens to subjects expressed by infinitive phrases, and again in Russian sentences with the verb "BE" in present tense as a predicate, this predicate may get omitted, causing the appearance of a dash. When a Russian learner of English constructs the direct equivalent of the Russian sentence of this type, it looks completely un-English (even though his and or her level of English proficiency may otherwise be high enough), as in this sentence: "In addition, the first small step towards public health—restrictions on easy availability of fast food." (It means that the first small step towards public health IS to impose restrictions on . . .)

Still another point of difference between English and Russian punctuation rules concerns specific constructions for which these two languages choose different punctuation marks. Quite a few comparative constructions operate differently punctuation-wise: comparison with "than" never requires a comma in front of "than" in English, but in its Russian equivalent a comma is always required before "чем;" in the construction with two forms of the comparative degree of adjectives or adverbs, the common punctuation mark in English is a comma, which is sometimes used in Russian too, but the use of dashes between the two groups with the comparative degrees is more common in Russian, as in this: "The more money, the better for them." "Чем больше денег – тем лучше для них." OR "Чем больше денег, тем лучше для них."

Finally, the choice of the punctuation mark when something has been omitted from the second (or third) clause is also different in the two languages—a comma in English, but a dash in Russian (see examples in the last row in Table 9.8).

Conclusions

Data from the learner corpus clearly indicate that Russian learners had serious problems in the use of punctuation while writing in English, as about a third of the sentences on average may at best look strange and at worst confuse a reader to the extent of becoming incomprehensible. Even one redundant comma in a simple sentence like "We couldn't figure out, when the change started—it was unbearable." may lead the reader to the meaning that the people in the sentence couldn't figure out something that was discussed before this sentence, while the clause introduced with "when" may be understood as referring to the time of change as unbearable, while the author clearly meant that they couldn't figure out when the change started, and that was unbearable. As a result, the Russian rule of separating all clauses in the sentence with commas may be the cause of confusion when writing in English.

To consider punctuation an area that should only be taught to students mastering the highest levels of proficiency in English means to seriously hinder students' development in the acquisition of the target language. Being accustomed to rigorous observance of punctuation rules in their mother tongue, Russian learners are probably compelled to pay more attention to the use of punctuation marks in the foreign language they are trying to master than many other learners. Besides, when some conventions in the use of punctuation are the same, learners may well generalize the sameness to the areas that are subject to rules different from those in the native language. Instead of meeting those needs, the Russian tradition of teaching English as a foreign language has largely neglected many areas where punctuation plays a role in overcoming ambiguity and confusion in order to get the idea through to others efficiently. The result is that Russian learners suffer from insufficient exposure to existing standards and conventions and therefore develop lower resistance to interference coming from their native language.

Punctuation similarities and differences between the native and the target languages have to be revealed to the learners explicitly, and the mere exposure to authentic materials is hardly enough to acquire the necessary skills, as the percentage of errors in writing production at the intermediate to upper-intermediate level of proficiency in English shows. In Elkılıç et al. (2009), the authors state in their conclusion that in order to avoid L1 interference, Turkish EFL students should be taught English punctuation explicitly and in comparison with Turkish punctuation conventions. Similar to the goals of our research, the authors made an attempt to identify which areas of punctuation uses have to be taught in comparison with and in contrast to the Turkish punctuation rules.

We do not mean to say that the problem of teaching too little punctuation is only a problem in the Russian EFL tradition. Learners of English with many different L1s have complained about poor exposure to punctuation conventions in the national traditions of teaching English: there has been a discussion on the internet over the last few years about the fact that Chinese EFL professionals teach almost no punctuation. We can see it, for example, in the following Quora thread, "First of all, it's a language education failure—no systematic course to emphasise the importance of punctuation in English, only a few students self-study after class" (Li, 2015). It does not take much effort to find similar complaints expressed online by learners of English with other native languages.

The attitude to punctuation on the part of English-speaking cultures also plays a role in insufficient attention to punctuation for learners of English. As was demonstrated in the beginning of this paper, many speakers of English think that the context is enough for the reader to work out the meaning without thinking about punctuation marks in the text. Some say that punctuation is gradually dying or fading out in English, especially in the era of very short messages that the new communication technologies dictate. But one should not forget that the people saying it are those who, back when they were young children, had years of constant processing of conventionally used punctuation without even realizing what the conventions themselves were. This is what learners of English need to work very hard at if they ever want to catch up on what they did not get as children. So, learners need help, they need focused exposure, they need EFL professionals patiently pointing out all the commas, colons, semicolons, and dashes used in authentic texts and misused by learners. The teaching traditions in Russia—and all around the world—will do more good for learners of English if they become more punctuation-friendly!

References

Elkılıç, G., Han, T., & Aydin, S. (2009). Punctuation and capitalisation errors of Turkish EFL students in composition classes: An evidence of L1 interference. In Padem, H. (Ed.), *Proceedings of International symposium on sustainable development* (pp. 279–284). International Burch University. http://tara.sdu.edu.tr/vufind/Record/95849.

Granger, S. (2012). How to use foreign and second language learner corpora? In A. Mackey & S. G. Gass (Eds.), *A guide to research methods in second language acquisition* (pp. 7–29). Basil Blackwell.

Hitchings, H. (2011). *The language wars: A history of proper English.* John Murray Publishers.

Huddleston, R., & Pullum, G. K. (2002). *The Cambridge grammar of the English language.* Cambridge University Press.

Israel, R., Tetreault, J., Chodorow, M. (2012, June 3). *Correcting comma errors in learner essays, and restoring commas in newswire text* [Paper presentation]. Conference of the North American Chapter of the Association for Computational Linguistics: Human Language Technologies (pp. 284–294). https://dl.acm.org/doi/10.5555/2382029.2382065.

Jones, B. (1997). *What's the point? A (computational) theory of punctuation* [Unpublished doctoral dissertation]. Centre for Cognitive Science, University of Edinburgh.

Markov, I., Nastase, V., & Strapparava, C. (2018). Punctuation as native language interference. *Proceedings of the 27th International Conference on Computational Linguistics* (pp. 3456–3466). Association for Computational Linguistics. https://aclanthology.org/C18-1000/.

Mingjie, L. (2015, May 1). Why do Chinese people constantly mix up English style punctuation with Chinese style? [Online forum comment]. Message posted to https://www.quora.com/Why-do-Chinese-people-constantly-mix-up-English-style-punctuation-with-Chinese-style.

Moore, N. (2016). What's the point? The role of punctuation in realising information structure in written English. *Functional Linguistics. 3*, 6. https://functionallinguistics.springeropen.com/articles/10.1186/s40554-016-0029-x.

Rudling, J. (n.d.) "Beginner's Guide to English Punctuation." *Curious.com*. Retrieved September 6, 2021 from https://curious.com/howtospell/series/beginners-guide-to-english-punctuation.

Straus, J., & Kaufman, L. (2008). *The blue book of grammar and punctuation.* Jossey-Bass.

Truss, L. (2003). *Eats, shoots & leaves: The zero tolerance approach to punctuation.* Gotham Books.

Part Four. Classroom Practice

10 From Secondary to Tertiary Education in Russia: Bridging the Academic Writing Gap

Tatiana Golechkova
NEW ECONOMIC SCHOOL, MOSCOW

In this chapter, I provide a case study of my experience helping Russian undergraduate students adjust to the requirements of higher education within first-year academic writing courses. Transition problems are largely accounted for by mismatches between students' and instructors' expectations, which originate from Russian historical features and educational policies. The mismatches include imposed lack of responsibility, poor commitment, misunderstanding the role of the instructors, grades, the writing process, and general unfamiliarity with academic conventions. Awareness of these mismatches can help instructors adjust their attitudes to undergraduates and adapt their teaching approaches. The author recommends a few easy-to-implement techniques which proved helpful in the classroom. By raising students' awareness of expectations at university, delegating some of the instructors' tasks to students, incorporating opportunities for making choices, encouraging independent work, and facilitating peer-assessment and reflection, academic writing instructors can help their learners become more responsible writers, which is likely to ensure their successful performance in the university.

There are many cases in which miscommunication takes place. The experience of not being heard and understood is not only uncomfortable for communicants from a psychological point of view but is highly unlikely to produce desired results. Unfortunately, this is what most university professors experience when working with first-year undergraduates in Russia (Maloshonok & Terentev, 2017). The process in a way resembles cross-cultural communication between representatives of two different cultures, who, being eager and generally effective communicators, have different backgrounds and experiences, and, consequently, different expectations. Unawareness of such "gaps and gulfs" (Clerehan, 2002, p. 72) can result in communicative failures which might lead to serious ramifications (Lowe & Cook, 2003). This miscommunication tends to be the case at the initial stages of Russian higher education and is also manifested in academic writing courses delivered to first-year undergraduates.

This "cognitive dissonance between the two parties of the learning process" (Leontyeva, 2018, p. 12) and its causes are more commonly referred to in the literature as a gap between two educational levels, secondary-tertiary transition, or underdeveloped academic literacies in first-year students (Agosti & Bernat, 2018; Chokwe, 2013; Parker, 2003; Wingate, 2012). Regardless of how it is described, transitioning from school to university has been a challenge not only for many students (Kyndt et al., 2017), but for all parties involved (Briggs et al., 2012).

Transition between educational levels is a complex process which is manifested in students' performance in various courses, including academic writing. Academic writing is not purely a written productive skill. Seen as a process, it encompasses and brings into play reading, listening, speaking, and then writing itself. From the perspective of academic study, these would be referred to as academic literacies in the British and European traditions. The concept of academic literacies is defined as a set of social practices associated with different cultures, situations, and communities (Lee & Street, 1998). Writing in this case is the culmination of a process involving academic reading, listening, discussion, and presentation. As a form of communication, or discourse, academic writing can be seen as a way to produce and share knowledge (Lea, 1998; Lea & Street, 1998, 2006), which is critical in academia for progress and achievement (Foster & Russell, 2002). It is not surprising that many first-year students have identified academic writing as their main challenge in adapting to the new stage of education and constructing their new identity as a university student (Gourlay, 2009; Miller & Pessoa, 2017). Consequently, helping students develop the necessary academic literacies significantly improves their performance as writers not only in academic writing, but also in other subjects. This strategy has been widely implemented in the Writing across the Curriculum pedagogy in the U.S. tradition (Russell et al., 2009).

In this essay, I will present the results of a case study conducted with first-year bachelor students during an introduction to academic writing course in a Russian university. This study enabled me to single out the problems the students felt they had with transition from secondary school into higher education. In an attempt to understand what causes difficulties in communication between professors and first-year students, I will start at the national institutional level and describe the situation with higher education and teaching academic writing in the Russian context. I will also present the preceding stages, namely, high school and standardized school-leaving exams. Finally, I will look at a profile of a first-year university Russian student that was developed as a result of the case study. I will identify the expectations with which students enter the university and compare them with the expectations of faculty. This information will help me discuss problems that arise in student-professor interactions and formulate some techniques that I found helpful in my teaching of academic writing courses to undergraduates. These are based on my own experience and observations and those of other instructors working in a similar context.

It is important to state that the aim of the paper is to present the challenges that university professors face with undergraduate students, so I do not cover the strengths and benefits of Russian secondary education in the current paper, which does not mean that there are none. Moreover, the presented tendencies by no means serve as indicators of the quality of Russian secondary school education. They attest more to the gap between the two educational levels, or as Smolentseva (2015) puts it, lack of consistency and continuity between them.

Higher Education in Transition

For the past 20 years, higher education in Russia has been going through a transition from the closed national model well-established in the Soviet Union to a more open and flexible model based on the Bologna system (since 1999), as it facilitates global integration. As I see it, there are two major trends that affect teaching academic writing at the university level.

One important trend is the shift from oral examinations as a dominant assessment form in the USSR to written examinations at the entrance level and within degree programs. For a long time, a discussion with the course instructor served as the main assessment tool. This discussion was graded based on the professor's impression. The test would start with one question and then might go in any direction determined by the professor or the student. As a result, at the undergraduate level, students could do without well-developed academic writing skills, as writing played a marginal role in assessment. The writing skill that was commonly required was summarizing and reviewing literature for the so-called report, so argumentative and research writing was rarely explicitly taught at the secondary school level with the exception of literary text analysis (see Chapter 2). It was not until the last decade that various kinds of essays became more widespread in multiple disciplines, causing the need for students to possess good academic writing skills and contributing to the gap between school and university.

The second trend affecting writing practices and requirements in higher education is the need to boost the visibility of Russian researchers in the global community. During the Soviet period, Russian research in several fields was barely available to the global audience, partly due to political reasons, which made Soviet academia quite a closed local community (see Chapter 1). In late 2013, the Russian government launched the Academic Excellence Initiative 5-100, which ensures financial support to leading Russian universities. The participating institutions are required, among other imperatives, to integrate into global research communities and to make Russian research more visible. These both require very high standards of research presentation, which sets the writing bar very high and puts extra pressure on academics. That is why as early as the undergraduate level, future academics could be required not only to conduct world-class research, but also to be able to present it well in writing.

Secondary Schools and University Admission

In Russia, as in many other countries, it is the last stage of secondary school that focuses on preparing students for university. After 9 years of instruction, more academically inclined students proceed to grades 10 and 11, which are generally equivalent to the sixth form and high school in the UK and US, respectively. The national syllabus for those two years is designed so that the learners revise and extend most of the knowledge they have gained in all subjects. At this stage, students do not usually have a choice of the subjects they focus on unless they transfer to a specialized school—an option that is not widely available and therefore not very common across the country. This has generally stayed the same throughout the transition from the Soviet to the Russian education system, while admission procedures have changed dramatically.

Historically, each university in the Soviet Union conducted a set of examinations for potential students. Although the exams were based on the national secondary school curriculum, they could take very different forms and require different skills; for example, some language and linguistics programs required an interview and a reading test, others just a grammar and vocabulary test; still others offered a more language theory-oriented exam. All these subjects are supposed to be covered at school, but there is no specific focus. That is why students had to first select a university, then find out entrance exam requirements, and only then could they start to prepare. On the one hand, this system kept leading universities elitist and contributed to de-massification (Smolentseva, 2016); on the other hand, students were encouraged to make a conscious decision about what university and what program they would like to apply to and to take more responsibility for the decision.

In 2009, a unified state exam was introduced, which marked a dramatic change in secondary school education. Now school leavers take written standardized tests to graduate and to enter universities. This test generally enables applicants from various backgrounds to apply to any university in the country and ensures fairer competition. However, along with the many benefits, one of the disadvantages has been that now high school education tends to focus on training exam skills rather than developing academic literacies. Like any test, it requires preparation for the test format, test-taking strategies, and endless drills. These skills have not necessarily been helpful in universities. Overall, the national school curricula did not change greatly because of the exam, and they still require a wide range of skills, including those necessary for higher education. However, since everyone has to take the unified state exams, high school has tended to focus on the exam rather than more abstract and less tangible academic literacies, which will be needed later.

The format of the English exam is similar to international language exams in that it consists of five parts: grammar and vocabulary, reading, listening, speaking, and writing. The writing part involves writing an informal letter and a short argumentative essay. The assessment rubric for the essay activities is designed so that the focus of assessment is mainly language and adherence to the guidelines (Federal Institute for Pedagogical Measurements, 2020). This focus is understandable for a national-level exam, as these criteria are the easiest to mark and to account for, but it means that students have gotten used to placing a lot of emphasis on accuracy and mechanics instead of content, which is paramount in university level courses, including academic writing.

Case Study

The case study was conducted in the 2018–2019 academic school year when delivering an Introduction to Academic Writing course to first-year undergraduates majoring in international relations and economics at one of the leading universities in Moscow, Russia. The entire program was taught in English, so it recognized academic writing in English as an essential part of the curriculum. The course was 102 academic hours long and started at the very beginning of the program, spanning the fall and spring semesters. The class was divided into three groups of students, so I shared the three sections with a colleague.

The case study involved 78 students, 52 females and 26 males, aged between 17 and 18, who joined the program right after high school. All students passed three unified state exams to enroll: English language, history, and Russian language. They had to achieve at least 70% in English and 60% in history and Russian.

Throughout the course, I observed students' attitudes to learning and expectations that they had formed prior to college. These observations were registered in my journal, which enabled me to identify key attitudes and expectations. These findings were further confirmed during unstructured or semi-structured interviews with individual students. One more step in validating the observations was a long semi-structured interview with my colleague who taught other sections of the course to the same class of students. After that, I matched the findings with the education trends in Russia in order to try to establish a rationale behind the observed attitudes and expectations of our first-year students.

Having established the expectations that were harming the learning process, I conducted a pilot study attempting to mitigate the effects of mismatches through classroom practices within the same introduction to academic writing course delivered in the 2018–2019 academic school year. Based on my prior experience of teaching in a similar context, I selected and implemented several classroom procedures and activities, observed their effect on students' behaviors, and then confirmed my observations with feedback from students. Since these mitigation attempts are not the key focus of the case study, I did not conduct additional quantitative assessment of their effectiveness. However, the results of the pilot study can serve as a starting point for further research into best practices, as they uncovered specific teaching techniques that helped my students overcome the secondary-tertiary gap in the context of the Russian education system.

Students in Transition and Education Trends: Case Study Observations

High school policies and university entrance requirements contribute significantly to the study patterns and expectations the students have (Laing et al., 2005). As a result of these, freshmen often come in with a pre-defined set of beliefs and attitudes, which are not necessarily helpful in undergraduate studies (Lowe & Cook, 2003). The discrepancies become apparent in students' work in academic writing courses, as, like I established earlier, successful performance in these courses requires well-developed academic literacies and academic skills other than writing.

The case study enabled me to uncover several expectations that first-year students have, and the following aspects of the Russian education seem to have shaped those expectations. The first is the optional status of higher education. Students seem to struggle with the fact that degrees are not compulsory, and those who decide to obtain them are expected to demonstrate a higher level of awareness and responsibility. Secondly, massification of higher education in the USSR led to the long-lasting belief that everyone should go to college regardless of their readiness, abilities, and inclinations; ideally, it would happen straight after high school. Thirdly, according to the students, both the secondary school teachers and the student's parents seem to place a great emphasis on the test score, rather than on the tested skills and knowledge. This attitude has also affected the perception of the teacher and their role. Finally, the standardized school-leaving tests have played a role in shaping students' attitudes to studying.

The students reported that getting a place in a university after leaving secondary school was crucial, and obtaining an actual degree seems secondary to that. This attitude appeared to be informed by what is probably the biggest issue underpinning the secondary-tertiary gap—the status of higher education in Russia. On the one hand, higher education is optional and is now becoming less accessible and more elitist. On the other hand, historically the USSR made significant effort to ensure massification of higher education, so that in the 1960s and 1970s it was one of the first countries to achieve this mass stage (Smolentseva, 2016). Yet, due to the massification propaganda, the idea that higher education is obligatory for any decent and respectable individual has now been firmly ingrained in Russian people's minds. As a result, university was seen as non-compulsory and compulsory at the same time in the sense that, unlike secondary school, a university degree was not part of compulsory education, but there was an assumption that those who do not hold a degree have failed just because of that. Moreover, students have believed that they have to do it straight after high school without having much time to properly consider this option. To prove that it is now not a necessity, but a belief held by students and their parents, the results of the unified state exams are valid for four years after obtaining them, so there is every opportunity to postpone the decision without the need to retake the exams (Federal Education Act, 2012).

This urge to get into a university brings about a few serious consequences. Since this step is more of a status move, students appear to treat entering the university as an end in itself, rather than the beginning of a challenging learning process. The case study showed that students have often come in unprepared for commitment and hard work. In addition, according to a survey at a Russian university, students might demonstrate high satisfaction rates when they do not have to put a lot of effort into studying (Chirikov, 2015), proving that they have not been ready to take responsibility for their own learning. Such limited responsibility could also be partly caused by the students' general immaturity and lack of informed decisions at the stage of choosing a university. Since the social pressure to get in has been very high, the students have opted for any program that would accept them regardless of whether this is something they want and have been inclined towards. This was hardly possible before the introduction of the unified state exam because of the differences in entrance exam formats, which required special preparation for each particular program. During this targeted preparation the students had a chance to become more conscious and responsible about choosing a program. Now, according to my observations, having secured any place in any program, the students relax and believe their goal to be fully achieved. Another study showed clearly that Russian first-year undergraduates tended to expect education to happen to them, which was manifested in their unwillingness to participate actively in classes. The students expected to sit through classes and be passive recipients of knowledge (Maloshonok & Terentev, 2017) or at the very best to be guided by the instructors. This is partly something that they would have been used to in the controlled environment of secondary school. However, this expectation does not appear to be common only among Russian students. Similar attitudes to self-regulation and increased workload were reported among British students (Money et al., 2019).

Apart from this passivity, Russian students bring from secondary school a firm belief in do-overs and make-ups, which was another observation that became apparent in the case study. This seems connected with high school being compulsory, meaning that there is no selection and mixed-ability classes. In this case teachers tend to help learners by giving them an opportunity to study more, rewrite tests, and make up assignments. However, being helpful in the short term, it can prove counterproductive in the long run. My experience teaching first-year students has shown that this practice has encouraged some learners not to take tests seriously and, therefore, not to prepare well, hoping that they will pass somehow. They believed that there would be another chance if they did not get away with little preparation the first time, and they could put in real effort at that point. This sounds very logical from the students' point of view, and since they have been given these opportunities, they take advantage without thinking about their responsibility to study well all the time. Moreover, students seem to have found it acceptable to ask explicitly for a make-up if they are not satisfied with the test result. This practice also has taught them not to respect the time it takes to design several versions of tests and to mark them.

One of the reasons for frequent requests for a make-up in case of a satisfactory or even good grade is attitude towards grades and grading systems. This attitude has been the second major issue underpinning the mismatch in student-professor expectations. The interviewed students noted that Russian school children have often been encouraged by the schools and families to get the highest scores possible and not to be content with anything less than excellent. This may be possible at secondary school where the amount of information to digest and the skills to develop are tailored to average abilities so that every child can exercise their right to secondary education. In this case, an excellent mark can be quite easily achievable and does not require outstanding performance, especially on the part of brighter, more academically inclined children. However, in highly specialized university programs, the amount of material and required depth of analysis is much greater, which means that each higher grade requires a substantial investment of effort and time. That is why a pass, not an excellent grade, should be treated as the baseline, while everything above is a significant achievement.

This mismatch in expectations has been supported by research. According to a survey carried out at a Russian university, 43% of first-year students overestimated the grades they were likely to obtain (Maloshonok & Terentev, 2017), as they were used to getting very high marks quite easily at school. Moreover, the researchers have proven statistically that the mismatch between expected and real grades affected students' academic performance (Maloshonok & Terentev, 2017). Compounded by the social pressure to get into a university and the consequent need to receive the highest scores possible on the unified state exam, the case study showed that the importance of assessment has tended to be inflated to the degree that it starts interfering with the performance. This attitude among students adds extra stress and shifts the focus from learning to scoring high on tests. Similar trends were reported in other higher education contexts (see DeFeo et al., 2020; Khan, 2014; Romanowski, 2004), making it a global problem that requires attention.

Another consequence of this shift in focus is the effect it has on relations with professors. The case study revealed that first-year students have tended to see teachers as grade-givers who introduce various assessments in order to prevent students from receiving the desirable highest grade. Indeed, when a grade has been treated as the ultimate goal of education, the role of the person who gives it is bound to change. Instead of mediators and facilitators of learning, teachers seem to become power wielders, sources of fear, and obstacles to getting a higher grade. Unfortunately, this attitude has not helped build a healthy student-professor relationship, which would involve open discussions, constructive debates, meaningful guidance, and advice-seeking. A study conducted at Russian universities reported that few students took advantage of professors' office hours to come and discuss research and professional questions: 18% of surveyed undergraduates discussed course concepts or ideas with their professors and only 6% talked about career plans (Chirikov, 2015), which indicates that students are unlikely to benefit from the opportunity to communicate with academic staff. In American and Australian universities, for example, attendance at office hours has also appeared infrequent (Briody et al., 2019; Robinson et al., 2014).

The last significant expectation that high school graduates in my class demonstrated was reluctance to engage with the class materials. The education trend accounting for this could be the impact of standardized tests and their format. While preparing for unified state exams in high schools, students are exposed to a large number of closed types of questions, such as gap fill, matching, and multiple choice. In any context, these are unlikely to encourage critical analysis of material widely required at universities (Watkins, 2018). On the contrary, these tests are likely to promote surface-level engagement and rote learning, which is what high school graduates seem to expect at university as well. Secondary school students have usually been geared towards clear-cut questions with straightforward answers. Additionally, being used to dealing with these closed questions, students in the case study showed a significant level of intolerance of ambiguity. Ability to operate in conditions of disorder and ambiguity is essential for formulating research questions, as well as conducting and writing up research, as this is one of the goals of academic study—to systematize, identify trends, classify, etc. the seeming chaos. In general, secondary school students tend to rely excessively on models, clear explanations, and well-documented expectations. If any of these are missing, students have appeared unable to cope by themselves and to formulate questions to professors that would guide them towards the necessary information. This does not seem to be a uniquely Russian issue, as similar attitudes have largely been present in various countries, for example, in Australian high school graduates (Clerehan, 2003).

Although the expectations of students participating in the case study presented above pertain to general academic literacies and can hinder undergraduates' performance in any subject, they appear to have been tackled explicitly mainly in academic writing courses in Russian universities. The students reported that in very few other subjects were they explicitly taught to present their thoughts in a well-structured, coherent way that was consistent with academic conventions. To be able to demonstrate these skills, students need to overcome the fixation on mechanics and grades, develop deeper and more active learning, become self-sufficient, take responsibility for their own learning, and be ready to build a partnership with the instructor. Lack of these abilities in high school graduates presents serious obstacles for their successful performance in academic writing, which encompasses all academic literacies.

Apart from poorly developed general academic literacies, secondary school graduates have tended to have specific expectations of writing in English. Preparation for the unified state exam in English appears to have notably affected the students' general perception of writing in English. The participants of the case study had to pass this exam in order to be enrolled in the bachelor of arts program. The exam requires a short, very controlled essay of 200–250 words. This is a task designed to test the learners' ability to write in a language accurately and within the given limits. The assignment clearly specifies the type and the structure of the essay down to the number of paragraphs, number of supporting ideas, and the way ideas should be organized into paragraphs (Federal Institute for Pedagogical Measurements, 2020). Any deviation results in a score deduction, so the focus of the task is often shifted from informing, convincing, etc., to getting the grammar and order of paragraphs right at the very best. This essay might serve the purpose of assessing writing proficiency, but students get used to it, and for them an essay becomes writing for the sake of writing or a formality. Later on, it takes time to convince students that the essay is a form of thinking and a manifestation of their thought process, so the target audience is actually interested in their ideas. Besides, this national exam essay, like in almost any international exam, does not require knowledge of academic conventions, research, or analytical skills. However, these are the pillars university-level academic writing is based on.

Faculty Expectations

Like students whose behaviors are largely shaped by the expectations formed in secondary school (Lowe & Cook, 2003), faculty also have specific ideas concerning what qualities and skills students should possess to do well at the university level. Wong and Chiu (2018) present an up-to-date comprehensive overview of professors' expectations of what they call an "ideal student." The researchers believe that such an articulation of the characteristics that are valued by lecturers can help students focus their efforts and not only build effective relations with the faculty, but eventually become better learners.

Although in their study Wong and Chiu (2018) interviewed academics in British universities, they show that the characteristics they uncovered seem to be shared by professors of different disciplines in different countries (Abdulghani et al., 2014; Thinyane, 2013; Thunborg et al., 2012; Vinther & Slethaug, 2014; Wong & Chiu, 2018). These findings are in line with my experience and appear as an accurate summary of the opinion of Russian university instructors.

Wong and Chiu (2018) divided the U.K. professors' expectations into two groups related to either personal or academic skill sets. The former involved characteristics often associated with the general maturity of an individual. Mature students were expected to perform well and to take full responsibility for their learning. According to the surveyed professors, this should be implemented in their preparation for teaching sessions, which mainly involved topic awareness through assigned reading or presentation slides. The professors also noted that today, academic reading has declined substantially among undergraduates, and this has complicated teaching. The second highly desirable characteristic was engagement in learning and motivation to work independently beyond regular classes and assignments. This proactive approach leaves the instructor in the role of facilitator and mentor rather than knowledge resource and manager. Students are also expected to manifest commitment, work ethic, and good time management skills so that the work is done to a high standard and no disciplinary measures are required.

The second group of skills was academic (Wong & Chiu, 2018). Students should be able to engage in analysis of concepts, not only description. They should be willing to critically evaluate and challenge ideas both orally and in writing rather than perform passive representation of information. Apart from critical thinking and analysis of course content, students are expected to be critical of their own work. They should have the ability to reflect on their performance, identify flaws, and try to take care of them, thus developing a sense of self-awareness of their progress. This awareness should enable students to learn to improve their skills continuously as a life-long process. At the same time, students should be able and willing to accept suggestions for improvement from their instructors and should not take them as personal criticism, which is also a sign of maturity.

Interestingly, university professors appeared less interested in test performance and resulting grades than secondary school teachers, which was partly caused by the national education assessment system. Schools are generally ranked by the attainment of their graduates, while at a university, students' GPA plays a relatively small role in the university's standing. Another important explanation is that in tertiary education, the learning process is often more important and has more educational value than the product. That is why an ideal university student, according to Wong and Chiu (2018), should make an effort and engage in the learning process rather than just produce results, however good they are.

Possible Solutions to Transition Problems

The practices Russian students are used to at the secondary level are the expectations they tend to transfer to their university studies. Since these appear to be different from what is actually expected at the university level, these mismatches cause problems for students when moving from secondary schools to university.

In general, the problems of transition from secondary to higher education are faced by schoolchildren in most education systems. To varying degrees, this seems to be a global concern that requires special attention. The most commonly identified issues have included unrealistic pre-transfer expectations, secondary-tertiary gap in learning approaches, cognitive challenges, uninformed decision-making, poorly developed academic literacies, and emotional challenges (Briggs et al., 2012; Lowe & Cook, 2003; Money et al., 2019).

To solve transition problems, a range of initiatives have been widely implemented in different countries, of which Britain and Australia have appeared to be the leaders (Agosti & Bernat, 2018). These initiatives are introduced by universities and vary in focus, duration, set-up, participants, and types of support. Clerehan (2003) identifies six main approaches to facilitating transition. The most common strategy is running orientation sessions lasting from one day to about a week. Their primary aim is to familiarize new students with university policies, while more extended orientation programs can focus on some academic conventions as well. A longer version of this initiative is a British and Australian foundation course, British pre-sessional course or American pathways program, which normally runs for up to a year and aims at preparing students for university in a broader sense. It includes content knowledge building and general academic literacies development. Both initiatives, shorter orientation sessions and longer courses, take place before the beginning of the main undergraduate program.

Besides or in addition to pre-course programs, some universities have offered support throughout the academic year. This support can take the form of mentoring by a professor or an older student, who is available to help individual students deal with the academic problems they may face. Another approach has been building academic literacies development into the curriculum or into content discipline syllabi, in which students have been offered either a series of focused sessions to develop the necessary skill set throughout the year or the skill set development has been integrated into core disciplines. In the latter case, subject professors have had to be trained to do it consistently and effectively. In fact, professional development of faculty in this area is a standalone initiative that can significantly improve students' experience, especially during the first stages of transition. Apart from professor- or mentor-led adaptation, universities may also provide a variety of offline and online support materials that can be accessed by students on their own (Laing et al., 2005).

In North American universities, traditionally the problem of adaptation to post-compulsory education has been dealt with through rhetoric and composition courses. Each program, regardless of the major, offers an early introduction to academic writing course, which may focus on discipline-specific genres or on writing as a way to process information and produce knowledge. The latter is known as writing across the curriculum (WAC), as it focuses on academic writing as a broad discourse type that enables students not only to join the academic community, but also to process information better. The first approach is referred to as Writing in the Disciplines (WID), and courses within this framework introduce first-year undergraduates to the conventions of research and analytical writing dominant in a particular field of research. WAC and WID pedagogies make it possible to combine teaching essay writing and broader academic literacies that are required to perform well in the particular field (for example Enoch & VanHaitsma, 2015). Writing courses delivered at the start of a program can prepare students for more complex and research-intensive disciplines, thus facilitating the transition process.

Perhaps due to this focus on first-year writing, pre-program initiatives appear to be less relevant in the American context. Agosti and Bernat (2018) provided an overview of global pathway programs and noted that 12% of all English-speaking programs were offered in the US, while Britain and Oceania account for the remaining 88%—72% and 16%, respectively. The pathway programs that were introduced in the US were modelled on the UK and Australian transition initiatives described above (Agosti & Bernat, 2018).

Overall, the choice of transition initiative depends on the understanding of whose responsibility it is to ensure access to university and a smooth transition from secondary school to university. Historically, as higher education was perceived as elite, it was believed that if the student was not adapting well, it was their fault, and this fact served as a direct indication that they were unsuitable for higher education altogether. Later on, with the adoption of the more constructivist view of learning as a social contextual practice (Clerehan, 2003), global massification of higher education (Agosti & Bernat, 2018), and the changing of its role to service provision, the responsibility for ensuring access and support was shifted to the universities, motivating much of the research on transition. However, there is an opposing opinion that if students do not realize that preparing for university, adapting to its culture, and devoting more effort to studying is their personal responsibility, neither staff or peer support nor training in academic skills will solve the transition problem. The latter view has been generally supported by university content lecturers (for example, Kajander & Lovric, 2005).

In Russian education, very little has been done on the government or institutional levels (Smolentseva, 2019) to ensure smooth transition from secondary school to universities. Existing pre-program courses for high school students planning to pursue degree programs are geared towards helping students pass the unified state exam and being admitted. It is also consistent with the idea that the focus here seems to be on getting in rather than getting through higher education. Some universities have offered inductions or mentoring schemes by older students, but these have been few and far between.

Proposed Solutions within Academic Writing Courses

The second part of the case study was a small pilot study of possible classroom practices that could help mitigate the mismatched expectations that seemed to affect students' performance. It had the following stages: identifying and grouping expectation mismatches, determining teaching techniques that have the potential to mitigate the effects of the mismatches, implementing them in the remaining part of introduction to academic writing, observing their effects, and collecting students' feedback.

After comparing the differences in students' and university professors' expectations of one another and the learning process, I can single out five key groups of mismatches typical of the Russian education system: general behavioral expectations, students' engagement, approaches to learning, roles of teachers, and grades (see Table 10.1).

Table 10.1. Expectation Mismatches Between
First-Year Students and Faculty

Students' expectations	Professors' expectations
Behavioral expectations	
Choices are imposed on students by the parents or by the system, causing lack of responsibility.	Students should make informed decisions and are prepared to take responsibility for consequences.
Students tend to look for shortcuts in the form of cheating or finding loopholes.	Students should demonstrate commitment to studying and high work ethic.
Students are used to clarity and straightforward answers to questions.	Students should be tolerant of ambiguity and able to accept that not every question has an answer.
Expectations of teachers	
Teachers serve as controllers and assessors.	Teachers serve as facilitators of learning.
Students are over-reliant on the teacher to take charge and manage learning.	Students should engage in independent and self-directed learning.

Students' expectations	Professors' expectations
Grading	
Students can learn solely to get a grade.	Students are less focused on grades and attainment.
Students are content only with excellent grades.	Passing grades are the baseline with higher grades requiring more investment of time and effort.
Involvement and focus	
Students expect to be taught and to be passive recipients of knowledge.	Students should participate actively in learning.
Students focus on the mechanics of the task.	Students should pay attention to content and topic development.
Learning process	
Students place the focus on product regardless of the way it was produced.	Students should be able to value the learning process.
Students expect rote learning.	Students should be able to challenge the concepts.
Students expect mechanical repetition and memorizing.	Students should be able to apply analytical approaches.
Students are familiar with simplified secondary school requirements.	Students should be familiar with academic culture and conventions.

Each group of mismatches was a point of departure in building a facilitation strategy that would help students adapt to higher education. Each of the problems presented a research question in itself, but this part of the essay does not attempt to provide a research-informed comprehensive overview of possible solutions. Here I summarize my experience in dealing with the identified mismatches within the case study. The proposed solutions may seem obvious and be already widely used in some education systems, but in Russian universities they have appeared less frequently. I based the choice of techniques on my own classroom observations and the students' feedback. However, to prove conclusively the effectiveness of the presented teaching techniques, a separate study should be conducted comparing skills and attitudes before the measures were taken and after.

Transition effects have been shown to last for at least one semester, as this has been the period during which secondary school study habits persist (Lowe & Cook, 2003), but it has taken as long as the first two or three semesters (Clerehan, 2003), making the first years of undergraduate programs critical (Briggs et al., 2012) and particularly susceptible to their negative effects. The conclusion to draw here is that the mismatches in expectations have to be dealt with very early to minimize their effects on the students' subsequent performance. From this point of view, my mitigation attempts in the first-year academic writing courses appear relevant and timely.

In this case study, mitigation of the secondary-tertiary transition problem took two main directions: through targeted training or by raising awareness. The latter proved effective with expectation mismatches in which no habits or skills were involved. Simply by raising awareness of what was actually expected at the tertiary level and showing how it was different from what the students were used to, professors could help them adapt to the new learning environment and its requirements.

These five groups of suggestions and recommendations by no means constitute an exhaustive list. These particular recommendations and techniques were selected because they appeared to involve very little administrative effort. Not every professor has the opportunity to change the syllabus, and even if they do, they might not have the resources. That is why the proposed solutions were chosen due to their ease of use. These ideas do not entail changes in course focus, outcomes, or topics; in most cases materials and activities stay the same. Only the format of in-class activities, interaction patterns, and home assignments needs amending, which should not add significantly to professors' workload.

All these techniques have been tried out and proven effective in my introduction to academic writing classes at a Russian university. I am aware that other contexts might already rely on these practices in regular teaching, so some amendments or completely different approaches might be required in such cases. At the same time, the proposed techniques seem in line with the learning styles of current generation Y and Z students described in the literature. It is believed that these cohorts have required greater clarity in course structure and assessment, they have wanted rationale for professors' decisions, they have appreciated opportunities for student initiative and choice, they have needed to make an impact and have required recognition through feedback, they must synthesize and experience knowledge in order to understand it, and they have liked assignments that connect course content to problems that require a solution (Purcell, 2019; Thacker, 2016; Wilson & Gerber, 2008).

Mitigating Expectations of the Learning Process

Raising awareness appeared particularly effective in dealing with expectation mismatches connected with the perceptions of the learning process in the case study. According to students, it seems that Russian secondary education instills the idea that education is mainly about increasing their knowledge base, which can be done mechanically. That is why the expectations that they come into university with are those of mechanical repetition, rote learning, and reproducing a required product. The university professors, in my experience, on the contrary, have tended to expect students to actively engage in the process of producing knowledge, rather than regurgitating it. That is why students are encouraged to challenge concepts, analyze phenomena, and develop their own well-grounded opinion that they would be ready to defend. Although the value of the product of these thought processes cannot be underestimated, the actual thinking, questioning, analysis, synthesis, and other higher-order thinking skills involved have tended to be the major focus of the learning process. As a result, students are likely to present different products, each having no less value than others. For Russian students this fact has appeared very confusing. In my course, I had to devote a sizeable part of class time to spelling out my expectations. Initially, when giving instructions for assignments, I not only commented on the procedures and outcomes, but also raised their awareness of the skills that we were developing through these assignments; for example, writing a summary was meant to develop information analysis and synthesis skills. In addition, I showed students examples of different approaches to the same task and commented on the results, highlighting the fact that all are acceptable despite the differences. It seemed important to help students understand that it is the process of arriving at a solution that they are likely to need in their further studies or work, as the tasks and problems are going to be different. This skill and approach can be transferred to other situations, while the product, be it an essay, presentation, study project, cannot. My students reported that they found these comments, examples, and explanations helpful and that understanding the priorities helped them to avoid frustration.

In addition, freshmen students come in with little to no familiarity with academic conventions, so in the first year, a major task for their instructors is to make the students aware of academic requirements. This gap may seem obvious, as the secondary school has not been expected to be responsible for building this culture, so it has had to be built at the university level. However, in my experience, Russian professors have been likely to assume that this culture will develop by itself without explicit instruction. Such an approach has been generally less effective and takes a lot of time.

Familiarizing students with academic culture is fully in line with the key objectives of academic writing courses. While preparing to write academic essays, students can and should get acquainted with a range of concepts and develop multiple skills, ranging from basic writing conventions (rhetoric, text organization, referencing, etc.) to research ethics and academic integrity. Therefore, it seems reasonable to add extra emphasis on building general academic culture within writing courses in the first year, to make teaching this as explicit as possible, and to highlight the fact that this culture is relevant not only to all other subjects, but also to academia in general. Within the introduction to academic writing course, the students and I focused on and tried to understand the rationale behind referencing conventions, standards for academic communication, academic genre features, and the target audience.

Mitigating Mismatches in Behavioral Expectations

Work ethic and commitment are one of the general expectation mismatches that I have identified, the others being taking responsibility for decisions and tolerance of ambiguity. Similar to overcoming learning process related mismatches, the first technique that proved helpful in the case study was raising students' awareness of these differences and reminding them of the expectations and rationale behind them. I explained to my students that at the level of higher education, which aims at preparing students for further graduate-level education or employment, they should be ready to accept ambiguity and lack of universally correct solutions. Since it is quite different from straightforward problems dealt with within secondary education, initially, this fact caused frustration, which was to be expected. Taking responsibility for decisions and actions appeared to be a more complex challenge connected with students' psychological development and general maturity, but addressing it also seemed to start with raising awareness of the issue. The students in my course were very familiar with work ethic, commitment and responsibility, but did not fully understand what was involved and somehow did not expect it to apply to them directly. The latter could stem from their expectation of multiple opportunities for make-ups, which I discussed earlier.

Students' general behavioral expectations can also be modified through a set of measures and classroom practices. Avoiding commitment and low academic integrity has been generally eliminated by watertight course regulations that clearly stipulate intolerance of such practices and impending consequences. Unfortunately, at the Russian university level enforcement has proved more challenging, as it usually has involved a lot of effort and patience on the part of the professors due to students' prior experiences.

Meeting the second expectation, that of students' being able to bear consequences for decisions, can also be encouraged through classroom practices. My case showed that students tended to come in unable and unwilling to participate in constructing their learning partly because all these choices were made for them by parents and secondary school teachers. I observed that first-year undergraduates genuinely did not expect to be involved in such decisions, which university professors, who expect more initiative and responsibility, have found quite annoying. This mismatch could be mitigated by explicitly giving students opportunities to make decisions and then dealing with their consequences. I started with offering my students minor classroom choices (e.g., about the order of activities, interaction patterns, topics, tests, or deadlines): Would you like to do a discussion or further language practice at the end of the class? Would you like to work individually, in pairs or in larger groups? Would you prefer to discuss this or that topic? Would you prefer to write the test next week or the week after? Although initially my students looked confused and unwilling to participate in the classroom decisions, with time, they got used to this practice. The students even mentioned that they felt more respected, they saw that their opinion on what happens in class mattered, so they were willing to play a more active role. These choices encouraged students not only to take ownership of their learning, but also to negotiate decisions with others, who were likely to have other preferences.

Apart from smaller classroom choices, students can be encouraged to take responsibility for adjusting the course syllabus wherever possible before finalizing it. Quite often, syllabi allow for flexibility in the order of topics, practice activities, types of essays, input formats, etc. If the changes proposed by students cannot be implemented, this discussion will be a good opportunity to get them on board by explaining the rationale behind the policies. When the students have been involved in such seemingly big decisions, they have tended to be more motivated and engaged.

Since Russian education has a long history of very teacher-centered instruction, it appears difficult for teachers to implement fully student-centered teaching. It becomes particularly apparent when delegating choices to students about the courses, as even when delegating, it seems that teachers try to claim control. However, when training students to become more responsible and active learners, it is essential to step back and not to interfere while students are trying to deal with negative outcomes of their seemingly poor choices and to let students own the consequences. In my course, some of these situations included choosing an inefficient number of students for a small group that complicated assignment completion, leaving more challenging activities for the end of the class when everyone was tired, and postponing tests after material revision. At first, careless poor decisions negatively affected the class, but with time and practice, students took this responsibility more seriously and started making more thought-out choices in order to avoid undesirable consequences. These student-centered teaching techniques have been widely encouraged within such approaches as active learning, universal design for learning, differentiated instruction, and flipped classroom, as they rely on students' responsible choices and active role, which prove helpful in mitigating this behavioral mismatch. Towards the end of the course, my students visibly manifested higher levels of responsibility and engagement in the ways they made classroom choices, selected materials, participated in assessment criteria development, and gave peer feedback to each other.

The third general mismatch is connected with tolerance of ambiguity. Apart from raising awareness, I encouraged my students to overcome frustration with everything ambiguous by offering them more activities that either have several right solutions or do not have any correct answer by definition. The activities the students found helpful included making lists of associations, brainstorming, organizing and structuring information, creating mind maps, classifying, interpreting verbal or visual cues, personalizing information or applying what has been learnt to their own lives, and trying to prove and disprove statements. Once the students saw that ambiguity can be acceptable, they showed more tolerance and were ready to produce deeper and more creative responses instead of looking desperately for the one correct solution.

Mitigating Mismatches in Expectations of Teachers' Roles

In higher education, professors have been expected to play the roles of facilitator and mentor. Surprisingly, at the beginning of the case study, students showed two extreme opposing views on the teachers' role: depending on students' previous experience, they tended to treat professors either as the ultimate authority who has the final say in everything or as someone with limited credibility deserving of little respect on their part. As a result, their attitudes can potentially create an atmosphere either of fear or excessive familiarity. Either way, none of the scenarios involve self-regulation, trust, and willingness to build a constructive dialogue with professors. The latter can seriously hinder learning and should be addressed as early as possible. In my course, one of the most effective ways to show that the dialogue between the professor and the student could be constructive was individual tutorials. They are not very common at Russian secondary schools and universities. Partly because of that, students tended to apprehend tutorials as an opportunity for me to point out mistakes and scold. However, they appreciated friendly meetings with the focus on areas for improvement, ways to achieve it, and general recommendations for becoming more effective autonomous learners. My case study demonstrated that it is advisable to make the first tutorials obligatory to encourage students to come to the office so that they could overcome their fear and see that individual feedback sessions could be helpful. Once they saw it, most of my students sought individual feedback sessions after each paper, which contributed to our constructive dialogue.

Tutorials help to reinforce the role of the professor as a mentor. Establishing the professor as a facilitator is closely related to promoting self-directed learning and learner autonomy in students, which will in fact enable the professor to facilitate learning instead of imposing it. Introduction to academic writing has lent itself well to this task. I found a few techniques especially suitable for reaching this goal. The first technique was individual reflective home assignments based on a prior writing assignment, in which students selected one of their weaknesses, analyzed it, and took measures to eliminate it. It involved the following: they identified a weakness they wanted to focus on, read theory if applicable, and then did practice activities of their choice. My students valued this opportunity. According to their feedback, they perceived it as something that catered for their specific challenges and therefore had immediate benefits, unlike general home tasks that were set to the whole class. Another effective way to promote self-sufficiency and responsibility was giving non-specific assignments, such as asking students to find some information in any source of their choice as opposed to retaining teacher control over assigned reading down to pages. When the goal was clear, but the way to achieve it was not specified, students tended to display higher levels of autonomy in working with sources. The work proved effective, as this information prepared at home was successfully used to complete a class assignment. Depending on the group level, this assignment could be broken into stages of first getting the professor's approval on the sources and selected information, and only then sharing it with other students. Eventually, the pre-approval stage could be eliminated and, ideally, the class verification and practice should be omitted as well, leaving only students' individual self-sufficient work.

Mitigating Involvement and Focus Mismatches

The above-mentioned activities not only develop higher self-sufficiency, they also ensure more active participation. Having shifted the perception of professors from authoritarian figures to facilitators who support learning, students need to see what it means to be active in a way that is conducive to learning. In the case study, to get students more involved in a productive way, I occasionally delegated to them preparing inputs, managing classes, and selecting topics and materials. I discussed the last two in the previous sections. In case of the first technique, I assigned to students the input, or mini-lectures in class, that I would normally give myself. They had to take full responsibility starting from familiarizing themselves with the topic and finishing with presenting it to other students. My experience showed that it is advisable to select topics relevant to key course theory so that subsequent work depends on everyone's understanding of this theory; otherwise, students were not motivated to apply themselves. Students found guidelines for delivering this input helpful, including the time limit, key points to be covered, and other requirements. The amount of detail in my task instructions depended on the students' maturity and responsibility and was greater towards the beginning of the course, going down towards the end. This peer-teaching appeared to be effective in motivating the students as well. It is worth noting that my students reported that they preferred delivering these presentations in smaller groups rather than as open-class talks, because it not only made them feel more confident but also helped establish better interaction with other students in the small group and offer necessary clarifications.

A sadly common misconception that students often bring from secondary schools is the focus on mechanics and accuracy rather than content and development. It is no secret that assessing the former and accounting for the resulting grade is much easier. The number of language errors, formatting, punctuation, word count, and other features that go into the mechanics section are easily quantifiable and hardly lend themselves to misinterpretation. According to the students, these safe assessment criteria tend to be relied upon in school, so it takes some time to shift the focus to ideas and reasoning. Having raised their awareness of this focus, I drew the students' attention to assessment rubrics. The assessment supported this shift by assigning much more weight to the content criteria compared to the grammar and mechanics sections. Initially, I even removed mechanics from the assessment criteria altogether to show more clearly where the priorities lay. Another technique that I used was stressing content aspects at feedback sessions and elaborating on them more, which reinforced their value and significance, compared to mechanics which could be mentioned briefly at the end. My observations showed that it took about two months to shift this focus.

Mitigating Expectations in Grading

Grading is perhaps the most sensitive issue of all because mismatches in expectations here not only cause demotivation, but they can also affect students' GPA, rating, scholarship, or even lead to expulsion. The general trend has been that current generations of students want to know their grades at any point in time, and they have been used to frequent feedback, possibly due to the development of digital tools with frequent automated feedback (Wilson & Gerber, 2008).

I stated earlier that one of the most common misconceptions has been misinterpretation of the grade value. When "good" and "satisfactory" are taken as a disaster, students tend to expect only very high grades. In the case study I used the awareness raising approach to mitigate this expectation. I continuously reminded the students of the real value of each grade (in Russia it is "excellent," "good," and "satisfactory") and explained that "satisfactory" means that they have mastered the required amount knowledge and developed skills to the required standard; therefore, there is no need to stress over grades that are lower than "excellent." Students should also understand that compared to secondary school, the courses tend to be more challenging and more intensive, so it is next to impossible to excel in all of them. Overall, this attitude to grades has seemed to take a very long time to overcome, as even at the end of the year-long introduction to academic writing course, a lot of students still struggled with accepting "satisfactory" and "good."

Conclusion

In this essay, I presented a case study conducted at a Russian university in Moscow in the 2018–2019 academic year. The study enabled me to describe expectations that Russian students have brought into higher education and to match these with trends and features of the national education system. I saw that students' expectations differed from those of university professors in five areas: learning process, students' involvement and focus, the role of teachers, grading, and general behavioral expectations. The major mismatches lie in students' insufficient responsibility, limited commitment and work ethic, low tolerance of ambiguity, inadequate self-sufficiency, unwillingness to participate in learning, overreliance on grades, underdeveloped analytical thinking, and unfamiliarity with academic culture. I am not trying to say that secondary school in Russia is incapable of preparing students for universities. I am fully aware that school teachers' work in different circumstances and have to adjust learning goals and approaches to teaching to the general mixed-ability student population. University professors, on the other hand, deal with selected cohorts, so they have tended to assume that students enter universities possessing the necessary academic literacies and are fully prepared for learning. Unfortunately, these differences in expectations persist and can cause miscommunication and lack of understanding, which can eventually build up and start affecting learning outcomes.

However, it seems that just by being aware of these gaps and expectation mismatches, as well as the underlying reasons and circumstances that brought them about, university professors can not only better understand the origins of some potential problems but also help undergraduates deal with them and be ready to support students in the most effective ways. If we are aware of these "gaps and gulfs" (Clerehan, 2002, p. 72), we as professors can be more understanding of where our students' attitudes and behaviors come from. This awareness can spare us a lot of frustration, annoyance, and anger, as these negative feelings tend to come from lack of understanding. In this case, we will be better equipped to facilitate the secondary-tertiary transition, as it will put us in a better position to establish and maintain a productive dialogue with students that is conducive to learning. Awareness is the first step in eliminating communication challenges. Apart from adjusting our expectations, we can potentially raise our students' awareness of their own beliefs, so that they start shifting them to those more appropriate for a mature university-level student.

Awareness of the mismatches can also help us adjust our teaching techniques to help our students get from where they are to where they are supposed to be without lowering the bar. Universities should not have to lower requirements for first-year undergraduates to mitigate the effects of transition problems, as has been sometimes suggested. After all, higher education is higher education, and it is meant to take the students to the next level not only academically or professionally, but also personally.

To facilitate this process, in the pilot study I applied several teaching techniques that appeared effective, according to my observations and the students' feedback. I have shared this set of simple, non-intrusive techniques that can complement raising awareness and can both demonstrate to students what they should be focusing on and help them develop the missing skills. Overall, involving students in planning the course, encouraging them to engage with each other and the materials through group work and peer-teaching, setting out clear rules and following them consistently, and showing to them that professors are there to help them become better and more independent learners can eventually help ease the transition and maximize the learning. Overcoming mismatches in expectations among professors and students involves regular, consistent and step-by-step work, which can take time and effort, but can potentially reduce the stress that builds due to miscommunication in all the parties involved.

This problem has seemed to be particularly important in the first semesters of a bachelor's program, in which introduction to academic writing courses are taught, making mitigation efforts appropriate and timely. Ultimately, as Hyland (2013) puts it, we are what we write, so if the students become more mature and responsible writers in our classes, we can hope that they will generally perform better as students of other disciplines.

References

Abdulghani, H. M., Al-Drees, A. A., Khalil, M. S., Ahmad, F., Ponnamperuma, G. G., & Amin, Z. (2014). What factors determine academic achievement in high achieving undergraduate medical students? A qualitative study. *Medical Teacher, 36*(1), S43-S48. https://doi.org/10.3109/0142159X.2014.886011.

Agosti, C. I., & Bernat, E. (2018). University pathway programs: Types, origins, aims and defining traits. In C. Agosti & E. Bernat (Eds.). *University pathway programs: Local responses within a growing global trend* (pp. 3–25). Springer. https://doi.org/10.1007/978-3-319-72505-5_1.

Briggs, A. R. J., Clark J., & Hall, I. (2012). Building bridges: Understanding student transition to university. *Quality in Higher Education, 18*(1), 3–21. https://doi.org/10.1080/13538322.2011.614468.

Briody, E. K., Wirtz, E., Goldenstein, A., & Berger, E. J. (2019). Breaking the tyranny of office hours: Overcoming professor avoidance. *European Journal of Engineering Education, 44*(5), 666–687. https://doi.org/10.1080/03043797.2019.1592116.

Chirikov, I. (2015). The mystery of Russian students: Poor learning experience, high satisfaction. *Higher Education in Russia and Beyond, 1*(3), 10–11. https://herb.hse.ru/data/2015/01/27/1105213149/HERB_03_view.pdf.

Chokwe, J. M. (2013). Factors impacting academic writing skills of English second language students. *Mediterranean Journal of Social Sciences, 4*(14), 377–383. https://www.mcser.org/journal/index.php/mjss/article/view/1617.

Clerehan, R. (2003). Transition to tertiary education in the arts and humanities: Some academic initiatives from Australia. *Arts and Humanities in Higher Education, 2*(1), 72–89. https://doi.org/10.1177/1474022203002001007.

DeFeo, D. J., Tran, T. C., & Gerken, S. (2021). Mediating students' fixation with grades in an inquiry-based undergraduate biology course. *Science & Education, 30*, 81-102. https://doi.org/10.1007/s11191-020-00161-3.

Enoch, J., & VanHaitsma, P. (2015). Archival literacy: Reading the rhetoric of digital archives in the undergraduate classroom. *College Composition and Communication, 67*(2), 216–242. https://www.mcser.org/journal/index.php/mjss/article/view/1617.

Federal Institute for Pedagogical Measurements. (2020). *Единый государственный экзамен по английскому языку* [Unified state examination in English]. https://fipi.ru/ege/demoversii-specifikacii-kodifikatory#!/tab/151883967-11.

Foster, D., & Russel, D. R. (2002). *Writing and learning in cross-national perspective: Transitions from secondary to higher education.* Routledge. https://lib.dr.iastate.edu/engl_books/5.

Gourlay, L. (2009). Threshold practices: Becoming a student through academic literacies. *London Review of Education, 7*(2), 181–192. https://doi.org/10.1080/14748460903003626.

Hyland, K. (2013). Writing in the university: Education, knowledge and reputation. *Language Teaching, 46*(1), 53–70. https://doi.org/10.1017/S0261444811000036.

Kajander, A., & Lovric, M. (2005). Transition from secondary to tertiary mathematics: McMaster university experience. *International Journal of Mathematics Education in Science and Technology, 36* (2–3), 149–160. https://doi.org/10.1080/00207340412317040.

Khan, M. (2014). Students' passion for grades in higher education institutions in Pakistan. *Procedia - Social and Behavioral Sciences, 112,* 702–709. https://doi.org/10.1016/j.sbspro.2014.01.1220.

Kyndt, E., Donche, V., Trigwell, K., & Lindblom-Ylanne, S. (Eds.). (2017). *Higher education transitions: Theory and research.* Routledge.

Laing, C., Robinson, A., & Johnston, V. (2005). Managing the transition into higher education: An on-line spiral induction programme. *Active Learning in Higher Education, 6*(3), 243–255. https://doi.org/10.1177/1469787405059575.

Lea, M. R. (1998). Academic literacies and learning in higher education: Constructing knowledge through texts and experience. *Studies in the Education of Adults, 30*(2), 156–171. https://doi.org/10.1080/02660830.1998.11730680.

Lea, M. R., & Street, B. V. (1998). Student writing in higher education: An academic literacies approach. *Studies in Higher Education, 23*(2), 157–172. https://doi.org/10.1080/03075079812331380364.

Lea, M. R., & Street, B. V. (2006). The "academic literacies" model: *Theory and applications. Theory Into Practice, 45*(4), 368–377. https://doi.org/10.1207/s15430421tip4504_11.

Leontyeva, E. (2018). How secondary school practices contribute to the acceptance of plagiarism in Russian HEIs. *Higher Education in Russia and Beyond, 3*(17), 11–12. https://herb.hse.ru/data/2018/10/04/1157617623/1HERB_17_view.pdf#page=11.

Lowe, H., & Cook, A. (2003). Mind the gap: Are students prepared for higher education? *Journal of Further and Higher Education, 27*(1), 53–76. https://doi.org/10.1080/03098770305629.

Maloshonok, N., & Terentev, E. (2017). The mismatch between student educational expectations and realities: Prevalence, causes, and consequences. *European Journal of Higher Education, 7*(4), 356–372. https://doi.org/10.1080/21568235.2017.1348238.

Miller R. T., & Pessoa S. (2017). Integrating writing assignments at an American branch campus in Qatar: Challenges, adaptations, and recommendations. In L. Arnold, A. Nebel, & L. Ronesi (Eds.), *Emerging writing research from the Middle East-North Africa region* (pp. 175–199). The WAC Clearinghouse; University Press of Colorado. https://doi.org/10.37514/INT-B.2017.0896.2.08.

Money, J., Nixon, S., & Graham, L. (2019). Do educational experiences in school prepare students for university? A teachers' perspective, *Journal of Further and Higher Education, 44*(4), 554–567. https://doi.org/10.1080/0309877X.2019.1595547.

Parker, J. (2003). Access and transition to higher education: A forum: Introduction. *Arts and Humanities in Higher Education, 2*(1), 63–64. https://doi.org/10.1177/1474022203002001005.

Purcell, M. A. (2019). Teaching PSC to gen Z. *Journal of Political Science Education, 16*(3), 335–343. https://doi.org/10.1080/15512169.2019.1568881.

Robinson, R. J., Culver, D., Schertzer, M. J., Landschoot, T. P., & Hensel, E. C. (2014). Understanding the causes for low student office hour attendance. In *ASME International Mechanical Engineering Congress and Exposition, Proceedings: Education and Globalization* (Vol. 5): V005T05A028. ASME. https://doi.org/10.1115/IMECE2014-38698.

Romanowski, M. H. (2004). Student obsession with grades and achievement. *Kappa Delta Pi Record, 40*(4), 149–51. https://doi.org/10.1080/00228958.2004.10516425.

Russell, D. R., Lea, M., Parker, J., Street, B., & Donahue, T. (2009). Exploring notions of genre in "academic literacies" and "writing across the curriculum": Approaches across countries and contexts. In C. Bazerman, A. Bonini, & D. Figueiredo (Eds.), *Genre in a changing world* (pp. 395–423). The WAC Clearinghouse; Parlor Press. https://doi.org/10.37514/PER-B.2009.2324.2.20.

Smolentseva, A. (2015). Bridging the gap between higher and secondary education in Russia. *International Higher Education, 19,* 20–21. https://doi.org/10.6017/ihe.2000.19.6863.

Smolentseva, A. (2016). The expansion of higher education and the transformation of the institutional landscape in Post-Soviet Counties. *Higher Education in Russia and Beyond, 2*(8), 6–7. https://herb.hse.ru/data/2016/06/14/1116816162/1HERB_08_view.pdf#page=6.

Smolentseva, A. (2019). Field of higher education research, Russia. In J. C. Shin & P. Teixeira (Eds.), *Encyclopedia of international higher education systems and institutions* (pp. 1–8). Springer. https://doi.org/10.1007/978-94-017-9553-1_189-1.

Thacker, D. (2016). Preparing your sales course for generation Z. *Business Education Innovation Journal, 8*(2), 198–204. Retrieved form: http://www.beijournal.com/images/824V8N2_final-20.pdf.

Thinyane, H. (2013). Academic perceptions of the ideal computer science student. *South African Computer Journal, 50,* 28–40. https://doi.org/10.18489/sacj.v50i1.165.

Thunborg, C., Bron, A., & Edström, E. (2012). Forming learning identities in higher education in Sweden. *Studies for the Learning Society, 2*(2–3), 23–34. https://doi.org/10.2478/v10240-012-0002-5.

Vinther, J., & Slethaug, G. (2014). Changing conceptions of the international classroom and the good student? *Hermes, 53*(3), 25–42. https://doi.org/10.7146/hjlcb.v27i53.20948.

Watkins, P. (2018). *Teaching and developing reading skills. Cambridge handbooks for language teachers.* Cambridge University Press.

Wilson, M., & Gerber, L. (2008). How generational theory can improve teaching: Strategies for working with the "millennials." *Currents in Teaching and Learning, 1*(1), 29–44. https://tigerweb.towson.edu/garcia/past%20semesters%20of%20intro/intro/2011%20fall%20intro/wilson%20and%20gerber.pdf.

Wingate, U. (2012). Using academic literacies and genre-based models for academic writing instruction: A "literacy" journey. *Journal of English for Academic Purposes, 11*(1), 26–37. https://doi.org/10.1016/j.jeap.2011.11.006.

Wong, B., & Chiu, Y.-L. T. (2018). University lecturers' construction of the "ideal" undergraduate student. *Journal of Further and Higher Education, 44*(1), 54–68, https://doi.org/10.1080/0309877X.2018.1504010.

Федеральный закон Об образовании в Российской Федерации. [Federal Education Act] (2012). http://pravo.gov.ru/proxy/ips/?docbody=&firstDoc=1&lastDoc=1&nd=102162745.

11 Transcending Authorities: Literature and Performance in an Integrated Reading-writing Classroom in Russia

Irina Kuznetsova-Simpson
NEW ECONOMIC SCHOOL, MOSCOW

Writing a composition on a literary topic has traditionally been an integral part of Russian education. However, as this chapter argues, the methods of writing pedagogy in literature classes both in first language (L1) and foreign language (FL) instruction have not evolved much since the Soviet times. Most students are still used to passive learning and to prescriptive teaching models. Similar to Russian youth back in the 1990s, today's students seem to have learned that there are authorities that shouldn't be questioned: the authority of the author, of a renowned literary critic, of a tradition, or of a teacher. Even when they formulate their thoughts autonomously, they often seem to search for one "true" interpretation, as well as for one main didactic function of the text. In this chapter, I examine the challenges that my students meet while confronting Western methods of writing pedagogy and advocate for substituting the traditional methods of teaching literature and writing with more liberating and creative practices. In particular, I discuss how I attempt to break with students' perception of a teacher as knowledge-producer and encourage them to challenge and question traditional "authorities" and interpretations. Drawing on my experience of teaching a comparative literature class, "Drama and theatre," I argue that a reader-response approach to interpreting literature in tandem with performance theory and practice can have a transformative impact on students' writing, facilitating their interpretative, analytical, and creative skills.

Writing a composition on a literary topic has traditionally been an integral part of Russian education (see Chapter 2). In the Soviet Union, students practiced writing such essays beginning in middle school. Those who aimed for an advanced degree in the humanities were required to write a literary essay as a part of their entrance exam to the university. Yet, the teaching methods on how to write such essays differed significantly from those associated with Western-style pedagogy. I experienced an extreme example of the approach practiced at the time during a tutoring session with a professor of Russian literature at one Moscow university. In preparation for the university entrance exam, she handed out a printed copy of a paper on Griboyedov's *Woe from Wit* and asked me to learn it by heart for our next tutoring session. Puzzled by my bewildered expression, she explained that rote learning is the most-effective way to teach a student to write an excellent essay during the exam. She meant that I had to know precisely what to say about the topic, who to cite, and what language to use.

Twenty years later, while teaching literature and writing courses in English at the New Economic School in Russia, I often wonder whether the methods of teaching literature and writing in Russian schools, both in a native and foreign language classroom, have progressed much since the Soviet period. Most students starting our courses, it seemed, are still used to passive learning and to prescriptive teaching models. When dealing with literary texts, they assume that there are authorities who should not be questioned: the authority of the author, of a renowned literary critic, of a tradition, or of a teacher. Even when they formulate their thoughts autonomously, they often search for one true interpretation, as well as well as for one main didactic function of the text.

Indeed, the research I conducted for this project shows that whereas literature still plays an integral part in acquiring literacy, both in first language (L1) and foreign language (FL) instruction, the methods of teaching literature still favor traditional approaches. Namely, in L1 classrooms, author-centered and text-centered approaches to interpreting literature have dominated; in FL instruction, literary texts have served the primary goal of improving students' overall linguistic proficiency. Thus, interpretation of these texts has been secondary to language-oriented priorities. These traditional methods create significant hurdles when students confront core-literature courses conducted exclusively in the target language. Moreover, they hinder the development of important critical, interpretative, and creative writing skills that the study of literature should facilitate.

In this essay I would like to advocate for substituting a linguistic approach to teaching literature in upper-level foreign language classes in Russia with a reader-response approach, better suited for the integrated reading-writing classroom. I should note that this approach could also be used in combination with other methods—textual, contextual, personal-response, and linguistic—as some studies have contended (Bloemert et al., 2017; Gilroy & Parkinson, 1996). A discussion of integrating these approaches is, however, beyond the scope of this chapter. I will further argue that engagement with performance in literature courses could serve as a very effective bridge between both skills—reading and writing—as well as a tool for sharpening students' analytical, creative, and independent writing skills. To illustrate this last point, I would like to draw on my experience of teaching a comparative literature class called Drama and Theatre, conducted in English, and to discuss some writing practices that enabled us to unite reading, writing, and performance successfully.

Literature and Writing Pedagogy in the Soviet Union

Reverence toward literature and literary study has always been one of the distinctive features of Russian culture. Therefore, in the USSR, the practice of writing a composition (сочинение) was primarily associated with an essay on a given literary topic (see Chapter 2). Anyone who studied in the Soviet Union had to write numerous compositions during his or her years of education in Russian schools, including as university entrance exams. As Irina Korotkina has already pointed out in Chapter 1 and in her previous work, this composition assignment was based on a literary text from the prescribed reading list. It primarily tested students' knowledge of the text, their ability to reproduce quotes by heart (during in-class composition writing), as well as their ability to interpret the text *correctly*, as prescribed in the teacher's manual (Korotkina, 2014). Spelling and punctuation were among the major grading criteria in assessing such essays. Further, as Korotkina (2014) stated, "the paper is considered excellent if the student uses elaborate language, quotes the prescribed critics beyond the manual, and expresses the prescribed ideas passionately, as if they were their own" (p. 3). The organization of the essays was assessed only marginally—it was sufficient to have an introduction, main thesis, and conclusion). Overall, the number of mistakes the student made and the instructor's subjective opinion on whether the topic of the essay was sufficiently covered or not (тема раскрыта или не раскрыта) would determine the failure or success of the given task.

The skills involved in writing compositions were not explicitly taught in Russian schools. As a student in humanities, with literature as a core component, I do not remember a single seminar devoted to writing per se. Whereas, undoubtedly a lot depended on individual literature teachers, the idea that was often transmitted in schools suggested that good writing—both creative and academic—was something innate, and that neither Dostoevsky nor Tolstoy were taught how to write.

What the instructors taught us, however, was how to interpret literary texts. The offered methods of interpretation favored predominately contextual author- and text-centered analysis of literary works, which according to recent teaching manuals, are still practiced in Russian schools (Chertov & Ippolitova, 2018; Kohanova, 2011). In other words, a successful literary essay pursued the goal of deciphering the author's ideas and intentions within a certain historical and socio-political context, with the help of famous and *recommended* literary critics. The degree of individual input in such compositions, let alone genuine critical analysis, was scanty.

The situation with teaching literature in a foreign language classroom—the primary focus of this paper—was similar. Traditionally, both in the Soviet Union and in the West, literary texts were "a staple of foreign language instruction" (Hirvela, 2001, p. 110). Especially during the era of the grammar translation method, literature was the main source of input for teaching the target language. Hirvela (2001) has stated the following reasons for using literature in FL classrooms back in the 1950s to 1970s, which were not much different from the ones considered in the USSR. First, the focus in foreign language classrooms was on practicing reading and writing. Second, literary texts served as models of the target language in use, offering, as in Coleridge's famous quote, "the best words in the best order" (as cited in Hirvela, 2001, p. 111). Third, the ability to read literary texts in a foreign language was indicative of reaching the pinnacle in foreign language proficiency (Hirvela, 2001). In the Soviet Union, in addition, the ultimate goal of learning a foreign language was the ability to understand and translate complex texts: literature always offered good examples of the required complexity.

In the West of the 1970s, however, with the introduction of the communicative method of teaching and the advent of English for specific purposes (ESP), literature was knocked off the pedestal (Hirvela, 2004; Khabit, 2011). With more practical goals in mind, foreign language instructors started discarding literary texts as being too difficult, too "deviant," "neither everyday, nor academic," and therefore "too remote from the learners' experience" (Gilroy & Parkinson, 1996, p. 214).

The Russian system of education, in contrast, retained its attitude of exaltation toward literature. Thus, literature continued to serve the purpose of enhancing overall language proficiency, but it was also recognized as essential for developing cultural competence. Yet, these two skills—linguistic and cultural—were often addressed in separate literature courses. For example, in the 1990s, the English department at Moscow State Pedagogical University, aside from general English practice courses, offered a lecture course on British literature conducted in Russian, and a literature course called Home Reading conducted in English. The latter emphasized a language-based approach and utilized literary texts to practice vocabulary and grammatical structures. The discussion of literary works in such classes thus involved summarizing the plot, characterization of the main heroes, reading comprehension questions, sentence completion exercises, etc. The lecture courses in Russian, however, informed students of the major names, texts, contexts, and literary movements associated with British literature and required one term paper at the end of the semester. In general, literature in Russia in the English as a Foreign Language (EFL) context, even at specialized linguistic institutions, was employed primarily for the enhancement of the mechanics of reading and writing in a foreign language. Good writing in the FL therefore was equated with grammatical and lexical accuracy and did not pursue any cognitive or argumentative goals. Individual experiences could vary, but in general, these literature classes, with this linguistic emphasis in mind, hardly offered the practice of textual, stylistic or cultural analysis of literary works, and thus failed in developing other important competencies—interpretative and critical thinking skills.

Literature and Writing Pedagogy in Modern EFL classroom in Russia

Presently, there are few studies of the contemporary use of literature in the EFL classroom in Russia and how the methods of working with literary texts have evolved since the Soviet period. The most recent and most comprehensive research in this regard is probably that of Raees Calafato (2018). His study, based on questionnaires collected from 152 Russian EFL teachers, attests to the fact that the major goal of using literary texts in the EFL classroom is advancing linguistic skills, yet it confirms the fact that many instructors recognize the importance of literary texts for the development of students' cultural awareness and critical thinking (Calafato, 2018). Further, Calafato contends, "there are notable shifts in teachers' attitudes towards learner interest and ability that reveal evolving teacher priorities and motivations" (2018, p. 92). What the scholar means by this is that many English instructors try to employ learner-centered approaches to teaching and choosing literary texts. For example, some university instructors employ modern literary texts from the twentieth and twenty-first centuries to teach English (Calafato, 2018). Yet, Calafato argues, "literary works that were popular during Soviet times [Jerome K. Jerome, John Galsworthy, Somerset Maugham, and others] continue to be used, although contemporary American students, might not know them" (2018, p. 95). As for the practices of teaching literature, they still include sentence-completion exercises, summary writing, etc., namely, exercises aimed at improving language proficiency (Calafato, 2018). Overall, Calafato concludes that even though the use of literature in the EFL context evolved after the collapse of the Soviet Union, traditional Soviet practices have continued to influence language classrooms.

I drew conclusions similar to Calafato's (2018), having reviewed ten different reading guides, teaching manuals[1] and other online resources from several major foreign language departments in Russian universities. First, I have noticed that not all language programs have offered literature classes. Whereas the B.A. in EFL teaching at Moscow State Linguistic University offers only one course, History of Literature, during the fourth year of study, (Moscow State Linguistic University, 2020), the English program at Moscow State Pedagogical University no longer offers any literature courses per se (Zvjagintseva & Borisova, 2019). This does not mean, however, that literary texts have not been employed in other courses of study. The potential exists that these texts might play a complementary function in general linguistic instruction.

In comparison, the Herzen State Pedagogical University of Russia—allegedly the best pedagogical university in the country—offers courses on foreign literature for future FL teachers in Russian. A teaching manual at a branch of this university, entitled *Contemporary Methodologies and Techniques in Teaching Foreign Language and Literature in School and at a University* (Murtazaeva et al., 2012) states the following goals of the target language literature course: "historical and literary process, connected to English literary canons," and "development of students' knowledge about English literature as an integral part of the European literary process"[2] (Kostareva, 2012, p. 69). The first assignments that this teacher's manual offers, however, are to summarize and compare the interpretations of Shakespeare's character Hamlet by Vissarion Belinsky (a famous Russian literary critic of the nineteenth century) and another famous Russian writer, Ivan Turgenev (Kostareva, 2012). Other suggested assignments include compiling "a terminological dictionary" of literary terms and "writing a reading journal," which should include biographical information about the author, as well as information about the publication of the work, its main characters, etc. (Kostareva, 2012, p. 71).

Furthermore, my review of other reading guides for intermediate, upper intermediate, and advanced students of English revealed that the literary texts

---

1   Generally, these reading guides and teaching manuals are published by universities and kept at universities. Therefore, it is difficult to get public access to such publications.

2   All citations from N. L. Kostareva are translated by Kuznetsova-Simpson.

often offered for reading are the same as the texts popular in the 1990s: short stories by Jeffrey Archer (Beljaeva & Petrischeva, 2016), Maugham's *The Painted Veil* and Wilde's *Ideal Husband* (Rokosovskaya, 2006), Sheldon' *Rage of Angels* (Tarverdjan & Ustinova, 2013), Arthur Hailey's *Airport* (Kosheleva, 2013). Notably, some of these manuals list as their goals "the development of oral and written, creative and analytical skills" (Tarverdjan & Zueva, 2012, p. 3). Yet, they provide exercises for practicing mainly grammar and vocabulary without any communicative context and often ask students to translate sentences and word expressions from Russian into English and vice versa (Beljaeva & Petrischeva, 2016; Danchevskaya, 2012; Tarverdjan & Ustinova, 2013; Tarverdjan & Zueva, 2012). Most of the questions formulated in these manuals target primarily reading comprehension, and few questions, if any, elicit literary analysis and interpretation. For example, the manual compiled by Beljaeva and Petrischeva (2016) offers the following assignments for text analysis:

> Give the summary of the story. – What is the turning point of the story? – What kinds of narrations are used (description, a dialogue or any other)? – What kind of atmosphere do you feel in the story" (p. 98)

and the following questions for general discussion:

> What do you think about the title of the story?
>
> What is the message of the story? (p. 127)

Even though the manuals available for review offered many useful exercises for the advancement of grammatical and lexical skills, these materials lack assignments that encourage text analysis, creativity, and genuine discussion. Moreover, they indicate that in Russia, EFL teachers generally do not gain proper training in how to work with literary texts, although there exist good materials on the subject published in Russian (for example, Natalia Smetannikova's *Strategic Approach to Teaching Reading* [Strategialjnij podohd k obucheniu chteniju], 2005). Therefore, these teachers can transmit to the classes they conduct only the experiences they gained during their own study. I admit though that more empirical research is necessary to properly evaluate the use of literature in the FL context in Russia.

Reader-Response Approach in the Literature Classroom

The English language program for bachelor's students at the New Economic School (NES) offers a different approach to teaching literature in a language classroom. Following the model of a Western-type liberal arts education, the English professors conduct literature classes in the target language from the second semester of study on, resembling the practices of the monolingual English-speaking classroom. The requirement for taking these classes is an upper-intermediate or advanced level of English, as well as successful completion of the advanced college writing course in English. These literature courses continue to develop students' overall linguistic and cultural competencies, yet they also emphasize the enhancement of students' analytical and interpretative reading and writing skills.

The use of literature in foreign language instruction, as well as in L1 and L2 composition, has long been a topic of debate in Western scholarship (Belcher & Hirvela, 2000). In EFL and ESL instruction, literature, as mentioned earlier, has often been dismissed due to its lexical, syntactical, grammatical, and cultural difficulties (Hirvela, 2004). Similarly, in L1 composition classrooms, literary texts are often viewed as irrelevant to students' practical needs and overall academic writing practice. As Vandrick (2018) writes, "those against including literature claim that academic discourse, not literature, should be the focus of writing classes" (p. 2).

Yet, there have been multiple studies that have viewed literature as an integral part of language teaching and as a domain offering not only culturally authentic texts, but also rich material for teaching both reading and good writing (Gilroy & Parkinson, 1996). As scholarship attests, one should teach these two skills—reading and writing—together (Carson & Leki, 1993; Hirvela, 2004; Vandrick, 2018). Both activities are processes of "composing" and "meaning construction" (Tierney & Person, 1983, p. 568); they both are closely linked and enrich each other (Vandrick, 2018). As Hirvela (2004) points out,

> Writing with or from source texts is an act of reading as well as writing, since it is through reading that the required writing material is appropriated. . . . students' performance as readers is bound to have an important effect on their performance as writers. Students who do not read texts well are not likely to write about them successfully. (p. 109)

In other words, students' performance as readers and writers is recursive, and each skill affects, informs, and enhances the other.

Following this teaching philosophy, we emphasize both reading and writing in the literature courses we offer at NES. Even though the overall language proficiency of students taking these courses is high, we still frequently confront hurdles. For example, as my personal teaching experience has shown, the majority of Russian students often believe in one true interpretation of a literary work, which they search for while deciphering the author's intentions in the background of the text's social and historical context. They also often assume that a literary text should have a didactic function, strengthening our *ethical* and *moral values* and admit to enjoying texts which have main characters they can identify with. Such an attitude to literature has been particularly noticeable when students have struggled to provide brief personal responses to any scenes, themes, characters, or other issues raised by the readings. The reverence they feel toward classical texts, their authors, and what famous critics had to say about them, makes these tasks especially challenging. Furthermore, I've noticed that students often expect to be lectured on the material and find it difficult to explore the writer's techniques or various interpretations through close reading of the texts. Being used to assigned lists of essay topics, learners struggle to articulate their own research questions and arguments and often have asked me to write some sample essay questions for their projects.

I have tried to resolve this problem by practicing the so-called *reader-response approach* to interpreting literary texts. Even though Barthes's idea of the *death of the author* still resonates as alien among Russian learners, especially in a non-specialized literary institution, the concept of readers' active contributions to a literary text often excites students. As Gilroy and Parkinson (1996) write,

> Reader response theory . . . challenges text-oriented theories, claiming that a text has no real existence until it is read. By completing meaning, thus actualizing or realizing it, the reader does not take a passive role, as was traditionally thought, but is an active agent in the creation of meaning. (p. 215)

So, reader-response theory appears to be especially advantageous for undermining students' reverence toward the authority of the text. Instead of decoding what the author or text says and responding to meanings presumably rooted in the text, learners in reader-response theory play an active and creative role in the production of meaning through interacting with the text. Thus, the reader-response approach elevates reading as a productive activity. As Hirvela (1996) argues, "Reading here creates meaning, meaning produced by and reflecting the learner and how he or she read and transformed the original text, as opposed to passively locating meaning conveyed by the text" (p. 132). In other words, the reader-response method puts emphasis on "telling a story of reading" (Hirvela, 1996 p. 131), and it acknowledges that readers are not subordinate toward the text, "but the text serves, and is secondary to, the learner/reader" (Hirvela, 1996 p. 130). Since learners contribute different impulses to the text in the process of reading, their interpretations reflect both the readers and the text simultaneously (Hirvela, 1996).

The reader-response approach certainly helps to develop students' literary competence and more independent interpretative skills. As Gilroy and Parkinson (1996) have already suggested, being involved in reading as a dynamic process, learners have opportunities to acquire new information and revise their positions, thereby producing diverse responses to texts. Students' ability to produce such responses makes reader-response theory especially well-suited for integrated reading-writing literature instruction both in EFL and in a native language classroom.

Practicing *Complex Seeing*: Dramatic Performance and Writing Pedagogy

Aside from the reader-response approach to literature, I have found working with a theatre performance in a literature classroom especially productive for breaking habits of author-based and text-centered interpretations. Any performance based on literature already presents an artistic interpretation and the embodiment of a director's reading of a literary text, rather than the author's. Watching and analyzing a performance involves an endeavor in reconstructing this interpretation. This task, according to the experience with my students—who are the products of a predominantly visual culture—appears to generate a higher volume of motivated responses than a literary text on its own. These responses eventually bring along students' independent interpretations of both the text and the play.

The interconnection between literature and theatre, composition and performance, has already been addressed in multiple studies. Collie and Slater (1987), for example, provide useful activities for incorporating a play in a language classroom, including "a staged reading of a play" (pp. 165–166). In her study, Deb Margolin (1997) shared the experience of teaching a performance composition class, where, through a series of diverse and often very personal writing and acting exercises, students managed to reach the synergy between both creative acts. Fishman et al. (2005), in their famous Berkeley experiment, demonstrated that "student writing is increasingly linked to theories and practices of performance" (p. 224). Manis (2009) and Werry and Walseth (2011) have also addressed the productive role of composition in the performance classroom. In accordance with this research, my experience has demonstrated that the introduction of elements of performance into an integrated reading-writing classroom also could be beneficial for the advancement of writing skills.

The close connection between performance and composition goes as far back as ancient Greece, where writing practically emerged and developed out of acts of performance (Manis, 2009). Dramas, poems, and speeches at the time were first performed in front of an audience, before being documented as written texts. Consequently, Aristotelian rhetorical concepts and canons of argumentation, still employed for constructing written arguments, were first primarily concerned with the art of public speaking. After rhetoric disconnected from performance and became an integral part of composition, writing and performance continued to intersect productively in multiple ways. As Werry and Walseth (2011) write, referencing the theory of embodiment, "both writing and performing are bodily practices and forms of corporeal intelligence" (p. 187). As scholars have agreed and Manis (2009) nicely has stated,

> both fields pay a great deal of attention to audience, both emphasize the importance of process, both understand themselves as ways of knowing and of coming to know, both are invested in their creative power, both struggle with the question of "authenticity." (p. 142)

Furthermore, composition and performance, as products of creative endeavor, strive for synergy between content and form; they both can be simultaneously collaborative as well as individual, public as well as intimately personal projects. In general, as Werry and Walseth (2011) contend, "both writing and performance provide rich opportunities for enacting critical and emancipatory pedagogies, and for training students to become critical thinkers and engaged cultural citizens" (p. 187).

I find Bertolt Brecht's (1964/2014) ideas on the epic theatre particularly beneficial for addressing and practicing students' critical skills. Whereas European drama since Aristotle has invited spectators to identify and empathize with the destiny of its main characters, in pursuing the so-called cathartic experience, Brecht's drama, in contrast, has attempted to examine rather than to stimulate emotions. As Brooker (2006) writes, Brecht's theatre "sought to produce a knowledge of the 'causal laws of development,' to divide rather than unify its audience, to intervene in and so transform ideas and attitudes" (p. 213). The dialectical theatre that Brecht proposed (Brecht, 1964/2014) confronts the audience with a performance full of effects—*alienation effects*—which would enable critical detachment: an epic play would always remind its audience of the artificial nature of the theatrical performance and make it confront and recognize alternatives to the portrayed actions.

This alienation effect (Verfremdungseffect) enables the presentation of the familiar as strange and the strange as familiar. It brings the needed rupture into performance, undermining the spectators' common practice of identifying with the characters and actions on stage. It objectifies itself in the innovative method of acting (an actor turns into a *demonstrator*); in the narrative form of the performance and songs; in the elements of the stage design, such as placards, decorations, and film projections on the screen; but also in new expectations from the audience.

The theatre that Brecht advocated required a new type of spectator. Brecht (1964/2014) wrote that the form of narration that his theatre adapts turns "spectators into critical observers," but also "awakens their activity" and "forces them to make decisions" (p. 1643). As Benjamin (1966/1998) famously wrote, "Brecht has attempted to make the thinking man, indeed the wise man, into an actual dramatic hero" (p. 17). "The art of the epic theatre consists in arousing astonishment rather than empathy. . . . instead of identifying itself with the hero, the audience should learn to feel astonished at the circumstances under which he functions" (Benjamin, 1966/1998, p. 18). In other words, Brecht's plays were designed to challenge the audience to think, to recognize alternatives not in opposing characters and scenes, but often embodied in one person and one action; they were produced to expose possibilities for change. Brecht believed that the plays he wrote, with proper distancing effects designed, forced spectators to "adopt a watching-while-smoking attitude" and thus engendered what he called *complex seeing*: "Complex seeing must be practiced. . . . thinking across the flow [of a play] is almost more important than thinking in the flow" (Brecht, 1964/2014, p. 1818). This *complex seeing*, as Raymond Williams (1961) wrote, was Brecht's "most original dramatic contribution" (p. 156).

Some of Brecht's ideas on the theatre could well be applied to reading, interpreting, and writing about literary texts as well. First, Brecht's theatre (1964/2014), much more strongly than naturalistic theatre, emphasized its audience. Whereas an actor in a naturalistic play is divided from his or her audience with the so-called *fourth wall*, an epic actor often interacts directly with spectators. Watching and discussing this interaction, I have tried to convey to my students that similar awareness of the audience can be applied to the writing process. Further, in my classes, I have encouraged students to sustain critical distance while working with texts rather than to empathize with characters and situations. My students also practiced looking at the texts anew—even in a strange and unfamiliar way—allowing for new meanings and alternatives to emerge.

The exercise in *complex seeing* is also rewarding in academic writing, since the formulation of an argument rests on seeing and recognizing different alternatives and counterarguments. As Manis (2009) already suggests, Brecht's

(1964/2014) concept of *not-but* could well be applied to writing instruction and to teaching students to acknowledge counterarguments productively in their papers. Brecht (1964/2014) introduced the concept of *not-but* as a means for the actor to "fix" or "freeze" the alternatives that may be communicated (p. 2609). He writes:

> When they appear on the stage, besides what the actors actually are doing they will at all essential points discover, specify, imply what they are not doing; that is to say, they will act in such a way that the alternative emerges as clearly as possible. (Brecht, 1964/2014, p. 4326)

Thus, the main idea of this *not-but* is to demonstrate that nothing is fixed and inevitable and to expose the choices that an actor or character might face. As Brecht writes: "Whatever he [the actor] does not do must be contained and conserved in what he does. In this way every sentence and every gesture signify a decision; the character remains under observation and is tested" (Brecht, 1964/2014, p. 4330). So, as Manis (2009) writes, the act of recognizing alternatives is also integral to constructing counterarguments. "Brecht's theorization of how to render deliberate decision making clear as an actor portraying a character provides an excellent way of thinking about acknowledging counterarguments and establishing authority as a writer aware of the many contingencies informing one's topic" (Manis, 2009, p. 144).

Overall, I believe that teaching literature and writing through the study of theatre and performance has a transformative and productive character. The study of performance theory and practice can help students to develop skills in both creative and academic writing. Performances in general resonate more powerfully in students' memories and thus provide additional motivation to write about them, as was manifested in the writing assignments I gave in my drama and theatre class.

During the semester of teaching the drama and theatre course, my students—independently and as a group, together with me—attended and discussed several productions in Moscow theatres, ranging from classical to post-modern. Most of the productions we watched were based on the texts we read in class. We saw plays staged by some of the most famous Russian directors (Yuri Lubimov, Konstantin Raikin, Yuri Butusov, Konstantin Bogomolov, and others), but also the productions of British theatres—Barbican, Old Vic, National Theatre—broadcasted in Moscow through Theatre HD. Toward the end of the semester, the students had to write a review of one of the productions of their choice (Assignment #1). I encouraged them to evaluate the play while assuming the role of a distant spectator—a spectator who could both enjoy and critically analyze the production. The assignment was to examine in an objective manner the success or failure of a given production, as intended for its target audience. In particular, they had to provide an interpretation and evaluation of the staging, acting, directing, etc., while concentrating on a few important and interesting aspects and critical or problematic points that the performance illustrated.

I always encouraged my students to attend plays with an open mind and willingness to accept the play as the director has presented it in the production, as well as to try to find good explanations and interpretations for what they considered a deviation from a standard or classical performance. The questions they had to address during their analysis also included the following: "How would you account for the choice of costumes, set designs, special effects, etc.? Did the director miss anything important you were able to see in your reading of the play? What are the new or different insights that the director tried to convey?"

In comparison to earlier assignments given in class, based on the reading and interpreting of a literary work, I felt that my students were more motivated to conduct the analysis of an adaptation of a literary text. They seemed to have less anxiety about expressing their judgments about a theatrical production, rather than about a text itself, scrutinized by intellectuals over centuries, and they honestly felt they could say something new. The immediacy of the performance and their own preconceptions of what this performance should have been like provided additional ground for forming their own judgments of the production. They were learning to disagree and to analyze in an objective manner rather than just to criticize what they had seen. Overall, this assignment provided them with the liberty to formulate their own opinions concerning the performance. I felt that my students were finally getting into the position of authority—the authority of the critic, knowledgeable about the text, and capable of judging how well the text was adapted for the stage. Moreover, I believe this assignment also encouraged them to conceptualize themselves as artists and producers of the performance, which prepared them for other more creative writing assignments.

The next writing project I assigned to my students (Assignment #2) was to take upon themselves the role of a contemporary theatre director and to express in writing their ideas about staging one of the dramas we discussed in class. The target audience for this production, as the assignment suggested, were primarily spectators of the same generation as my students. The learners also had to speculate about why the particular play they chose would resonate with younger audiences in Russia and how the questions or issues it addressed could potentially be relevant to or interesting for contemporary spectators. Their concept proposal also had to address the elements of the production itself (the setting, costumes, music, stage design, etc.), as well as other theatrical techniques that the student-directors wanted to employ. The participants also had the liberty to choose either a classical or an experimental stage interpretation; an *epic theatre*, an absurdist, or a naturalistic production, as well as to alter the original text, if they wished. As Pope (1995) wrote in his book *Textual Intervention*, "the best way to understand how a text works, . . . is to change it: to play around with it, to intervene in it in some way (large or small), and then to try to account for the exact effect of what you have done" (p. 1). Even though intervention in the original text of the drama was allowed, it was not a required task. Yet, my students' papers demonstrated that they found this choice particularly exciting and productive.

As a result, in the conception of one student, the absurdist situation of Didi and Gogo from Beckett's *Waiting for Godot* turned into a "waiting for promotion" of two miserable analysts who hated their positions in a bank but would not dare to change anything in their lives (Sample 3).[3] In the conception of another student, the same characters represented two Russians—an intellectual and a philistine—waiting for the political change that never occurred. Another conception looked at Tom Stoppard's *Rosencrantz and Guildenstern are Dead* as a precursor to the post-modern concept of precariat (social class characterized by lack of job security, affecting both the material and psychological spheres of life) and moved the setting of the play from the palace to "a front office of some big corporation," retaining, however, most of the absurdist dialogues between the characters. One of the conceptions, based on Ibsen's *A Doll's House*, reflected on what gender dynamics would look like in the contemporary world and how politics can affect the life of a simple family (Sample 2).

In the end, what these students finally produced were proposals of quite independent dramas. Most of the essays offered either the modernization of a classical text, relocated the characters to altered yet similar circumstances, or visualized new dramas, which combined in a creative manner several texts through references and citations in a manner typical of post-modernism. Most importantly though, the majority of the student-directors tried to stress that they targeted critical and distant spectators and suggested several alienation effects that their dramas could employ, as well as alternative situations that spectators could elicit from their dramas. For example, a student working

---

3   See Appendix. The sample demonstrates an excerpt from students' play that grew out of the drama conception (Assignment #1) and the performance that I will discuss later in the chapter.

on Chekhov's *Three Sisters* moved the focus of the play from the Prozorov sisters to Natasha (probably the most unpleasant character in the drama) and suggested an alternative view on her, challenging traditional interpretations of the play. Stressing Natasha's ambitiousness and resourcefulness in comparison to the inertia and arrogance of the sisters, the student drew attention to the outcomes of the shifts in the social, class, and value system of the society. The aforementioned play, called *Waiting for Promotion*, attempted to create "a higher sense of absurdity" with the following alienating technique: "[analysts'] faces are colored in white and there are big black circles under the eyes. . . . Overwork is highlighted by the size of the objects of stage design: all the office staff—pens, paper piles, computers and chairs—are abnormally big" (from the conception on which Sample 3 was based). In the actual performance of the play, the students also critically juxtaposed their made-up absurd situation with those in Beckett's *Waiting for Godot* and Chekhov's *Three Sisters*, having started Didi and Gogo's dialogue with an altered version of Chekhov's famous lines, projected on the screen.

> The time will come, and all will know what these sufferings [are] for, there will be no secrets, but now we need to live . . . we need to work, work harder. Tomorrow I will again sleep 4 hours, will work at the bank and will sacrifice my life to those who may need it. It's autumn now, soon it'll be winter with the snow, but I will be working, will be working. Good God, let alone being a man, it would be better to be an ox, better to be a simple horse, as long as one can sleep, rather [than] be a young man who finishes his work at 2 in the morning, spends 2 hours on a way back home, sleeps for 2 hours and then convulsively drinks coffee to be in shape. (Sample 3)

The adaptation of Wilde's *Salome* was conceptualized in a truly metatheatrical manner as a rehearsal of the play, reflecting the predicament of a director and his actors to present a performance that could be contemporary and innovative, yet would touch upon the eternal artistic, philosophical and gender issues addressed in Wilde's text. This predicament was signaled with the following alienation technique, as the stage directions to the actual play demonstrate:

> In "STOP" moment the sound of the cassette rewinding appears. The sound is annoying and short, presenting "interruption" in its most direct and explicit form. It is important that a preceding action may be reversed and played one more time in

a "distorted" version. Our aim is to "overfeed" a spectator with contemporary allusions and distortions, to create a feeling of the cumulative "awkwardness" with each new director's insertion. (Sample 1)

Even those students who at the beginning of the semester had advocated for classical adaptations of literature, chose to experiment creatively with canonical texts, unveiling both for themselves and for me as a reader latent themes and ideas they had discovered in these texts.

The writing assignment discussed above also laid the foundation for the final creative group project in my class—a 20-minute performance. My students had a choice to present a scene or scenes from one of the dramas we had covered in class or their own short play. Several groups chose to stage a play, drafted earlier by one of the students for Assignment #2, and to work together on its development. Thus, many of the students' ideas, expressed in Assignment #2, received practical realization on the stage of our classroom.

After the performances, my students had to submit scripts of their plays (Assignment #3). While I was reading these scripts, I found it fascinating to trace how students had distilled and re-conceptualized in writing some ideas that they earlier had tried to express during the production. Both performance and writing, it seemed, stimulated their critical awareness and editing initiatives, making them discern the conceptions that appeared awkward and unproductive during the play. Overall, I believe, throughout these activities (evaluating a play, conceptualizing one's own performance, staging it, and documenting it), my students got a taste of a genuine artistic process which always involves research, reflection, recording, and revision.

The major problems that I encountered during these assignments were the following. I noticed that some students found it difficult to carry through their ideas to their logical end, to connect conceptually all the elements of the production, and to interpret the choices they had made. Yet, taking into account that my students were future economists, rather than actors or directors, the overall result of this creative work truly exceeded my expectations. I also felt that the three essays discussed surpassed the previous class assignments in grammatical and lexical accuracy. This could have been the result not only of improvement through writing progression, but also the outcome of higher personal motivation associated with the creative task itself and the opportunity to choose the texts and themes the students found most engaging. I found it difficult, however, to establish proper evaluation criteria for the performances and the scripts because of the artistic nature of the assignment and the issue related to group-authorship. But since the performing project accounted for only one-fourth of the course grade, I felt that participation in this creative collaborative work was more essential than each individual's contribution.

The feedback I received from students indicated that the majority of the class found creative writing assignments especially interesting and rewarding. Some of the students wrote in their evaluations that it was "cool" to go to the theatre and to be able to produce in writing a critical and informed judgment of a performance. Out of all literature and writing classes I have taught, I received more comments stating that students not only "improved," but "truly enjoyed writing" only in this class. Further, I believe this assignment provided my students with the long-desired liberty and space for shaping their thoughts; it encouraged them to experiment with new ideas and to subvert creatively the authority of traditional Russian stage interpretations.

Conclusion

Russian universities have consistently offered very strong education in foreign languages and linguistics. Yet, there is further potential to train students not only to succeed in the formal elements of writing in a foreign language, but also in the mechanics of thinking and argumentation, as well as in creative use of language. Yet, the integrated reading-writing literature instruction in the target language in the EFL context is only possible if FL instructors similarly receive proper training in teaching literature along with linguistic education.

Literature presents a crossroads of various discourses; therefore, its study offers rich opportunities for enhancing students' linguistic, cultural, and interpretative competencies along with analytical and creative writing skills. As Myles Chilton (2016) writes—and I can only agree with this—

> When we teach literature in a language foreign to that of our students, we are initiating and maintaining the circulation of not only a text, but also responses to the text. These responses too can be literature; these too can create knowledge, rather than merely regurgitate readings and interpretations that come from a professor of literature, an "authority." (p. 137)

The experience I had in my drama and theatre course demonstrated that through engagement with performance, my students not only sharpened their literary competencies, but also acquired their autonomous voices: the creative freedom they gained in this class was an effective step in overcoming former dependences upon assigned essay topics, authorial intentions, and authoritative teaching models. Most importantly, theatre enabled my students to understand more sharply the dramas we had been reading, to draw connections between writing and performance, and to create their own literary texts.

References

Belcher, D., & Hirvela, A. (2000). Literature and L2 composition: Revisiting the debate. *Journal of Second Language Writing, 9*(1), 21–39. https://doi.org/10.1016/S1060-3743(99)00021-1.

Beljaeva, O. V., & Petrischeva, O. S. (2016). *Anglijskij Jazik:* Uchebnoje posobije po domashnemu chteniju po rasskazam Jeffrey Archer [English: A reading guide to short stories by Jeffrey Archer]. MGIMO University.

Benjamin, W. (1998). *Understanding Brecht.* (A. Bostock, Trans.). Verso. (Original work published 1966). https://www.scribd.com/document/138098970/Benjamin-Walter-Understanding-Brecht.

Bloemert, J., Paran A., Jansen E., & van de Grift, W. (2017). Students' perspective on the benefits of EFL literature education. *The Language Learning Journal, 47*(3), 371–384. https://doi.org/10.1080/09571736.2017.1298149.

Brecht, B. (2014). *Brecht on theatre.* (M. Siberman, T. Kuhn, & S. Giles, Eds.) (Davis, R. Fursland, & S. Giles, Trans.) [Kindle edition]. Bloomsbury. (Original work published 1964). https://www.amazon.com/Brecht-Theatre-Development-Aesthetic-Bertolt/dp/0809005425.

Brooker, P. (2006). Key words in Brecht's theory and practice of theatre. In P. Thomas & G. Sacks (Eds.), *The Cambridge companion to Brecht* (pp. 209–224). Cambridge University Press. https://doi.org/10.1017/CCOL0521857090.

Calafato, R. (2018). Literature in language education: Evolving language pedagogies and text preferences in contemporary Russia. *Voprosy obrazovaniya [Educational Studies], 2,* 91–116. https://doi.org/10.17323/1814-9545-2018-2-91-116.

Carson, J. G., & Leki, I. (1993). *Reading in the composition classroom: Second language perspectives.* Heinle & Heinle; Wadsworth.

Chertov, V. F. (Ed.). (2018). *Programmi obscheobrazovateljnih uchrezdenij*: Literatura, *5–11 classi,* [Comprehensive school programs: Literature, grades 5–11]. Prosveschenije. https://www.sinykova.ru/biblioteka/chertov_literatyra_5-11kl/.

Chilton, M. (2016). *English studies beyond the "center:" Teaching literature and the future of global English.* Routledge.

Collie, J., & Slater, S. (1987). *Literature in the language classroom: a resource book of ideas and activities.* Cambridge University Press.

Danchevskaya, O. E. (2012). *"The magician" by W. S. Maugham: Uchebnoe posobie po domashnemu chteniju* [*The magician* by W. S. Maugham: Reading guide]. Flinta.

Fishman, J., Lunsford A., McGregor B., & Otuteye M. (2005). Performing writing, performing literacy. *College Composition and Communication, 57*(2), 224–252. http://www.jstor.org/stable/30037914.

Gilroy, M., & Parkinson, B. (1996). Teaching literature in a foreign language. *Language Teaching, 29*(4), 213–225. https://doi.org/10.1017/S026144480000851X.

Hirvela, A. (1996). Reader-response theory and ELT. *ELT Journal, 50*(2), 127–134. https://doi.org/10.1093/elt/50.2.127.

Hirvela, A. (2001). Connecting reading and writing through literature. In D. Belcher & A. Hirvela (Eds.), *Linking literacies: Perspectives on L2 reading-writing connections* (pp. 109–34). University of Michigan Press.

Hirvela, A. (2004). *Connecting reading and writing in second language writing instruction.* University of Michigan Press.

Kohanova, B. A. (Ed.). (2011). *Technologii in metodiki obuchenia literature. Uchebnoe posobie dlja bakalavrov* [Methodologies and strategies of teaching literature. A study manual for bachelor students]. Flinta.

Korotkina, I. (2014). Academic writing in Russia: Evolution or revolution? Social Science Research Network, https://doi.org/10.2139/ssrn.2435130.

Kosheleva, I. N. (2013). *Anglijskij Jazik: Uchebno-metodicheskoje posobije po domashnemu chteniju po romanu A. Hailey's Airport* [English: Reading guide to A. Hailey's *Airport*]. MGIMO University.

Kostareva, N. L. (2012). O formah i vida vneauditornoj samostojateljnoj raboti v kursah disziplin po zarubeznoj literature. [Types and forms of independent study in foreign language literature courses] In M. M. Murtazaeva, S. G. Filipova, A. U. Sapoznikova, U. P. Bolotina, O. D. Ermakova, & N. L. Kostareva (Eds.), *Sovremennie metodiki in technologii obuchenia inostrannomu jaziku i literature v shkove in v vuze* [Contemporary methodologies and techniques in teaching foreign language and literature in school and at a university] (pp. 68–76). Lema.

Manis, S., (2009). Writing as performance: Using performance theory to teach writing in theatre classrooms. *Theatre Topics, 19*(2), 139–151. https://doi.org/10.1353/tt.0.0072.

Margolin, D. (1997). A perfect theatre for one: Teaching "performance composition." *The Drama Review, 41*(2), 68–81. https://www.jstor.org/stable/1146625.

Moscow State Linguistic University. (2020). *Bachelor degree program: Linguistics 45.03.02. Theory and methodology of teaching foreign languages and cultures.* Moscow State Linguistic University. https://linguanet.ru/en/studies/programmes-courses/bachelors/linguistics-45-03-02-theory-and-methodology-of-teaching-foreign-languages-and-cultures/.

Murtazaeva, M. M., Filipova, S. G., Sapoznikova, A. U., Bolotina, U. P., Ermakova, O. D., & Kostareva, N. L. (Eds.) (2012). *Sovremennie metodiki in technologii obuchenia inostrannomu jaziku i literature v shkove in v vuze* [Contemporary methodologies and techniques in teaching foreign language and literature in school and at a university]. Lema.

Pope, R. (1995). *Textual intervention: Critical and creative strategies for literary studies.* Routledge.

Rokossovskaya, N. K. (2006). *Anglijskij Jazik: Uchebnoje posobije po domashnemu chteniju dlja studentov vtorogo kursa fakuljteta mezdunarodnih ekonomicheskih otnoshenij* [English: Reading guide for second-year students of international economic relations]. MGIMO University.

Smetannikova, N. N. (2005). *Strategialjnij podohd k obucheniu chteniju* [Strategic approach to teaching reading]. Shkoljnaja Biblioteka.

Tarverdjan, A. S., & Ustinova, E. V. (2013). *Anglijskij Jazik: Uchebnoje posobije po domashnemu chteniju. "Rage of Angels" by S. Sheldon* [English: Reading guide to "Rage of Angels" by S. Sheldon]. MGIMO University.

Tarverdjan, A. S., & Zueva, V.V. (2012). *Anglijskij Jazik: Uchebnoje posobije po domashnemu chteniju к sborniku rasskazov "Crime never pays"* [English: Reading guide to the collection of stories "crime never pays"]. MGIMO University.

Tierney, R. J., & Pearson, P. D. (1983). Towards a composing model of reading. *Language arts, 60*(5), 568–580. http://www.jstor.org/stable/41961506.

Vandrick, S. (2018). Reading and writing connections in writing about literature. In D. Belcher & A. Hirvela (Eds.), *The TESOL encyclopedia of English language teaching* (pp. 1–6). John Wiley & Sons.

Werry, M., & Walseth, S. L. (2011). Articulate bodies: Writing instruction in a performance-based curriculum. *Theatre Topics, 21*(2), 185–197. https://muse.jhu.edu/article/449857/pdf.

Williams, R. (1961) The achievement of Brecht. *Critical Quarterly, 3*(2), 153–162. https://doi.org/10.1111/j.1467-8705.1961.tb01157.x.

Zvjagintseva, A. V., & Borisova, E. Y. (2019). *Raspisanie uchebnih zanjatij instituta inostrannih jazikov na 2019–2020 uchebnij god* [Course schedule of the Department of Foreign Languages for school year 2019–2020]. Moscow State Pedagogical University. http://mpgu.su/wp-content/uploads/2019/10/Расписание-английское-отделение.pdf.

Appendix: Excerpts from students' theatrical adaptations (Assignment #3)

Sample 1

Salome
(an adaptation of Oscar Wilde's *Salome*)
Notes*:*
In "STOP" moment the sound of the cassette rewinding appears. The sound is annoying and short, presenting "interruption" in its most direct and explicit form. It is important that a preceding action may be reversed and played one more time in a "distorted" version.

Our aim is to "overfeed" a spectator with contemporary allusions and distortions, to create a feeling of the cumulative "awkwardness" with each new director's insertion. Increasing discomfort eventually evolves in so-called "catharsis" both on spectators' and actors' side.

– The director sits on the side of the scene at the table. She is creating a new play. The scene with the actors illustrates the flow of her imagination.

– Black screen with white text on the background:

Salome
well-known contemporary director.

DIRECTOR. *(hectically, stands up)* I am a <u>contemporary</u> director. I need to write a play. I want my play to be <u>contemporary</u>. I want my play to be <u>eternal</u>. I want my play to be <u>relevant</u>. I want my play to be <u>experimental</u>.

– *Leans on the table*

I have a deadline in a month!

Herodias, Herod, Salome . . . Ok, ok . . . the setting—the moon, the palace.

– *Sits at the table, dreams*

– Herod, Herodias, and Salome appear, sit on three chairs. They wear blankets, under the blankets are casual contemporary clothes (not seen).

HEROD (imperatively, expressively acting). Dance for me, Salome, I beseech thee. If you dance for me you may ask of me what you want, and I will give you thee. Ask of me what you wilt, and I will give it thee. Yes, dance for me, Salome, and whatsoever you shall ask of me I will give it thee, even the half of my kingdom.

SALOME. (standing up). Will you indeed give me whatsoever I shall ask of you, Tetrarch?

HERODIAS. I will not have her dance.

HEROD. Whatsoever thou shalt ask of me, even the half of my kingdom.

STOP (cassette rewind). Characters freeze up.

DIRECTOR: This will not work. The costumes, I should change the costumes. The costumes must be <u>contemporary</u>. I want the young audience to relate.

– Characters take blankets off. Stay in casual clothes.

– (cassette rewind)

HEROD. Whatsoever thou shalt ask of me, even the half of my kingdom.

SALOME. You swear it, Tetrarch?

HEROD. I swear it, Salome.

HERODIAS. Peace. Let her alone.

SALOME. By what will you swear this thing, Tetrarch?

HEROD. By my life, by my crown, by my gods. Whatsoever thou shalt desire I will give it thee, even to the half of my kingdom, if thou wilt but dance for me. O Salome, Salome, dance for me!

SALOME. You have sworn an oath, Tetrarch.

HEROD. I have sworn an oath.

SALOME. Whatever I wish, be it even the half of your kingdom?

HERODIAS. I do not want her dancing.

SALOME. I will dance for you, Tetrarch.

HEROD. You hear what your daughter says. She is going to dance for me. And when you have danced for me, forget not to ask of me whatsoever you want. And I have never failed of my word. I am not of those who break their oaths. I am the slave of my word, and my word is the word of a king. The King of Cappadocia had ever a lying tongue, but he is no true king. He is a coward. Also he owes me money that he will not repay.

STOP (cassette rewind).
DIRECTOR (highbrow speech). No Cappadocia here, it is not <u>relevant</u>. My play must be <u>relevant</u>. I want <u>politics</u> here. As Brecht said, "Art is not a mirror with which we reflect reality, but a hammer with which we shape it" (expressively admires herself while quoting Brecht). Yes, more politics.
– (cassette rewind)
– On the screen: the photo of "United Russia" (leading political party). The photo is intentionally awkward and obviously does not fit the play.
HEROD. The King of Cappadocia had ever a lying tongue, but he is no true king. He is a coward. Он должен знать, что будет уничтожен. А мы, жертвы агрессии, мы как мученики попадем в рай, а они просто сдохнут, потому что даже раскаяться не успеют.
HERODIAS. (a bit confused after Herod's speech, still not showing confusion explicitly). Do not dance, my daughter. I will not have her dance while you look at her in this fashion. In a word, I will not have her dance.
HEROD. Do not rise, my wife, my queen. I will not go till she had danced. Dance, Salome, dance for me. I will not go within till she hath danced. Dance, Salome, dance for me.
SALOME. I am ready, Tetrarch.
– Salome takes a veil, puts it on.
– Salome starts performing "Dance of the Seven veils," taking the veil off.
STOP (cassette rewind).
DIRECTOR. Ok, why does Salome take off her veil? It must have a <u>sense</u>! A deep social sense is indispensable in my play. She is taking of her veil, because . . . it is warm, because of . . . global warming! This is definitely missing! (expressively presses the cassette rewind button)
– (cassette rewind)
– On the screen: melting ice, poor polar bears and penguins, stock posters about global warming with "Go vegan" calls
SALOME. I am ready, Tetrarch. It's warm here.
First, how warm? (change in tone)
If we act NOW, the worldwide temperature increases will be kept to 2 degrees Fahrenheit per year, and the damages—though significant—will be manageable. But if we don't act, and the temperature increases by 9 degrees by the end of the century, the damage will be CATASTROPHIC and IRREVERSIBLE (expressively).
Our biosphere is being sacrificed to our needs. We need to keep fossil fuels in the ground. And if solutions within the system are so impossible to find, maybe we should change the system itself.
[inciting the audience, frantically] We have run out of excuses and we are running out of time. I'm here to state that change is coming, whether you like it or not. The real power belongs to the people.

...

STOP (cassette rewind).

DIRECTOR. Something is missing here. I need more . . . something . . . I had ecology, feminism, philosophy . . . But the play is still not contemporary enough! I want to be an <u>innovator</u>! The time for <u>innovation</u> has come, the time for fear is over! My Salome will be experimental! My Salome will be a . . . MAN!

– Herod takes Salome's place, repeats her words and tries to kiss Iokanaan

– (cassette rewind)

HEROD[SALOME]. You didn't want me to kiss your mouth, Iokanaan. Well! I will kiss it now. I will bite it with my teeth as one bites a ripe fruit. Yes, I will kiss thy mouth, Iokanaan.

– Herod stops, realizing that something goes wrong.

HEROD. What is going on here? Does anybody understand?

HERODIAS. Not really.

SALOME. I do not know.

HERODIAS. Do not you think that everything became senseless?

HEROD. Yeah, it was too much.

SALOME. I feel that I lost myself.

HERODIAS. I feel that someone distorted our personalities, interfered the whole story.

HEROD. Alas, poor Wilde! I knew him, Herodias: a fellow of infinite jest, of most excellent fancy.

SALOME. Here hung those lips that I have kissed I know not how oft.

HEROD. Now everything is wasted, everything is ruined . . .

HERODIAS. BECAUSE OF HER (notices director, points at the her)

– Characters start screaming simultaneously. They approach the director, who is still sitting at the table on the side of the scene.

SALOME. YOU RUINED MY PERSONALITY!

HEROD. WHAT DID YOU DO TO US!

HERODIAS. I HATE YOU!

– The director anxiously presses the "cassette rewind" button, the sound plays, but the characters do not stop.

– The characters come close to the director, slam her with the plaster bust and kill her. The director falls from her chair and silently pronounces her last words.

DIRECTOR. I just wanted to be contemporary . . .

– The characters silently put the blankets on, sit on their chairs and take their initial positions. Herod starts . . .

HEROD. Dance for me, Salome . . .

Sample 2

Nora's House
(an adaptation of Henrik Ibsen's *A Doll's House*)
Space is separated in two parts, one has a bench or chairs and a kitchen table with a lamp on it (Torvald's room, far from the door), one has nothing but a chair and a table.
SCENE 1.
[Enter NORA, well-dressed woman, dressed as a business lady, powerful, practical, a bit sentimental. She has a small red book in her hands, military ID. She is checking her phone.]
[On the screen appears twitter account of Torvald with an avatar of Russian bear, he has twitted something related to the celebration and patriotic with lots of Russian flag smiles and stuff.]
NORA. [Coming to the door of Torvald.] Is that my lark twittering there? [No answer.] Good, he is still not here.
[She's putting the pass to the drawer, going to Torvald's room, putting a cover to the table, putting drinks and food there. She is about to take a selfie for her husband, but the doorbell rings.]
NORA. Oh, he's coming! [She runs to the door, opens it, hesitates and steps back a bit surprised].
[Enter CHRISTINA, a woman (possibly played by a man), dressed fancy, tastelessly and weirdly, with lots of make up on her face.]
MRS. LINDEN. [Screaming and acting actively.] How do you do, Nora?
NORA. [Doubtfully.] How do you do?
MRS. LINDEN. I see you don't recognize me!
NORA. No, I don't think—oh yes!—I believe—[Suddenly brightening.] What, Christina! Is it really you?
MRS. LINDEN. Yes; really, I!
NORA. Christina! And to think I didn't know you! But how could I—[More softly.] How changed you are; Christina!
MRS. LINDEN. Yes, no doubt. In twenty years after graduation—! Skin got a bit wrinkly; voice got a bit lower, but all in all it's still old crazy me, remember? [*Shows* NORA *photo on her phone, on the screen photo of young* NORA *with a good looking, young girl, on the background NES signs.*]
NORA. Yes, now I can see the dear old face again. It was only at the first glance—But you're a little paler, Christina—and perhaps a little thinner.
MRS. LINDEN. And much, much older, Nora.
NORA. Yes, perhaps a little older—not much—ever so little. And now you have come to town? You were in Norway, as I remember. All that long journey in mid-winter!

[*She suddenly checks herself; seriously.*] Oh, what a thoughtless wretch I am! Here I sit chattering on, and [*Softly.*] Poor Christina! I forgot: you are a widow.

MRS. LINDEN. [*Recklessly.*] Yes; my husband died three years ago.

NORA. I know, I know; I saw it on Facebook. Oh, believe me, Christina, I did mean to write to you; but I kept putting it off, and something always came in the way.

MRS. LINDEN. I can quite understand that, Nora dear.

NORA. No, Christina; it was horrid of me. Oh, you poor darling! how much you must have gone through! So utterly alone! How dreadful that must be!

MRS. LINDEN. He left me nothing, we had no children, and I had not even a sorrow or a longing to dwell upon. I didn't really care about him.

NORA. [*Looking at her incredulously.*] My dear Christina, how is that possible?

MRS. LINDEN. [*Smiling and stroking her hair.*] Oh, it happens so sometimes, Nora. You know, it's so horrible in that place Norway. I was going there for a brawny, handsome, bearded Viking, who would be a proper man, and you know what? All the men there are just pussies. Women, and I say it again, women should do all men's job, women should start flirting in a bar [*she's making* NORA *sit down and acting out everything she's saying*] buy them drinks and so on. And men are just hesitating, pretending to be shy, putting on an act, and you literally need to do all the work, can you imagine that? And if I come there dressed up fancy, you know, in my best possible outlook, all shining and glimmering, none, none of them wouldn't even try to talk to me, I'm not talking about flirting or something.

NORA. Now tell me, is it really true that you didn't love your husband? What made you marry him, then?

MRS. LINDEN. Oh, he was some old minister who adored Russian women. He was so brilliant and popular, I thought, he would be perfect. And of course, money and residency, it is all important. But he turned out to be a fraud, he signed some important papers with fake signatures and sold to a Stock Exchange speculator a Cabinet secret. Then, it all was published because of some sort of lady [Cheveley] or something, and he died of a heart attack, not such a big deal.

[*Pause.*]

MRS. LINDEN. Anyway, I want you to tell me—[*Pause.*] How is your life going?

NORA. I have three of the loveliest children. I can't show them to you just now; they're out with their nurse. And I love my husband very much. He sa—

MRS. LINDEN. [*Interrupting.*] I've seen your Instagram post last week, about your great stroke of fortune. That you became a manager in BCG.

NORA. In McKinsey. And a partner, not a manager.

. . .

NORA. Yes indeed. But now let me tell you, Christina—I, too, have something to be bothered with.

MRS. LINDEN. And what is that?

NORA. My family might be torn apart.

MRS. LINDEN. What? Your family?

NORA. Yes, by our damned government and its damned regulations.

MRS. LINDEN. But how is that possible?

NORA. Last week I have found out an email from the recruitment office where it was stated that according to a new law, my husband should immediately come to the office and serve in the military.

MRS. LINDEN. Oh, this law that forces every man, who is younger than 60 and unemployed, to serve in the military for five years.

NORA. Exactly. And you know, the demand on the military ID is extremely high because of that, they are really strict with all the fake IDs, and in order to get one, you need to spend a fortune on it, even for me it's unaffordable.

MRS. LINDEN. Yes, that must be really expensive. So would he go to the army then?

NORA. No, I wouldn't allow that, my family is sacred for me.

MRS. LINDEN. How do you want to prevent it?

NORA. I did. It's already done.

MRS. LINDEN. Of course you couldn't bribe them.

NORA. No? Why not?

MRS. LINDEN. A person of your position can't bribe others as it might put all your career under threat.

NORA. Yes, it's true. But what can I do if they want to take my husband from my family. Should I just silently agree to all the decisions of those idiots who are sitting up there?

MRS. LINDEN. So you did ...

NORA. I never said that I bribed somebody. But using some connections, making some Agreements of Cooperation. There are many ways I may have got it. I may have got it from some admirer. When one is so attractive as I am—

...

SCENE 2

[*ENTER TORVALD AND RANK. TORVALD is played by a woman.*]

RANK. You know, I want to be honest with you. When I was in a soviet army, it was exactly as you described: the army was a forge of masculinity, it was strong, it was prestigious, it made a man out of a boy, it disciplined you and gave you a military spirit. If you said something wrongly, you would always get your face punched. But now, let me tell you something, now, it's completely different. It's all corrupt, dirty, older generations are humiliating younger ones, and one just returns from there lacking all the skills he was supposed to get.

TORVALD. General, you're wrong. Our army is still strong, we showed them all who is dominating in the world. Everybody has seen our new tanks and weapons, and that it's better to not play around with us.

RANK. Dominating? Sending couple of generals and some weapons to Syria is dominating for you? In former times, people were dying as heroes. They were fighting against bloody fascists, and we still sing praises to them. When we won the war, we were happy. And what the point in the army now? People have nothing to fight against. There's no proper war, Hitler is dead, nothing. With whom are you fighting now?

TORVALD. All our western enemies, States, they all want us to be weak, terrorists in Syria and—.

RANK. It's all crap. They are all made up and exaggerated as hell. What is going on now, can you tell me?

TORVALD. [*Angrily.*] Our soldiers are the bravest—

RANK. [*Interrupting.*] I'll tell you what's going on now. This government is as much corrupt as the army. Sick and old people who are supposed to die are not dying, look at me. So the government can't afford to keep everybody anymore. They perfectly understand that our people would do everything to protect their home and families, though they can't do practically anything in case of the potential attacks, and there's nobody to defend against. And that's why we have all these new rules about sending men to the army. They simply hope that they would die there, meaninglessly, like some sort of animals. And then they would call it a heroic death.

Sample 3

Waiting for Promotion
(an adaptation of Samuel Beckett's *Waiting for Godot*)
Text on the screen:
"Office of an Invest Bank.
Two analysts: Vladimir and Estragon"
The dialogue from Chekhov's *The Three Sisters*:

ESTRAGON (puts his head on Vladimir's chest): придёт время, все узнают, зачем все это, для чего эти страдания, никаких не будет тайн, а пока надо жить . . . надо работать, только работать! Завтра я опять посплю 4 часа, буду работать в банке и всю свою жизнь отдам тем, кому она, быть может, нужна. Теперь осень, скоро придет зима, засыплет снегом, а я буду работать, буду работать . . .". Боже мой, не то что человеком, уж лучше быть волом, лучше быть простою лошадью, только бы хоть иногда поспать, чем человеком, который заканчивает работать в 2 часа ночи, 2 часа едет до дому, 2 часа спит а потом судорожно пьет кофе чтобы быть в форме.

ESTRAGON: The time will come, and all will know what are these sufferings for, there will be no secrets, but now we need to live ... we need to work, work harder. Tomorrow I will again sleep 4 hours, will work at the bank and will sacrifice my life to those who may need it. It's autumn now, soon it'll be winter with the snow, but I will be working, will be working. Good God, let alone being a man, it would be better to be an ox, better to be a simple horse, as long as one can sleep, rather than be a young man who finishes his work at 2 in the morning, spends 2 hours on a way back home, sleeps for 2 hours and then convulsively drinks coffee to be in shape.

VLADIMIR: Если бы знать, если бы знать!

Estragon begins to rummage through a huge pile of papers (instead of a boot).

ESTRAGON: (giving up again). We need to work harder.

VLADIMIR: (advancing with short, stiff strides, legs wide apart). I'm beginning to come round to that opinion. All my life I've tried to put it from me, saying Vladimir, be reasonable, you haven't yet tried everything. And I resumed the struggle. (He broods, musing on the struggle. Turning to Estragon.) So, you finished the report.

ESTRAGON: Did I?

VLADIMIR: I'm glad to see you back. I thought you were gone forever.

ESTRAGON: Me too.

VLADIMIR: (hurt, coldly). Where did you spend the night?

ESTRAGON: In the office.

VLADIMIR: And they didn't give you another report?

ESTRAGON: Beat me? Certainly, they gave me another report.

VLADIMIR: The same lot as usual?

ESTRAGON: The same? I don't know. Ah stop blathering and help me off with this bloody thing.

VLADIMIR: Hand in hand graduates of the New Economics School. Among the first in the rating. We were respectable in those days. Now it's too late. They wouldn't even let us up. (Estragon is crying over the pile of papers) What are you doing?

ESTRAGON: For the tenth time redoing the same report, that no one needs. Did that never happen to you?

VLADIMIR: It hurts?

ESTRAGON: (angrily). Hurts! He wants to know if it hurts!

VLADIMIR: (angrily). No one ever suffers but you. I don't count. I'd like to hear what you'd say if you had to do their presentations as I do.

ESTRAGON: It hurts?

VLADIMIR: (angrily). Hurts! He wants to know if it hurts!

ESTRAGON: Why don't you help me?

VLADIMIR: Sometimes I feel it coming all the same. Then I go all queer. (He takes off his jacket, peers inside it, feels about inside it, shakes it, puts it on again.) How shall I say? Relieved and at the same time . . . (he searches for the word) . . . appalled. (With emphasis.) AP- PALLED. AP- PALLED. AP- PALLED. We need to work harder. (Estragon with a supreme effort succeeds in finishing the first part of his report. He peers inside it, staring sightlessly before him.) Well?

. . .

ESTRAGON: Charming spot. (He turns, advances to front, halts facing auditorium.) Inspiring prospects. (He turns to Vladimir.) Let's go.
VLADIMIR: We can't.
ESTRAGON: Why not?
VLADIMIR: We're waiting for Promotion.
ESTRAGON: (despairingly). Ah! (Pause.) You're sure it was here?
VLADIMIR: What?
ESTRAGON: That we will get a promotion
VLADIMIR: He said in the office. (They look around.) Do you see any others?
ESTRAGON: What is it?
VLADIMIR: I don't know.
ESTRAGON: Where are other workers?
VLADIMIR: It must be dead.
ESTRAGON: No more weeping.
VLADIMIR: Or perhaps it's not the season.
ESTRAGON: Looks to me more like a cage.
VLADIMIR: A prison
ESTRAGON: A cage.
VLADIMIR: What are you insinuating? That we've come to the wrong place?
ESTRAGON: The promotion should be here.
VLADIMIR: He didn't say for sure it'd come.
ESTRAGON: And if it doesn't come?
VLADIMIR: We'll stay here tomorrow.
ESTRAGON: And then the day after tomorrow.
VLADIMIR: Possibly.
ESTRAGON: And so on.
VLADIMIR: The point is—
ESTRAGON: Until it comes.

§ Contributors

Olga Aksakalova holds a Ph.D. in English from The Graduate School and University Center of the City University of New York (CUNY). She founded and directed the Writing and Communication Center at the New Economic School in Moscow, and she currently serves as associate professor of English at LaGuardia Community College (CUNY), where she teaches writing and literature courses and coordinates the Collaborative Online International Learning (COIL) program. Her research is in transnational writing pedagogies, virtual exchange as a form of internationalization of higher education, twentieth-century American literature, and autobiography studies. Her work appears in edited collections *Willa Cather and Aestheticism: From Romanticism to Modernism* (Fairleigh Dickinson University Press, 2012), *Next Steps: New Directions for/in Writing about Writing* (Utah State University Press, 2019), *Civic Engagement in Global Contexts* (forthcoming, Utah State University Press), and in the journals *Contrastive Linguistics* (Ural State Pedagogical University) and *The Writing Center Journal* Special Issue: Transatlantic Writing Centers (forthcoming).

Svetlana Bogolepova is Associate Professor at the School of Foreign Languages at HSE University. She holds a Ph.D. in language theory from the Russian Academy of Sciences. She teaches advanced English, language teaching methods and research methods to linguistics students. Her interests lie in the fields of academic writing, course design and assessment. Svetlana has authored more than 30 publications both in national and international journals. She is a co-author of the "English for Academics" course published by Cambridge University Press.

Elena Getmanskaya holds a Ph.D. in pedagogical science and holds the rank of Professor in the Department of Literature Teaching Methodology at the Moscow State Pedagogical University, where she directs the master's program, active processes in philological education. The main directions of her scientific interests are the history of Russian literary education and world models of the study of literary texts in high school. She is the author of more than two hundred scientific works, including her doctoral thesis, *Continuity of Secondary and Higher Literary Education in the Russian Methodological Tradition* (Moscow, 2013), and the textbook, *Methods of Teaching Literature: Twenty-first century* (Saint-Petersburg, 2019).

Tatiana Glushko grew up in Russia, where she received her education in teaching English as a foreign language and taught English at the college level. Her interest in teaching academic writing flourished when, in 2006, she moved from the bitter cold eastern Russia to hot and humid Mississippi. There she pursued her graduate degree while also working in a writing center as a graduate peer tutor and later as coordinator. Besides teaching writing one-to-one in the writing center, she has also taught freshman composition. For the past five years, she has been collaborating with writing center director Kathi Griffin to research and write about local composition histories within national and international contexts, the effectiveness of writing center pedagogy, and the role of writing centers in liberal arts education. Together they have published in *Composition Studies, Praxis: A Writing Center Journal*, and in the blog *Connecting Writing Centers Across Borders*.

Tatiana Golechkova is Assistant Professor in the Department of Humanities and Languages at the New Economic School, Moscow, Russia. She holds a Ph.D. in cognitive linguistics from Moscow Linguistic University and a Cambridge Delta teaching diploma. Her areas of interest include cognitive semantics, developing academic literacies, effective academic communication, and genre features of English academic texts.

Anna Guseva is Associate Professor in the School of History, Faculty of Humanities, at HSE University in Moscow, where she has been a faculty member since 2014. She also directs a master's program, "History of Art Culture and the Art Markets," in the same department. Her research interests span both art and urban history in Russia and Asia in relation to architecture and garden history. She graduated from the Lomonosov Moscow State University with a degree in art history in 1998 and received her Ph.D. in architecture from the University of Tokyo in the Fujimori-Muramatsu Lab in 2011. She has organized architectural exhibitions as an independent curator, including *My Melnikov* (2013) and *Environmentally Friendly Japanese Architecture* (2013), both at the Moscow Architectural Institute, and the latter also at the House of Architects in Nizniy Novgorod. She also writes reviews for professional journals and trade publications on architecture and Asian art.

Irina Korotkina is Dean of the Interdisciplinary Department of English at the Moscow School of Social and Economic Sciences (Russian-British university), and Director of the Academic Writing and Communication Center at the Russian Presidential Academy of National Economy and Public Administration, Moscow, Russia. She holds two Russian doctoral degrees in education, candidate's (2008) and doctor's (2018), both dissertations being devoted to developing academic writing in Russia. A structural linguist by education (Moscow State University, 1977), she worked as a translator in science and technology and an editor of a scholarly edition at the Academy of Sciences, but in 1993 changed her career and devoted herself to teaching

English, focusing on academic literacy and writing, and aiming at introducing writing as a discipline into Russian education. She has taught ESAP and academic writing for over two decades in English and twelve years in Russian, published over 80 research papers, 11 books and designed an online course in Russian for research publication purposes. Her manuals *Academic Vocabulary for Social Sciences* (2016), *Academic Writing: Product, Process and Practice* (2015, in Russ.), *English for Public Policy, Administration and Management* (2015), and monograph *Academic Writing Teaching Models: International Experience and National Practices* (2018, in Russ.) are widely used by teachers, researchers and experts around the country.

Irina Kuznetsova-Simpson is Assistant Professor in the Department of Humanities and Languages at the New Economic School. Since 2012 at NES Irina has taught academic writing, comparative literature, drama, English- and German-language courses, and held several administrative positions. She received her Ph.D. in German from the University of Virginia, USA (2012) and two MAs: one in German studies from California State University, Long Beach, USA (2003) and one in linguistics from Moscow State Pedagogical University, Moscow (2000). Her research interests include literature and writing pedagogy, performance studies, and late-nineteenth/early-twentieth century Russian and European literature. She has several publications on Dostoevsky and Thomas Mann in international journals.

Viacheslav Lanin is Senior Lecturer of IT in the business department at HSE University, Perm, Russia. His areas of expertise and interest include semantic tagging, multiagent systems, and document management systems.

Veronika Smilga is a research intern at the Research and Studying Laboratory of Learner Corpora (Department of Humanities, HSE, Moscow). Her responsibilities include providing the consistency of manual annotation of punctuation errors in essays written in English by Russian university students, which are collected in REALEC (Russian Error-Annotated Learner English Corpus).

Elizaveta Smirnova holds a Ph.D. in philology and now is Associate Professor in the foreign languages department at HSE University, Perm, Russia. Her areas of expertise and interest include EAP, ESP, corpus linguistics, learner corpora, and functional grammar. Her works have also appeared in *RELC Journal, Lingua, Metaphor*, and *The Social World*.

Natalya Smirnova is Associate Professor and Deputy Chair of the Department of Foreign Languages, HSE University, St. Petersburg, Russia. She holds a Ph.D. in TESOL and has designed and taught courses in research writing, political rhetoric, argumentation and writing. She has designed an innovative online writing for publication module for junior scholars and Ph.D. students. She is currently doing her doctoral work in applied linguistics at the Open University, UK. Her current research interests lie in the field of writing for publication in the global context. She draws on the academic literacies research tradition and the conceptual frame of the geopolitics of academic writing (Th. M. Lillis, M. J. Curry) which provide strong theoretical and methodological grounds for exploring the publishing experiences of scholars.

L. Ashley Squires received her Ph.D. in English from the University of Texas at Austin in 2012 and currently serves as Assistant Professor and Director of the Writing and Communication Center at the New Economic School, where she has worked since 2013. In addition to writing studies and the internationalization of higher education, she has research and teaching interests in American literary and religious history, American realism and naturalism, medical humanities, and digital humanities. She is the author of *Healing the Nation: Literature, Progress and Christian Science* (Indiana University Press, 2017) and articles in journals such as *Nineteenth-Century Literature*, *Book History*, and *American Literary Realism*.

Svetlana Strinyuk holds a Ph.D. in philology and now is Associate Professor in the foreign languages department at the Admiral Makarov State University of Maritime and Inland Shipping, Saint Petersburg, Russia. Her areas of expertise and interest include Irish literature, teaching EAP and ESP, corpus linguistics, and learner corpora.

Svetlana Suchkova is Associate Professor, teacher trainer, and Cambridge ESOL examiner. Currently, she directs the Academic Writing Center at HSE University, Moscow. She holds a Ph.D. in philology. She has authored and co-authored a number of EFL course books for university students and researchers, among them the *English for Academics* series (CUP, 2014, 2015). She has participated in presentations and workshops at numerous national and international conferences and edited the Scopus-indexed *The Journal of AsiaTEFL*. Her areas of expertise are academic writing, writing for research and publication purposes, public speaking, and teacher training.

Anna Viklova graduated with honors from the Institute of Linguistics, Russian State University for Humanities, in 2005. Besides teaching English in various institutions from 2006 to 2016, she participated in a project on publishing Mikhail Prishvin's Diaries, for which she became the recipient of the Alexander Blok Award in 2011. She has been a freelance translator for *National Geographic* magazine in Russia since 2010. She joined the School of Linguistics, HSE University, as a senior lecturer teaching English to bachelors students in 2019. The same year, she became a researcher at the Research and Studying Learner Corpora Laboratory.

Olga Vinogradova defended her Ph.D. dissertation in 1982 in the area of the languages of the Caucasus. She worked as a senior researcher in information retrieval systems, then as a senior EFL instructor at the Russian State University for the Humanities, as an associate professor at the MBA program of the California State University in Hayward (Moscow outreach), and has been Associate Professor in the School of Linguistics at HSE University, Moscow, since 2011, teaching courses on *Preparation for IELTS*, *Computer Methods of Learning Foreign Languages*, and *Debating in English*. She is also a researcher at the Research and Studying Laboratory of Learner Corpora, HSE, since 2019.

www.ingramcontent.com/pod-product-compliance
Lightning Source LLC
Chambersburg PA
CBHW030230100526
44583CB00013BA/648

A MOMENT JUST FOR YOU

Powerful Daily Affirmations for a Positive Life

DR. DHANVANTRI N

Copyright © 2025, Dr. Dhanvantri N
All rights reserved.

No part of this publication may be reproduced or transmitted in any form or by any means, electronic or mechanical, including photocopy, recording or any information storage and retrieval system now known or to be invented, without permission in writing from the publisher, except by a reviewer who wishes to quote brief passages in connection with a review written for inclusion in a magazine, newspaper or broadcast.

Published in India by Prowess Publishing,
GJ Complex, Thadikara Swamy Koil St, Alandur,
Chennai, Tamil Nadu 600016

ISBN: 978-1-5457-6348-3

Library of Congress Cataloging in Publication

Table of Contents

Dedication vii

Introduction: Every day is a new beginning ix

Part 1: Awakening to Self 1
Chapter 1: I Am Enough Exactly As I Am 3
Chapter 2: My Home is a Haven of Peace and Happiness ... 9
Chapter 3: I Prioritize My Physical and Mental Well-being ... 15
Chapter 4: I Am Calm and Peaceful in Every Situation ... 23
Chapter 5: I Trust Myself 29

Part 2: Cultivating Connection 35
Chapter 6: Gratitude Fills My Heart and Mind 37
Chapter 7: I Am Strong and Resilient 43
Chapter 8: I Love and Appreciate Myself 49
Chapter 9: My Thoughts Are Positive and Empowering ... 55
Chapter 10: I Am Deserving of Happiness and Success ... 61

Part 3: Embracing Growth 67
Chapter 11: I Release Self-Doubt and Negativity 69
Chapter 12: I Am Unique and Special 75
Chapter 13: I Prioritize Self-Care and Self-Love 81

Chapter 14: I Am Confident in My Abilities — 89
Chapter 15: I Focus on the Present Moment — 95

Part 4: Living with Purpose — **101**
Chapter 16: I Am Worthy of Love and Respect — 103
Chapter 17: I Cultivate a Growth Mindset — 109
Chapter 18: I Am at Peace with Myself and Others — 115
Chapter 19: I Trust the Universe and Its Plan — 121
Chapter 20: I Am Strong and Capable — 127

Part 5: Sustaining Joy — **133**
Chapter 21: I Prioritize Positivity and Joy — 135
Chapter 22: I Let Go of Fear and Anxiety — 141
Chapter 23: I Am Deserving of Abundance and Prosperity — 147
Chapter 24: I Trust My Intuition and Inner Wisdom — 153
Chapter 25: I Am Grateful for My Blessings — 159

Part 6: Embarking Anew — **165**
Chapter 26: I Am Confident in My Decisions — 167
Chapter 27: I Prioritize My Well-being — 173
Chapter 28: I Let Go of Negativity and Limitations — 179
Chapter 29: I Am Worthy of Love and Connection — 185
Chapter 30: I Am at Peace with My Journey — 193

Epilogue: The Ever-Unfolding Path — 199

Dedication

"To the pillars of my life, whose unwavering presence and love have shaped my journey and illuminated my path: my father, my guiding light and motivator; my mother, my rock and support system; my son, the rhythm of my heart; my husband, my beloved companion; and my brother, my cherished confidant. This book is a reflection of the love, support, and motivation I have received from each of you. I dedicate it to you, with all my love and gratitude."

Introduction

Every day is a new beginning

The First Dawn

The world awakens, a canvas fresh and new,
A quiet breath, a moment just for you.
No need to rush, no battle to be won,
Just peaceful presence, beneath the rising sun.
Embrace your power, gentle and serene,
A living masterpiece, beautifully convened.
The journey calls, with whispers soft and low,
Inviting you to bloom, and simply grow.

The Power of Daily Positive Affirmations

In a world swirling with challenges, stress, and moments of self-doubt, finding a way to anchor your mind in positivity can be truly transformative. Each new sunrise offers a fresh opportunity to fill your mind with words that uplift your spirit, sharpen your focus, and remind you of your boundless potential. Daily positive affirmations are more than just encouraging phrases—they are a powerful practice that can rewire your thinking, boost your confidence, and help you create a life you truly love. For those on a path of healing, they offer comfort to the heart, restore hope, and bring the inner peace needed to navigate life's challenges. With every mindful reflection, you set the tone for happiness, resilience, and the strength to rise above obstacles, emerging wiser and stronger than before. Begin your day with this gentle ritual, and watch as your mindset—and your life—blossom in beautiful, unexpected ways.

The Quiet Promise

Imagine a trusted friend sitting beside you, offering a quiet hand, a moment of understanding. That's the spirit of this book. Within these pages, you'll find thirty powerful daily positive affirmations, each a soft lamp illuminating a path towards greater self-awareness, unshakable confidence, and a deep, abiding peace.

These aren't stern commands or complex theories. They are gentle echoes of timeless wisdom, designed to resonate with the innate knowing already deep inside you. There's no pressure here, no need to rush. Growth, like a flower unfurling, happens at its own perfect pace. Approach each day's offering with an open heart, a curious mind, and a generous dose of kindness for yourself.

Here, you will uncover the secrets to:

- ♣ **Embracing your authentic self:** Unearthing the unique brilliance that makes you, uniquely, you.

- ♣ **Creating pockets of peace:** Transforming your surroundings and your mind into serene sanctuaries.

- ♣ **Nurturing inner resilience:** Learning to bend without breaking, to flow with life's unpredictable currents.

- ♣ **Unlocking your true purpose:** Discovering what truly ignites your spirit and gives your life meaning.

- ♣ **Living with effortless joy:** Finding gratitude and delight in the simplest moments, cultivating a heart that overflows.

This is not a race, but a tender unfolding. Let these gentle whispers guide you, day by day, towards a life brimming with presence, purpose, and profound well-being. Your journey to inner harmony begins now.

May this book become a constant, comforting presence in your life, a wellspring of quiet inspiration and steady support as you navigate the beautiful tapestry of your experiences. May you emerge from each reflection feeling more rooted, more vibrant, and more profoundly at peace with the extraordinary unfolding story of your being.

Part 1
AWAKENING TO SELF

Chapter 1

I Am Enough Exactly As I Am

Cultivating Joy: The First Step

Close your eyes for a moment and picture a magnificent ancient tree. Its roots run deep, anchoring it firmly to the earth, drawing strength from unseen sources. Its branches reach towards the sky, bearing witness to countless seasons, storms, and sunny days. Does it judge its own knots or the way its leaves unfurl? No. It simply *is*. In its quiet power, it stands whole and complete, exactly as nature intended.

Now, turn that gentle gaze inward. Like that resilient tree, you are already whole, complete, and perfectly unique, right here, right now. Your worth isn't something you need to earn, achieve, or prove. It's not dependent on external validation, fleeting accomplishments, or the shifting opinions of others. It is an inherent, unshakeable truth woven into the very fabric of your being.

This journey begins with a radical act of self-acceptance, dropping the heavy burden of self-criticism, releasing the relentless pursuit of an imagined "perfect" self, and simply embracing the magnificent human you already are. Every scar, every quirk, every triumph, every lesson learned – they are all threads in the rich tapestry of your unique existence, making you wonderfully, beautifully, unequivocally *you*.

Positive Affirmation
"I love and accept myself just as I am."

Reflection: Standing Tall in Your Own Truth

Imagine a majestic mountain. It doesn't try to be taller or smoother or prettier than the mountain next to it. It simply is a mountain, with its rugged peaks, deep valleys, and ancient rocks. Its strength comes from its unwavering presence, its natural form. How often do we try to sculpt ourselves into something we think others want us to be, rather than standing tall in our own authentic form? This moment is an invitation to shed those external expectations. What would it feel like to stand as tall and as unyielding as the mountain in your own skin, fully embracing your natural contours and expressions? When you truly see and accept yourself, the need for external approval begins to fade, replaced by a quiet, profound inner knowing. This is where true peace blossoms.

Mindful Moment: A Gentle Hand on Your Heart

Place your right hand gently over your heart. Feel the warmth, the soft pressure. Close your eyes and take three slow, deep breaths, feeling your chest rise and fall beneath your hand. As you breathe, silently offer yourself a simple phrase: *"May I be kind to myself. May I be at peace."* This small gesture sends a powerful message of comfort and acceptance directly to your nervous system.

Just Like a Seed, You Grow

A seed, before it sprouts, looks unremarkable. It holds all the potential of the magnificent plant it will become, yet it is raw, unformed, and far from perfect. It doesn't question its worth or wish it were already a blooming flower. It simply rests, holds its potential, and waits for the right conditions to unfurl. You, too, are always in a state of becoming, always holding immense potential. Embrace your current "seed" state – *perfectly imperfect, infinitely capable*. Trust the process of your own growth without needing to be fully bloomed right now.

Gentle Self-Talk

"Today, I will speak to myself with the same gentle kindness I offer a beloved friend."

"I love and accept myself just as I am."

✦

POSITIVE AFFIRMATION

note to self

Pen Your Thoughts

1 What is one aspect of yourself that you have been most critical of?

2 How can you offer that part of yourself a moment of acceptance today?

3 Think of a time when you felt truly authentic and at ease. What was it about that experience that allowed you to feel that way?

Your Space to Reflect

Chapter 2

My Home is a Haven of Peace and Happiness

My Space Reflects My Calm

Step into a bustling city market, filled with sounds, sights, and endless activity. Now, imagine walking from that chaos into a quiet, sunlit room, simply furnished, with a single vase holding a fresh bloom. Can you feel the subtle shift within you? The calming of your breath, the softening of your shoulders, the clearer space in your mind?

Your physical environment is not just a backdrop to your life; it's an active participant in shaping your inner world. A cluttered, chaotic space can drain your energy, scatter your thoughts, and leave you feeling overwhelmed. Conversely, a space that feels harmonious, intentional, and inviting can act as a powerful anchor for your peace, clarity, and well-being.

This chapter is an invitation to become the mindful architect of your surroundings. It's about more than just tidiness; it's about curating a living space that truly reflects and supports the calm you wish to cultivate within. When you create pockets of peace in your external world, you're simultaneously building a sanctuary for your inner landscape.

Positive Affirmation

"My home is filled with love, laughter, and positivity."

Reflection: The Stream's Clear Path

Imagine a clear mountain stream, its waters flowing smoothly over pebbles and stones, reflecting the sky above. Now picture that same stream choked with debris – fallen branches, litter, and stagnant pools; the flow is disrupted and the reflection obscured. Your living space can be like that stream. When it's clear, intentional, and clutter-free, your thoughts and energy flow more freely. When it's filled with unnecessary items or disarray, it can create internal friction and mental fog. This isn't about perfection, but about the gentle act of releasing what no longer serves you, making space for breath and clarity. Each item you thoughtfully release is a small act of freedom for your mind.

Mindful Moment: The Sensory Scan of Your Space

Choose one small, designated area in your home or workspace (e.g., your bedside table, a favorite chair, or a small shelf). Take a moment to simply observe it with all your senses. What do you see? What textures do you feel? What sounds are present? What scents can you detect? Notice how your body responds to the current state of this space. Now, if it feels right, make one small, intentional adjustment – remove one item, straighten something, add a small touch of beauty. Feel the subtle shift as you interact consciously with your environment.

Declutter: The Simplicity of the Desert Bloom

In the stark, captivating beauty of the desert, life is sparse yet remarkably resilient and vibrant. A single cactus flower, blooming against a vast, open expanse, embodies pure, uncluttered elegance. It flourishes not by abundance, but by clarity—holding only what is essential for survival and growth. Likewise, when we declutter our physical spaces—removing the excess and keeping only what is meaningful—we invite a striking simplicity and a profound sense of peace. It's not about going without, but about living with intention, allowing the true beauty of what remains to shine.

Gentle Self-Talk

"Today, I will bring intentional calm to one small, beloved corner of my world."

"My home is filled with love, laughter, and positivity."

✦

POSITIVE AFFIRMATION

note to self

Pen Your Thoughts

1 Describe your ideal "sanctuary" space. What qualities does it possess?

2 What is one area in your home or workspace that, if cleared, would bring you the most immediate sense of relief or calm?

3 Beyond physical items, what "clutter" (e.g., unfinished tasks, old thoughts) might be lingering in your mental space, and how might you begin to address it?

Your Space to Reflect

Chapter 3

I Prioritize My Physical and Mental Well-being

Honoring Your Body: The Foundation of Well-being

Your body is the sacred space where your life unfolds—a vessel that carries your thoughts, emotions, and experiences. Prioritizing your physical well-being means embracing simplicity, presence, and gentle care in every moment.

♣ **Move with Intention**

Movement is not just exercise but a mindful practice. Whether you walk slowly feeling each step, stretch gently with awareness, or engage in flowing movements, moving with calm focus turns every action into a meditation. Listen deeply to your body's signals and respond with kindness, honoring its needs without judgment or haste.

♣ **Nourish with Mindfulness**

Every meal is an opportunity to connect with the essence of life. Eat with quiet intention, fully aware of each bite's texture, color, and flavor. Let this mindful practice awaken gratitude and respect for the nourishment your body receives.

In this simple act, you honor your body's needs and align with a deeper sense of purpose, bringing harmony to both your inner and outer worlds.

♣ Rest and Restore

True well-being thrives in the harmony of activity and rest. Honor your body's natural rhythms by allowing moments of stillness and quiet. Rest is not a withdrawal but a vital replenishment—a peaceful pause that nurtures strength and clarity. Like a calm pond reflecting the sky, stillness restores and renews.

♣ Breathe to Reconnect

Your breath is a gentle anchor to the present. Deep, steady breaths release tension, invite calm, and reconnect you to your body's wisdom. When overwhelm arises, pause and breathe fully, letting each inhale and exhale ground you in peace and clarity.

Nurturing Your Inner Garden

Imagine your inner world as a secret garden, a lush, vibrant expanse filled with endless possibilities. In this garden, seeds of joy, resilience, wisdom, and compassion lie dormant, waiting for your gentle touch to awaken them. Just as a dedicated gardener carefully tends to their plants—watering them, providing sunlight, protecting them from harsh elements—you too must lovingly nurture this precious inner landscape.

This isn't a passive dream; it's an active, ongoing practice. It means consciously choosing which thoughts you water with your attention and which beliefs you allow to take root. It's about becoming mindful

I Prioritize My Physical and Mental Well-being

of the "weeds" of self-doubt, fear, or negative comparison, and gently uprooting them before they overshadow the beautiful blooms of your authentic self. When you commit to tending this inner sanctuary, you lay the foundation for profound well-being, allowing your true essence to flourish and radiate outwards, transforming your entire experience of life.

Positive Affirmation

"I nourish my body and mind with healthy choices."

Reflection: The Gardener's Art

Think of a seasoned gardener. They understand that growth is a continuous cycle, not a one-time event. They don't get frustrated if a seed doesn't sprout overnight; instead, they continue to provide consistent care, knowing that patience and persistence yield the most beautiful blooms. Your inner world demands this same unwavering, gentle attention. What "seeds" (positive qualities, aspirations, or dreams) have you been wishing to cultivate? What "weeds" (negative thought patterns, limiting beliefs, or old wounds) have been hindering their growth? This moment is an invitation to step into your role as the conscious gardener of your mind, choosing to nourish the seeds of positivity, self-compassion, and gentle optimism. Every breath, every conscious choice, is an opportunity to plant a new seed or lovingly care for an existing one.

Mindful Moment: Reflecting on Your Inner Flow

Find a comfortable position, perhaps with a soft blanket or cushion. Gently close your eyes. Imagine your breath as a clear, refreshing stream of living water, flowing effortlessly. As you inhale, visualize this stream entering your inner garden, gently watering the seeds of peace, joy, and calm. Feel the warmth and nourishment spreading. As you exhale, imagine the stream washing away any weeds of worry, doubt, or tension, carrying them away. Feel your inner garden becoming more vibrant, more alive, and more deeply nourished with each flowing breath. Continue this visualization for 2-3 minutes, basking in the sensation of inner vitality.

Nature's Wisdom: The Resilience of the Wildflower

Consider the wildflower—blooming brilliantly in unexpected places, breaking through pavement cracks and thriving in dry, rocky soil. It doesn't wait for perfect conditions; it adapts, draws strength from its surroundings, and flourishes with grace. Like the wildflower, we are meant to thrive not in spite of challenges, but through them. Our inner landscape doesn't need perfection—it needs presence, care, and intention. Tend to your roots, honor your strength, and trust that you are always capable of blooming where you are.

Start with a 10-minute walk outside, breathing deeply and letting your body reconnect with the rhythm of nature.

Gentle Self-Talk

"Today, I will consciously nurture one positive thought or feeling, allowing it to bloom."

"I nourish my body and mind with healthy choices."

POSITIVE AFFIRMATION

note to self

Pen Your Thoughts

1. What "flower" (a positive quality, a cherished dream, or a feeling you desire) in your inner garden are you most eager to cultivate and see flourish right now?

2. Identify one recurring "weed" (a negative thought pattern, a self-limiting belief, or a fear) that you are ready to gently uproot today. How might you begin this process?

3. What small, consistent act of self-care can you offer yourself today to nourish your body and mind?

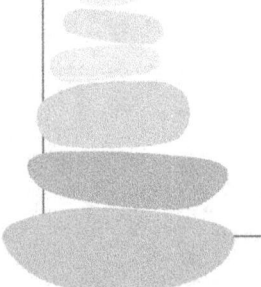

Chapter 4

I Am Calm and Peaceful in Every Situation

Finding Stillness Amidst the Current

Have you ever watched a magnificent river, its surface rushing with incredible force, yet somehow, beneath that powerful current, there are deep, undisturbed pools of serene calm? Life often feels like that river – a relentless, powerful current of demands, responsibilities, and constant movement. It's easy to feel swept away, tossed and turned by the ceaseless activity, leaving you feeling overwhelmed and disconnected.

This chapter is your invitation to discover and intentionally create those "pools of stillness" within your own day, no matter how turbulent the surface might appear. Finding stillness isn't about stopping the world from spinning; it's about shifting your internal focus, learning to drop anchor in the present moment, and accessing a profound wellspring of quiet calm, even amidst the busiest of days. These moments aren't a luxury; they are essential anchors that ground you, allowing you to observe your thoughts and feelings without being consumed by them. By consciously seeking stillness, you cultivate a deeper awareness, a clearer mind, and a more peaceful engagement with every aspect of your life.

Positive Affirmation

"I remain calm and centered, even in chaos."

Reflection: The Unshakeable Roots of the Ancient Tree

Imagine a colossal, ancient tree standing tall on a windswept cliff. Its massive branches dance and sway with every gust, but its deep, intricate roots grip the earth with unwavering strength, anchoring it firmly. The tree doesn't resist the wind; it yields to its movement, yet its core remains utterly unshakeable. Similarly, the "winds" of daily life may bring external pressures and constant motion, but you possess the ability to cultivate deep inner roots of stillness. This means consciously choosing to pause, to breathe, and to connect with the quiet, unmoving core of your being, regardless of external circumstances. It is in these moments of inner stillness that you gain perspective, clarity, and a profound sense of rooted strength, allowing you to navigate challenges with grace.

> ### Mindful Moment: Unshakable Stillness
>
> Close your eyes and take a slow, steady breath. Feel your body soften with the exhale. Picture yourself as a still lake—undisturbed, reflective, clear. No matter what stirs around you, your surface may ripple, but your depth remains untouched. In this moment, whisper gently to yourself: "I am calm and peaceful in every situation." Let this affirmation anchor you. You are the calm within the storm, the breath between thoughts, the quiet strength that steadies every step. Return to this stillness any time—it's always within you.

Calm Thinking – Reframing the Mind

Your thoughts are powerful messengers. But they aren't always truthful. Often, our stress stems not from reality, but from the stories we tell ourselves.

Use this framework to gently shift your mindset:

- ♣ Stress Thought: *"I can't handle this."*
- ♣ Reframe: *"This is challenging, but I've handled tough things before."*
- ♣ Affirm: *"I am calm and peaceful in every situation."*

Gentle Self-Talk

"Today, I will deliberately create one small island of stillness in my busy day."

"I remain calm and centered, even in chaos."

✦

POSITIVE AFFIRMATION

note to self

Pen Your Thoughts

1 When do you most feel overwhelmed by the "current" of your daily life? What specific situations or times trigger this feeling?

2 What is the smallest, easiest action you could take right now to create a brief moment of stillness for yourself, even if it's just a single conscious breath?

3 How does connecting with that inner stillness change your perception of a challenging situation or a busy moment?

Your Space to Reflect

Chapter 5

I Trust Myself

Trusting the Inner Compass

Imagine standing at a crossroads, with countless paths stretching before you, each promising something different. The world often shouts its opinions, offering a dizzying array of directions. But what if the most accurate map, the truest guide, isn't found outside, but pulses quietly within you? This is your inner compass, your intuition, your unwavering sense of knowing.

Trusting yourself isn't about having all the answers or never making a mistake. It's about cultivating a deep, abiding faith in your own judgment, your values, and your ability to navigate the landscape of your life. It's about quieting the external noise and tuning into that subtle whisper of wisdom that guides you toward your highest good and your most authentic path. When you trust yourself, you unlock a profound sense of empowerment, knowing that you are capable of choosing wisely and moving forward with courage and conviction.

Positive Affirmation

*"I trust myself to make wise decisions
and take positive actions."*

Reflection: The River's Knowing Flow

Consider a river, carving its path through mountains and plains. It doesn't question its direction; it simply flows, adapting to the landscape, finding its way to the ocean. It trusts its inherent nature, its purpose. Similarly, your inner wisdom, your intuition, has an inherent knowing, a natural flow. How often do we second-guess this flow, allowing external doubts or fears to divert us? This reflection invites you to observe moments when you felt a strong inner pull or a clear "yes" or "no" from within, even if logic argued otherwise. What happens when you honor that inner voice? Trusting yourself is an ongoing practice, a gentle surrender to your deepest knowing, allowing your life to flow with greater ease and purpose, much like the river moving steadily towards its destination.

Mindful Moment: The Intuitive Breath

Sit comfortably and close your eyes. Place both hands over your lower abdomen, a traditional energetic center for intuition. Take a few deep, slow breaths, focusing on the gentle rise and fall of your belly. Now, bring to mind a small, low-stakes decision you've been pondering (e.g., "Should I wear X or Y today?"). Without overthinking, simply ask your inner self.

I Trust Myself

> Notice any subtle sensations, a feeling of expansion or contraction, a warmth, a lightness, a gentle tug in one direction. Don't force an answer; just observe. This practice helps to build your sensitivity to your own intuitive signals.

The Spider's Web:

The spider, with innate wisdom, spins its intricate web without a blueprint or external instruction. It trusts its instinct, its unique design, to create a structure that is both delicate and incredibly strong, perfectly suited for its purpose. It doesn't need to consult other spiders or external sources. You, too, possess an innate wisdom to construct your life's path, to weave your experiences into a strong and beautiful tapestry. Trusting your inner compass is akin to trusting the spider's innate knowing – you have everything you need within you to build the life meant for you.

Gentle Self-Talk

"Today, I will listen for the quiet whispers of my inner wisdom before seeking external advice."

"I trust myself to make wise decisions and take positive actions."

✦

POSITIVE AFFIRMATION

note to self

Pen Your Thoughts

1 When have you trusted your gut feeling, and it led you to a positive outcome?

2 What is one small decision you can practice trusting your intuition on today?

3 What does "trusting yourself" truly mean to you, beyond just decision-making?

Your Space to Reflect

Part 2
CULTIVATING CONNECTION

Chapter 6

Gratitude Fills My Heart and Mind

Gratitude Is a Powerful Practice

Close your eyes and imagine the warmth of the morning sun on your skin, the scent of fresh rain on earth, or the sound of a loved one's laughter. In those moments, what swells within your chest? It's gratitude – a powerful, life-altering force. We often rush through our days, ticking off tasks, focused on what's next or what's missing. But imagine deliberately pausing, even for a breath, to truly *feel* the blessings that already surround you.

Gratitude is more than just saying "thank you." It's a profound recognition of the good in your life, big or small, a conscious choice to appreciate the present moment and all it offers. When you cultivate a heart full of thanks, you don't just acknowledge blessings; you *attract* more of them. It shifts your perspective from lack to abundance, from hurriedness to grace, transforming your inner landscape into a vibrant, joyful space. This chapter is an invitation to open your heart wide and let the gentle rain of appreciation nourish your very soul.

Positive Affirmation

"I am grateful for all the blessings in my life."

Reflection: The Dewdrop's Reflection

A single dewdrop, tiny and unassuming, can perfectly reflect the vast morning sky, the intricate branch it clings to, and even the distant sun. It doesn't need to be a grand ocean to hold immense beauty and perspective; it simply reflects what is present. Similarly, cultivating gratitude allows you to see the immense beauty and abundance in the seemingly small, everyday moments of your life. It's about shifting your inner lens. What subtle blessings are present in your day that you might be overlooking, much like the dewdrop reflecting an entire world in its tiny surface? This reflection invites you to become a collector of these small, precious moments, allowing them to fill your heart and mind with expansive appreciation.

Mindful Moment: The Gratitude Stone

Find a small stone, crystal, or even a smooth button that you can carry in your pocket today. Hold it in your hand for a moment. As you do, think of one thing you are truly grateful for right now. Feel that gratitude. Place the stone in your pocket. Throughout the day, whenever your hand touches the stone, pause for a moment and bring another blessing to mind. Let this simple object be a tangible anchor for your gratitude practice.

The Unfurling Leaf

Every leaf on a tree unfurls with simple perfection, drawing nourishment from the sun and rain, contributing to the life of the whole. It doesn't strive to be more, it simply is. It receives what it needs and expresses its unique form. Gratitude is like this acceptance of life's gifts. It's the conscious act of recognizing the nourishment you receive, the beauty you witness, and the simple existence that is yours. When you approach life with such open hands, you become a vibrant part of the interconnected flow, just as a leaf contributes to the thriving forest.

Gentle Self-Talk

"Today, I will actively look for and appreciate five small things that bring me joy."

"I am grateful for all the blessings in my life."

✦

POSITIVE AFFIRMATION

note to self

Pen Your Thoughts

1. What is one unexpected blessing from the last 24 hours that you can acknowledge with gratitude?

2. How does practicing gratitude shift your mood or outlook, even slightly?

3. Think of a person who brings positive energy into your life. What specifically about them are you grateful for?

Your Space to Reflect

Chapter 7

I Am Strong and Resilient

Bending, Not Breaking

Have you ever witnessed a majestic willow tree in a fierce wind? It doesn't rigidly stand against the gale; instead, its branches sway and bend, sometimes almost touching the ground, yet it rarely breaks. When the storm passes, it gently springs back, still rooted, still whole. Life, much like that wind, will inevitably bring storms – unexpected challenges, setbacks, and moments that test your very core.

This chapter is about cultivating your inner willow tree, developing the profound strength of resilience. Resilience isn't about avoiding difficulty or pretending pain doesn't exist. It's about learning the art of bending without breaking, finding your inner flexibility to adapt, to learn from setbacks, and to return to your natural strength after facing adversity. It's about recognizing that every challenge, though difficult, holds within it a seed of growth, an opportunity to discover capabilities you never knew you possessed. By embracing this truth, you transform from merely surviving life's storms to skillfully navigating them, emerging stronger and more deeply rooted than before.

Positive Affirmation

"I can overcome any obstacle and challenge."

Reflection: The River's Persistent Path

Consider a river flowing towards the sea. When it encounters a massive boulder, it doesn't stop or despair. It simply flows around it, perhaps eroding it slightly over time, or creating new channels. It finds a way to continue its journey, demonstrating incredible persistence and adaptability. Similarly, when you encounter an obstacle in your path, rather than seeing it as a dead end, can you approach it with the river's mindset? How can you flow around it, find an alternative route, or patiently work to wear it down? This reflection invites you to tap into your innate resourcefulness, to remember that like the river, you have the power to adapt and find a way forward, even when the path isn't clear.

Mindful Moment Practice: Rising Like the Sun

Sit comfortably, letting your spine lengthen gently and your hands rest in your lap. Close your eyes or soften your gaze, and begin to breathe slowly and deeply. With each inhale, feel a quiet strength begin to rise within you—like the sun cresting the horizon. As you exhale, imagine releasing doubt, fear, or resistance. Picture the sun: it does not rush, it does not question its place—it simply rises, every day, no matter the weather. Let that image mirror your own strength and certainty. Whisper to yourself, syncing the words with your breath: *"I can overcome any obstacle and challenge."*

I Am Strong and Resilient

> Let each repetition anchor you more deeply in confidence. Sit with this feeling for a few more breaths, then gently bring your awareness back to the room, carrying with you the unwavering power of a new day.

The Fire-Adapted Seed

Some pine cones, found in certain forests, are designed to only release their seeds and reproduce after a forest fire. The intense heat cracks them open, allowing new life to spring forth from the ashes. This powerful example from nature teaches us that sometimes, the most profound growth and new beginnings emerge directly from periods of intense challenge or even destruction. It's a reminder that what feels like an ending can often be the fertile ground for an extraordinary new beginning, revealing untapped potential and strength.

Gentle Self-Talk

"Today, I will meet any challenge with a curious mind and a resilient spirit."

"I can overcome any obstacle and challenge."

✦

POSITIVE AFFIRMATION

note to self

Pen Your Thoughts

1 Describe a past challenge that, in hindsight, taught you something valuable about your own strength.

2 What is one current challenge you are facing? How can you approach it with the "bending, not breaking" mindset?

3 What small act of self-compassion can you offer yourself when you feel overwhelmed by a difficulty?

Your Space to Reflect

Chapter 8

I Love and Appreciate Myself

Embracing Your Own Radiance

Imagine a sunflower, not comparing itself to the rose's delicate petals or the oak's towering strength. The sunflower simply turns its face to the sun, absorbing light, and radiating its own bold, golden brilliance. It doesn't apologize for its height or its vibrant color; it simply *is* magnificently itself. Yet, how often do we, dim our own light, trying to fit into a mold, or compare ourselves to others' perceived perfections?

This chapter is a gentle but firm invitation to embrace your own inherent radiance, to recognize the unique beauty, talents, and worth that reside within you. Self-love isn't vanity; it's a fundamental acceptance and appreciation of who you are, flaws and all. It's about tending to your own needs, speaking to yourself with kindness, and acknowledging your deservingness of all good things. When you truly love and appreciate yourself, you become a source of light, not only for yourself but for everyone around you, inspiring them to embrace their own inner glow.

Positive Affirmation

"I am worthy of love, care, and respect – from myself and others."

Reflection

Recognizing your own worth is a journey that reaches far beyond the self—it connects you to something greater, to the vast and mysterious universe that surrounds us all. Each time you affirm, "I am worthy of love, care, and respect—from myself and others," you align with the natural order of things, where every being has its place and purpose.

In the quiet moments of mindfulness, you may sense how deeply you are a part of this cosmic tapestry. Just as the stars shine without needing permission, so too do you deserve to be seen, cherished, and valued. When you treat yourself with kindness, you honor not only your own spirit but also the universe that brought you into being.

There is wisdom in understanding that your unique presence matters—not just to those around you, but to the grand unfolding of life itself. When you respect yourself, you open the door for others to do the same, creating ripples of compassion that flow outward, touching lives in ways you may never see.

Let this affirmation remind you that you are as essential as the air, the earth, and the sky. You are a living expression of the universe's creativity, deserving of all the love, care, and respect you can give—and receive. Stand tall in this truth, and let it guide you toward a life filled with purpose, joy, and a deep sense of belonging to the world around you. The universe celebrates your worth, and when you do too, you inspire others to join in this beautiful dance of existence.

Mindful Moment: The Inner Glow

Find a quiet space and sit comfortably. Gently close your eyes. Take a few deep, settling breaths. Now, bring your attention to your heart center. Imagine a soft, warm, gentle light beginning to glow there. This is the light of your own self-love and appreciation. With each inhalation, imagine this light growing brighter, expanding to fill your chest, then your entire body, radiating outwards from your fingertips and toes. Feel the warmth, the peace, the deep acceptance this light brings. Rest in this feeling for a few moments, knowing this glow is always within you.

The Unfolding Blossom

A flower doesn't force itself open; it simply unfurls at its own perfect pace, responding to the sun and warmth. It doesn't compare its petals to the one next to it or try to be a different color. It simply blooms in its own magnificent way, fulfilling its own nature. Similarly, your own unique beauty and radiance are meant to unfurl naturally. There's no need to force yourself to be anything other than who you are. Trust your own unfolding, allowing your unique essence to bloom in its perfect time, sharing its beauty effortlessly with the world.

Gentle Self-Talk

"Today, I will celebrate one small, unique aspect of myself without judgment."

"I am worthy of love, care, and respect – from myself and others."

✦

POSITIVE AFFIRMATION

note to self

Pen Your Thoughts

1 What is one quality or talent that you genuinely love about yourself, even if it feels small?

2 When do you tend to feel most critical of yourself? What is one gentle counter-thought you can offer in that moment?

3 How might treating yourself with more love and care impact your interactions with others?

Your Space to Reflect

Chapter 9

My Thoughts Are Positive and Empowering

Sowing Seeds of Positive Thought

Imagine your mind as an incredibly fertile garden, constantly ready to receive seeds. Every thought you entertain, every belief you nurture, is a seed planted in this garden. If you continuously sow seeds of worry, doubt, or criticism, that's what will inevitably grow. But what if you consciously chose to plant seeds of positivity, empowerment, and possibility?

This chapter is about becoming the deliberate gardener of your mind, understanding the immense power of your thoughts to shape your reality. It's about recognizing that you are not merely a passive recipient of thoughts, but an active participant in cultivating your mental landscape. By choosing to focus on positive and uplifting thoughts, you begin to rewire your brain, create new neural pathways, and build a vibrant inner world that supports your highest aspirations. This isn't about denying challenges, but about empowering yourself to approach them with a mindset that fosters growth, resilience, and inner peace.

Positive Affirmation

"I choose to focus on positive and uplifting thoughts."

Reflection: The Artist's Vision

An artist begins with a blank canvas, but in their mind, they hold a vision, a positive image of what they intend to create. They don't dwell on what might go wrong or what they lack; they focus on the beauty they wish to bring forth. Their every brushstroke is an act of bringing that positive vision into reality. Your mind is your canvas, and your thoughts are your brushstrokes. What vision are you holding for your life? This reflection invites you to become a conscious artist of your thoughts, deliberately painting a picture of positivity, possibility, and joy. When you choose uplifting thoughts, you are not just thinking; you are actively creating the masterpiece of your life, one conscious brushstroke at a time.

> **Mindful Moment: The Thought Cloud Release**
>
> Sit comfortably and close your eyes. Imagine your mind as the vast, open sky. Now, notice a negative or worrying thought that might be present. Picture this thought as a small cloud drifting across the sky. Don't engage with it or judge it. Simply observe it. Now, with your exhale, imagine a gentle breeze catching the cloud, slowly pushing it away, until it drifts out of sight. Breathe in light and clarity. Repeat for any other challenging thoughts, allowing them to gently dissipate into the vastness of your mental sky.

The Bees and the Blossoms

Bees are inherently drawn to the sweetest nectar of flowers. They don't waste time on thorns or dried leaves; they seek out the blossoms. Our minds can be like bees. If we train them to seek out the "nectar" – the positive, the uplifting, the grateful – they will naturally gravitate towards it. This doesn't mean ignoring reality, but consciously choosing where you direct your focus. When you intentionally seek out the good, you nourish your spirit and contribute to the flourishing of your inner world, just as bees contribute to the life of the garden.

Gentle Self-Talk

"Today, I will pause and intentionally choose an uplifting thought whenever I catch myself spiraling into negativity."

"I choose to focus on positive and uplifting thoughts."

✦

POSITIVE AFFIRMATION

note to self

Pen Your Thoughts

1 What is one negative thought pattern that you often find yourself repeating?

2 If you were to replace that negative thought with a positive one, what would it be?

3 How might cultivating more positive thoughts impact your energy levels and your overall sense of well-being?

Your Space to Reflect

Chapter 10

I Am Deserving of Happiness and Success

Welcoming Abundance, Deserving Joy

Imagine standing by a flowing river, its waters rich with life, constantly moving and nourishing the land around it. You don't question if the river has enough to give; you simply observe its inherent abundance. Yet, when it comes to our own lives, we often find ourselves clinging to a mindset of scarcity, worrying about what's missing, or feeling unworthy of true joy and success.

This chapter is an invitation to shift your perspective from lack to limitless possibility, to truly believe that you are deserving of all the good that life has to offer – not just material wealth, but abundance in love, health, connection, and purpose. It's about understanding that happiness and success aren't elusive prizes to be won, but natural states that unfold when you align with your inherent worthiness. When you genuinely believe you deserve a happy, successful, and fulfilling life, you open yourself to receiving it, creating a magnetic field that attracts positivity and abundance into your experience.

Positive Affirmation

"I deserve to live a happy, successful, and fulfilling life."

Reflection: The Ocean's Limitless Generosity

The ocean is a vast, boundless expanse, capable of holding untold depths, sustaining countless forms of life, and offering its waves and tides without reservation. It doesn't hold back; it expresses limitless generosity. Our universe, too, is inherently abundant, constantly creating and expanding. How often do we, in our own lives, act as if there's not enough, or that we are not enough to receive from this boundless source? This reflection invites you to consider the ocean's limitless nature. What would it feel like to approach your life with the same expansive belief, knowing that you are connected to an infinite source of possibility, and that you are inherently worthy of receiving its gifts? When you embody this deservingness, you open yourself to the vast, generous flow of life.

Mindful Moment: Receiving with Open Palms

Sit comfortably, with your spine tall. Gently close your eyes. Turn your palms upwards, resting them gently on your knees, in a gesture of receiving. Take a few deep, deliberate breaths. As you inhale, imagine drawing in all the abundance you desire – joy, peace, health, connection, financial ease – feeling it fill you from the tips of your toes to the crown of your head. As you exhale, simply release any tension or doubt. Rest in this posture for 2-3 minutes, visualizing yourself as a vessel ready and open to receive the vast generosity of the universe.

I Am Deserving of Happiness and Success

The Apple Tree's Harvest

An apple tree, once mature, doesn't produce just one apple; it produces hundreds, far more than it could possibly consume itself. It offers its abundance freely, trusting in its own nature to continually produce. It doesn't worry if its apples are "good enough" or if there will be "enough" for everyone. It simply gives. This teaches us about the natural state of abundance. When we tap into our own inherent capacity to create, to give, and to receive without judgment, we align with this natural flow, allowing our lives to blossom with effortless prosperity and joy, just like the bountiful apple tree.

Gentle Self-Talk

*"Today, I will release any feelings
of unworthiness and open myself fully
to receiving joy and abundance."*

"I deserve to live a happy, successful, and fulfilling life."

POSITIVE AFFIRMATION

note to self

Pen Your Thoughts

1 What does "happiness, success, and a fulfilling life" truly mean to you, beyond societal expectations?

2 Identify one small area in your life where you tend to feel a sense of lack. How can you shift your perspective to one of abundance in that area?

3 What is one thing you can do today, even a tiny act, that makes you feel more deserving of joy?

Your Space to Reflect

Part 3
EMBRACING GROWTH

Chapter 11

I Release Self-Doubt and Negativity

Releasing the Unseen Chains

Imagine holding a handful of dandelion seeds, ready to be carried away by the slightest breeze. Yet, if you cling to them tightly, they cannot fly, cannot fulfill their natural purpose of spreading new life. In much the same way, we often hold onto invisible chains – self-doubt, past mistakes, limiting beliefs, or even old grievances – that prevent us from truly soaring.

This chapter is an invitation to feel the lightness that comes from letting go. It's about recognizing that what once served you might now be holding you back. It's about understanding that releasing doesn't mean forgetting, but rather freeing your energy to create something new. When you consciously unburden yourself from these unseen chains, you create space for new growth, for clarity, and for the authentic confidence that allows your spirit to truly expand. This is a gentle liberation, a quiet shedding of what no longer serves your highest good.

Positive Affirmation

"I let go of self-doubt and negativity, embracing positivity and confidence."

Reflection: The River Meeting the Ocean

Think of a river. As it flows towards the ocean, it eventually merges, releasing its individual identity into the vastness. It doesn't cling to its riverbanks or its past journey; it gracefully lets go and becomes part of something larger. This act of merging is not a loss, but a powerful expansion. What "riverbanks" are you clinging to? What old stories, fears, or doubts are preventing your own expansion? This reflection invites you to consider the river's surrender. What might it feel like to gently release those mental ties, to allow yourself to merge with a larger sense of possibility and freedom? When you release, you don't diminish; you expand, becoming more of who you are meant to be.

Mindful Moment: The Releasing Breath

Sit comfortably and close your eyes. Take a deep breath in, imagining you are gathering up any tension, self-doubt, or old worries. Hold it for a moment. Now, slowly, gently, exhale, imagining you are releasing all of it, letting it float away on your breath. Feel the lightness as you empty. Repeat three times, or as often as needed, until you feel a sense of inner spaciousness.

I Release Self-Doubt and Negativity

The Shedding Snake Skin

A snake regularly sheds its old skin. It doesn't cling to the scales that are too tight or worn. It simply moves forward, rubbing against a surface to loosen the old layer, revealing fresh, vibrant skin underneath. The snake doesn't dwell on the past skin; it embraces the new. This act of shedding is essential for its growth and vitality.

Trust your own process of release, knowing that letting go makes space for renewal and a more vibrant, authentic you.

Gentle Self-Talk
"Today, I will gently loosen one invisible chain that binds me."

"I let go of self-doubt and negativity, embracing positivity and confidence."

POSITIVE AFFIRMATION

note to self

Pen Your Thoughts

1 What is one specific self-doubt or negative thought you are ready to gently release today?

2 How does holding onto old beliefs or worries impact your energy or your ability to move forward?

3 Imagine what it would feel like to be completely free of this burden. What new possibilities emerge?

Your Space to Reflect

Chapter 12

I Am Unique and Special

My Unique Melody

Imagine a vast orchestra, where every instrument, from the deep cello to the soaring flute, plays its distinct part. No instrument tries to be another; each contributes its unique voice, and together, they create a rich, harmonious symphony. You, too, are an essential instrument in the grand symphony of life, playing your own unique melody.

This chapter is a vibrant celebration of your individuality, your distinct talents, quirks, passions, and perspectives. In a world that sometimes encourages conformity, embracing your unique melody is an act of courage and profound self-love. It's about recognizing that your authentic expression is not just valid, but vital. There is no one else exactly like you, and your particular blend of experiences and gifts is precisely what the world needs. When you fully embrace and express your unique melody, you not only light up your own life, but you also inspire others to play their own beautiful tunes.

Positive Affirmation

"I celebrate my uniqueness and individuality."

Reflection: The Irreplaceable Star

Look up at the night sky. Each star, from the brightest to the most distant twinkle, holds its own unique luminosity and position. No star tries to outshine another by becoming something it's not; each simply burns with its own particular intensity, contributing to the awe-inspiring tapestry of the cosmos. If even one star were missing, the pattern would be subtly incomplete. This reflection invites you to recognize your own irreplaceable contribution to the tapestry of life. What unique light do you bring? What talents or perspectives are distinctly yours? When you stop comparing your light to others and simply allow yourself to shine, you illuminate your own path and contribute to the collective brilliance in a way no one else can.

Mindful Moment: The Inner Rhythm Dance

Stand up (or sit) and gently close your eyes. Bring awareness to your natural rhythm – your heartbeat, your breathing, the subtle sway of your body. Imagine that these rhythms are creating a unique, internal melody. Allow yourself to gently move or sway to this inner tune, if it feels comfortable. This isn't about formal dance; it's about connecting with your own unique inner flow and expression. Feel the freedom in simply being in your own rhythm.

The Fingerprint of the Leaf

Every single leaf on every tree, even on the same branch, possesses a unique pattern of veins, an individual fingerprint. No two are precisely identical. Yet, each leaf performs its essential function perfectly. Nature celebrates individuality, understanding that unique forms contribute to the overall health and beauty of the ecosystem. Like the leaf, your unique pattern, your individual design, is not a flaw but

I Am Unique and Special

a masterpiece. Embrace your distinct "fingerprint," knowing that your specific contributions and your authentic way of being are invaluable to the world.

Gentle Self-Talk

"Today, I will bravely express one small aspect of my authentic self."

"I celebrate my uniqueness and individuality."

POSITIVE AFFIRMATION

note to self

Pen Your Thoughts

1 What is one unique quality that you possess that you often downplay or hide?

2 How might fully embracing this unique aspect of yourself empower you or bring you more joy?

3 What is one small way you can celebrate your individuality today, even if no one else notices?

Your Space to Reflect

Chapter 13

I Prioritize Self-Care and Self-Love

The Art of Gentle Nurturing

The quiet strength of a well-lived life begins in the unseen spaces — the moments when you choose to care for yourself as you would for someone you deeply love. Your mind, body, and spirit are not separate entities competing for your attention; they are three threads of the same cloth. When one is frayed, the whole fabric feels it. When each is treated with patience and care, your life becomes softer, yet stronger.

Positive Affirmation

"I nurture my mind, body, and spirit with love and care."

Living the Affirmation

When you say, *"I nurture my mind, body, and spirit with love and care,"* you are making a quiet promise to live gently but intentionally. This is not about perfection, but about presence. It is about showing up for yourself as you would for a dear friend, and remembering that caring for yourself is not selfish — it is the root of your strength and the source of your joy.

Every breath, every choice, every small act of kindness toward yourself weaves together into a life that feels whole. You become your own safe harbor. And from that place, you can meet the world with clarity, energy, and grace.

Reflection: Living in Gentle Harmony

Your mind, like still water, clears when you release unnecessary thoughts and let only what is true remain. Your body, like a trusted companion, moves with grace when you treat it with patience, strength, and rest. Your spirit, like a lantern in the night, glows brighter when you feed it with purpose and joy.

Understand that each breath, each action, and each choice is part of a harmonious circle — what you give to yourself ripples into the world. When you care for your mind, you sharpen your clarity; when you care for your body, you deepen your vitality; when you care for your spirit, you keep your heart light.

Life is not about rushing to the finish, but about finding beauty in each step, each sip of tea, each moment of stillness. When you nurture yourself with love and care, you are already living fully — not someday, but now.

Mindful Moment: The Inner Garden Visualization

Find a comfortable position. Close your eyes gently and take a few slow, deep breaths. Imagine yourself walking into your own serene inner garden. What does it look like? Perhaps there are gentle streams, blooming flowers, ancient trees, or simply open, peaceful spaces. Notice the colors, the scents, the sounds, the feeling of the air. This is your space. Spend a few moments simply being present in this inner sanctuary, feeling its calming energy. Know that you can return here whenever you need solace or clarity, simply by closing your eyes and returning to your breath.

I Prioritize Self-Care and Self-Love

> As you breathe, imagine filling your mind
> with clarity and kindness.
>
> Shift your awareness to your body — sense
> the gentle rise and fall of your breath,
> the steady beat of your heart.
> Picture your body absorbing strength and ease.
>
> Finally, turn inward toward your spirit — that quiet,
> glowing center that feels light, peaceful, and whole.
> Feel your spirit glowing brighter, warmed by
> your own compassion.
>
> Rest in this feeling for a few heartbeats.
>
> Carry it with you as you move through
> the rest of your day.

The Lotus's Journey

The lotus blooms only when it is ready.

It rises slowly from the depths, nourished by the mud that once weighed it down.

Each petal opens in its own time, never rushed by the world around it.

You, too, deserve the same patience and care.

Your self-care is the water that keeps you alive.

Your self-love is the sunlight that warms your growth.

When you give yourself both, you bloom naturally — not for others, but for your own joy.

A Moment Just For You

The lotus does not compare its petals to another's; it simply opens. So can you.

Gentle Self-Talk

"Today, I will create one small, sacred pause to connect with my inner peace. I will choose actions that make me feel cared for, valued, and at peace."

"I nurture my mind, body, and spirit with love and care."

POSITIVE AFFIRMATION

note to self

Pen Your Thoughts

1 What is one gentle way you can care for your mind today?

2 What is one tender, supportive act of care you can offer your body today?

3 What is one nourishing practice you can embrace for your spirit today?

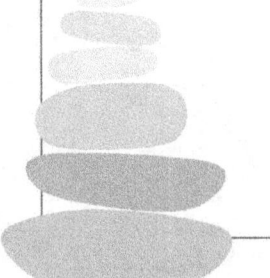

Your Space to Reflect

Chapter 14

I Am Confident in My Abilities

The Unwavering Core of My Being

Imagine a magnificent ancient tree, standing for centuries, weathering countless storms, droughts, and changing seasons. While its leaves may fall and regrow, its branches may bend, its core, its mighty trunk, remains unwavering. It holds its strength, its wisdom, and its essence through all transformations. Similarly, beneath the shifting currents of daily life – your roles, your emotions, your experiences – lies an unwavering core of your being.

This chapter is an invitation to connect with that deepest, most authentic part of yourself. It's the part that holds your innate strength, your deepest values, and your unique purpose. It's the part that knows who you are, beyond external labels or temporary circumstances. When you anchor yourself in this unwavering core, you gain a profound sense of stability, clarity, and peace. You realize that while life will always bring change, your essential self remains constant, resilient, and always connected to a boundless source of wisdom and courage.

Confidence is a powerful catalyst for success and fulfillment. Like a mountain standing firm against the winds, you too can cultivate a sense of stability and trust in your abilities. By acknowledging your strengths and accomplishments, you'll build confidence and develop a deeper understanding of your capabilities

Positive Affirmation

"I trust myself and my capabilities."

Reflection: The Steadfast Mountain Range

Consider a grand mountain range. Individual peaks may be climbed, valleys may be explored, and weather patterns may shift around them, but the fundamental structure of the mountains remains steadfast, unyielding. They have stood for millennia, a silent testament to enduring strength. Similarly, your life might have many "peaks" of joy and "valleys" of challenge, but beneath it all, your unwavering core remains. This reflection invites you to feel into that deep, stable part of yourself. What does it feel like to know that, despite external changes, your true self is inherently strong and resilient? When you connect with this steadfastness, you gain a quiet confidence to navigate any landscape, knowing your core remains unshakeable.

By trusting yourself and your abilities, you'll unlock your full potential and live a life that reflects your passions and values. With confidence, you'll be more resilient, adaptable, and better equipped to face life's challenges with courage and determination. By believing in yourself, you'll achieve great things and live a life that is authentic, meaningful, and fulfilling. Your confidence will shine like a beacon, inspiring others and guiding you towards your goals.

I Am Confident in My Abilities

> ## Mindful Moment: The Inner Anchor
>
> Find a comfortable position. Close your eyes gently. Imagine a strong, golden cord extending from the base of your spine, rooting you deeply into the earth. Feel yourself connected, stable, and secure. Now, bring your awareness to your heart. Imagine a warm, glowing light there – this is your unwavering core. With each breath, feel this light expanding, filling your entire being with a sense of quiet power and stability. Rest in this feeling for a few moments, knowing your anchor is always present.

The Ocean's Deep Current

On the ocean's surface, waves crash and winds howl, creating a visible turbulence. Yet, far beneath the surface, there are deep, powerful, and utterly calm currents that move with immense purpose, unaffected by the surface chaos. These deep currents represent the unwavering forces of nature. Your unwavering core is like this deep current within you. No matter how much turbulence or superficial chaos might be happening on the "surface" of your life, there is always a deep, calm, purposeful current within that remains constant. Trust this deeper flow; it will always guide you home. Believe that YOU are capable!

Gentle Self-Talk

"Today, I will act from my deepest wisdom, trusting my inner strength."

"I trust myself and my capabilities."

✦

POSITIVE AFFIRMATION

note to self

Pen Your Thoughts

1 When you think of yourself as a mountain, what "peaks" (joys) and "valleys" (challenges) have shaped you most?

2 When have you felt most connected to your inner strength and clarity, and how can you return to that stability the next time life feels uncertain?

3 What is one way you can practice showing confidence in your everyday actions this week?

Your Space to Reflect

Chapter 15

I Focus on the Present Moment

The Ever-Present Moment

Imagine holding a single, perfectly ripe piece of fruit in your hand. Feel its weight, its texture. Notice its vibrant color, its subtle aroma. When you are truly present with that one piece of fruit, savoring it fully, you are experiencing the richness of the ever-present moment. Yet, how often do we rush past such moments, our minds either reliving the past or anxiously planning the future?

This chapter is an invitation to reclaim the profound power and beauty of the now. The past is a memory, and the future is a dream, but the present moment is the only place where life truly unfolds, where joy can be felt, and where action can be taken. Learning to live fully in the "here and now" is not about ignoring life's responsibilities, but about engaging with them with greater clarity, peace, and appreciation. When you embrace the ever-present moment, you unlock a deep sense of serenity, realizing that true peace is always available, right where you are.

A Moment Just For You

Positive Affirmation

"I live in the present, letting go of worries about the past or future."

Reflection: The Single Melody Note

Think of a beautiful piece of music. Each note is played in its perfect, singular moment. The musician doesn't dwell on the note that just passed or rush to the one coming next; they simply play the current note with full attention. It is in this full presence with each individual note that the entire melody becomes harmonious and beautiful. How often do we "miss" the current "note" of our lives by dwelling on past errors or fearing future uncertainties? This reflection invites you to become the mindful musician of your own existence, savoring each moment, each breath, each experience as if it were a single, perfect note. When you do, the entire symphony of your life flows with grace and beauty.

Mindful Moment: The Five Senses Anchor

Pause wherever you are. Take a deep breath. Now, consciously engage your five senses, one by one, to anchor yourself in the present:

♣ **See:** Name five things you can see around you.

♣ **Feel:** Notice four things you can feel (e.g., fabric on skin, air temperature, feet on floor).

♣ **Hear:** Identify three sounds you can hear.

I Focus on the Present Moment

- ♣ **Smell:** Recognize two things you can smell.
- ♣ **Taste:** Acknowledge one thing you can taste (even if it's just the residual taste in your mouth). This practice quickly brings your awareness back to the tangible reality of the present.

The Bud, Blossom, and Decay of a Flower

A flower lives fully in each stage of its existence. A bud is simply a bud, holding its potential. A blossom is fully open, vibrant in its present beauty. And a decaying flower gently releases its form. At no point does the bud wish it were a full blossom, nor does the blossom cling to its vibrancy. Each stage is fully present and accepted. Nature teaches us that life is a continuous cycle of becoming and releasing, and true peace comes from embracing the completeness of this moment, whatever stage it may be.

Gentle Self-Talk

"Today, I will bring my full attention to one simple, everyday activity."

"I live in the present, letting go of worries about the past or future."

POSITIVE AFFIRMATION

note to self

Pen Your Thoughts

1. What is one recurring thought about the past or future that often pulls you away from the present?

2. Choose one routine activity you do today (e.g., drinking water, walking). How can you bring your full, mindful attention to it?

3. How does being fully present, even for a moment, change your experience of that moment?

Your Space to Reflect

Part 4
LIVING WITH PURPOSE

Chapter 16

I Am Worthy of Love and Respect

Acknowledging My Inherent Worth

Imagine a vast, ancient forest where every tree, from the towering oak to the smallest sapling, plays a crucial role in the ecosystem. Each one contributes oxygen, provides shelter, and enriches the soil, simply by existing. No tree needs to prove its right to be there; its worth is inherent, foundational to the health of the whole. You, too, possess an inherent worth that is fundamental to your being, independent of your achievements, failures, or external opinions.

This chapter is a deep invitation to acknowledge and truly embody this profound truth: you are intrinsically valuable, simply because you exist. Your worth is not a fluctuating currency based on performance; it is a timeless, unwavering core of your identity. When you truly acknowledge your inherent worth, you unlock a powerful sense of self-respect, self-compassion, and confidence that ripples through every area of your life. It allows you to set healthy boundaries, pursue your dreams with conviction, and receive love and respect from others, because you first offer it to yourself.

Positive Affirmation

"I am worthy of love and respect, just as I am."

Reflection: The Sun's Unconditional Giving

The sun shines on everyone and everything, without judgment or condition. It doesn't ask if a flower is "worthy" of its light, or if a person has "earned" its warmth. It simply radiates its energy, enriching all life. Similarly, your inherent worth is like the sun's unconditional light – it doesn't need to be earned or qualified. It simply is. How often do we block our own light, believing we need to "earn" love or "deserve" respect? This reflection invites you to bask in the truth of your own unconditional worth. What would it feel like to allow yourself to receive love, care, and respect as freely as the earth receives the sun's warmth, knowing you are inherently deserving? When you radiate this truth, you naturally draw the love and respect you truly deserve.

Mindful Moment: The Truth

Close your eyes.

Take a deep breath in...

And slowly breathe out.

Feel your body grounded in the present moment.

Gently place your hand over your heart.

I Am Worthy of Love and Respect

> Repeat silently or out loud:
>
> **"I am worthy of love and respect, just as I am."**
>
> Let this truth settle into your body like sunlight on your skin.
>
> There is nothing to prove. Nothing to earn.
>
> You are enough — right here, right now.

The Mountain and the Breeze

The mountain does not chase the breeze, nor does the breeze try to move the mountain. Both exist in perfect harmony, simply being what they are — complete, whole, and at peace.

You are like that mountain, steady and rooted. Or like the breeze, gentle and free. There is no need to become anything else. Just by existing, you hold value. You are worthy of love and respect, without striving or change.

Breathe deeply. Let yourself simply be.

Gentle Self-Talk

"Today, I will treat myself with the kindness and respect I would offer a cherished loved one."

"I am worthy of love and respect, just as I am."

✦

POSITIVE AFFIRMATION

note to self

Pen Your Thoughts

1. When do you tend to feel less worthy? What specific triggers or situations bring up this feeling?

2. What is one small act of self-care or self-respect you can practice today that acknowledges your inherent worth?

3. What new possibilities open when your sense of worth guides the way you face challenges and connect with others?

Your Space to Reflect

Chapter 17

I Cultivate a Growth Mindset

The Curious Learner's Path

Imagine a child discovering the world for the very first time – wide-eyed, filled with wonder, asking endless questions, unafraid to explore, and learning rapidly from every new experience. This innate curiosity, this eager desire to understand and grow, is a powerful engine for evolution. Yet, as adults, we sometimes lose this playful wonder, settling into routines and believing we already know enough.

This chapter is an invitation to rekindle that childlike curiosity, to step onto the path of the curious learner. It's about approaching life with an open mind, a willingness to explore new ideas, and a joyful embrace of growth. Every challenge becomes a puzzle to solve, every new encounter a lesson, and every misstep an opportunity for deeper understanding. When you walk the curious learner's path, you not only expand your knowledge but also keep your spirit vibrant, adaptable, and forever open to the exciting possibilities that life continually offers.

Positive Affirmation

"I am open to learning, growing, and evolving."

Reflection: The River That Carves Mountains

A river, over millennia, can carve canyons and shape entire mountain ranges, not through brute force, but through persistent, continuous flow and the cumulative effect of small, consistent actions. It learns the path of least resistance, adapting to the terrain, always moving forward. Similarly, your journey of learning and growth is a continuous flow, a persistent carving of your own unique path. What "mountains" in your understanding are you ready to explore or reshape? This reflection invites you to approach your own learning with the river's patient persistence. Every new piece of knowledge, every new experience, however small, carves a deeper channel for your wisdom, shaping the landscape of your understanding in profound ways.

As you cultivate a growth mindset, you'll discover new opportunities for growth and development. Like a lotus flower blooming in the muddiest of waters, you'll rise above challenges and emerge stronger and wiser.

Mindful Moment: The Beginner's Mind

Choose one everyday object around you – a pen, a cup, a leaf, a stone. Look at it as if you've never seen it before. What details do you notice? What is its texture, its color, its form? How does it feel in your hand? Allow yourself to observe it with pure, open curiosity, without labeling or judgment. This practice trains your mind to see the world with fresh eyes, fostering a "beginner's mind" open to new discoveries.

The Root Seeking Water

A plant's roots tirelessly seek water, even through dense soil and around obstacles. They are not deterred by darkness or difficulty; their innate drive is to find what they need to grow and thrive. This ceaseless seeking, this inherent curiosity, ensures the plant's survival and flourishing. You, too, have an innate drive to seek knowledge and wisdom, to grow and to thrive. Embrace this natural inclination within you. Allow your "roots" of curiosity to explore new depths, to find new sources of nourishment, and to push beyond perceived limitations.

Gentle Self-Talk

"Today, I will approach one new situation or idea with an open, curious mind."

"I am open to learning, growing, and evolving."

✦

POSITIVE AFFIRMATION

Pen Your Thoughts

1 What is one topic or skill you've always been curious about but haven't explored?

2 How might approaching a current challenge with a "learner's mindset" change your experience of it?

3 What small question can you ask today that sparks a new thought or insight?

Your Space to Reflect

Chapter 18

I Am at Peace with Myself and Others

Harmony in Every Breath

Imagine the rhythmic dance of the tides, the gentle rise and fall of the ocean, perfectly balanced, creating a soothing melody of movement and stillness. This natural rhythm brings harmony to the vast waters. Similarly, within you, your breath is a constant, rhythmic anchor, a direct link to a profound sense of inner harmony and peace.

This chapter is an invitation to reconnect with the simple, yet profound, power of your breath. In moments of stress, our breath often becomes shallow and rapid. But by consciously slowing down, deepening, and simply observing your breath, you can instantly calm your nervous system, quiet your mind, and restore a sense of balance. Your breath is your most accessible tool for cultivating peace, love, and positivity, radiating outward from your very core. When you consciously breathe with awareness, you don't just take in air; you invite harmony into every cell of your being, creating a resonant vibration of peace that extends to the world around you.

Inner peace is a profound state of being that transcends life's challenges. Like a serene mountain lake, you'll reflect the calmness and tranquility that comes from within. By letting go of conflicts and negativity, you'll cultivate a sense of harmony and balance that radiates outward, touching the lives of those around you.

Positive Affirmation

"I radiate peace, love, and positivity."

Reflection: The Rhythm of Day and Night

The world experiences a continuous, balanced rhythm of day turning into night, and night into day. There is no resistance, no argument; just a perfect, harmonious flow. Each part serves a purpose – the light for activity, the dark for rest and renewal. Similarly, your life experiences its own rhythms of action and pause, effort and surrender. This reflection invites you to find the harmony in these natural cycles within yourself. What does it feel like to release the need to constantly do, and instead, to simply be in rhythm with your own needs? When you align with your natural rhythms, you radiate a deep sense of balance, much like the planet itself.

With inner peace, you'll navigate life's challenges with greater ease, clarity, and purpose, living a life that is authentic, meaningful, and fulfilling. Your presence will uplift and inspire others, creating a ripple effect of peace and positivity.

Mindful Moment: The Four-Count Breath

Find a comfortable seat. Gently close your eyes. Breathe in slowly for a count of four. Hold your breath gently for a count of four. Exhale slowly for a count of four. Pause before the next inhale.

I Am at Peace with Myself and Others

> Repeat this cycle 3-5 times. Notice how the rhythmic, balanced breathing brings a sense of calm and clarity to your mind and body. This simple practice is a powerful way to re-center yourself.

The Interconnected Forest

In a healthy forest, trees communicate and share resources through a vast underground network of roots and fungi. They exist in a beautiful harmony, each contributing to the well-being of the whole. There's a natural give and take, a balance that creates a thriving ecosystem. This intricate interconnectedness reflects the harmony within you and your connection to the world. When you radiate peace, love, and positivity, you become part of this larger harmonious network, contributing to the well-being of your community and the planet, just as each tree contributes to the vitality of the forest.

Gentle Self-Talk

"Today, I will return to my breath whenever I seek harmony or peace."

"I radiate peace, love, and positivity."

POSITIVE AFFIRMATION

note to self

Pen Your Thoughts

1 How does your breath change when you feel stressed or anxious versus when you feel calm and relaxed?

2 What is one small, simple moment today when you can consciously pause and take three deep, calming breaths?

3 How might radiating peace, love, and positivity impact your interactions with others, even subtly?

Your Space to Reflect

Chapter 19

I Trust the Universe and Its Plan

Surrendering to the Flow of Life

Imagine a leaf falling from a tree in autumn. It doesn't fight the wind or try to reattach itself to the branch. It simply lets go, surrendering to the breeze, allowing itself to be carried wherever the natural flow takes it, eventually landing softly on the earth. This act of surrender is not about giving up; it's about trusting the larger forces at play, releasing the need for control, and embracing the wisdom of allowing.

This chapter is an invitation to release the tight grip of needing to control every outcome, every detail, every aspect of your life. It's about cultivating a profound trust in the inherent intelligence of life itself. When you surrender to the flow, you become like that autumn leaf – gracefully carried, navigating twists and turns with ease, and finding a deep sense of peace in knowing that everything truly is working out for your highest good. This surrender liberates immense energy, transforming anxiety into a quiet confidence and effort into graceful movement.

Positive Affirmation

"I trust that everything is working out for my highest good."

Reflection: The Ship Navigating the Ocean

A ship on the ocean doesn't try to control the waves or the currents; it uses them. The captain steers, adjusts the sails, and navigates with skill, but ultimately trusts the vastness of the ocean to carry it to its destination. The ship surrenders to the ocean's power while skillfully working with it. Similarly, you are the captain of your life's ship. You set intentions, you take action, but you also learn to trust the vast, unpredictable "ocean" of life to carry you. What "waves" are you trying to control, rather than skillfully navigating? This reflection invites you to steer your ship with intention, but also to surrender to the powerful currents, trusting that even unforeseen detours are part of the journey leading you exactly where you need to be.

Mindful Moment: The Unclenched Hand

Make a fist with one hand, clenching it tightly. Feel the tension in your knuckles, your forearm. This is what it can feel like when we try to control everything. Now, slowly, consciously, gently unclench your hand, finger by finger, until your palm is soft and open. Feel the release of tension, the lightness. This simple physical act is a powerful reminder of how releasing control brings ease. Practice this whenever you notice yourself gripping tightly to a situation or outcome.

The River's Bend

A river flows ceaselessly towards the sea. When it encounters an obstacle, it doesn't fight it; it simply flows around it, creating a new bend in its path. It adapts, it yields, and it continues its journey. The bend becomes a natural part of its flow, adding to its beauty and uniqueness. Similarly, when you surrender to the flow of life, you allow for "bends" and detours. These unexpected turns are not failures but natural evolutions of your path, often leading you to new perspectives and unforeseen opportunities that ultimately serve your highest good.

Gentle Self-Talk

"Today, I will release one thing I'm trying to control and trust the unfolding."

"I trust that everything is working out for my highest good."

POSITIVE AFFIRMATION

note to self

Pen Your Thoughts

1 What is one specific area of your life where you feel a strong need for control?

2 What is one small step you can take today to practice letting go and trusting in that area?

3 How might surrendering to the flow of life create more ease or unexpected opportunities for you?

Your Space to Reflect

Chapter 20

I Am Strong and Capable

Unearthing My True Inner Strength

Imagine a small, resilient seed pushing through hardened earth, defying gravity and darkness to reach the sunlight. Or a tiny sapling bending in a storm, only to straighten and grow stronger, its roots deepening with every challenge. Within each of us lies a similar, profound inner strength – a wellspring of resilience, courage, and unwavering capability.

This chapter is an invitation to unearth and fully embrace this powerful inner resource. It's about recognizing that strength isn't always loud or externally visible; often, it's found in quiet persistence, in choosing compassion over criticism, and in rising again after a fall. You possess an innate capacity to face challenges, to learn from experiences, and to grow beyond your perceived limitations. When you tap into this inner strength, you realize you can handle any challenge that comes your way, not by avoiding difficulty, but by meeting it with an empowered spirit and unwavering self-trust.

Positive Affirmation

"I can handle any challenge that comes my way."

Reflection: The Mountain's Steadfast Presence

A mountain stands tall, enduring centuries of changing weather, tectonic shifts, and the passage of time. It doesn't flinch in the face of a blizzard or crumble under the weight of a storm. It simply is – steadfast, unwavering, and powerful. Its strength is in its sheer presence and resilience. How often do we underestimate our own capacity to stand firm in the face of life's "storms"? This reflection invites you to connect with the mountain's steadfastness within you. What challenges have you already overcome that prove your resilience? What unwavering qualities lie beneath the surface of your daily life? When you connect with this deep, inherent strength, you realize that like the mountain, you are equipped to face anything that comes your way, not by brute force, but by your deep, unwavering presence.

Mindful Moment: The Warrior's Breath

Stand tall, with your feet hip-width apart, arms relaxed at your sides. Take a deep, intentional breath. As you exhale, imagine a soft, audible sigh, releasing any tension or fear. With each inhalation, imagine drawing in courage and strength. With each exhalation, release doubt. Feel your rootedness, your inherent power. Repeat 3-5 times, embodying a quiet, inner warrior ready to meet the day.

I Am Strong and Capable

The Tree's Deep Roots

A tree's visible strength is in its trunk and branches, but its true power lies unseen, in its deep, intricate root system. These roots anchor it, draw nourishment, and allow it to weather the fiercest storms without being toppled. The deeper the roots, the stronger the tree. Similarly, your inner strength is cultivated through your experiences, your lessons learned, and your connection to your core self. The more you explore and acknowledge this inner foundation, the more resilient and powerful you become. Every challenge overcome deepens your roots, making you unshakeable.

Gentle Self-Talk

"Today, I will trust in my capacity to handle whatever unfolds."

"I can handle any challenge that comes my way."

POSITIVE AFFIRMATION

note to self

Pen Your Thoughts

1 Recall a specific challenge you faced that, at the time, felt insurmountable. What inner strength did you discover in overcoming it?

2 What is one current situation that feels challenging?

3 How can you approach it by consciously tapping into your inner strength?

Your Space to Reflect

Part 5
SUSTAINING JOY

Chapter 21

I Prioritize Positivity and Joy

Choosing Light, Choosing Bliss

Imagine a garden filled with vibrant, sun-kissed flowers, each one turning its face towards the warmth, absorbing light and radiating color. Even on a cloudy day, they hold the memory of the sun, ready to bloom the moment the light returns. You, too, have the power to choose where you direct your focus, to turn towards the light, and to cultivate a life filled with joy, bliss, and laughter, no matter the external weather.

This chapter is an invitation to consciously choose happiness, to seek out moments of lightness, and to embrace the healing power of joy. It's about understanding that happiness isn't just a fleeting emotion; it's a practice, a deliberate cultivation. By intentionally focusing on positivity and seeking out moments that uplift your spirit, you don't just experience joy; you become a source of it, illuminating your own path and brightening the world around you. This conscious choice transforms your daily experience into a vibrant canvas of delight.

Positive Affirmation

"I choose to focus on positivity and joy."

Reflection: The Stream's Merry Dance

Observe a stream, not a mighty river this time, but a small, bubbling brook. It dances over pebbles, gurgles around roots, and sparkles in the sunlight. It doesn't question its path; it simply flows with an inherent lightness and joy. Even when it encounters a small obstacle, it finds a way around, often creating a playful splash. How often do we let small obstacles dampen our spirits? This reflection invites you to embody the stream's merry dance. What small moments of joy are you overlooking? How can you approach your day with more lightness and playfulness, allowing your spirit to bubble and sparkle? When you choose joy, you create a ripple effect, much like the stream bringing life and cheer to its surroundings.

Mindful Moment: Heal With a Smile

Think of a time when you laughed so hard your belly hurt, a truly genuine, unrestrained laugh. Recall the feeling of that joy in your body. Now, gently smile. Even if it feels a little forced at first, allow your lips to turn upwards. Notice how a small smile can begin to shift your internal state. You can also listen to something that genuinely makes you laugh – a favorite podcast, a silly video, or a memory of a loved one's humor. Let laughter be your medicine, echoing within you.

I Prioritize Positivity and Joy

The Sunflower's Face

A sunflower doesn't force itself to be happy; it simply turns its face towards the sun throughout the day, absorbing its light and energy. Its very nature is to seek the light. You, too, have an innate inclination towards joy and positivity. It's about consciously turning your "face" towards what uplifts you, just as the sunflower turns towards the sun. When you make this conscious choice, you draw in the energy you need to bloom brightly, radiating your own vibrant joy to the world.

Gentle Self-Talk

"Today, I will actively seek out and appreciate at least one moment of pure joy or laughter."

"I choose to focus on positivity and joy."

✦

POSITIVE AFFIRMATION

note to self

Pen Your Thoughts

1 What is one simple activity that consistently brings a smile to your face?

2 When do you tend to feel least joyful? How can you gently shift your focus in those moments?

3 How might consciously choosing positivity and joy impact your energy levels and your interactions with others?

Your Space to Reflect

Chapter 22

I Let Go of Fear and Anxiety

Gentle Breezes, Peaceful Mind

Imagine a summer day, with a gentle breeze rustling through the leaves, carrying away the heat and creating a sense of refreshing calm. This soft, consistent movement brings peace to the landscape. Our minds, too, often carry a "heat" of worries, anxieties, and constant thoughts, but just like the breeze, we have the power to invite a cooling, calming presence.

This chapter is an invitation to release the grip of fear and anxiety, allowing a gentle breeze of peace to soothe your mind. It's about understanding that worries are often like clouds, transient and ever-changing, and you don't need to be consumed by them. By consciously returning to your breath, to the present moment, and to a sense of inner spaciousness, you can allow anxieties to gently dissipate, leaving behind a profound sense of tranquility. This is a practice of quiet liberation, a gentle letting go that opens your heart to an abiding sense of calm.

Positive Affirmation

"I release fear and anxiety, embracing calm and peace."

Reflection: The Floating Cloud

Look up at the sky. Notice a cloud. It drifts effortlessly, without holding onto any shape, constantly changing, eventually dissolving. It doesn't resist the wind; it simply allows itself to be carried. Our fears and anxieties are often like these clouds – shapeless, transient, and if we don't cling to them, they will naturally drift away. How often do you grasp onto a "cloud" of worry, making it feel solid and real? This reflection invites you to observe your worries as passing clouds. Can you allow them to simply float by, without needing to control them or judge them? When you release your grip, the vast, clear "sky" of your mind reveals itself, vast and peaceful.

Mindful Moment: Breathe Out Worries and Anxiety

Sit or lie down comfortably. Close your eyes. As you inhale, imagine drawing in cool, calm air, filling your lungs with a sense of peace. As you exhale, imagine breathing out any worries or anxieties, like soft grey clouds dissipating into the sky. Feel the space that is created with each exhalation. Repeat for 2-3 minutes, focusing on the release of tension with each outgoing breath.

The Stillness of the Deep Forest

Deep within a forest, even when winds howl at the canopy, there is often a profound stillness and quietude on the forest floor. The ancient trees act as protectors, creating a calm sanctuary. This teaches us that even when the "winds" of fear and anxiety swirl on the surface of our lives, there is always a deep, calm, protective sanctuary within. By connecting with this inner stillness, you create a haven where worries gently fade, much like the quiet calm on the forest floor.

Gentle Self-Talk

"Today, I will gently release one small worry and replace it with a calm breath."

"I release fear and anxiety, embracing calm and peace."

POSITIVE AFFIRMATION

note to self

Pen Your Thoughts

1 What is one specific fear or anxiety that often occupies your mind?

2 What is the smallest, simplest action you can take to invite a sense of calm into that situation today?

3 How might releasing fear and anxiety create more space for other positive emotions in your life?

Your Space to Reflect

Chapter 23

I Am Deserving of Abundance and Prosperity

The Flow of Endless Possibility

Imagine a vast ocean, stretching endlessly beyond the horizon, holding untold depths, diverse life, and boundless potential. Its currents move with power and grace, constantly reshaping, constantly creating. It doesn't question its own capacity; it simply *is* a magnificent embodiment of limitless possibility. You, too, are connected to such an ocean of endless potential within your own being.

This chapter is an invitation to open yourself to the vibrant flow of abundance and prosperity in all its forms. It's about recognizing that abundance isn't just about money; it's about a richness of experiences, loving connections, vibrant health, and a profound sense of well-being. When you truly believe that you are deserving of this endless flow, you begin to align with the natural generosity of the universe. This isn't about striving or forcing, but about opening your hands and heart to receive, trusting that there is always more than enough, and that countless possibilities are constantly unfolding for your highest good.

Positive Affirmation

"I welcome abundance and prosperity into my life."

Reflection: The Ever-Replenishing Spring

Think of a natural spring, bubbling up from the earth, its water pure and clear, flowing continuously without effort. It doesn't worry about running dry; it simply flows, providing life to everything around it. This spring represents the ever-replenishing source of abundance that is available to you. How often do we block this flow with doubts or limiting beliefs? This reflection invites you to see yourself as connected to this endless spring. Simply allow the flow of abundance – in all its forms – to pour into your life. When you trust in this endless source, you become a channel for prosperity, much like the spring nourishing its surroundings.

Mindful Moment: The Open Hand Gesture

Sit comfortably, perhaps in a peaceful spot. Gently open your hands, resting your palms upwards on your lap, in a gesture of receiving. Take a few slow, deep breaths. As you breathe in, imagine a gentle, golden light of abundance (whether it's joy, opportunity, connection, or resources) flowing into your open palms, filling your entire being. As you breathe out, simply release any resistance or feeling of unworthiness. Practice for 2-3 minutes, reinforcing your openness to receive.

The Fertile Soil

Fertile soil doesn't question its ability to grow life; it simply receives seeds, water, and sunlight, and responds by nurturing vibrant growth. It is inherently abundant, capable of supporting endless cycles of life. This teaches us that we, too, possess an inherent capacity for abundance. When we cultivate fertile "soil" within our minds – through positive thoughts, gratitude, and a belief in possibility – we create the perfect conditions for prosperity and joy to flourish effortlessly.

Gentle Self-Talk

"Today, I will recognize and celebrate one form of abundance already present in my life."

"I welcome abundance and prosperity into my life."

POSITIVE AFFIRMATION

note to self

Pen Your Thoughts

1 What does "abundance" truly mean to you, beyond just material possessions?

2 What is one belief you hold about success that might be limiting your experience of abundance?

3 What are the things that make you feel abundant and prosperous right now?

Your Space to Reflect

Chapter 24

I Trust My Intuition and Inner Wisdom

Listening to the Deepest Whisper

Imagine standing in a bustling city, full of sounds and distractions. Yet, if you quiet yourself and truly listen, you might still catch the faint, unique melody of a distant bird's chirping. Your inner guidance, your intuition, is often like that faint, clear melody – a quiet, profound whisper amidst the noise of the world.

This chapter is an invitation to tune into that deepest whisper, to cultivate your intuition as your most reliable guide. In a world full of advice and external pressures, it's easy to lose touch with your own inner knowing. But your intuition is a powerful, wise compass, leading you towards choices that truly resonate with your authentic self and your highest good. By learning to listen, to trust, and to honor this inner voice, you gain unwavering clarity, make decisions with greater confidence, and navigate your life's journey with a profound sense of inner alignment.

A Moment Just For You

Positive Affirmation

"I trust my inner guidance and intuition."

Reflection: The Compass Needle's True North

A compass needle, no matter how much you spin the compass, always returns to true north. It doesn't waver or get confused; it simply points to its inherent direction. Your inner guidance, your intuition, is like this compass needle. It always points you towards your "true north," your authentic path, your highest good, even when the world around you feels chaotic. How often do we override this inner wisdom, relying on external maps or the opinions of others? This reflection invites you to observe your own inner compass. What does it feel like to simply trust its unwavering direction, knowing it will always guide you home? When you honor this inner truth, your path becomes clearer, and your steps more confident.

Mindful Moment: Building Trust in Your Inner Guidance

Sit comfortably and gently close your eyes. Take three slow, deep breaths. Feel your body begin to settle. Now, bring a simple decision to mind — something light and present (e.g., "Should I take a break now or finish one more task?"). No need to analyze.

Just ask the question gently in your mind. As you hold the question, tune into your body. Notice any sensations — a softening, a tingle, a quiet yes or a subtle tension. Let your body speak before the mind jumps in. This is the language of your intuition. Trust it. It may not always be loud, but it's always there — steady and wise. The more you listen, the clearer it becomes.

The Bird's Migratory Instinct

A bird knows when to migrate, which direction to fly, and where to find food, even across vast distances, guided by an innate, powerful instinct. It doesn't need maps or lessons; it simply trusts its inner wisdom. You, too, possess an innate wisdom, a deep inner knowing that guides you. This wisdom reminds you that you have an inherent capacity to navigate your life's journey. When you quiet the external noise and listen to your deepest whisper, you activate this powerful inner guide, allowing yourself to fly with purposeful direction and unwavering trust, just like the migrating bird.

Gentle Self-Talk

"Today, I will pause and listen to my intuition before making a decision."

"I trust my inner guidance and intuition."

✦

POSITIVE AFFIRMATION

note to self

Pen Your Thoughts

1 When have you ignored your gut feeling, and later wished you had listened?

2 What is one small decision you can consciously use your intuition for today?

3 How might trusting your inner guidance more impact your confidence or your sense of peace?

Your Space to Reflect

Chapter 25

I Am Grateful for My Blessings

A Heart Overflowing

Imagine a calm, clear lake, so full that its waters gently spill over, nourishing the surrounding land, creating lush greenery and vibrant life all around it. The lake doesn't hold back; it simply overflows with its abundance, sharing its life-giving essence. You, too, have the capacity for a heart overflowing with gratitude, compassion, and joy, naturally spilling out to enrich your own life and the lives of others.

This chapter is a profound invitation to cultivate a heart that overflows with thankfulness and appreciation for all the blessings in your life. It's about moving beyond simply acknowledging gratitude, to truly embodying it – allowing it to become a vibrant, expansive feeling that radiates from your very core. When your heart overflows, you not only attract more good into your life but also become a powerful source of positivity and inspiration for the world. This practice transforms your daily experience into a continuous flow of giving and receiving, creating a life rich in connection, joy, and profound fulfillment.

Positive Affirmation

"I am thankful for all the blessings in my life."

Reflection: The Bees and the Blossoms

Observe a bee moving from flower to flower. It gathers sweet nectar, but in doing so, it also spreads pollen, aiding the growth of the plants. It both receives and gives, in a perfect, harmonious exchange. Similarly, when your heart overflows with gratitude, you not only receive the sweetness of life's blessings, but you also naturally give back, spreading positivity and kindness, creating a beautiful cycle of abundance. What "nectar" are you receiving in your life? How can your overflowing gratitude become a "pollen" that nurtures those around you? When you live with a heart overflowing, you become a vital part of life's interconnected dance, enriching yourself and the world.

Mindful Moment: The Gratitude Ripple

Sit comfortably. Take a deep, gentle breath. Think of one person or experience that fills your heart with deep gratitude. Feel the warmth of that feeling. Now, imagine that feeling radiating outwards from your heart like gentle ripples in a pond, touching everyone around you, then extending further, touching your community, and then the entire world. Feel the expansive, overflowing nature of your gratitude. Hold this feeling for 2-3 minutes.

The Bountiful Harvest

A healthy harvest is a testament to abundance. A single seed, tended with care, can produce hundreds or thousands of new seeds, far more than was originally sown. Nature is inherently generous, designed for overflowing bounty. This teaches us that abundance is not a scarce resource, but a natural state. When we approach life with a heart overflowing with gratitude, we align with this natural law, recognizing the endless harvest of blessings available to us and becoming ourselves a source of bountiful generosity.

Cultivating gratitude is a powerful practice that shifts your focus to the good things in life. Like a garden blooming with vibrant flowers, your heart will overflow with appreciation and joy. By focusing on the blessings in your life, you'll attract more positivity and abundance.

Gentle Self-Talk

"Under the sky's wide gaze, I remember that life is full of quiet gifts. Today, I will share the overflowing gratitude in my heart with someone else."

"I am thankful for all the blessings in my life."

✦

POSITIVE AFFIRMATION

Pen Your Thoughts

1. What is one specific blessing you can name right now that truly makes your heart feel full?

2. How does expressing gratitude, either silently or aloud, change your feelings or your perspective?

3. Is there something you often take for granted — a person, moment, or part of daily life — that you'd like to notice and appreciate more consciously today?

Your Space to Reflect

Part 6
EMBARKING ANEW

Chapter 26

I Am Confident in My Decisions

Navigating with Inner Clarity

Imagine a ship at sea, not tossed aimlessly, but sailing purposefully, guided by a clear compass and the captain's steady hand. Even when the horizon is unclear or storms gather, the inner navigation system ensures its direction. You, too, have an inner navigation system – a profound clarity that resides within, capable of guiding you through life's vast and sometimes unpredictable waters.

This chapter is an invitation to cultivate and trust this inner clarity, empowering you to make wise decisions and move forward with confidence. In a world full of conflicting information and endless choices, it's easy to feel lost or overwhelmed. But by quieting the external noise and tuning into your own deep knowing, you can access a clear sense of direction that aligns with your true values and purpose. When you navigate with inner clarity, your path becomes less about external maps and more about a profound trust in your own inner compass, leading you steadily towards your desired destination with peace and conviction.

Embracing confidence in your decisions is a journey of self-trust and empowerment. Like a tree standing firm in its roots, you'll make choices that reflect your values, wisdom, and inner guidance. By trusting yourself, you'll navigate life's challenges with clarity and purpose.

A Moment Just For You

Positive Affirmation

"I trust myself to make wise and informed decisions."

Reflection: The Crystal-Clear Mountain Lake

Think of a mountain lake on a calm day, its waters so clear that you can see the depths, the stones, and the fish swimming below. It perfectly reflects the sky and the surrounding peaks, offering pure, unclouded vision. Our minds, when clear, are like this lake. When we quiet the surface ripples of busy thoughts, the deeper truths and the right decisions become perfectly visible. How often do we allow the "wind" of distractions or anxieties to cloud our inner lake? This reflection invites you to seek out moments of stillness, allowing your inner lake to become perfectly clear. When you connect with this profound clarity, your decisions flow effortlessly from a place of deep knowing.

Mindful Moment: The Decisive Breath

When faced with a decision, even a small one, pause. Close your eyes. Take three deep, conscious breaths. As you inhale, imagine drawing in clarity and discernment. As you exhale, imagine releasing confusion or doubt. Now, ask yourself: "What is the next wise action?" Listen for the first subtle knowing, not the overthinking. Trust the first gentle whisper that arises.

I Am Confident in My Decisions

The Salmon's Return

A salmon, despite vast ocean journeys, instinctively knows its way back to its birthplace to spawn, guided by an unwavering inner compass and a powerful sense of purpose. It doesn't question its direction; it simply follows its innate clarity. This teaches us about the power of an inherent, clear knowing. You, too, have a powerful inner drive and a clear sense of "home" – your true purpose and alignment. When you trust your inner guidance, you move with the same unwavering clarity and determination, always finding your way to where you are meant to be. By believing in yourself, you'll become more decisive, resilient, and empowered to create the life you desire. You'll learn from your experiences, grow from your mistakes, and make informed decisions that support your growth and well-being. With confidence in your decisions, you'll live a life that is authentic, purposeful, and fulfilling.

Gentle Self-Talk

"Today, I will trust my inner voice to guide my decisions. I choose with confidence, knowing my path is mine to walk."

"I trust myself to make wise and informed decisions."

POSITIVE AFFIRMATION

note to self

Pen Your Thoughts

1 What is one decision, big or small, that you need to make today? How can you approach it with inner clarity?

2 When do you tend to feel least clear about a path forward? What factors contribute to that feeling?

3 How might having more inner clarity impact your ability to act with confidence and intention?

Your Space to Reflect

Chapter 27

I Prioritize My Well-being

My Sacred Wellspring of Care

Imagine a hidden wellspring, deep within the earth, continuously bubbling forth with pure, refreshing water, sustaining all life around it. This wellspring doesn't deplete; it constantly replenishes itself, a vibrant source of nourishment. You, too, possess such a wellspring within your own being – a sacred source of care, compassion, and renewal for your physical, emotional, and mental well-being.

This chapter is a profound invitation to prioritize and protect this sacred wellspring of self-care. In a world that often demands constant output, it's easy to neglect our own needs, draining our reserves until we feel empty. But true self-care is not selfish; it's essential. It's about consciously replenishing your energy, nurturing your spirit, and honoring your own unique needs. When you consistently draw from your sacred wellspring, you ensure you have an abundance of energy, resilience, and compassion, not only for yourself but also to share generously with the world around you.

Positive Affirmation

"I take care of my physical, emotional, and mental well-being."

Reflection: The Gardener's Loving Touch

A dedicated gardener knows that to have a thriving garden, they must actively nurture it. They don't just admire the flowers; they water, weed, provide sunlight, and protect their plants from harm. They understand that consistent, loving care yields the most beautiful blooms. How often do we treat our own being with less care than we would a beloved garden? This reflection invites you to become the conscious gardener of your own well-being. What specific acts of nourishment – for your body or mind – are you ready to provide today? When you commit to this loving touch, your inner garden flourishes, vibrant and resilient, naturally overflowing with peace and joy.

Mindful Moment: Reclaiming Your Energy

You carry a lot — responsibilities, emotions, expectations. But today, even for a moment, you're invited to pause and check in with yourself. Not to fix or change anything, but to notice:

How does your body feel?

What emotions are quietly asking for space?

Where is your mind pulling your energy?

I Prioritize My Well-being

> Taking care of yourself isn't a luxury. It's a quiet form of strength. When you care for your body, you create energy. When you tend to your emotions, you restore balance. When you give your mind moments of rest, you renew clarity.
>
> This moment is yours. A small pause to remind yourself: You matter. And the way you care for yourself — in big and small ways — ripples into everything you do.

The Forest's Regeneration

After a storm, a forest doesn't instantly repair itself. It undergoes a process of regeneration, slowly healing, replenishing, and growing stronger over time. It allows for rest and natural processes of recovery. This teaches us about the wisdom of taking time to heal and replenish. You, too, need seasons of rest, renewal, and deliberate care, especially after periods of challenge. Honor your body's need for rest, your mind's need for quiet, and your spirit's need for nourishment. This conscious regeneration strengthens you, allowing you to flourish anew.

Gentle Self-Talk

"Today, I will offer myself one small act of loving self-care."

"I take care of my physical, emotional, and mental well-being."

POSITIVE AFFIRMATION

note to self

Pen Your Thoughts

1. Which area of your well-being — physical, emotional, or mental — could use more support and care right now?"

2. What is the smallest, most accessible act of self-care you can do for yourself in the next hour?

3. How might consistent self-care improve your overall capacity to handle daily life or engage with others?

Your Space to Reflect

Chapter 28

I Let Go of Negativity and Limitations

Unfurling to What Can Be

Imagine a tightly closed flower bud, holding within it the promise of vibrant petals and sweet fragrance. It doesn't force itself open; it simply unfurls at its own perfect pace, responding to the warmth of the sun and the gentle nourishment of rain. It trusts its innate nature to fully bloom into its magnificent potential. You, too, hold immense potential within you, waiting to unfurl.

This chapter is an invitation to release any negativity or limiting beliefs that might be holding you back, and instead, to gently unfurl towards the vast possibilities that lie ahead. It's about understanding that growth is a natural process, and that by releasing what no longer serves you, you create space for new beginnings, exciting opportunities, and a vibrant expansion of who you are. When you consciously embrace this unfurling, you step into a powerful alignment with your true self, allowing your unique brilliance to blossom and illuminate your path forward, opening you to a future richer than you can imagine.

Releasing negativity and limitations is a liberating experience that opens doors to new possibilities. Like a bird taking flight, you'll soar above restrictive thoughts and beliefs, embracing positivity and growth. By letting go of what's holding you back, you'll unlock your full potential and live a life that is authentic, meaningful, and fulfilling.

Positive Affirmation

"I release negativity and limitations, embracing positivity and growth."

Reflection: The Caterpillar's Transformation

A caterpillar transforms into a butterfly not by clinging to its old form, but by completely surrendering to the process of change within the chrysalis. It lets go of its past identity to unfurl into something entirely new and beautiful. How often do we resist our own transformations, clinging to old habits or fears, even when we yearn for something more? This reflection invites you to consider the caterpillar's profound surrender. What "old skin" or limiting beliefs are you ready to shed, allowing your own beautiful transformation to unfold? When you release the past and embrace the inherent process of change, you allow yourself to unfurl into the magnificent, winged potential that awaits you.

Mindful Moment: Letting Go and Growing Forward

Find a comfortable position and gently close your eyes. Take a slow, deep breath in… and exhale fully, releasing tension. Allow yourself to settle into the present moment.

As you breathe, imagine a gentle breeze sweeping through you — clearing away any heaviness, self-doubt, or limiting beliefs. You don't need to hold onto what no longer serves you. You are safe to let go.

I Let Go of Negativity and Limitations

> Now, picture that same breeze making space for lightness — new thoughts, fresh energy, a sense of possibility. Growth doesn't require perfection, only willingness.
>
> With every breath, you release.
>
> With every breath, you open.
>
> You are choosing expansion over fear, hope over heaviness — and in doing so, you create space for who you're becoming.

The Melting Snow

Snow, when it melts, doesn't resist its transformation. It simply softens, turns into water, and flows, nourishing the earth and eventually becoming part of streams and rivers. It releases its solid form to embrace a fluid new state, bringing life. This teaches us about the beauty and necessity of releasing old forms – old ideas, old identities, old limitations – to embrace a new flow of being. When you allow yourself to "melt" away what no longer serves you, you create space for new life, new growth, and a beautiful unfolding of your true potential.

Gentle Self-Talk

"Today, I will open myself to a new possibility or idea. Like trees shed their leaves, I release what no longer serves me, trusting that new growth will follow."

"I release negativity and limitations, embracing positivity and growth."

POSITIVE AFFIRMATION

note to self

Pen Your Thoughts

1. What is one limiting belief you hold about yourself or your capabilities that you are ready to release?

2. What is one new possibility or dream that you are excited to unfurl towards?

3. How might embracing positivity and growth change your outlook on challenges or setbacks?

Your Space to Reflect

Chapter 29

I Am Worthy of Love and Connection

The Weave of Connection

Imagine a vast, intricate tapestry, woven with countless threads of different colors, textures, and origins. Each thread is unique, but together, they create a beautiful, cohesive pattern, stronger and more vibrant than any single thread alone. Your life, too, is part of a grand tapestry, interwoven with countless connections – to loved ones, community, nature, and the larger human experience.

This chapter is an invitation to cultivate these connections with an open heart, recognizing that our lives are enriched by the threads that bind us. It's about valuing empathy, practicing active listening, and extending kindness, understanding that every interaction, however small, creates a ripple effect. When you consciously nurture these relationships, you not only strengthen your own sense of belonging and well-being but also contribute to a more compassionate and harmonious world. This is the art of weaving a life rich in shared experiences, mutual growth, and profound, meaningful relationships.

A Moment Just For You

Positive Affirmation

"I deserve meaningful relationships and connections."

Reflection: The Interconnected Forest

Consider a healthy forest, where trees are connected by an invisible, underground network of roots and fungi. They share nutrients, communicate, and support each other's growth, making the entire forest stronger and more resilient. No tree stands truly alone. Similarly, your connections to others are like this unseen network. How often do we forget that our well-being is intertwined with the well-being of those around us? This reflection invites you to feel into this interconnectedness. When you consciously nurture your connections, you strengthen not only yourself but also the entire "forest" of your community, creating a vibrant ecosystem of care.

Embracing your worthiness of love and connection is a journey of self-discovery and empowerment. Like a blooming flower, you'll attract positive relationships and connections that nourish your mind, body, and spirit. By believing in your worthiness, you'll cultivate deep and meaningful relationships that bring joy and fulfillment to your life.

Rooted in Worth, Open to Connection

There's a quiet strength in knowing you don't need to chase connection — only to be fully present, and fully yourself. When you slow down and align with what feels true, the right people begin to gather around that calm center. Meaningful relationships aren't built from striving, but from showing up with sincerity, patience, and presence. Just as a tree does not rush its blooming, trust that connection unfolds in its own time — when there is mutual purpose, care, and space for both silence and growth. You are already worthy of connection that feels natural, fulfilling, and aligned with your deeper sense of self. Let your presence be your invitation.

Mindful Moment: Creating Space for Meaningful Connection

Take a moment to sit quietly. Let your hands rest gently in your lap. Close your eyes and take a slow, steady breath in… and a long, gentle breath out. Bring your awareness to the space around your heart. Imagine it softening — not to give more, but to receive.

You don't need to reach or strive. The connections that are meant for you arise from stillness, from authenticity, from simply being who you are.

Let this moment remind you:

You are worthy of relationships that reflect peace, presence, and mutual growth. You don't have to chase — only align.

Breathe here a little longer. In this calm, you're already attracting what belongs.

Quiet Belonging

The mountain does not seek to be seen, yet it is always there — steady, present, complete. The cherry blossom doesn't bloom for applause; it simply opens when the moment is right.

In the same way, you do not need to prove yourself worthy of love and connection. You are already whole. Meaningful relationships come not through striving, but through stillness — the kind that invites others to meet you as you truly are.

Let your presence be enough. Let your quiet truth be the offering. The love you deserve is not rushed or loud — it arrives gently, in its own time, like rain returning to the earth that has always been ready to receive.

Gentle Self-Talk

The love and connection I deserve will meet me where I am — calm, open, and true.

"I deserve meaningful relationships and connections."

✦

POSITIVE AFFIRMATION

note to self

Pen Your Thoughts

1 What does meaningful love and connection look like for you — emotionally, spiritually, and in daily life?

2 How do you feel when you're around people who truly see and value you? (What qualities or energy do they bring?)

3 What small shift can you make to open yourself more fully to the relationships you deserve?

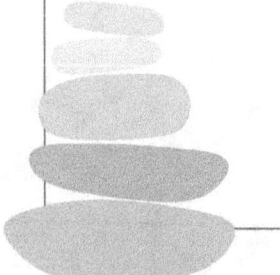

Your Space to Reflect

Chapter 30

I Am at Peace with My Journey

Journeying with a Tranquil Heart

Imagine a serene mountain lake, its surface perfectly still, reflecting the vast sky, the soaring peaks, and the quiet beauty of the world around it. It holds all the beauty and complexity of its surroundings within its calm depths, without judgment or resistance. You, too, can cultivate such a tranquil heart, journeying through life's diverse landscapes with a profound sense of inner peace and acceptance.

This final chapter is an invitation to embrace peace with your entire journey – every triumph, every challenge, every bend in the road. It's about cultivating a deep sense of trust that everything is unfolding as it should, even when the path is unclear. By embracing the present moment, finding solace in stillness, and releasing the need to control every outcome, you step into a profound alignment with the natural flow of existence. When you journey with a tranquil heart, you not only experience a deeper sense of inner peace and well-being but also radiate a quiet strength and confidence that allows you to navigate life's adventures with grace, wisdom, and an unshakeable sense of calm belonging.

Embracing peace with your journey is a profound act of trust and surrender, allowing you to flow like water in the stream of life. Like a tranquil garden, you'll cultivate a sense of harmony and balance, finding solace in the present moment. By trusting in the journey of life, you'll discover a deeper sense of inner peace and alignment with the natural flow of existence.

Positive Affirmation

"I trust that everything is unfolding as it should."

Reflection: Trusting the Unfolding

There is no need to rush the river. No leaf opens before its time. In the stillness of nature, nothing is hurried — and yet everything is completed.

So too with your life.

When you release the need to control every detail, you create space for grace to flow. Trust doesn't mean having all the answers — it means being willing to sit in the unknown without fear. It means allowing life to unfold like a path in the mist, revealed only step by step.

What is meant for you will not pass you by. What is not meant will gently fall away. Let this moment be enough. Let it be your teacher.

Your journey is not behind or ahead — it is here. And it is unfolding exactly as it should.

When you live with this profound trust, your journey becomes less about struggle and more about graceful movement, filled with an unshakeable inner peace.

I Am at Peace with My Journey

> **Mindful Moment: The Deep Peace Hand**
> ....
> Place your right hand over your left hand, palms touching, and bring them gently to your chest, over your heart. Close your eyes. Take a deep, slow breath, feeling your heart gently rise and fall beneath your hands. As you breathe, silently repeat the affirmation: "I trust that everything is unfolding as it should." Feel the words resonate in your heart, releasing any tension or doubt. Rest in this feeling of deep trust and inner peace for 2-3 minutes.

The Cycle of Seasons

The seasons unfold in a perfect, inevitable cycle – spring blossoming, summer thriving, autumn releasing, winter resting. Each season is essential, and there is no resistance to the next. Nature trusts this continuous unfolding. This teaches us that life, too, has its seasons of growth, activity, release, and rest. When we resist these natural cycles, we create friction. When we trust that every phase, every experience, is part of a larger, wise unfolding, we find a profound sense of peace and belonging in the natural rhythm of our own journey.

Gentle Self-Talk

"Today, I will release the need to control and simply trust the flow of my journey."

"I trust that everything is unfolding as it should."

POSITIVE AFFIRMATION

note to self

Pen Your Thoughts

1 What does "peace with your journey" truly feel like to you?

2 What is one specific situation where you can practice trusting that everything is unfolding as it should?

3 How might embracing this trust reduce stress or bring a greater sense of freedom to your daily life?

Your Space to Reflect

Epilogue

The Ever-Unfolding Path

With every step, you've claimed your way
Affirmations guiding you, day by day
Success, peace, happiness, and calm reside
In your heart's core, where love abides.
May these treasures stay with you, always near
Bringing joy and strength, dispelling fear
And as you walk, your path aglow
May your spirit soar, in all you know.

www.ingramcontent.com/pod-product-compliance
Lightning Source LLC
Chambersburg PA
CBHW070056080526
44586CB00013B/1086